Software Performance Engineering

*A comprehensive guide for
high-performance development*

Alon Rotem

bpb

www.bpbonline.com

First Edition 2025

Copyright © BPB Publications, India

ISBN: 978-93-65895-445

To View Complete
BPB Publications Catalogue
Scan the QR Code:

www.bpbonline.com

Dedicated to

Antonia and Benji

About the Author

Alon Rotem is a soulful geek and musician. His encounters with code go back to his teenage years in the mid-1980s, where he discovered the ATARI 800 8-bit computers and the BASIC programming language. His days in the actual tech industry, all around software engineering, go back to the mid-1990s, the days of DOS, Windows 3.1, and prehistoric Red Hat distributions.

Since then, he has worked as a quality assurance engineer, a software engineer, a lecturer, an educational manager, a solutions consultant, a team lead, a tech lead, a solution enterprise architect and a senior engineer at one of the most well-known database companies, the **MariaDB Foundation**. He has been managing a team of software architects for one of the big four global accounting companies, **KPMG**. He also established and created a certification program for one of the biggest enterprise-level content management systems, **Sitefinity**, being one of the senior engineers who had built it firsthand for the most successful Bulgarian software company, **Telerik**.

Apart from his work, he is an active hacker and developer, always exploring technological solutions, workarounds, free alternatives, and hacks, and is an avid supporter of Linux and open-source software.

He studied computer science at the *Open University of Israel*, and in recent years has been living and working on both ends of East and West Europe.

He is also an electro-acoustic musician whose works can be found on all major streaming platforms, as well as on his personal site.

About the Reviewers

❖ **Martin Yanev** is a highly accomplished software engineer with nearly a decade of experience across diverse industries, including aerospace and medical technology. Throughout his illustrious career, Martin has carved out a niche for himself in developing and integrating cutting-edge software solutions for critical domains, including air traffic control and chromatography systems. Renowned as an esteemed instructor and computer science professor at Fitchburg State University, he possesses a deep understanding of the full spectrum of OpenAI APIs and exhibits mastery in constructing, training, and fine-tuning AI systems. As a widely recognized author, Martin has shared his expertise to help others navigate the complexities of AI development. With his exceptional track record and multifaceted skill set, Martin continues to propel innovation and drive transformative advancements in the field of software engineering.

❖ **Tareq** is a performance engineering senior architect with nearly 15 years of experience in quality engineering, including a decade specializing in performance engineering. He focuses on optimizing system performance, API tuning, and architectural design. His expertise spans tools like JMeter, LoadRunner, AppDynamics, DataDog, and New Relic. He was a speaker at the Xpand Conference 2024, where he talked about Observability in an Age of Microservices. He is an active reader, enjoying comics, manga, science fiction, and IT-related books, and continuously shares best practices and insights on software performance through various platforms.

Acknowledgement

As someone who has been deeply immersed in the tech industry for almost four decades, I have taken on many roles and undertaken a wide variety of tasks. I have written blog posts, recorded training videos, and tech videos, but I have never written an entire book. This was a golden opportunity, brought to me by BPB Publications, and I am immensely grateful for it. Their guidance and expertise in bringing this book to reality cannot be emphasized enough. Their patient support and assistance were invaluable in navigating the complexities of the publishing process. My experience was intriguing, interesting, and educational, all of which I am grateful for.

I would like to acknowledge the reviewers, technical experts, and editors who provided valuable feedback and contributed to the refinement of the book's contents through their insights and suggestions, which significantly improved its quality. Not to mention their patience with my constant corrections and additions, as technology has been running forward, even while I was researching and writing.

Special thanks to my literary editor, to whom I have given a whole lot of painstaking, fine-tuned work, which she has executed meticulously and flawlessly, and made this book so much better.

Lastly, I would like to express my gratitude to the readers who have shown interest in this book. Your support and encouragement are warmly appreciated.

Thank you to everyone who has played a part in making this book a reality.

Preface

Performance engineering is a broad and elusive subject on which several books can be written, and indeed, quite a few have been. Commonly, users do not give a lot of thought to how fast their app runs before they intuitively sense it is slow. Many moving parts contribute to how well an app performs: from the architecture of the CPU cores and the hardware setup, through the optimization of the code, the underlying runtime environment, efficiency of algorithms, data structures, databases, storages and strategies, all the way to the broad worldwide deployment and scaling schemes of services, networking components and security constraints. This renders performance and efficiency complex cross-cutting concerns throughout the entire process of producing and running software in our modern era.

Since ENIAC, the very first digital computer, was introduced just 80 years ago, in the 1940s, the performance and capabilities of computers have been evolving astronomically, in the endless race to accommodate ever-heavier tasks. Unlike in the old times, software today is expected to be operated by hundreds of millions of users, literally around the world, to process vast amounts of data records, while remaining pleasing, easy, and quick to use, all the way down to the single user's experience. The evolution of big data, with machine learning and artificial intelligence, keeps pushing even the most powerful supercomputers to the edge of their abilities, while on the other hand, quantum computers advance in lightning speed towards a completely new world of computing. We really are living in the future that science fiction has charted for us.

As the topic is so broad and versatile, this book covers some of the practical aspects of developing and delivering performant software in the modern world of technology, while mentioning other areas as knowledge pointers, in order to help direct the curious readers to acquire more knowledge, with the intention to provide a wholistic understanding of performance engineering, right from the standard processes of inception, production, testing and delivery, to the high level runtime view and analysis. This book is current. It talks about the past, but looks into the future, demonstrating current trends, tools, programming languages, frameworks, and platforms, to provide a strong base for people who are interested in learning the basics of performance engineering.

Chapter 1: Introduction to Performance Engineering- This chapter presents some of the aspects of performance engineering to understand its broad meaning in today's world, in order to acquaint the readers with the concept itself, which not many are aware of, at least not in depth. We look at how it is integrated in our modern-day software development lifecycle processes, we discuss principles of modern software delivery, in light of the evolution of computers, and some of the performance concerns software must accommodate nowadays, and why they count.

Chapter 2: Performance Driven Development- In many ways, performance-oriented development is baked into the software delivery methodology itself. In this chapter, we get into more refined details of the current-day processes of software delivery. We look at the evolution of various methodologies, each with its advantages and flaws, and learn how applications are being planned, built, provisioned, and delivered with modern tools, in order to get the most out of them. We also mention different types of tests that help us evaluate the quality of our software and to understand how well it is performing in comparison to our expectations and requirements.

Chapter 3: Non-functional Requirements Definition and Tracking- Performance planning is a first-class citizen in the functionality of our application, how it is perceived, how it functions, how it reacts, and responds. However, it comes with a detailed underlying, well-defined set of requirements that we need to plan and take into account, attributes such as security, maintainability, and compliance, as well as considerations related directly to runtime performance features. This chapter looks at ways we can structure our non-functional requirements' definitions as part of our product plan.

Chapter 4: Workload Modeling and Projection- Continuing the analysis and breakdown of the features in our software, in this chapter, we look at how we identify and map use cases, usage flows, and workloads, in order to understand how and by whom our application is expected to be used. We discuss future load projection methods and performance measurements.

Chapter 5: High Performance Design Patterns- In this detailed technical chapter, we take a closer look at software and system design. We review the evolution of software architecture and approaches throughout the decades and how modern architectural design accommodates modern requirements. We discuss and review in detail several software design principles, which are directly related to scalability and performance enhancements.

Chapter 6: Performance Antipatterns- In continuation of the discussion of useful design patterns, in this chapter, we look at potential pitfalls of common design, which are sometimes overlooked by software architects and developers. Accompanied by concrete code examples, we take a deep technical look at a number of antipatterns, discuss their flaws, and why and how to avoid and mitigate them, in order to improve the performance and overall quality of our application.

Chapter 7: Performance in the Clouds- Cloud platforms are all the rage in modern software development and delivery. We discuss advancements in high-power computing, which is made accessible to all through the cloud, as well as a look into the future of quantum computing, which is, in fact, already the present, and becoming available as we speak. We discuss the advantages of running our microservice applications in the cloud, we look at scalability, elasticity, and large data management.

Chapter 8: Designing Performance Monitoring- Once we have our application running, we want to make sure it runs smoothly. Monitoring its performance metrics and telemetry, following detailed logs and runtime traces, gives us real-time insights into issues and helps us design and plan for improvements. This chapter explains the concepts, tools, and methodologies to monitor our app, to ensure it lives up to the promises we had made for it.

Chapter 9: Tools and Techniques for Code Profiling- Looking deeper into the code of our application, in this practical chapter, we take a technical dive into the analysis of our code, in development as well as during execution. We discuss static vs. dynamic profiling, we look at code profiling tools such as cProfile, pyinstrument, line profiler, VisualVM, pprof, and eBPF, by going through detailed code examples and walkthroughs, to understand how to put them to use in the real world.

Chapter 10: Performance Testing, Checklist to Best Practices- After learning about tools for optimizing our code, in this chapter, we look at what we can do once it's already built. Testing is a crucial pillar of software development and improvement, and performance counts for quality. In this chapter, we look at different types of performance tests, how they are executed, and the importance of test environments, conditions, and practices.

Chapter 11: Test Data Management- Still in the realm of testing, data is at the heart of any modern-day application. Providing proper quality data for testing is just as important as the test itself, and the area of test data management (TDM) has been marked as a core emerging technology by Gartner's hype cycle for Agile and DevOps. This chapter explains test data management, strategies for good quality test data, as well as practical demos for automated test data production, in order to achieve the most from our tests.

Chapter 12: Performance Benchmarking- Another aspect of understanding how well our application runs is benchmarking and execution analysis over time. In this chapter, we revisit the different types of performance tests while practically looking at runtime test tools, such as Locust and JMeter. We differentiate benchmarking from baselining and discuss the important aspect of continuous performance monitoring and validation, using an automation server (Jenkins) and containers (Docker).

Chapter 13: Golden Signals, KPI, Metrics, and Tools- As we run tests and benchmarks to monitor and get acquainted with our application's performance, we also want to refer to a well-defined set of measurable metrics, in order to actually know how well we are doing. In this chapter, we understand key performance indicators (KPIs). We map different types of metrics to different levels of roles; we discuss monitoring tools and take a practical example with the ELK stack and the Elastic Application Performance Monitoring suite.

Chapter 14: Performance Behavioral Correlation- Continuing the discussion on metrics and runtime monitoring, in this chapter, we look further into how to better understand the reports of our monitoring tools. While discussing practical examples, we investigate root cause analysis, data correlations, behavioral analytics, as well as strategies for future predictions, and practical code examples of mapping and charting them. We also talk about how to follow up on issues and the process of closing and completing them.

Chapter 15: Post-Production Management- As the previous chapters focused on delivering the software, making sure it complies with our requirements, code quality, performance definitions, test requirements, and runtime measurements, this chapter looks at the next day: once we have our app up and running in a live production environment. We look at managing dashboards and alerts, about the endless, continuous journey of improvement, we discuss the different stakeholders and different levels of ownership and responsibility, and briefly look at predictive analytics for the future.

Code Bundle and Coloured Images

Please follow the link to download the
Code Bundle and the *Coloured Images* of the book:

https://rebrand.ly/rdwrm8j

The code bundle for the book is also hosted on GitHub at
https://github.com/bpbpublications/Software-Performance-Engineering.
In case there's an update to the code, it will be updated on the existing GitHub repository.

We have code bundles from our rich catalogue of books and videos available at
https://github.com/bpbpublications. Check them out!

Errata

We take immense pride in our work at BPB Publications and follow best practices to ensure the accuracy of our content to provide with an indulging reading experience to our subscribers. Our readers are our mirrors, and we use their inputs to reflect and improve upon human errors, if any, that may have occurred during the publishing processes involved. To let us maintain the quality and help us reach out to any readers who might be having difficulties due to any unforeseen errors, please write to us at :

errata@bpbonline.com

Your support, suggestions and feedbacks are highly appreciated by the BPB Publications' Family.

Piracy

If you come across any illegal copies of our works in any form on the internet, we would be grateful if you would provide us with the location address or website name. Please contact us at **business@bpbonline.com** with a link to the material.

If you are interested in becoming an author

If there is a topic that you have expertise in, and you are interested in either writing or contributing to a book, please visit **www.bpbonline.com**. We have worked with thousands of developers and tech professionals, just like you, to help them share their insights with the global tech community. You can make a general application, apply for a specific hot topic that we are recruiting an author for, or submit your own idea.

Reviews

Please leave a review. Once you have read and used this book, why not leave a review on the site that you purchased it from? Potential readers can then see and use your unbiased opinion to make purchase decisions. We at BPB can understand what you think about our products, and our authors can see your feedback on their book. Thank you!

For more information about BPB, please visit **www.bpbonline.com**.

Join our book's Discord space

Join the book's Discord Workspace for Latest updates, Offers, Tech happenings around the world, New Release and Sessions with the Authors:

https://discord.bpbonline.com

Table of Contents

CHAPTER 1
Introduction to Performance Engineering

Introduction

Many people in the IT world know about software engineering and the practices and roles that take part in building a software project. Many also know about performance and why it is important, although this aspect often gets sidelined and not properly addressed.

However, not many know about performance engineering as a thing, all the more so as a field with specialized professionals and structured methodologies.

Performance engineering, nevertheless, is a wide field with many faces, which touches on many aspects and concepts. Some of which are project management, system design, software engineering practices, hardware architecture, testing and automation, and others. This chapter introduces the tip of the iceberg of performance engineering before going deeper into explanations.

Structure

This chapter will cover the following topics:

- The story of performance engineering
- Modern principles of software engineering

Objectives

In this chapter, we will get acquainted with the concept of performance engineering in the light of software engineering. We will briefly review modern concepts and practices of software development and project management. We will understand what performance engineering is, why it is important, what its challenges, objectives, and risks (as well as the risks of neglecting it) are, and what we can benefit from it.

The story of performance engineering

Putting first things first, let us first understand what exactly we are talking about here, what performance engineering is.

About performance engineering

Intuitively speaking, proper **engineering** (i.e., designing, outlining, implementing, testing, and delivering) of software, considering its **performance**. That is, how well it executes under various conditions, mostly in terms of (but not limited to) speed and efficiency.

In contrast to classic methodologies of software engineering, with their patterns and rules, where it is clear who (the developer) does what (writes the code), performance engineering is a broad set of processes and techniques that are to be applied during the entire software development lifecycle. It is rooted in processes, people, and technologies, and has an impact on the optimization of an application's performance prior to product deployment, as well as following up on it afterwards.

Alongside a software's feasible, operational, user-facing interactive **functional** features, its buttons, menus, and interactive and responsive behavior, there is often a list of **non-functional** requirements: supporting features that are transparent to the user but are required to keep the app and its data stable, reliable, durable, and secure.

Performance is a non-functional feature, which is sometimes included in the list of requirements, and sometimes omitted. Concerns such as how much time a page should take to load, how quickly data should be retrieved, what should be the throughput of records per second, how it should handle multiple users and heavy load, etc.

As a small side note from my own personal experience on industrial software projects over more than 27 years, some software applications, like those that deal with finance and regulations, come with hard, specific performance requirements, as processed data needs to be delivered at a specific rate, at specific times. Some systems require the data delivery to be instantaneous (or at least pseudo-instantaneous). Those are intrinsic performance features that come pre-baked in the product's list of requirements, as the integrity and regulatory nature of the system rely on it. Of course, in many cases, performance is *not the most important* aspect of the software. Other properties, such as compatibility, functionality, maintainability, modularity, profitability, and usability, are at the base of any application, as they are its selling points. But performance is sometimes compared to a currency, with which we can *trade* other properties of the application. For example, we can sacrifice performance in favor of making the code more readable, or sacrifice performance in order to make sure our program is secure, etc.

Speaking of currencies, putting efforts into improving performance does translate directly to money, as it may take more time and manpower to build highly performant code, as well as compatible tests and monitoring, and integrate the whole chunk of work into the development process.

On the flip side, in many cases, a software project is born from a functional idea, and not a regulatory need. Thus, the focus of the development process is to make the dream and vision come to life. This leans mostly on *what* we want the app to do, rather than *how, how well*, or *how fast*. Building software in this mindset is incredibly common, and performance comes last on the list of features, if at all. Considering performance as a feature means utilizing efforts and resources, which, in many cases, is transparent to the developers, too. They would rather put their work into tangible, functional fruits, and sometimes think of performance as an extra that may not be worth their time, or do not think about it at all. Project managers await visible features they can show and talk about, and many people in the development circle would consider working on performance features a needless hassle, until they have to.

Life is short; time is money. On the other side of the application sits a user, staring at progress bars (which are made to comfort them that everything is fine: things are happening, work is being done), waiting for data to be submitted or retrieved, or worse: staring at a blank, unresponsive page. While performance is not at the top of the list of many application developers, it is right in front of the users' eyes, and, depending on the complexity of the application, it is very noticeable.

Given this common progression, it is not uncommon practice to start noticing and considering performance when the project already stands, and not while planning and designing it. This can be metaphorically compared to making fundamental construction changes to a house while planning and building it, vs. a renovation, after it is already built and standing. Doing this in advance can save a lot of trouble and extra work and produce a smoother, holistically better-integrated result.

Hence, considering performance engineering as part of the initial requirements and integrating performance practices and relevant quality tests into the software development lifecycle may be beneficial, even if performance is not one of the topmost considered priorities for the project, especially if future scale and growth are desired.

There are a few (albeit not too many) books, tutorials, and courses discussing the topic of performance engineering out there, and it is indeed a wide topic, to say the least. Spanning from hardware and processor architecture and utilization, through coding principles, patterns, and antipatterns, programming language-specific tricks and pitfalls, design of services and cloud integration, various types of tests and benchmarks, tools for analysis and monitoring, and more.

This book will provide a modern view of performance engineering aimed at the current day's developers in mind. It will discuss common patterns, solutions, and methodologies. Performance is a theory with many faces, and hopefully, this book will put the perplexed software engineer in the right mindset, using simple, down-to-earth words.

Modern principles of software engineering

Software has existed since the beginning of digital computers. In the beginning (the 1940s), software was written with binary code, directly to the heart of the computer, which was a room-sized mainframe (the term **mainframe** comes from the large cabinet which was housing the computer, the main frame). Binary code is still used today, as this is the only language computer processors can understand, but it is written indirectly. Layers of compilation and interpretation separate the code the developer writes from what the processor eventually reads. Those layers create much more sophisticated and elegant ways to model our programs and build them in a more natural linguistic manner (mixed with mathematical logic), and programming languages, much like natural human languages, evolve and grow, become more elaborate, creating a universe of frameworks, methodologies, and practices of design and implementation. The computer processors have also grown immensely in capabilities, and smaller in size, to say the least.

In this segment, we will look a bit into this evolution and where it has brought us to today.

The modern era

The ever-evolving craft of software engineering has grown over the years into a wide variety of programming languages, frameworks, development and runtime environments, technologies, techniques, tools, and purposes.

Some languages are driven by object-oriented design; others are procedural. Some are strongly typed, while others are completely fluid. Some are interpreted, making them executable on multiple platforms, while others are compiled into binary executables for a specific operating system on a specific processor. Some would argue that declarative languages may not be programming languages at all, but in effect, they certainly are (just to add to the mix).

While the Assembly programming language has always been (and will probably remain) the closest wrapper representation to actual binary machine code, it too has evolved quite a lot over the years, as computer processors and their respective architectures have. Going through the specs of Assembly language keywords for x86 processors will reveal a long list of added instructions on every consequent generation.

Processors themselves have been keeping up nicely with Moore's law in the past decades. In 1965, *Gordon Moore* predicted that the number of transistors in an integrated circuit would double every 18-24 months (thereby increasing processing power exponentially). This prediction of growth, referred to as *Moore's law*, has been consistently confirmed over the years. If we compare the first microprocessor, Intel's 4004 from 1971 with 2,300 transistors and a clock speed of 750KHz, to today's latest technology of a TSMC's N3 processor, with the modern advanced 3-nanometer technology, with more than 314 million transistors, and clock speed of 3.16GHz, we see a growth of density of more than 136,000 times, and speed of more than 4,000 times. This rate of growth is incomparable to any other technology in any field.

It is not uncommon to argue that Moore's law has reached its end of potential, as modern processors are already pushing the limits of physics itself. The density of transistors is already literally bordering mere atomic scale, resulting in potential temperatures as hot as the surface of the sun (or much worse: the temperature of a slice of tomato inside a pressed grilled cheese sandwich!). In light of the physical limits of the processor itself, modern-day computers' CPUs are getting not only dense in themselves, but each modern CPU now packs multiple processors (cores) at once and uses additional architectural tricks, such as various data caches, in order to get as performant as possible.

Moore's law is well known and mentioned everywhere. Let us look at yet another, less-known law related to microprocessor's evolution: *Dennard scaling*, established in 1974 by *Robert Dennard*; in simple words, it states that as the transistors get smaller, their density on the chip grows, but the power consumption per surface area remains the same. This means that despite the greater (to say the least) processing horsepower, electric power consumption does not grow remotely as much.

Alongside all those evolutions, other shifts have taken place. Software projects have grown bigger in scale (with the potential to scale-grow indefinitely upon need). Data has grown tremendously, and the collection of big data has allowed the creation of enormous data models to be crunched by machine learning algorithms and artificial intelligence engines. Software still runs on the user's computer, but also inside their web browsers, on remote servers, in large cloud clusters of computers around the globe, inside databases, on mobile devices, on smart home appliances' microcontrollers, and in IoT. Software is not just for nerds who are hacking the local traffic lights system from their moms' basements, but for everyone, everywhere, all at once.

Interestingly enough, some companies, running large data centers, chose to place them in naturally cold locations, such as *Canada* (*CLUMEQ silo* in *Quebec*), *Scandinavia* (Google's Hamina data center in *Finland*, Facebook's data center near the *Arctic Circle* in *Lulea, Sweden*), to help the hardware cool while lowering energy costs.

Amid the rapid and ongoing advancements in both software and hardware, we have yet to even approach the early stages of quantum computing—an area that once seemed like a distant vision but is now steadily becoming a reality.

Our modern computing realms have gotten us to develop accommodating methodologies and principles, too. Since we are dealing with large volumes of data, with wide globally distributed computer systems, and dependent services, patterns of architecture for software solutions, services, and good coding were developed. Many also come to accommodate proper performance needs. Also, proper processes come into play in the development of complex systems and solutions.

In the next section, we will list a few commonly followed principles in software engineering, both at the project/process level and at the architecture/design/code level. As this is not the focus of this book, only some are mentioned here, with short (much-)simplified explanations. Of course, those principles are not mutually exclusive, and in many cases, coexist. We will also revisit some of the important ones, relevant to our discussions, in greater detail in the following chapters.

Development process principles and practices

The common **software development life cycle** (**SDLC**) is a methodology with clearly defined processes for creating high-quality software. The current standard process adopted by many organizations, as the work itself tends to run and be managed in iterative cycles, is (but not limited to) SCRUM. Basically, the SDLC methodology focuses on a few well-defined, structured phases that work in sequence:

Analysis of demands and requirements, feature planning, architectural design and initial documentation, development of features, testing (which may circulate between development and testing, when bugs are reported), deployment (depending on the nature of the product), and a potential step of maintenance, for features for which no further development is pending. A point to note is that documentation, in all its forms, is a crucial integral part of all phases of the development process, not just for architectural design, in order to keep track and to give context to anyone involved with the project, currently and in the future: from documenting the business proposal, requirements and analysis at the planning phase, through documentation of the code, APIs, build scripts, libraries and tools during the development stage, documentation of test plans and test cases, as well as the scripts written at the test phase, deployment scripts and pipelines at the deployment phase and maintenance plans as well as incidents which were found and handled during maintenance. We will review the modern software development practices in more detail in the next chapter, *Performance Driven Development*.

Keeping the cycle running helps ensure that requirements are understood, listed, and followed, with persistent improvement, stability, and quality. Since the process is iterative, it is also delivering features in an incremental manner and removing bugs. Both feature and bug handling are based on priority. The following figure shows the modern software development lifecycle, and typical stages it may include, which one leads to which, and how the cycle iterates in loops:

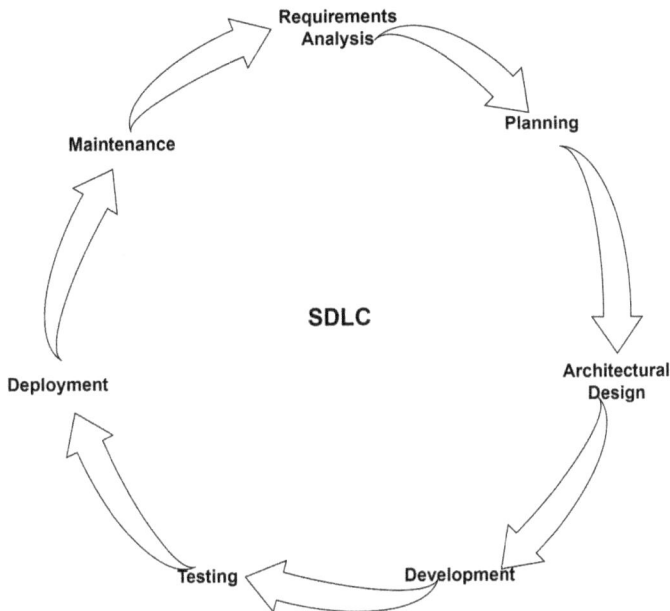

Figure 1.1: Typical flow of the software development lifecycle

In terms of the development process itself, there are a few (some more, some less) commonly followed principles to note:

- **Architecture first**: Robust, resilient, secure, software, spanning multiple services, clients, big quantities of data and high availability requires strong foundations. Following the Architecture-first principle helps making the right decisions, by considering the architecture... first! Researching tools and technologies, listing communications, data volumes, and designing the system as much as possible. That is before implementation starts.

- **Round-trip engineering** (RTE): Not the most common of methodologies, but in some cases of complex object-oriented systems, specifications of objects, get reflected into auto-generated code skeletons, whereas changes in code get reflected back to specifications (e.g. UML diagrams, depicting the current objects and their relations).

- **Domain driven design** (DDD): With DDD, the application follows the real-world models which it comes to serve. Names of classes, objects, methods, properties, imitate the real-world objects which they represent (e.g. bank, branch, bank account, balance, withdrawal, etc.). The models (i.e., data models) that are used also follow the same principle.

  Domain-driven design helps grasp and follow projects that come to serve real-world systems.

- **Test-driven development (TDD) and quality tests**: Testing, a core part of any healthy software development lifecycle, is the most important factor to ensure quality and proper behavior. Different types of tests are defined, built, and executed at different levels and areas of the project and at different stages:

- ○ **Unit tests**: To ensure that code components behave and react as expected in different scenarios. With **test-driven development** (**TDD**), unit tests can be written before the code is written to ensure the functionality matches the expected results, though many times, TDD is not practiced, and tests are written during development.

  All other test types mentioned below, are written and maintained during the different development cycles, mostly after the features are already implemented.

- ○ **UI tests**: To ensure parts of the user interface are displayed and react according to their design.

- ○ **Integration tests:** To make sure the entire system is intact and works properly as a whole.

- ○ **Regression and smoke tests**: To ensure no new bugs were unexpectedly introduced. Regression tests ensure that recent code changes haven't negatively impacted existing functionality in a software application. It involves retesting previously working features to confirm that they still function as expected after modifications. Smoke tests are preliminary tests to verify the basic functionality of the software. They check whether the most critical features work correctly, often before more detailed testing begins. Smoke tests serve as a quick check to determine if the software build is stable enough for further testing.

Despite being an effective, efficient way to ensure expected behaviors, high quality, and make tests an integrated first-class part of the development process itself, TDD is not common enough. However, the importance of tests is clear.

Software design principles

It is worth mentioning a few modern common principles of software engineering design, which are good practices to be aware of and follow:

- • **Abstraction**: In the base (pun not intended) of object-oriented design, which is the hierarchy of classes and interfaces, keeping things in order, and on a need-to-know basis. Functionality and information are kept in isolation, accessible only to those they may concern, at different levels. This is the base for other principles, such as SOLID (see below), refined as guidelines.

- • **SOLID**: No list of modern software development principles is complete without mentioning SOLID, one of the most well-known code guidelines, tightly related to good practices of object-oriented design and proper abstraction. This set of principles helps keep things in place, making sure that the structure is understandable and ordered, neat and maintainable. It consists of the five basic ideas, which create the acronym SOLID.

The SOLID principles dictate how software classes and interfaces relate to one another, and how to build them properly, in order to keep things in abstraction and separation on a need-to-know basis, in order to avoid one part of the code meddling with the other. The five principles, shortly explained and put into simple words:

- **S: The single responsibility principle**: Every class has just one area of responsibility (e.g., a class that contains functionality for user management will not start handling unrelated functionality, like sending notifications).

  This keeps functionality separated with clear borders, to avoid confusion and complication on which part does what.

- **O: The open-closed principle**: Software entities are open for extension but closed for modification. This idea keeps software classes intact and keeps them from changing in an unpredictable way. Functionality, which is relevant for a specific software class, stays within that class. If any additional functionality is required to be implemented, a different class should extend the original one with its own variant of the function, rather than changing the code of the original one. This gives clarity and predictability.

- **L: Liskov substitution principle**: A common idea of abstraction and extension of classes in inheritance. According to this principle, a base class contains an abstraction of a function to be overridden/implemented by a derived class. The base does not care about its derivatives.

  For example, the base/abstract class **Bird** has an abstract function **Fly** (given that all the birds we are dealing with can fly), which is then implemented concretely differently by derived birds, such as **Flamingo** or **Duck**.

  If an abstract object of type **Bird** is at hand, pointing to any of the concrete birds, we can invoke the method **Fly**, without caring which bird we are actually dealing with. Also, different birds can be substituted, without breaking the base abstraction of the **Bird** class.

- **I: Interface segregation principle**: Put simply, create minimal interfaces in a proper context.

  For example, Our interface, **IBird**, defines functions of **Bird** activities, which do not include unrelated functions, which are not relevant to all birds, because then you would be forcing all birds to implement irrelevant (or empty/invalid) operations. Keep common activities (e.g., **Eat**) in the common interface (**IBird**), and special activities (**Hunt**) in specialized interfaces (**IBirdOfPrey**).

- o **D: The dependency inversion principle**: Depending on your class relations on abstractions, not concrete implementation. The idea here is not to base classes on other classes, but on higher-level abstract ones, or interfaces. This principle decouples concrete classes and makes sure that they do not *know* about each other. Instead, the relation is made by using an interface, higher in the chain of abstraction. This helps implement another common feature of object-oriented systems: dependency injection (also commonly related to inversion of control). If you are a user of a class, you do not need to know its details, only its base interface. That way, the actual object we use can be dynamically set or changed, if it complies with the interface.

- **KISS**: **Keep it simple, stupid**: Another one of those principles that cannot be omitted from such a list. This is a general principle that calls to keep your program simple. It is not always easy, if you implement complex algorithms, recursive structures, or build hacks to improve performance, but in general, one should try to, for example, **write smaller, minimized, neat programs**. Remove unnecessary, unused, unreachable code. Keep your code readable, give your variables and methods clear names (choosing names is sometimes one of the most difficult tasks). Use SOLID principles to structure your classes correctly and with minimum confusion.

- **DRY**: **Don't repeat yourself:** Again, one of the most well-known and discussed principles of modern software engineering. Avoid duplicate code, modularize your functionality in a way that every operation has just one place in which it is implemented. This helps not just simplify and minimize the code, but also makes it maintainable, since if we need to make a change, there is only one place to apply it.

Importance of performance engineering in software development

As mentioned in the beginning, in some cases, performance is baked into the base requirements, when runtime is of the essence, for example, due to financial or regulatory reasons, or as a defined goal stated from the start (Explicit SLA, as elaborated ahead). However, this is not always the case.

As it is sometimes considered to be less crucial, performance engineering may be of importance for several reasons, which extend across various domains. Here are some key reasons why one may deem performance engineering an essential feature:

- **User experience, customer satisfaction, business reputation**: We have already mentioned the poor users, watching their lives slip away, staring at blank pages and progress bars. Performance directly impacts the user's experience. Faster response times and efficient software operation contribute to a positive user experience, leading to increased user satisfaction and engagement.

Happy users make satisfied customers, who are more likely to continue using a software product or service and may become advocates, positively influencing others to use the product.

This enhances the reputation of a business. Conversely, poor performance can lead to negative reviews, complaints, and potential loss of customers. Also, well-performing software allows users to complete tasks more efficiently, leading to increased productivity in various domains, including business, education, and entertainment.

- **Competitive advantage**: In continuation to the previous bullet: in a competitive market, superior performance can be a differentiator. Users are more likely to choose a product that performs well over alternatives with slower response times or unreliable operation.

- **Cost saving**: This bullet already comes to the hands of project managers, developers, testers, dev-ops, and all stakeholders involved in the development process. Identifying and addressing performance issues early in the development process can be more cost-effective than fixing them after the software is deployed. It reduces the likelihood of emergency fixes and unplanned downtime.

Analysis and fixing a high-complexity, low-performance app may be quite a time-consuming project in itself.

- **Scalability**: Performance engineering ensures that a system can scale to handle increased workloads. This is crucial for accommodating growth in the number of users or transactions without compromising performance.

- **Efficient resource utilization**: Optimizing the use of hardware resources (CPU, memory, network) ensures cost-effective operation and can lead to energy savings, particularly in cloud computing environments.

The realm of heavy-duty performance engineering includes utilizing modern processor's architecture to the fullest (smartly using parallel processing on all cores, caches, registers etc.), but even when we leave this aspect aside, in today's world where apps run in data centers, on cloud servers, where every processor minute, every bit of memory and disk usage are counted and paid for, an efficient application may be much more cost effective than a badly performing resource hog.

- **Reliability and stability**: Performance engineering helps identify and address issues related to system stability and reliability. Reliable software reduces the risk of crashes, errors, and disruptions, contributing to a more dependable system.

The testing and monitoring practices that performance engineering brings help identify potential issues before they impact users. This proactive approach helps prevent performance bottlenecks and downtime.

- **Compliance with service level agreements** (**SLAs**): As mentioned above, many organizations have SLAs that define acceptable levels of performance. Those usually come with predefined performance rules that should be met. Meeting or exceeding these SLAs is crucial for contractual obligations and customer satisfaction and may cost money to the software/service provider.

Objectives of performance engineering

The objectives of performance engineering complement the important items listed in the previous section and revolve around ensuring that a software application or system meets specific performance criteria and provides a positive user experience.

By achieving these objectives, performance engineering aims to deliver software that not only functions correctly but also meets the performance expectations of users, stakeholders, and business requirements. Let us take a look at the following:

- **Identify and remove bottlenecks**: Identify and eliminate performance bottlenecks within the software, such as slow database queries, inefficient algorithms, or resource constraints.

- **Prevent performance regressions**: Conduct continuous performance testing to ensure that software changes and updates do not introduce performance regressions or degrade the overall system performance.

- **Optimize response time**: Minimize the time it takes for the software to respond to user inputs, requests, or transactions to enhance user satisfaction.

- **Ensure scalability**: Design and optimize the system to scale efficiently, accommodating increased workloads or user demand without a significant decrease in performance.

- **Optimize resource utilization**: Ensure efficient use of hardware resources, including CPU, memory, and network bandwidth, to minimize resource contention and enhance overall system performance.

- **Enhance reliability and stability**: Identify and address issues related to system crashes, errors, or instability to improve the reliability and stability of the software.

- **Mitigate risks**: Proactively identify and mitigate risks related to performance issues, especially in high-stakes applications or systems with critical dependencies.

- **Adhere to SLAs**: Meet or exceed performance targets defined in SLAs to ensure contractual obligations and customer satisfaction.

- **Plan for future growth**: Consider future scalability needs and design the software to handle increased user loads and data volumes over time.

- **Comply with industry standards**: Ensure that the software complies with industry standards and best practices related to performance, security, and reliability.

- **Provide actionable insights**: Utilize performance testing, monitoring, and profiling tools to gather actionable insights into the software's performance characteristics and areas for improvement.

Common performance issues in modern applications

Performance has always been something to aspire to. As we mentioned in the beginning, some compare performance to a currency. Developers can *trade* some base features of their code for performance. As it is commonly stated, one can never be too rich, too thin, or too performant.

However, performance is not a luxury. Modern applications, with their complex architectures and dynamic environments, can face various performance issues. Identifying and addressing these issues is crucial to ensure optimal user experience and system efficiency. Addressing them requires a combination of effective performance testing, continuous monitoring, code optimization, and architectural improvements. Regular performance assessments and proactive measures can help ensure that modern applications deliver the expected speed, responsiveness, and reliability.

- **Suboptimal resource allocation and utilization**: This is a deeper pit than it looks. Hardware is handy and available today more than ever. Spinning up a cloud monster server is literally a matter of a few careless clicks, and the options are endless. Be it in the cloud or on-premises, it is important to consider and make the right choices to match the requirements and the case, and use them wisely.

  Problems may rise, starting from allocating a machine not suitable for the job, insufficient or inefficient CPU, memory, and storage resources, all the way through how well the code utilizes its hardware resources, memory usage, inadequate or inefficient algorithms, or not using the hardware properly, for example with parallel execution on multiple CPU cores, or hardware caching (this is a rather special case, when such processing is needed and built with the right software components).

- **Concurrency issues**: Again, taking advantage of the power of modern hardware. Concurrency and building multiprocessing/multithreading applications are not new concepts. Of course, most server applications are built in a multithreaded manner to respond to multiple concurrent calls. But one must tread carefully when working the threads and building parallelly executable code.

  We mentioned the multi-core parallel execution above, but also mentioned this is a rather special case, in which developers are usually quite aware of what they are doing. More commonly, building multithreaded code is for efficient execution, running code in a background thread, while other things take place. It is not uncommon to run into concurrency bugs (which come with a higher toll of complexity and difficulty to analyze and debug than *regular* streamlined execution bugs). Poor management of execution exclusions, a proper locking mechanism, and shared resource access may lead to low-performance code, problematic race conditions, and ultimately deadlocks.

- **Slow response times**: The number one symptom in a heavy distributed internet-based system. Delays in responding to user interactions or requests, leading to a sluggish user experience. This is normally caused by inefficient code, slow database queries, network latency, or resource contention, as described in the other sections.

- **High latency and network issues**: Extended delays in data transmission between components, impacting real-time or interactive applications. Not everything can be real-time, but network latency, inefficient data processing, or excessive round-trip times can be quite a nuisance. This is not always the case, but may be due to network-related problems, such as packet loss or unreliable connections causing network congestion, insufficient bandwidth, or suboptimal routing.

- **Poor scalability**: The inability to handle increased workload or user demand without a proportional decrease in performance. Nowadays, we want applications to be available globally (physical location of the server in the world also counts) and respond quickly. We also have the option to scale our resources to handle greater loads without effort. Scalability refers to either **horizontal scaling**: adding more machines or nodes to a system (simply put, more servers), or **vertical scaling**: adding more power (CPU, RAM, storage, etc.) to an existing machine.

  Building the right infrastructure, be it cloud hosted or on premise, can help plan scaling (manual or automatic) properly upon need, improve performance, resilience, and durability of any distributed system.

- **Bottlenecks in database access**: Data is at the core of every application. That is the base of what we want the computer to compute. Data keeps growing, applications become more data-hungry, hence planning the right database to use, how to build and serve its queries, procedures, data relations, indexing, and partitioning/sharding of the data, are crucial aspects to maximize data usage. Slow retrieval and storage of data from databases affect the entire system performance. Developers usually have limited knowledge of the ins and outs of databases; many times, a professional DBA must step in in order to keep everything running smoothly.

- **Inefficient algorithms**: With great code comes great responsibility. Poor algorithm selection, lack of optimization, or outdated algorithms, usage of algorithms with high time or space complexity, impact the speed of critical operations. This again comes joined with the volumes of data saved and processed.

- **Inadequate caching strategies**: Reusability of data can come in handy in many occasions. Caching data close to heart helps reduce unnecessary retrievals and processing, and insufficient or inappropriate use of caching, leads to frequent redundancies. This can be caused by lack of caching mechanisms, incorrect cache expiration policies, or improper cache invalidation.

- **Third-party integration problems:** We mentioned above that with great code comes great responsibility, but one cannot always be responsible for other people's code. Nobody wants to (or should) reinvent all the possible wheels. The modern world of app development is not complete (to say the least) without utilizing available APIs of existing services, using frameworks, libraries, or SDKs.

Take an example any Python app, which almost always would depend on a selection of packages available through the pip package manager, or any Node app, which right from the start depends on a number of pre-build packages from the vast npm market, making the infamous `node_modules` directory bloat into monstrous sizes. Taking advantage of such useful, dependent, external libraries is easy, saves time and effort, and it is free and legal to use.

Many public APIs are available out there to be used whenever needed, to retrieve time zone data, financial information, AI integrations, or any other possible purpose and service. All this results in great richness and a boost in productivity for any software developer, but also makes their code depend on other people's work. This includes third parties who inevitably create bugs or inefficient code. Some external library issues go unnoticed for years before they are even detected.

In late 2021, a vulnerability issue was detected in a popular Java library, Log4j. However, popular is an understatement here. Yes, it is considered quite a standard among Java developers for managing and creating logs, but it is also integrated as part of the Apache Logging services, which are integrated by default into the Apache HTTP server. Just to set the numbers straight, in 2009, Apache became the first web server to serve more than 100 million websites, and as of March 2022, *Netcraft* estimated that Apache served 23.04% of the million busiest websites. Under some estimations Apache runs more than 30% of the Internet's websites today. That is an astronomical figure. Hence, Log4j as an externally integrated logging library has been incredibly popularly used, both explicitly and implicitly.

The Log4j vulnerability (which was nicknamed Log4Shell) was a serious security threat, as it allowed opening a backdoor to execute any arbitrary malicious code right on the server's computer (also known as **arbitrary code execution**), a serious back door to an open buffet. When discovered, in 2021, it was found that this dangerous security breach had been present unnoticed since 2013, thus affecting literally millions of servers worldwide.

A code may not be perfect, even if it is open source, known to all, and used by the biggest corporations and the brightest software engineers.

Such radical security bugs are extreme, but on a lower note, dependency of libraries brings with it all the bugs packed in them, including, but not limited to, performance issues (or, as people use libraries not really knowing how they internally work, may contain an implementation not suitable for the use, which may cost in performance as well).

- **Security and other overheads**: Speaking of security, high standards are important nowadays, and they are needed everywhere. User accounts, profiles, passwords, fingerprints, data encryption, and secure channels for communication with services. Security measures add up to extra processing and require consideration on how to implement them in an optimal way, when and what to cache or encrypt; otherwise, they may result in low performance.

- **Inefficient frontend rendering**: In the early days of the web, sites were simple enough, or they used overly complex external integration such as ActiveX or Flash, but under the hood of the browser's abilities, there were no more than simple HTML and CSS, and occasionally a script for simple interactions, and for making (synchronous or asynchronous) server calls upon need.

  Nowadays, the web is the face of the internet for many people, and sometimes the face of applications, whether people are aware of that or not (as they are wrapped to appear as native apps). Websites should be responsive to render properly on any screen and any device, frontend frameworks become more and more capable and sophisticated, allowing developers to build complex components, using local browser cookies, storage, frontend-databases, and worker processes.

  We tend to attribute performance issues to the backend, server, and desktop applications, but today's web frontend is a complicated monster.

  Classic web challenges such as caching, file size optimizations, minimizing requests and HTTP traffic, while providing optimal user experience and decreasing load times, are topped by the complexity of hardcore coding, ever-evolving JavaScript (and its underpinning standard ECMAScript, and new variants such as TypeScript), and the abundance of tools and frameworks trying to take control of the power of the web, make web applications at least as complex as standard desktop ones, if not more, adding challenges of performance at all levels.

Consequences of downtime and performance impact

We have been mentioning here applications in general, talking about the importance of performance and the risks of lacking it, but those are understatements in today's connected world. Applications are at the heart of businesses in the modern economic landscape and are expected to perform well and be available 24/7. This is almost taken for granted, and it is vital to the business reputation. Any major online service, website, social network, shop, forum, or chatting app taken down immediately gets ripples worldwide, saying the service is unavailable. Any downtime, also for smaller apps/companies, may immediately be noticed and take its toll as the spoiled people of today are used to gratification without delays, and may immediately turn to an alternative. Uninterrupted availability is the baseline of delivering a good service, proper user experience, on both ends of the business, staff, and customers alike.

The reasons for downtime may vary, from software issues, hardware issues, operational issues, or malicious attacks. Companies make efforts to always keep their services up, regardless of usage load, global location, and even during maintenance, patch installations, upgrades, and updates. But downtime does not have to be a completely unavailable service. Low performance may give an equally bad impression. According to a survey conducted by **digital.com** at the beginning of 2022, 25% of online shoppers will just abandon pages that do not load within 4-6 seconds. 48% will try refreshing the page a few times before leaving the site, but 14% of them will immediately leave and not look back.

As the app is the face of the business, the immediate impact that comes to mind due to downtime (or a service which appears to be dead enough, that is again- a matter of just a few critical seconds) is *loss of revenue*, both with active customers, and potentially new ones. This may *damage the business reputation* too, either directly or indirectly. Fewer people would trust a business with downtime service, which also contributes to a negative perception of a brand, as users may associate slow or unreliable applications with incompetence or a lack of investment.

In business and enterprise environments, downtime affects the staff providing the service, too. It *disrupts workflows*, leading to a *loss of productivity* among employees who rely on the affected systems. Sluggish performance can hinder productivity as users experience delays in completing tasks, leading to frustration and inefficiency. Hence, the loss counts both from the customer and the staff sides of the barricade.

We also mentioned in earlier sections, performance issues in certain industries may have legal consequences, especially if it results in *data breaches, SLA violations*, or *non-compliance* with industry regulations. Specifically, for example, fin-tech and reg-tech companies have strict **regulatory requirements** when it comes to data delivery times, and down or slow times have **legal implications**.

Bugs and software malfunctions also result in *operational costs*. Businesses may incur additional costs to address and recover from downtime, including expenses related to incident response, system recovery, and potential compensation to affected customers. Addressing performance issues may require investments in optimization efforts, infrastructure upgrades, or additional resources to meet user demands.

To mitigate these consequences, organizations often spin up multiple servers to back each other up, with proper load-balancing, and implement robust monitoring, preventive maintenance, disaster recovery plans, and performance optimization strategies to ensure the reliability and optimal performance of their software applications. Those concepts and strategies will be addressed and detailed throughout this book.

How performance engineering solves problems that software brings in

Including performance engineering as an active part of the software development process brings forward certain aspects of the application and mitigates some of the risks that we listed earlier. It *elevates the software quality* by detecting certain issues ahead of time, before things become critical, and fires need to be put out on a production server. Also, as mentioned, fixing performance issues in an already standing application may require deep changes that are not easy to apply, affect the foundation of the code, and entail heavy refactoring, which is both costly and requires heavy testing to detect regressions.

Performance engineering is an ongoing process that involves continuous testing, monitoring, and optimization efforts. This reflects *continuous improvement*, which ensures software *adaptation to changing conditions*, remains efficient, and provides a *positive user experience* throughout its lifecycle. Quality assurance par excellence.

Whether or not performance is considered on the server or the database, the impact of performance issues is user-facing. Thus, a good process of performance engineering puts the user experience as a first-class goal and first-class requirement of the application. Not only to make the application functionally proper, but also well behaving in the eyes of the users. One cannot be too rich, or too performant, there is no loss with a super-high-performance app.

In terms of optimization, as performance can be affected by many factors, hardware considerations, code efficiency, good use of algorithms, effective caching, optimal data modeling, distributing, sharding and indexing, all parts of the software benefit from including performance engineering into the development lifecycle, and they all get improved in quality. Speaking of quality, performance engineering relies on data from testing, monitoring, and profiling tools to make informed decisions. This kind of *test-data-driven decision-making* enables developers and operations teams to *identify trends, analyze patterns*, and implement *targeted optimizations*.

In summary, by incorporating performance considerations throughout the software development lifecycle, we contribute to the creation of robust, scalable, and efficient software systems.

Mindset for performance engineering adoption

Performance is not always thought about and considered, in many cases, until late in the delivery process. Adopting performance engineering involves both process changes and a shift in mindset within an organization.

First, in terms of process, since performance impact and considerations go deep, performance should be integrated into all phases of the software development lifecycle, from design to deployment, including, but not limited to- proper requirements, coding principles, hardware selection, testing on all levels, data modeling and database considerations, deployments and infrastructure architecture, logging and monitoring on live environments. This ensures that performance considerations are addressed early, reducing the risk of late-stage performance issues. This means a significant chunk of testing is included, by definition, from the early stages of the development, also sometimes referred to as **shift-left testing**, as the testing is pushed back (to the left, if you envision this as a left-to-right sequence) of the development process.

Also, performance testing must incorporate real-world test cases and scenarios and user behavior, which are not always considered. **Realistic testing scenarios** help uncover performance issues that may not be apparent in isolated tests, ensuring a more accurate representation of user experience.

In order to achieve this kind of optimization, testing should be continuous and automated, at different levels (unit tests, UI tests, integration tests). This is also some part of the mindset of the process, not always considered or included, but if included, it results in more accurate performance assessments and reports. As tests are performed at different stages and different areas, involving different professionals (project managers and business analysts, architects, developers, testers, DevOps), they promote collaboration between the different teams. Cross-functional collaboration ensures that performance considerations are addressed from multiple perspectives, leading to more comprehensive solutions.

At the final stage of the development, ensuring performance, as well as ensuring continuous uptime of the server/service/application, requires implementation of continuous monitoring and profiling on the live production environments. Real-time data allows organizations to identify and address performance issues in a live environment, leading to quicker resolution and improved user experience.

In terms of the organizational mindset, performance-focused development requires a shift from a reactive to a proactive approach, emphasizing the importance of performance from the beginning. Proactive engineering helps prevent issues rather than addressing them after deployment, leading to more stable and efficient systems. Also, treating performance simply as one of the features of the software ensures it receives the proper attention, but this requires having the right mindset as well and makes the engineering teams take ownership on performance needs.

Common challenges in performance engineering

It is easy to talk about performance and how proper engineering of it can make everybody's lives better, but there is a reason that performance engineering is not commonly an integrated part of the standard software development process. Performance is elusive, has many faces, and can be affected by many moving parts. It is not easy to define, not easy to debug, test, or code. Adding to this, amongst the biggest drives that reduce the investment in performance engineering: **time and budget constraints**. Developers do not want to invest their time in something that may or may not be an effective part of the application, unless it is defined as such.

Customers want their software, and they want it quickly. Even when the software itself is not quick, they want features. Ability over agility. Greed over speed. Analysis of performance and the skills it takes to address performance issues are not always for the faint-hearted juniors out there. It takes awareness, experience, determinism, and knowledge to build the right tests with the right tools, to know how to create the right reports, analyze them, and take the right measures. Identifying the root cause of performance issues (bottlenecks) in a complex system can be time-consuming and may require advanced monitoring tools. An extra point is to have tests against a live production deployment environment, which is the most sacred, delicate, sensitive environment of all, which should be left stable and untouched as much as possible. Planning all this in advance can help minimize the stress over the effort of integrating performance engineering into the "classic" engineering process. Additionally, Agile and DevOps practices often involve rapid development cycles and frequent releases. Ensuring continuous performance optimization without disrupting development timelines can be challenging.

That is, with the basic elusiveness of the process. Some performance issues may be intermittent and difficult to reproduce consistently. Identifying and addressing issues that occur sporadically can be challenging, to say the least.

Additionally, we face the challenges of modern software, which make handling performance even less sexy and accessible.

Modern applications often have complex architectures, involving microservices, APIs, and multiple layers. Testing and optimizing such intricate systems for performance can be challenging to say the least. Many moving parts resulting in a large number and types of tests to be conducted, and how to make something of it all in the end.

Speaking of modern times, the times of one app for a single system are over. Applications today must perform well for users on various devices, browsers, and network conditions. Considering how to minimize traffic and optimize behavior on a small screen of a handheld device is different than building it for a fully capable computer, be it a native app or browser-based, which comes with a different set of tools and options, solution structures, and in many cases in order to maximize the use of all available resources, apps are built on multiple channels, as responsive web apps, native desktop apps and native mobile apps, supporting multiple operating systems and architectures. If we aim for a good performant app, we may need to address all of those.

The overhead of the need to include security and privacy features in most modern apps, and the fact that they are built modularly, meaning that there are many points of communication between services that need to carry the same level of security, may introduce a challenging performance overhead. Balancing security requirements with performance goals is a delicate task. In general, for other features too, the pressure to deliver new features quickly may sometimes lead to compromises in performance. Balancing feature development with performance considerations is an ongoing challenge.

Early problem detection and anticipating failures

We already mentioned two famous laws commonly quoted in relation to modern computers' evolution: *Dennard scaling* and *Moore's law*. But there is one more law that governs almost any engineering process: *Murphy's law*. Things can and will go wrong, and that's expected. A flawless, bug-free system does not exist.

Not many people know, but the law is named after *Edward Murphy Junior*, an aerospace engineer, who was developing aircraft safety systems at the *Wright-Patterson US Air Force base*. While working on a high-speed rocket sled (i.e., a sliding platform for testing rocket propulsion), his remark *Anything that can go wrong will go wrong* (or variants thereof) was coined as *Murphy's law*. Failure is anticipated.

Early problem detection in relation to software performance involves identifying potential issues before the software is deployed or released to end users. This is crucial to prevent disruptions and ensure optimal performance.

The first step is understanding what we are after. Before starting to test, it is important to understand the performance requirements of the software. This includes response time or latency, load limitations, scalability, and potential bottlenecks. For instance, software should ideally have virtually imperceptible response times to end users. Similarly, enterprise applications should be able to handle a finite number of simultaneous users without performance degradation. This may or may not be defined as general rules or translated into metrics of exact numbers, such as latency (how much is the delay for receiving the response) and load times.

The way to maintain software at its desired quality is to keep testing it, and performance is an important aspect, as its effects can be revealed by testing, measuring, benchmarking, orchestrating, and simulating. It is important to produce test cases according to the pre-set metrics and standards and keep executing them to check for regressions on relevant configurations, upon code changes, environment changes, and new deployments, in order to detect issues as soon as they are introduced into the project. This should save a lot of trouble as the development continues. Just to say, those tests should be there as soon as possible and run in an automated manner as much as possible.

Another claim to mitigate is the infamous *it works on my machine*. Companies today have different organizational structures, some of which hold dedicated test engineers, and some leave testing in the hands of the developers who write the code, which makes them usually less independent and more biased. In any case, developers can run tests up to a point, normally to unit-test what they have cooked, including runtime estimations, to assess performance. The developer's runtime environment is built to support the written code, has all the relevant configurations to build and run it, therefore when trying to run the built app, or when running initial tests on it, it is better, when possible, to execute those in an environment as similar as possible to the designated live one (which is, in many cases, very different than the developer's machine), to simulate real world conditions, and avoid surprises later.

One option which is luckily becoming commonplace today, to equalize and mitigate differences between environments, is to use containers, which allow lightweight uniform virtualization of many environments, and can be uniformly customizable with ease, so that deploying and running the app behaves the same everywhere. This is also a measure of making sure we know how things are going to run.

Finally, load tests are a valuable measure to take (pun not intended) as a fundamental form of performance assurance. It involves understanding the system's behavior under a specific expected load, such as the expected number of concurrent users or transactions. As we first need to decide what those tested numbers should be, those metrics may be crucial for our system's performance. Getting down to the actual numbers by which we can test is important. This can be done either through systematic testing and learning from results or, for example, through studies, statistics, or machine learning. Such methods will be discussed in further chapters. Once we have expectations and numbers, methodic load testing provides insights and assists in identifying bottlenecks in both the application software and the hardware, and helps us foresee where and in what conditions we are bound to fail.

Creating sustainability in the digital landscape

One may find the subject of sustainability strange to be mentioned in a book about software and performance, but in fact, there is a tight coupling to note.

Sustainability is a buzzing topic in today's world's spotlight. Energy is one of the hottest topics (pun not intended). According to The **Energy Institute** (**EI**), the chartered professional membership nonprofit organization for people who work across the world of energy, global energy consumption has risen from 28,564 TWh in 1950 to 178,899 TWh in 2022. We already mentioned big companies, trying to reduce the energy consumption required to power (and cool down) their enormous number of computers in large data centers, for example, by using the naturally lower temperatures of cold places around the globe. Additionally, such tech giants are focusing on decarbonizing their data centers to reduce greenhouse gas emissions. Google has pledged to use completely carbon-free energy in its data centers by 2030. More than 100 organizations operating in Europe's data center sector have also agreed to make their infrastructure climate-neutral by 2030.

Hardware manufacturers themselves try to optimize power consumption of their components as well, there is no reason not to think about that when it comes to software too.

As we are talking about efficiency and performance, this translates directly to energy consumption, namely how hard should a server work, and for how long, in order to process what we need. Ecological and sustainable energy considerations apply to software, just as they do to any other field: software can be green too!

Optimizing software and system performance can lead directly to reduced energy consumption. Efficiently written code and optimized algorithms often require fewer computational resources, contributing to energy savings in data centers and cloud environments.

Performance engineering can also mean maximizing the efficient use of hardware resources. By minimizing resource wastage and ensuring optimal resource utilization, organizations can reduce the overall environmental impact associated with the production and operation of hardware. This relates again, directly to cloud resource usage. It is possible to consider consolidation of server resources, in order to reduce physical infrastructure usage. Also note that better working software, results in higher hardware lifespan, which means less replacements and more sustainability of hardware components.

One more interesting point is that efficient global cloud utilization and smart reuse of existing hardware reduce telecommuting, less required travel, thus less carbon emissions. It's not exactly a direct effect (to say the least), but it still shows how everything is related to everything, and while billions of people worldwide use software, every little thing adds up on a large scale.

Conclusion

In this chapter, we took a first glance at the different faces of performance engineering, its objectives, pluses and minuses, and the consequences of not adhering to it. We reflected on modern software engineering and how it came to be, and provided a brief overview of some of the common modern principles.

In the next chapter, we will take a closer look at how software projects are managed nowadays and what methodologies and tools are utilized for controlling, optimizing, and automating the process. We will present what types of tests are conducted and a bit more about how performance engineers do their estimates to help make software projects better.

Key learnings

In this chapter, we took a first look at the wide definition of performance engineering, what it consists of, why you would want to include it in your development lifecycle (and why it is not always included, to say the least).

- We defined what performance engineering is and its importance.
- We covered some modern principles of modern software development and how they come into play, both in the development lifecycle itself and in the design of software solutions.
- We covered some key points about why performance is important and what benefits it brings to a piece of software.
- We covered some of the objectives of performance engineering and what it tries to do and achieve.
- We looked at some common modern app performance issues and where they come from.
- We discussed some of the consequences and impact that low performance and downtime may cause.
- We discussed how performance engineering helps mitigate and resolve issues that software comes with.
- We covered some of the process keys and right mindset, which are required in order to adopt performance engineering into the development cycle.
- We spoke about some of the challenges in modern-day performance engineering.

- We spoke about early detection of issues, and again, the importance of integrating the right measures to prevent failures.
- We briefly discussed the topic of sustainability in the context of today's highly energetic (in the literal meaning) digital landscape.

Join our book's Discord space

Join the book's Discord Workspace for Latest updates, Offers, Tech happenings around the world, New Release and Sessions with the Authors:

https://discord.bpbonline.com

CHAPTER 2
Performance Driven Development

Introduction

In the previous chapter, we introduced the concept of **performance-engineering,** which is all about making performance a first-class citizen of our software development process, and not postponing it. The point of the former approach is to integrate performance as a first-class concern in the engineering process. In this chapter, we will take a closer look at this engineering/development process and the integration with performance considerations along the way, **performance-driven development** (**PDD**), a lesser-known, lesser-used methodology. In a PDD approach, developers actively consider and address performance requirements and potential bottlenecks during the design, coding, and testing phases. It emphasizes the importance of building systems that are not just functionally correct but also meet certain performance criteria. The idea is to minimize performance issues (and definitely zero performance issues for committed SLAs), awareness of known performance boundaries in advance, and less unplanned downtime right from the get-go. Just like with many things in life, awareness plays a big part.

We will examine the popular project management methodologies, their structures, advantages and disadvantages, and how to take specific aspects into account and integrate them in. We will look at tools both for the management of the **software development lifecycle** (**SDLC**), and for performance.

Structure

The chapter covers the following topics:

- Waterfall and Agile ways of delivering software
- DevOps
- Plan for performance in sprints
- The right tools at the right place
- Process management and Agile collaboration
- Controlling infrastructure
- Test automation
- Requirement engineering
- Design for performance and scalability
- Code optimization
- Performance validation and scalability optimization
- Capacity planning
- Performance engineering using Jenkins
- Velocity of performance bug fixes
- Roles and responsibilities of a performance engineer

Objectives

In this chapter, we will understand what PDD is, by first understanding the development process itself, and the entry points in which we can integrate performance as product requirements, testing, analysis, monitoring and improvement.

We will examine the different common methodologies of the modern SDLC, the modern role of DevOps and continuous delivery, different types of tools for fulfilling different purposes, and different types of tests we can perform. This will be mostly a light review of topics we will be diving into in the next chapters.

Waterfall and Agile ways of delivering software

There are a number of popular practices for software delivery, and as the demands from the software increase, applications become bigger and more complex, and the processes evolve too. Here, we will briefly introduce the most popular methodologies, their basics, advantages, and disadvantages, and how they came to be.

The Waterfall way

Figure 2.1 depicts why the name **Waterfall** was given to this system. One stage leads to the next (actually *fall* to it, there is no turning back) in a serial manner, every step is declared as *complete* before the next step is invoked until the work on the project is done.

The Waterfall methodology is considered to be old-fashioned and traditional, probably because it *is* old. It is commonly attributed to the American computer scientist *Winston Royce*, who mentioned it in an article from 1970, while in fact the idea had been already proposed as a software engineering process by *Herbert Benington* in a presentation in 1956.

The Waterfall is a one-way stream with a beginning and an end date, and this is what it is good for. A project where the lines are clear, dates and budgets are predefined, after which the project goes into maintenance mode to keep it stable by solving bugs that are revealed. Internally, each phase of the Waterfall has defined lines and boundaries, a start and an end date. Compared to more modern, flexible methodologies, the Waterfall is rigid. This also means that each phase is well-defined upfront. For example, all the project requirements are known in advance and are not flexible, the solution design, before coding starts, is final, etc.

The common stages in the Waterfall process are:

1. **Requirements analysis**: This phase outlines the features and requirements of the product. Here, we determine what the product comes to solve and what it will do according to the requirements outlined by a customer or a business analyst. People who follow the Waterfall methodology adhere to the belief that all project requirements can be gathered and understood upfront.

2. **Design**: In the design phase, the requirements, which were outlined by the previous step, are translated to a solution architecture, by the developers/architects, outlining the modules and how they communicate, data flows, which technologies to use, basically as much information as possible, which the engineers may need before they start their development work.

3. **Implementation**: Based on the previous step, we should now have a clear outline of requirements and system design. In this step, the engineers build the product accordingly, turning the idea into a reality.

4. **Verification**: This is basically testing, with or without the customer. This step verifies that the implementation fits the requirements and predefined scenarios and the product is ready to be launched.

5. **Maintenance**: At this point, it is believed that the product is built and ready, hence it gets released/launched/deployed. If defects are detected or specific change requests are raised, they are handled by an assigned team.

Here is a common representation of a waterfall process:

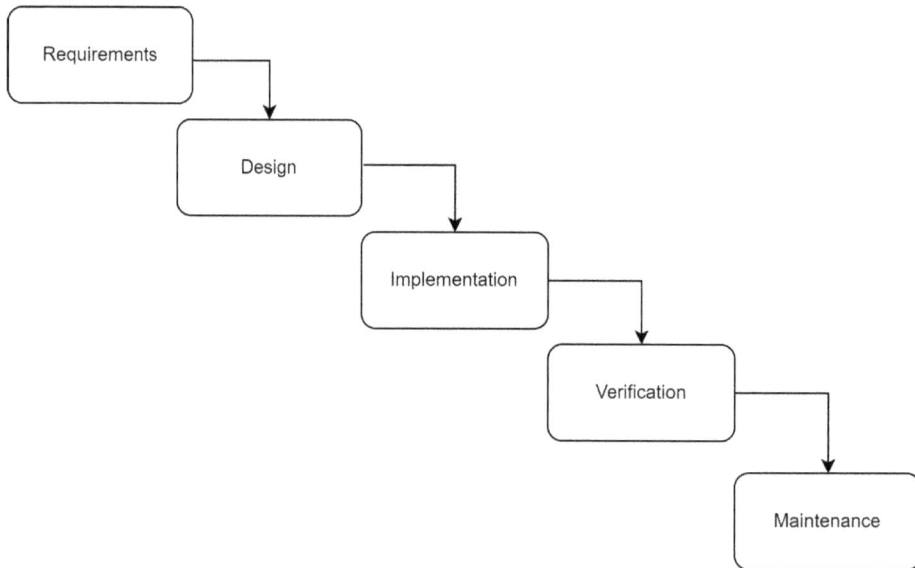

Figure 2.1: Common depiction of the Waterfall process

Advantages

The biggest advantage of the Waterfall system is determinism, as explained in the following points:

- The budget and timeline are known in advance.
- All the requirements are outlined in advance and do not change.
- The entire system design is completed before a single line of code is written. The painstaking work of research and design is complete and firm. This makes the implementation work well-defined, relatively quick, and easy. New requirements are not landed by surprise, which would require developers to start making retroactive changes.
- The end-to-end process gives all the stakeholders clarity and transparency in the process and sub-processes.

Disadvantages

The biggest disadvantage of the Waterfall system is that we are living in a reality (or inside a highly-performant computer simulation, although this is not 100% certain, as it is impossible to prove, and there would be no way to break out of the simulation, if it were proven), and reality is only rigid to a point. Let us look at the following:

- Many times, projects take longer than planned to be delivered. The dreadful deadline creep may be caused by delays, which may, in turn, cause delays of subsequent phases (and/or make them more stressful).

- Clients' requirements are not always fully defined to the very last bit. Minor details may be discovered or questioned during the design or implementation phases, which would require the involvement of all parties, but the Waterfall places hard borders of involvement between one stage and the next.

The Agile way

Software projects are alive. They evolve, change, and adapt. The Agile methodology accommodates the disadvantages of the Waterfall. Circular and iterative instead of sequential and linear. Flexible and quickly adapting to changes instead of being rigid and predefined.

While incremental, iterative methods were thought about and experimented with as early as the 1960s and 1970s, they were not commonplace. Voices and attempts towards lighter, more adaptive ways of managing projects were increasingly raised during the 1990s. In 2001, the manifesto of Agile software development was published by 17 engineers, which took flight from there into the 2000s as an increasingly popular method, significantly preferred, in comparison to the rigid old Waterfall.

The four core values of the Agile methodology, as per the manifesto, are (simplified) as follows:

- Since software is complex and sophisticated, prefer collaboration and co-working over hardcore, rigid processes and tools. Let departments collaborate and work in sync, rather than cutting phases between them.

- A working software is of high value. Let the developers do their work in smaller batches rather than dropping a bulk of documentation on their heads.

- Customers take part and collaborate in the process rather than providing a predefined, outlined contract. This helps fine-tune the software to match their exact needs, which may change.

- Flexibility and response to change. This is probably the biggest contrast to Waterfall. Rather than having everything dictated in advance and no changes accepted, Agile strives for continuous adaptive change. Each development cycle is a chance to reevaluate, review, correct, fix, and fine-tune.

Agile evaluations and discussions are cross-teamed and occur daily. A simple board shows which task is in which stage, while tasks are stacked in a central backlog list. Each part of the Agile process can change and adapt according to needs, requests, evaluations, and discussions.

The Agile SDLC is the process that takes place in small iterations (sprints), usually 2-3 weeks in duration. The stages are also not that rigid, and there may be slight variations from one implementation to the other. Otherwise, the stages may look familiar to those who know the Waterfall system. However, we are not talking about an entire end-to-end project here but about cycles, in which, in each, we address specific features or bugs to be worked upon.

A typical list of phases on an SDLC is as follows:

- **Requirements analysis**: Similar to Waterfall, feature requirements are defined and entered into the cycle here. In contrast to the Waterfall, we are talking only about features that are relevant to the sprint. Also, all relevant parties take part in the discussions, and requirements can always be discussed and tuned.

- **Planning**: In this part of the cycle, the requirements are processed, categorized, and collected at different levels as **stories** (under bigger **epics**), which are split into sub-*tasks*, each evaluated, prioritized, and estimated in terms of effort, manpower and time.

- **Architectural design**: Again, similarly to the Waterfall, features require a design effort before they get implemented. Technologies, tools, architectural design of the feature, structure, data flow are evaluated and documented at high and low level of details.

- **Development / Implementation:** Turns the feature design or the bug fix into code.

- **Testing:** Once new features and bug fixes get committed to the project by the developers, they go through a phase of testing to detect bugs, malfunctioning features that do not follow the requirements, user experience standards or other possible issues. Those are reported to the developers through the same stack of tasks to get prioritized and addressed accordingly.

- **Deployment:** Once the development and testing phases are complete, changes that were tested and approved are merged into the product's codebase. With the faith that it is stable enough and of good quality, a version is released / deployed, making it available to the world and / or to customers. Deployment of software to the live world production server can be a complex procedure, depending on the complexity of the architecture and infrastructure, and the production server is considered the most sensitive area. Automation may be considered here in order to make a clean, error-free deployment, which may or may not contain additional last-minute deployment validations in the form of quick tests. This job used to be under the responsibility of what used to be referred to as the **release engineering team**, and it is now under DevOps, which will be described in detail in the next section.

- **Maintenance:** Once the software is out there and available to whoever consumes it, there may be a need for maintenance cycles to help the world use the software, which may also help detect new issues. The software team provides ongoing support to keep the system running smoothly and resolve any new bugs. They are also on hand to offer additional training to users and ensure that they know how to use the product. Over time, new iterations can take place to refresh the existing product with upgrades and additional features.

Here is a common representation of an Agile SDLC process:

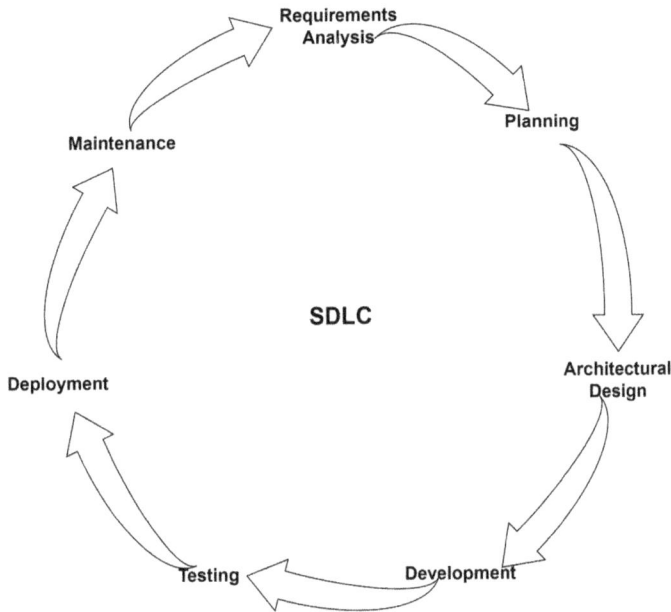

Figure 2.2: The Agile software development lifecycle

Once a cycle (sprint) is finished, a new one starts, and the cycle runs again through the phases, from planning to deployment, going through prioritizing tasks and bugs to handle, designing, implementing and deploying, and repeating again on future sprints, and so on and so forth.

Advantages

As the name implies, Agile is for agility and adaptability, responding to changes, and ever-fine-tuning the software. The following are some of its advantages:

- With Agile, the software gets refined over time. It is not expected to be complete or perfect, but it gets perfected in cycles. Basically, it makes it better and more capable all the time, and the response time to problems is relatively short and quick.

- Work is flexible. It addresses tasks and bugs by prioritizing the most critical ones at the beginning of every sprint, at which point a different focus may be set.

- Similar to Waterfall, with Agile we have definite stages of work, and each stage is fed by the previous step's activities, but the work in cycles provides feedback on short time ranges. Testers give feedback to developers, and the developers give feedback to architects and analysts, and so on.

- Requirements can get tuned, too. The software itself is responsive and, as the name implies, Agile.

Disadvantages

Agile is a really great system, and it is much superior and more fitting for today's software world than the traditional Waterfall, but even Agile is not perfect. Flexibility has its downsides, and managers need a good, long-term vision for the product and to actively work on communicating it.

Here are some of the drawbacks of the Agile methodology:

- With flexibility, some things get lost. As the focus is on implementation and delivery, some aspects can get sidelined. Things like documentation and non-functional requirements that are not at the top of the team's head, such as **performance**, may not be minded. **Working software is the primary measure of progress** and is one of the key values listed in the Agile manifesto.
- In contrast to Waterfall, which has a strict, clear end-to-end hard definition, Agile progress is more difficult to measure, as it may get extended or split across cycles.
- Projects can become everlasting because there's no clear end. Sometimes scope-creep, means expansion of the project's goals or requirements, may also add to the lack of clarity, as the project may not have strict lines.
- Focusing on features at a more micro level sometimes lacks prior design and overview at the macro level.

Scrum

Just one more word to avoid common confusion of terms. Many companies claim to be Agile in their process and use **Scrum**. Scrum is one of the **flavors** of Agile development, setting specific work standard rules, which help the teams **implement** the SDLC.

That is, Agile, the philosophy, the idea and base of how we work in cycles, can be implemented in practice in various ways. Scrum is one of those ways, which comes with a set of rules and outlined practices, such as: daily scrum (a quick daily mutual status update meeting), sprint planning (and how it is conducted), sprint review, sprint retrospective, etc.

DevOps

Now, we have defined the Agile process, by which we work in cycles, and we implement Scrum, which gives us a handy process and practical tools to realize it. We work fast, in cycles, and every 2-3 weeks at most, we have new deliverables to release. But with the growing pace of development across multiple teams, large software with many moving parts, and complex architecture, it is necessary to put everything in place, work with microservices (each of which may be built completely differently from the others), compile and package the code, deploy with or without containers, into complex clusters, on multiple servers, on different cloud environments and/or on-premise, that is a lot of heavy technical work, that has to be done quickly and professionally, and to be repeated whenever new resources join the game, or when the systems scale horizontally.

DevOps is a new concept that was introduced in 2009. DevOps is an evolution of software delivery practices rather than a new methodology. It comes to accommodate and complete Agile lifecycles, by making the bridge between the software engineering (**Dev**) and the infrastructure architecture and delivery procedures, practically handling **operations** of the different pieces (**Ops**). Before DevOps, we would need an operations team performing many tasks manually or in a semi-automated manner. DevOps takes this integration between the software development process and the operations to the next level of efficiency. In other words, unlike Waterfall vs Agile, DevOps is not a different system, but applies additional practices to the existing system (Agile-based, most likely), for quick and efficient delivery.

The keyword is speed. DevOps uses practices to automate processes that are crucial and used to be manual and slow. They use various tools to help automate their tasks and operate accurately, reliably, and quickly. While we run in cycles of development and delivery, we want to update the project on a regular basis, that is, to incorporate changes at all levels in a seamless manner. That is commonly referred to as **continuous integration**, which means that as soon as the developer pushes code changes (assuming they have been sufficiently tested on their machine, with proper unit tests or any other initial verifications), an automated process of building all the relevant parts of the project gets triggered. Then, it is tested accordingly to make sure the project as a whole still holds and works without regressions. The runtime/test/delivery environments are also ensured to match the developer's expectations, hence making sure the software runs in a similar proper manner. In today's world, containerization helps a lot to achieve this goal of uniformity, but it is not always used.

Once we conclude that the integrated version is stable and ready to be released to the world (working on a continuous integration environment and constantly running proper tests helps a lot), we can do just that. We want the release cycle to be smooth and deployed without effort whenever needed. This is known as **continuous delivery**. Continuous integration and continuous delivery are key terms in the DevOps world, also known as CI/CD.

Basically, with really good and polished CI/CD in place, fully automated procedures, which include immediate automated tests and results analysis, automated deployment from one environment to the next (e.g., development | testing | staging | production), delivery can be very fast, even a number of times a day, which is unheard of, in comparison to old practices.

Another buzz concept that is sometimes raised is **Infrastructure as Code**. In order not to handle infrastructure changes manually every time, tools used by DevOps take advantage of automation, using APIs and code libraries, and define their environments through different tools, scripts, configuration files, and custom programs. This requires a deep acquaintance with a variety of tools, runtime environments, scripting (for example, with Python, Batch, PowerShell, or Bash, depending on the environment, requirements, and available tools), working with APIs, security procedures, etc. For CI/CD, they need to know the runtime and deployment environments, to know the code repositories, and to be able to write code for build and deployment pipelines.

Plan for performance in sprints

Now that we understand the standard SDLC, and how it works in Agile sprints, with the additional power of DevOps and automation tools, we can talk about how performance engineering plugs into the stream.

The first stages of a sprint are requirements collection and planning, which are interconnected. We define the pending requirements, and then we sort, categorize, prioritize, and break them down into tasks that are to be worked upon. To integrate performance into the cycles, we first need to be aware of performance and include it as any other requirement. Some of the steps to take include the following:

1. **Clearly define tasks**: Similar to any other feature, we put performance into the backlog, but in order for it to be feasible, we define clear tasks related to it.

   Tasks are meant to be completed, and completion is an entire other iceberg of questions, such as - *what does complete mean? How does one declare a task as done? What are the parameters of success of the specific task?* That is usually defined under the **definition of done**, and the **acceptance criteria** of the feature.

   Project management jargon follows **user stories** format, which defines the requirement well and with reasoning. For example, they would say, *as a customer, I want the view report button to appear after logging in so that I can get to the complete report page*, telling the story of who performs what actions and what the expected outcome is. This way, architects and developers understand what has to happen, when, and why, and design and implement the feature accordingly. Then, upon verification, we can make sure that the task has indeed been followed and fulfilled the requirement.

2. **Cold hard metrics**: At this point, we would want to include **performance requirements** and equally important, **measurable metrics**, include the criteria of what we can expect in terms of performance, latency figures, how many concurrent connections should the app handle etc.

   This includes tasks for developers (create proper tests and quality gates, see Shifting left below), for QA (to define and run test cases), for DevOps [to set up tools such as **application performance monitoring** (APM) software which allows users to consistently track performance metrics for mobile, web-based, and desktop applications in real time], and any stakeholder who needs to be in the loop.

3. **Shifting left**: Testing is crucial for performance engineering. A single task on a single computer in isolation would normally run fine (as the developer meant for it), but in real conditions, performance is elusive and difficult to measure. The target of this shift-left approach is to find and fix all code-related performance (and other) defects as development is in process. For example, create tests to measure performance metrics on code units and set timeouts on API and database calls, as best practice, to observe errors in insufficient performance.

In the following sections and chapters, we will talk about some of these aspects in more detail.

The right tools at the right place

We now have an overview of how modern Agile projects are managed and run through the common phases, a rough understanding of the importance of performance, and basic steps to integrate performance metrics into the SDLC. This cannot be achieved without a little help from proper tools.

Choosing the right tools for the job is always important. When researching which tools and platforms to use, the selection is both endless and ever-changing. Tech fashions get discarded under the radar faster than any other fashion. A tech book can give recommendations, but one never knows when those will become obsolete (many irrelevant tech books on my shelf can confirm this). Principles, however, remain the same. So, rather than being a book that gives out fish, it is better to include a word about how to fish, explaining what the goal is and how it is achieved. Hence, in this section, we will list some of the tools we can use in order to make a healthy end-to-end setup and mention some that are in fashion nowadays. The functionality and purpose of each tool are important aspects. Therefore, it is important to emphasize the following:

- There are many alternatives to each tool, and picking one sometimes requires subtle research, and sometimes an arbitrary cold decision. Also, tools come and go, as mentioned above.

- System design and architecture are an entire universe in itself, we are not covering here even a small part of it, but some of the main areas which are relevant for the understanding of our topics.

- Each of the tools mentioned here can have (and probably has) a book (or a set of books) just for it. Here, their purpose is mentioned in just a few words, so this overview is incredibly shallow.

- In many cases, DevOps professionals are required to have multidisciplinary control over many of those tools, in different categories.

Process management and Agile collaboration

As there are many moving parts in the Agile-managed project, we would need to consider tools for project collaboration, management, the more intuitive and automated, the better. In this section we will examine some of these commonly used tools and explain what they are for and why they are among the most popular choices today.

Jira by Atlassian, and tools for SDLC management

One cannot make a list of dev aid tools and not mention Jira. According to the 2021 State of Agile Report, Jira is the most highly recommended Agile tool in the world. It has become the de facto standard project management and follow-up platform, and any tech professional, of any sort, they are most probably using it. Jira is built natively for Agile and contains a wide variety of tools specifically tailored for it. At the time of writing this, Jira offers options to be self-hosted and self-managed on a private data center or consumed on the cloud as a service, which also has a free tier.

Jira is an exemplary tool that helps project managers hold and manage the complete end-to-end Agile process. Jira also supports detailed flavors of Scrum, DevOps, Kanban, and others. It helps manage teams and roles, sprints with their phases gives hierarchical management of epics, features, user stories, bugs, and tasks, follows them all with personnel assignments, manages and tracks the status of each item, tracks bugs' statuses, and integrates into version control systems, to relate code changes (commits) to their respective tasks. It gives an easy overview of pending tasks (backlog) and allows building every possible custom report, tabular or graphical, for a team or an individual. A really handy Agile tool, and not for nothing, the standard. Jira also integrates with external systems, allowing a layer of automation in the process.

As previously discussed, Jira is an exemplary tool, and other tools may be considered, of course, depending on needs, time, budget, the size of the team, etc. **Asana** or **Monday.com** are also rising names at the time of this book as competing, capable tools. Other options are countless. Even extremely popular source/version control systems, such as **GitHub** or **GitLab**, have feature and issue-tracking systems. It is not as capable, but it is close to the code. Also, tools such as **BugZilla** can be used as bug trackers, but again, they are not remotely as holistic and comprehensive as Jira.

Confluence by Atlassian, or similar, for collaborative documentation

Never underestimate the power of documentation. Another popular creativity and collaboration tool to accompany projects is Confluence, with which an elaborate knowledge base can be constructed. Rich articles can be written and organized in any desirable way, split into separate areas (**spaces**). An approval workflow, collaboration, contribution, and commenting are some of the valuable features. Integration with Jira is native, too. When we talk about completing features in the SDLC, especially complex requirements like performance-related ones, documentation is definitely a crucial part of the process. That may include design documents, help articles, research, or any other to accompany the work done for future generations.

Confluence is an incredibly common tool, but for collaborative documentation, there are many options, including just saving documents in a common stash or centrally managed intranet, such as **Microsoft SharePoint**, or again working with the popular **GitHub/GitLab** to include help files in markdown format in the code repository, or building an entire **Wiki**, but those are partial to the collaborative effort recorded by tools like Confluence, or competitions like **Nuclino**, or **Quip**.

DevOps tools

Today's DevOps world is diverse and constantly growing in complexity and scale. Automation tools are in abundance nowadays, and it also depends on what we are trying to achieve. DevOps works closely with developers in order to get the services/modules/packages built and deployed correctly, with or without containerization, on a variety of environments, and puts additional tools in place. As in the previous segment, we will bring up a few common options, again emphasizing functionality and what we may need them for. Although there are many alternatives to choose from, each project, as the unique snowflake it is, should be researched, evaluated, and considered, which is the right one for it.

CI/CD tools, Jenkins, or similar

At the heart of the DevOps environment sits an automation server in charge of executing the software delivery process. As with other tools, there is a disclaimer that things may change, but at this time, **Jenkins** is one of the leading tools in the market. According to the Jenkins website, there are over 1 million active Jenkins users and more than 200,000 active installations worldwide, with the platform handling one million+ jobs per day. It had about 44% of the global market share for CI/CD in 2023, way above any competition. Jenkins has been around since 2011 and has many advantages, being a free (under MIT license), open source software, easy to install and use, but also very powerful, and has a large ecosystem of software plugins and prebuilt integrations. Jenkins can pretty much do anything.

The core of the automation environment is based on automation **pipelines**. A pipeline is a program built either with code or declaratively using a markup language. Jenkins supports both formats, and pipelines are coded with *Apache Groovy*, a flavor of the Java programming language.

A pipeline consists of a collection of stages that are executed one after the other. Pipelines can be parametrized and run a variety of actions: retrieve the code, build it, pack it, run it, run tests, deploy it, and run arbitrary actions, like invoking API calls and creating reports. Pipelines can also be triggered either manually or automatically, on a schedule, or as a response to an event (for example, code update on a specific repository in a specific branch), a high level of automated execution, simple and powerful, and also highly customizable. Pipelines can go to extremes, with complex features and very sophisticated UIs, pushing Jenkins to its customization limits.

Although Jenkins is the king of CI/CD, a couple of other noteworthy competitors of our time are: the cloud based **TravisCI**, the slightly older **TeamCity**, and hyped **GitHub Actions** and **GitLab Pipelines**. Each of which comes to serve the same purpose, with different implementations (yaml files mostly), but none of them possesses the magnitude, versatility and ecosystem of Jenkins.

Controlling infrastructure

Another big part of constructing an automated, hands-free empire is **Infrastructure as Code**. Tools that translate structured markup configuration files (yaml, JSON, or something else, backed up by an executing runtime, which can be extended, either Python, Ruby, or any other) into actual infrastructure, with specifically set configurations. The code dictates which resources are required and in what state.

The job of the Infrastructure as Code tools is to bring the environment to the expected state, and it is *smart* enough to know which parts are missed and what needs to be done. Create virtual machines, set up users, passwords, groups, and permissions, install applications, copy files, spin up clusters and containers, start services, etc. The idea is to have a bunch of configuration files safely stored under version control, and at the time of need, whenever an environment needs to be configured, the scripts are run to make sure the environment is up-to-date, in an incremental manner (i.e., take care only of what is missing). In contrast to the previous sections, the abundance of tools is greater here because this category is newer and growing.

As with the previous sections, the tools mentioned here are not a recommendation, but they are the common ones used today. **Ansible**, **Chef** and **Puppet** are three popular tools that help create and take control over multiple machines or virtual machines. They can handle everything from orchestration of resources, down to detailed configuration settings.

Terraform is another noteworthy tool. A point that makes Terraform different from the other tools mentioned is that it is specialized towards data centers, i.e., cloud resources, while being agnostic to the cloud provider. **Vagrant** is another infrastructure management tool, though focused more toward development environments.

It is also worth pointing out that the big cloud platforms come with their own APIs and resource management tools. Hence, if a project is bound to a specific cloud environment, it is possible to use the platform's native tools, such as **Azure Resource Manager** for Microsoft Azure, **AWS CloudFormation** for Amazon, and **Cloud Deployment Manager** for Google.

On top of all this, it is not uncommon to build services and code modules into containers. Containers are lightweight virtualization wrappers that help produce uniform preconfigured runtime environments, regardless of the host computer and how it is set. **Docker** is the most popular containerization framework, but there are others, such as **Podman** and **Containerd**. But a single container stands alone. It does not stand as a computer. A single container is meant to run one specific service or one specific app. Therefore, if we wish to spin up a controlled setup of an entire cluster of services with highly available redundancies and intercommunications, then we need a robust container orchestration tool. **Kubernetes** is probably the most popular of the bunch, but there are others, such as **Red Hat OpenShift** or **Nomad**. Once we have a cluster defined, there are specialized, complex deployment tools to help with the hard work of continuous delivery of big clusters, such as **ArgoCD** or **OctopusDeploy**.

If an orchestration tool like Kubernetes seems like overkill, there are light alternatives for running a number of containers together, such as **Docker Swarm** mode or **Docker Compose**.

As previously mentioned, this section can contain a much longer list of tools and native cloud services, and searching for alternatives for each of them would yield many options. It is up to the DevOps and infrastructure architects to decide what is best for them.

The differences between the tools are sometimes subtle, but when considering which one to use for a project, the differences must be researched in order to know what the best one for the job is. Also, we are only providing here a quick 2-word description of what is what, since this is far from the scope of this book, each of those tools is a whole world in itself, and a dedicated book can be written just for it.

Test automation

The next important subject is automated testing. In collaboration with other teams and previous stages, the engineers build sets of testable cases and translate those into automated scripts, which can be executed anytime.

Automated tests come in different flavors, a few of which are mentioned below. With the right setup, all tests can be run, both manually and automatically, in a proper environment, pre/post deployment, or even during, inside the pipeline.

Unit tests

Unit tests are written by the developers who write the code, and remain close to the code itself, covering various scenarios of method calls and asserting the expected outcome. If the code relies on other code, or on data, those get simulated (mocked) during the test.

The selection of a unit testing frameworks depends very much on the programming language in use, but the implementation is pretty much the same. For example, **unittest** and

PyTest frameworks for Python, **dotnet test** and **xUnit** for the Microsoft .NET framework, or **JUnit** for Java.

Unit tests are to be executed whenever changes are made to the code and should prevent merging the code back upon failure.

One more nugget to note here is that with the growth of web frontend frameworks in recent years, frontend unit testing is also in demand. Frontend code has become big and complex, and it is built now in encapsulated UI components, interacting with services, caches, local storage data, and other particles. This means that frontend code units should be tested similarly to backend code units. Suitable frameworks now exist exactly for this purpose. **Jest** and **Jasmine** are notable front-end testing frameworks. **Karma** is a testing framework built by the **AngularJS** team and is a native part of the Angular framework.

UI/integration/end-to-end tests

Those tests are written by QA test engineers and are executed against a user interface and simulate a user interacting with the system (be it a web, desktop, or mobile app). The simulation and tests run against a real environment in which the application is deployed, either on-screen or a virtual headless display. In any case, the application should behave as expected from it. According to the predefined test case, the test framework simulates clicking buttons, filling forms, inspecting fields, messages, texts, etc. There are a number of leading tools, some made for web testing through browsers and some for desktop native applications.

Selenium is one of the names which is heard a lot in this context in relation to web applications testing. Selenium, with its client libraries supporting the most popular programming languages and a collection of Webdriver extensions, which can execute automation procedures against any browser, is an easy tool to learn and use and has become pretty much a standard in its field. Selenium is open source and free under Apache 2.0 license. Its versatility also makes it independent of a specific operating system.

Selenium's biggest limitation is that it is built for web application testing and cannot be used for desktop applications, although many application's frontends are now web-based. Tools such as **Ranorex**, which is specialized for Windows, **TestArchitect**, which has Linux options, and **Appium**, which works on iOS, extend beyond Selenium's limitations.

Performance testing

Testing performance is obviously a topic which is going to be mentioned here a lot, as we already understand the rational and need for performance analysis and integration of performance requirements into the SDLC. Performance testing has a few faces and purposes, and different aspects of performance are to be tested in different ways on different parts of the lifecycle by different tools.

One distinction worthy of noting is between different common types of tests, which sometimes get confused. In these cases, we test the system's behavior against a simulated number of users/requests. We are testing the stability of the software and its response time under various types of loads.

Load tests

The term **load** refers to the number of sessions/users engaging with the system at once. Load tests make sure the system behaves as expected (i.e., does not crash and responds at the expected times, as defined in the performance requirements) under the expected load, that is, under an anticipated load of users/requests.

Stress tests

Stress tests try to overload the system, by exceeding the number of expected users/requests, in order to see at what point the performance deteriorates, or the system crashes. That is, trying to break the system by gradually increasing the load beyond the expected one, see how well it handles the growing load, and where it snaps.

For example, if the system is required to be able to handle 1000 simultaneous users and respond within two seconds, we can check it with 1500, 2000, 2500 etc. to see at what point the performance deteriorates, and at what load the system crashes.

Scalability tests

Similar to stress tests, we are again testing how the system reacts to an increasing load, but in addition, we scale the system resources to see how the performance scales in relation to horizontal or vertical scaling. Regardless of whether we are talking about manual or automatic scaling, we can check if the system responds accordingly.

For example, if a system is required to be able to handle 1000 simultaneous users and respond within 2 seconds, scale it up by doubling the number of servers, and see how the load corresponds. Check with 1500, 2000 and up, check if the response times are not impacted, and when the system crashes.

Scalability tests are meant to be performed once we have established performance metrics, and how they are kept up with initial setup vs. how they scale up when the system scales.

Endurance tests

With endurance testing, we also test the system under heavy load and see how it responds, similar to the previously listed test types. The difference here is that we are testing how the system can handle the load for long periods of time.

Volume tests or flood tests

Volume tests, also known as **flood tests**, check the behavior of the data layer by checking the system's performance with large data volumes.

For example, check the system's response time when many sessions push data at once, or add big bulks of data, make sure the database can handle them without crashes or delays, and while checking that resource utilization (e.g. CPU/RAM/storage) remains in the predefined boundaries.

This includes always verifying the data integrity and ensuring that no data gets lost.

Backend and code-related tests

Testing the system's response times with loading requests is one thing, but there are tests that can be executed on the server to measure execution at the code level. This is done with frameworks that help measure execution times of specific code blocks and tools that help analyze how the code gets executed, which methods take longer to execute, and which methods get called the most, perhaps more than planned.

The tools for the job

Now that we have an immediate understanding of the various performance tests we may want to execute, we can match a few tools to the pool. As with the other test tools sections, there is a disclaimer that these notable mentions are some popular picks but may not be relevant in the future.

Tools for load related tests

One popular performance test tool is the free, Java-based, open source (Apache license 2.0), **JMeter**, which allows testing load on web applications, as well as APIs and databases. JMeter allows creating multithreaded virtual users with various load parameters for requests, and an elaborate UI with many options, generating detailed reports.

Another popular tool is **Locust**, a Python framework. Locust is an open-source (MIT license) Python pip library, that allows creating test scripts with Python, then feeding the script with parameters, such as how many concurrent users should be simulated. It also runs its own localhost web interface, which makes interaction with the Locust test easy, and also gives real-time reports and graphs of the tests in progress, and generates detailed resolution reports too. We will look closer at Locust and demonstrate it in *Chapter 12, Performance Benchmarking*.

Another very popular load testing tool is **LoadRunner**, not free nor open-source, but a proprietary flexible tool, supporting many protocols, including various web, mail and database connections, as well as others such as SAP, and direct wrapping on Windows

Sockets. LoadRunner allows recording test scripts, or coding them directly in a proprietary development environment, offering plenty of runtime options.

For database load tests, a popular tool is **sysbench**, which is a free, open source (GPL-2.0 license) based on standalone binaries, executing test scripts in Lua language. It can connect and perform high load operations on popular databases, and give detailed performance reports.

Tools for code execution measurement

Once we have the collected information about the behavior of the application under load, we'd may want to analyze bottlenecks in the code, to check which functionality takes more time to execute and which methods are being invoked more than necessary: in general, which areas of our code have a negative impact on performance.

For example, in Python, the **timeit** library, which integrates into the code, helps measure and report execution time of code blocks. A more detailed code profiling analysis tool is **cProfile**, which measures execution times, as well as statistics on times and number of calls by files and functions. We will look closer at timeit and cProfile, and demonstrate them in *Chapter 9, Tools and Techniques for Code Profiling*.

Comprehensive tools

For more advanced performance profiling and analysis, there are quite a few wider platforms with smart continuous performance profiling and reporting, such as **Performance Pro**, **Performance Cloud,** or **Flood.io**.

Requirement engineering

It is important to plan projects and sprints ahead by first defining the right requirements, but requirements engineering is not a widely spoken field in itself.

Requirements engineering is a crucial aspect of software development that focuses on defining, documenting, and maintaining requirements throughout the engineering design process. This process which ensures that the developed software aligns with the needs and expectations of stakeholders, is developed within the stipulated timeframe, budget, and quality standards.

The requirements engineering process typically involves several key activities, some of which are:

- **Requirements elicitation**: It is the initial phase where the requirements are gathered from the stakeholders and existing systems. This process includes:
  - Identifying what the customer wants.
  - Understanding the associated constraints.

- **Requirements specification**: It follows elicitation, where the gathered requirements are formally written down.
  - o Usually, the specs are written in a natural language to avoid technical jargon and presented in a consistent format.
  - o Visual aids like diagrams and models are often used to effectively communicate these requirements.
- **Requirements verification** and **validation** come next.
  - o The specified requirements are checked for completeness, consistency, and accuracy.
  - o This step ensures that the requirements meet the desired conditions and can be practically implemented.
- **Requirements management**: It is the process of handling changes to the requirements throughout the development process.
  - o With the evolution of business needs, new requirements may emerge, and the priorities of existing requirements may shift.
  - o Effective requirements management is essential to keep the project on track.

Design for performance and scalability

Once we have the requirements, the next step is to build the system design while considering performance and scalability. This may vary by many factors of the project, but here are some key steps to consider:

1. **Identify performance goals:** Before starting the design process, clearly define your performance goals and requirements. Consider factors such as expected user load, response times, scalability needs, and resource utilization constraints. These goals will serve as benchmarks and guide your design decisions throughout the development lifecycle.

2. **Modularize your system:** Design your system with loosely coupled and cohesive components that can be scaled independently. This modular approach allows for horizontal and vertical scaling, enabling your application to handle increasing workloads and users.

3. **Distribute across multiple nodes:** Distribute your system across multiple nodes, servers, or regions to share the load and provide redundancy and fault tolerance. This strategy can significantly improve the performance and scalability of your application.

4. **Optimize for concurrency and parallelism:** Use techniques like multithreading, multiprocessing, or asynchronous programming to optimize your system for concurrency and parallelism. This can greatly enhance the performance of your application under heavy loads.

5. **Cache data and computations:** Implement caching to reduce the frequency and latency of accessing external resources. This technique can significantly improve the response time of your application.

6. **Choose suitable technologies and platforms:** Select the right technologies and platforms that match your system's needs and capabilities. This includes considering technologies like microservices, containers, and serverless computing that enable elasticity and handle varying loads efficiently.

7. **Design for user experience:** While designing for scalability and performance, it is also important to focus on the user experience. Users may have different performance expectations depending on the type of application. Understanding the user experience for every use case may allow the designers to make some trade-offs more easily.

8. **Integrate performance testing and monitoring:** Incorporate performance testing and monitoring as an integral part of your development and deployment pipeline. Regularly test your application under simulated loads and monitor key performance metrics in real time. This enables you to proactively identify and address any performance issues as early as possible.

Code optimization

After designing our features as per the requirements, we can start coding. Optimizing code for performance can be achieved in many ways, some of which were already mentioned in the previous chapter as good coding practices. Here are some points again:

- **KISS & DRY:** Keep your code as simple as possible. Simpler code is often more efficient and easier to debug. Minimizing the amount of code required to achieve a desired outcome can result in a more efficient program. Clean code is also easier to read, understand, and maintain, which is crucial for keeping your code running smoothly. Techniques such as refactoring, adhering to **Don't Repeat Yourself** (**DRY**) principles, and commenting can help make your code cleaner.

- **Optimize for speed:** Reducing the execution time of a program can be achieved through various methods such as caching, reducing the number of database queries, and minimizing the amount of code that needs to be executed. A profiler can help identify slow areas of your code, which can then be optimized.

- **Optimize for memory:** Reducing the amount of memory your code uses can be achieved by using fewer variables, minimizing data structures, and using memory-efficient algorithms. For instance, with certain languages and frameworks, manual garbage collection may be crucial for optimizing memory usage.

- **Consider the fastest operation:** One of the most important tricks is to realize that the fastest operation you can do is nothing. If you're struggling to improve the performance of some code, consider whether you need to be doing this at all. Sometimes, the best solution is to call a function less frequently or not at all.

All in all, performance optimization should be balanced with maintainability and readability. Always profile your code to ensure that your optimizations are actually improving performance and not degrading readability or maintainability unnecessarily.

Performance validation and scalability optimization

Next on the cycle is to ensure the system meets the performance requirements such as response times, throughput, and availability. This involves collecting and analyzing performance metrics, setting up alerts for data metrics, and diagnosing data performance issues. Regular review of collected data metrics helps pinpoint potential performance bottlenecks or degradation in data operations. Visualization tools or dashboards can be invaluable in this process, helping to highlight trends, bottlenecks, and outliers in data performance.

Scalability optimization, on the other hand, focuses on the ability of a system to handle increased loads by adding resources. This could be done vertically (adding more resources to the existing hardware) or horizontally (distributing the load across multiple machines). Vertical scalability can involve upgrading server hardware or optimizing software to use system resources more efficiently. However, it is subject to a physical limit imposed by the maximum possible hardware upgrades and can be expensive and require significant downtime to implement.

Both performance validation and scalability optimization are essential for ensuring the reliability, efficiency, and longevity of software applications. They help in maintaining a smooth and responsive user experience, supporting business growth and mitigating risks.

Capacity planning

While we are planning our system's runtime, performance capacity planning is the process of determining the necessary resources to prevent performance or availability impact on business-critical applications. It involves measuring and predicting the demand for resources based on past and anticipated usage patterns. The goal is to ensure that the system has enough capacity to handle the expected load without causing performance degradation or downtime. This is crucial in maintaining the reliability and efficiency of software applications. It involves several key activities:

- **Capacity utilization**: This metric assesses how much of the total available capacity is being used. It is a main indicator of production efficiency and operational effectiveness.

- **Throughput**: Measures the rate at which products or services can be delivered within a specific time period. This is particularly important in high-volume, high-traffic applications.

- **Work in progress (WIP)**: WIP represents the number of in-progress units within the production process. In a professional service setting, it shows the capacity of your team's workflow through the number of in-progress tasks.
- **Bottleneck analysis**: This is a management tool that examines potential disruptions to the workflow, the point at which they occur, and why. Identifying bottlenecks early can help optimize the system and avoid performance issues.
- **Performance metrics: Key performance indicators (KPIs)** help determine the resources required to meet demand and ensure optimal performance and resource allocation. Resource utilization and response time are critical capacity planning metrics for professional services and IT capacity planning.

Effective performance capacity planning requires regular monitoring and adjustment of resources based on changing demands and performance metrics. Tools like capacity planning software can help evaluate and optimize these metrics.

Performance engineering using Jenkins

Next on the lifecycle is delivery. Jenkins has been mentioned as one of the leading core tools of the automation world, including, but not limited to, CI/CD pipelines, which can pretty much do anything, and a wide ecosystem of plugins for any relevant purpose. Pipelines are powerful, simple to write and maintain, and have a wide variety of triggering options. building wrappers for running automated performance tests.

One powerful Jenkins plugin is the **Performance** plugin. This plugin allows users to run tests using popular open-source load testing tools, obtain reports from them, and output analysis and graphical charts. This is crucial for testing the stability of applications. By integrating this plugin with Jenkins, we can organize our software performance testing in each software build, thereby gaining insights into the stability of our application under load. Running performance tests in each build can help determine if recent changes are causing problems, if there is a more gradual degradation of system performance, or if our system is able to handle its traffic load optimally.

By using Jenkins along with the Performance plugin, we can automate performance testing as part of our continuous integration pipeline, providing valuable insights into our application's performance under different loads and conditions.

Velocity of performance bug fixes

On a running SDLC, velocity often refers to the speed at which tasks are handled, and bugs are fixed. It is a key performance indicator in Agile development methodologies like Scrum, where it measures the amount of work a team can handle during a sprint. Not only does it gauge the team's speed, but it also offers a projection of their potential output.

In Scrum, velocity is calculated by adding up the points of all user stories delivered by the development team at the end of the sprint. Bugs are often included in this calculation, meaning that the points of unfinished user stories or bug fixes should never be considered when calculating velocity.

Analyzing changes in velocity over time can provide insights into the team's ability to complete the remaining work. Sprints with reduced velocity can indicate reasons behind the negative trend, such as a change in capacity, inaccurate estimates, or more bugs in the sprint backlog.

Velocity is a valuable tool for evaluating the performance of a development team. It can show whether changes in the work processes have helped or not, and can be used for sprint planning by predicting how many user story points the development team can deliver.

One common misconception is the belief that higher velocity equates to better performance. While a higher velocity can indicate that a team is capable of completing more work in a given timeframe, it does not necessarily mean that the team is producing high-quality, reliable code. In fact, rushing to meet velocity targets can lead to compromises in code quality and potentially introduce more bugs.

Moreover, velocity should not be compared across different teams, as each team may have its own unique definition of story points, leading to differing velocities. Each team should aim for predictability rather than simply trying to maximize velocity. This predictability can provide better assurance to stakeholders about the team's ability to deliver on commitments.

While velocity can be a helpful metric, it is also crucial to consider other factors, such as code quality, test coverage, and overall system performance. These factors are equally important in maintaining a high-performing software system.

Roles and responsibilities of a performance engineer

We have covered here some of the main SDLC features and how they relate to performance. It is worth mentioning that some tech professionals are defined as proper performance engineers who are responsible for handling performance throughout the software lifecycle. Their primary responsibility is to help monitor, analyze, and optimize the performance of software applications under various loads and scenarios. They identify bottlenecks, performance issues, and areas for improvement and develop strategies to enhance the application's performance and scalability.

Performance engineers are sometimes part of the dev team or work closely with them to understand how changes in the codebase might affect the application's performance. They also collaborate with operations and infrastructure teams to ensure the application runs smoothly in production environments.

They are responsible for setting performance goals and establishing performance benchmarks, conducting performance testing, analyzing test results, and making recommendations for performance improvements. They also participate in incident investigations during outages and work with product management to prioritize performance improvements based on business impact.

In summary, performance engineers play a vital role in ensuring that software applications deliver high performance and a positive user experience.

Conclusion

In this chapter, we outlined some of the main aspects of the modern software development methodologies and matching tools. We discussed the cycle of the project, to its delivery, but starting from the importance of recognizing and defining its requirements, both functional, such as user-features, and non-functional, such as performance.

In the next chapter, we will explore the definition of non-functional requirements and how to consider, formulate, and manage them.

Key learnings

In this chapter, we have taken a closer look at the SDLC and how performance engineering can become part of the process.

- We presented the main methodologies of software projects.
  - o We outlined the Waterfall methodology, its properties, advantages, and disadvantages.
  - o We outlined the Agile methodology, how the SDLC operates, again with its properties, advantages, and disadvantages, and Scrum as one of its modern implementations.
  - o We talked about DevOps, and how DevOps enhances the efficiency of software delivery in a modern SDLC, by adding layers of automation to the process.
- We talked about considerations that should be included in the mindset of Agile sprint planners and the planned work.
- We outlined which tools would normally be included to aid the modern software delivery lifecycle for collaboration, creativity, documentation, CI/CD, infrastructure automation, and testing at all levels: unit tests, UI tests, and the different types of performance tests.
- We described in more detail the process of SDLC in reflection on performance:
  - o About requirements engineering
  - o About system design

- o About coding, good code practices, and optimization
- o About performance, scalability testing, and validation
- o About capacity and utilization planning
- o About automated delivery and tests with Jenkins
- o About the velocity of task handling and bug fixes
- • We described the main responsibilities of a performance engineer.
- • We listed the chapter's key learnings (pardon the recursion).

At this point, we have an eagle-eye-view (similar to bird-eye, but with finer details) of the process of delivering software in modern times, with and without relation to performance, as well as understanding the tools, responsibilities and methodologies involved.

Join our book's Discord space

Join the book's Discord Workspace for Latest updates, Offers, Tech happenings around the world, New Release and Sessions with the Authors:

https://discord.bpbonline.com

CHAPTER 3

Non-functional Requirements Definition and Tracking

Introduction

In the previous chapter, we looked at software development practices from various angles, such as processes, DevOps, automation, and project management, in the context of which we touched upon defining requirements. As people say, understanding the problem is already a major part of the solution. Similarly, in delivering a software solution, understanding what we want to build is a major part of accomplishing it. The devil is in the details and the craft of understanding what the customer wants and needs, covering what is actually needed in order to deliver the project, many times requiring experience, knowledge, and many times more than one iteration for refinement and clarification.

As we mentioned previously, requirements may be functional or non-functional. **Non-functional requirements (NFRs)** are more elusive and less trivial to define and detail, but performance requirements need not only to be well-defined and clear but also better when they consist of measurable metrics. Hence, in theory, they should be easier to clarify and understand, and easy to follow and implement. But as the famous saying goes, the difference between theory and practice is that in theory, there is no difference between theory and practice, but in practice, there is.

Structure

This chapter contains the following topics:

- Functional and non-functional requirements
- Types of non-functional requirements
- Defining attributes related to system performance
- NFR template
- Guidelines for defining NFRs
- Managing NFRs throughout the development lifecycle
- NFR tracing and management in GitLab

Objectives

By reading and understanding this chapter, you should know what functional and NFRs are and how to tell them apart. We will learn about different types of NFRs, how to define NFRs with a standard typical template, both in general and with specific relation to system performance, and see how we can define and manage NFRs.

Functional and non-functional requirements

Suppose you wish to buy a new smartphone. What qualities would you expect from it? You would surely want it to be comfortable, have the power button in a reachable location for an average human thumb, have a camera with a sensor of such-and-such megapixels, include a SIM card tray (or two), a Wi-Fi module, possibly with an option of a few colors, etc.

You would also want it to be secure so that your data is kept safe; you would want it to be fast and not laggy to respond quickly and potentially be able to play games on it, with an upgradable operating system, etc. In addition to thumb placement of the button, you may also want it to be blazing fast to load its home screen once you press it. These sets of features are less operational, that is, less describing what the phone does, but even so, they may many times set the border between picking one phone or the other.

The former set of features would be considered functional. In contrast, the latter would be considered non-functional (the phone's OS upgradability is debatable and may be considered non-functional, as it reflects the phone's reliability and maintainability, or it can be considered a functional requirement, as it defines a specific function or capability that the system must possess—in this case, the ability to undergo upgrades or updates).

NFRs were already mentioned in this book (and will be mentioned again, quite expectedly) as central properties of pretty much every software project. Typically, some non-functional concerns tend to be more obvious and trivial, hence naturally included in a software project's requirements (such as security, availability, or regulatory compliance - which is mandatory in specific cases), while others may be neglected until they are deemed necessary (e.g., performance and scalability).

As a quick recap, functional requirements define product features, which are set by how the users interact with the system by describing what the system does.

NFRs, sometimes referred to as quality attributes, define **properties** dictated by tech experts, architects, and policies by describing how the product works. NFRs are sometimes treated as desirable extras rather than core mandatory features.

In contrast to functional requirements, where we have a clear vision of the interactivity of actions and reactions, for non-functional ones, we need to make arbitrary decisions based on experts' consultation, business analysis, and research. Specifically, in fields such as performance, we need some form of technique to formulate clear, trackable requirements, not only ones based on guessing.

Features such as **user interface and user experience** (UI/UX), user authentication, integration with external systems, logging, and any operational features (like seeing and interacting with a product data page, managing a shopping cart, etc.) are considered functional requirements.

Features such as various performance metrics, security needs, scalability, reliability, maintainability, and accessibility are considered NFRs.

Of course, both functional and NFRs take equal parts and importance of the product we build, and the combination of both defines our project's acceptance criteria.

One can also say that functional requirements define what the system does, while NFRs define how the system behaves. In the next section, we will focus on NFRs and their different types.

Types of non-functional requirements

Any type of requirement naturally depends on the product and what is required of it. As we are talking about the capabilities of the system and not its functional features, those are sometimes referred to as "*-ities*" of the system (as they are normally morphologically formed as such. Examples include security, portability, compatibility, capacity, reliability. In fact, performance is an exception to this linguistic rule). Just like people, every project is a different, unique snowflake, totally like no other (NOT), but listed below are some typical NFRs, which are commonly included in projects of various sizes and considerations, but of course, this is a very partial exemplary list. However, it is important that anyone who talks about NFRs must know to mention at least these popular ones, how they are defined, and what they mean. As they may seem to be more abstract theoretical, elusive ideas rather than feasible functional features (*how does one define clear requirements for the application to* *be memorable or learnable?)*, a few base examples to demonstrate how those may be used as actual requirements of a project are also included.

Performance

Performance requirements are defined by specifying how well the system is expected to perform, including factors such as speed, response time, and throughput. To define performance, we follow a structured process:

1. **Quality definition**: We start by naming the requirement and identifying its scale and method of measurement. For example, we may call it **response time**, set the scale to milliseconds, and choose to measure it using benchmarking tools.

2. **Measurable values**: We quantify the NFR by defining the baseline (current measured value), target (value to achieve), and an added buffer, which results in a defined constraint (value that becomes unacceptable). For instance, if the current response time is 100 ms, the target could be 50 ms, and the constraint could be 150.

An example of specifying a performance requirement could be that the system must respond to user requests within 100 milliseconds under normal load, but should never exceed 150 milliseconds. This definition provides a clear standard against which the system's performance can be tested and evaluated.

Other examples of performance requirements may be (such metrics may also be agreed upon as part of a service level agreement, or SLA):

- **Transaction throughput**: The system must be able to process a minimum of 1000 transactions per second under normal operating conditions.

- **Page load time**: The website must load all pages within 2 seconds for 95% of the user base, measured under peak traffic conditions.

- **Data transfer speed**: The file transfer service must support transfers of files larger than 1 GB within 1 minute.

- **Latency**: The system must have an average latency of less than 50 milliseconds for read operations in the database.

- **Resource utilization**: The system must utilize no more than 80% of CPU capacity and 60% of memory usage under peak load conditions.

- **Concurrency handling**: The system must support a maximum of 5000 concurrent users without significant performance degradation.

- **Backup completion time**: The system must complete a full back-up within 4 hours without impacting the normal operation of the system.

Scalability

Tightly related to performance and commonly used to achieve the performance requirement goals, scalability as an NFR refers to the system's ability to handle increased loads without losing performance or becoming unusable. It is about the system's capacity to expand and grow to meet changing demands. As you will see below, definitions of scalability requirements also look somewhat like performance requirements.

There are two primary methods to achieve scalability:

- **Horizontal scaling**: Adding more machines to the server pool to distribute the load.
- **Vertical scaling**: Increasing the resources of existing machines, such as CPU and RAM, to handle more load.

When architecting scalability into a system, we should consider load patterns. That is, understanding the system's traffic fluctuations is crucial to determining how many resources are needed at different times. Patterns may vary from diurnal (traffic peaks at certain hours), global/regional (heavy usage in specific regions), to thundering herds (sudden spikes in traffic). Those can be identified and predicted in advance, to an extent (as we will see in the next chapter), and can be responded to elastically. They should be able to quickly add resources to handle sudden traffic surges and then release those resources when demand drops. Many tools and cloud platforms support automation for such adaptability. To approach scalability requirements effectively, we should:

- Define scalability expectations from a business perspective, considering future growth forecasts and market expansion plans.
- Consider industry-specific factors, such as the importance of user numbers for websites and apps or data volume for IoT systems.
- Quantify scalability requirements using specific metrics like the number of concurrent users, data volume, transaction rates, or response times.
- Set realistic goals based on realistic usage scenarios, considering expected growth patterns and peak demand.

An example of a scalability requirement could be that the website should be able to scale to accommodate a 300 percent increase in user traffic during holiday seasons or promotional events without any degradation in response time or service availability.

Security

Security as an NFR refers to the measures that a system must take to protect its data and users from unauthorized access, data breaches, and other security threats.

Security has many faces and is, of course, an infinitely wide topic that spans many disciplines, practices, areas, and needs. Among all NFRs, it is probably the most crucial one in our connected world. Everybody's information, identity, and sensitive data are everywhere, and security is so embedded into our software practices that many users take it for granted without even being aware of the layers of complexity that allow them a safe and worry-free experience (until a breach is exposed). Hence, it is an integral part of almost any software system. In some cases, security requirements are self-suggested, according to the understanding of the business analysts and consulting architects, but in some cases, security is regulated with specific compliance mandatory requirements, which dictate exact security standards and measures. Refer to the *Compliance* section.

Some security requirement areas may be:

- **Authentication**: The system should ensure users are who they claim to be, typically through mechanisms like passwords, biometrics, or two-factor authentication. Authentication is the simple case of allowing users to identify themselves and log in, for example, with a chosen username and password (and possibly another factor, such as a verification email). The person who types the password behind the keyboard may, in fact, be the actual account owner, but they might as well have created five additional fake accounts, or they may use somebody else's credentials altogether. The system only knows how to validate the given credentials and allow the user in upon request.

- **Authenticity**: To accommodate the drawbacks of simple authentication, by which the system cannot tell a real person from a fake or stolen account, authenticity involves a higher level of system authentication, that is, to actually verify the user's identity and ensure they are who they claim to be. It is not enough for an account owner to just create an arbitrary username and password; they must also provide proof of their real-world identity in the form of a government-issued identification card, a passport, a facial scan, a video call with a real person who represents the service, or any other hard proof of who they are.

- **Authorization**: The system should control access to functions and data based on user roles and permissions.

- **Confidentiality**: Data must be accessible only to those authorized to have access.

- **Encryption**: Data in transit and at rest must be encrypted to protect against unauthorized access and data breaches. This includes using secure communication protocols such as HTTPS for data in transit and disk encryption for data at rest.

- **Integrity**: The system must prevent unauthorized access or modification of software or information. This is in addition to the previously listed items. By preventing unauthorized personnel from accessing the system or performing certain actions, the system maintains its integrity as a **source of truth**, meaning the data it holds and serves is correct and not tampered with.

- **Nonrepudiation**: The system should provide a way to prove whether actions or events have taken place, typically through digital signatures or other mechanisms.

- **Accountability**: The system should be able to trace user actions to individuals or processes.

- **Auditability**: The system should maintain audit trails to track system activity and help investigate security breaches.

- **Legality**: The system must comply with laws and industry requirements, such as data protection laws like the European **General Data Protection Regulations (GDPR)** or the **California Consumer Privacy Act (CCPA)**.

- **Compliance**: The system must adhere to specific data protection standards or certifications, like the **Service Organization Control Type 2 (SOC2)** or China's **Personal Information Protection Law (PIPL)**.

- **Privacy**: The system should have the ability to hide transactions or sensitive data, often through encryption.

To approach security requirements effectively, we should, as with other NFRs, build a clear list of needs: define specific threats that we want our system to be protected from, such as the circumstances under which unauthorized access might occur and the types of malware attacks we want to prevent, expand NFRs to include comprehensive authorization and authentication schemes for each system actor, consider industry-specific security standards or regulations that the system must comply with, such as the American **Health Insurance Portability and Accountability Act (HIPAA)** for healthcare applications.

Usability

Usability is about ensuring that a software product is user-friendly and meets the user's needs. It involves several factors that contribute to a positive user experience. Those factors sometimes seem abstract. Hence, here, too, we need to think about a proper definition of how we want the system to behave to demonstrate good usability. Some usability factors include:

- **Learnability**: *How quickly can users understand how to use the system or application?* To address learnability, we define requirements for things like documentation, visual prompts, design consistency, intuitive navigation, feedback mechanisms, and clear error handling.

- **Efficiency**: *How quickly can users accomplish tasks with the system?* Efficiency is another face of performance, but is considered through the eyes of the user. Here, we measure page load and response times to keep the user from waiting, transaction speeds, data processing, system updates, etc.

- **Memorability**: *Can users remember how to use the system after some time away from it?* This is a tricky one, but it is sometimes mentioned in requirements such as having a consistent design across all parts and using familiar symbols, icons, and terminology. It is also known as recognizability.

- **Errors**: *How often do users make mistakes while using the system?* Here we include features such as error prevention (reduce the options to enter erroneous values by validation, autocompletion, on-screen guides, etc.), error recovery (backup features that help users not lose their work in case of failure or error), and error reporting (reporting errors to the user, so that they are always clearly informed on what went wrong).

Usability NFRs are often specified in terms of performance-based usability specifications, where the system's usability is measured against certain criteria. For example, an ATM might have a usability requirement that states it must allow users to withdraw cash within 30 seconds of first attempting to use it.

Usability testing is a crucial part of verifying and improving usability requirements. It involves real users interacting with the system to identify usability issues. Testing should be conducted throughout the development process, especially before the product is launched, to ensure that usability is perfected.

Reliability

The topic of reliability also became a thing and took flight in the new millennium. It started as a concept in the early 2000s and was adopted by *Google*, which also coined the new term for **site reliability engineers (SRE)**, who help in keeping the reliability of deployed software by tools such as automation, integration, and monitoring.

As a requirement, reliability specifies the probability of a system or its components functioning without failure for a given period under specified conditions. As with other NFRs, the approach with reliability features is that first, we would need to define our needs clearly, (for example, if we talk about uptime or failure rate, as listed below, we would need to define a clear goal, such as the system should be up and running 99.9% of the time, and a measurable period as a metric, such as over the course of a month, or a year), then we would need to propose the strategic operational that means to achieve this goal (e.g. by means of redundancy infrastructure architecture, monitoring tools and automated incident report and response tools).

Some examples of actual reliability requirements, which we may address in that manner, may be:

- **Uptime**: The system should have a specified percentage of uptime, meaning it should be operational and accessible without failure for a certain amount of time.
- **Failure rate:** The system should operate without failure for a certain percentage of its use cases during a specific period, such as 95% of use cases during a month.
- **Error handling**: The system should be able to handle and recover from errors without data loss or incorrect data processing, ensuring that critical transactions like financial transactions are processed accurately.
- **Critical failure detection**: The system should be able to detect critical failures, which could include the number of critical bugs found in production over a certain period or the time between critical failures.
- **Mean time to failure (MTTF)** is a measure of the average time between failures of a system or component. It is used to assess the reliability of the system.

Maintainability

Maintainability is an NFR that describes the ease with which a system can be updated, modified, and repaired. It is in the hands of the solution's architects and developers to deliver it that way. It is a crucial aspect of system design that ensures the system can be easily maintained over time, which is especially important for long-term projects or systems that require frequent updates or adaptations to changing environments. There are some best practices for keeping a software system maintainable. Here are some examples of maintainability requirements:

- **Modularity and testability**: The system should be composed of separate elements or modules that can be changed or updated independently with minimal impact on other components. This makes it easier to maintain and update the system. This is a best practice of solution architecture, which can and should be followed in most modern languages and technologies in order to increase the system's modularity for better and easier maintainability. That is, to make changing or correcting a single module/service/class as least disruptive as possible. This also helps test separate units of the system independently to make sure their integrity remains intact.

- **Documentation**: Documentation tends to be underrated by developers, but it is, in fact, extremely important to provide comprehensive documentation to facilitate maintenance and understanding of the system's architecture and functionality, as many times, the developers themselves tend to forget how things were implemented and why. Understanding the rationale of technical and architectural decisions that were taken can be a great help when functionality needs to be extended or fixed, especially with complex solutions.

- **Analyzability**: The system should be designed in such a way that it is easy to diagnose deficiencies or causes of failures or to identify parts to be modified. In terms of defining actual requirements, examples may be features such as error reporting and regular logging to gain insight into the running application.

- **Lifespan consideration**: The maintainability of a system should be considered in relation to its expected lifespan. For example, for a **minimum viable product** (**MVP**), there may be no need to invest in high maintainability if the product is only meant for testing assumptions.

Portability

Portability as an NFR measures the ease with which a software system can be transferred from its current hardware or software environment to another environment. It is a key aspect of transition requirements, which also include installability, interoperability, and reusability.

When defining portability requirements, it is important to consider the specific environments in which the software will be used and to design the software in a way that allows for easy adaptation to those environments. This can involve using standard protocols, avoiding platform-specific APIs, and providing clear documentation and support for different environments.

Some portability requirements may be:

- **Device independence**: The software should be able to run on different operating systems and hardware without the need for significant changes. For example, a web application should be accessible and function correctly across various browsers and devices. Another common example is modern interpreted high-level programming languages, such as **JavaScript** and **Python**, which depend on runtime binaries that are available for a wide variety of operating systems and hence, can be run similarly on almost any device.

- **Cross-platform compatibility**: The software should be compatible with different platforms, such as mobile, desktop, and server environments. This is particularly important for applications that are expected to be used on a variety of devices. In contrast to device-independent software (which runs on any device that supports its runtime without changing the code), here we would need separate native configurations for the various platforms. They may share code libraries between them, but eventually, they would have to be built independently.

- **Version compatibility**: The software should be able to work with different versions of the same operating system or other software. This is crucial for ensuring that users do not have to upgrade or change their systems to use the software.

- **Migration effort**: The effort required to move the software to a new environment should be minimized. This includes the ease of migrating data, configuration settings, and any dependencies the software may have.

- **Documentation and support**: The documentation and support provided for the software should be able to be adapted to the new environment without significant changes. This ensures that users can effectively use and maintain the software in the new context.

Compliance

Compliance NFRs are specifically related to the legal and regulatory requirements that a system must adhere to. These requirements ensure that the system is designed and operates in a way that meets the standards and laws of a particular industry or jurisdiction. Of course, based on the system's purposes, target audience, location, and other factors, compliance is mandatory. In contrast to other NFRs, many compliance-related ones are usually well defined, as they have strict, clear requirements, like which data to store, what it means, for how long, etc. Some examples of compliance requirements are:

- **Data protection and privacy**: Systems must comply with data protection laws such as the European GDPR, the HIPAA, or the CCPA, which dictate how personal data can be collected, stored, and processed. Those laws are usually clearly dictated and are followed as a standard.

- **Accessibility**: Systems must meet accessibility standards like the **Web Content Accessibility Guidelines** (**WCAG**) or the **Americans with Disabilities Act** (**ADA**), ensuring that they are usable by people with disabilities. For example, government websites, portals, and digital services are often required to comply with accessibility standards to ensure equal access to information and services for all citizens. Anyone who builds a public system should consider accessibility standards to ensure that users with disabilities can access and interact with the content. This includes online platforms for e-commerce, information sharing, social networking, and more.

- **Security**: Systems must adhere to security standards, such as ISO/IEC 27001, which outlines best practices for information security management.

- **Quality management**: In industries like medical devices, systems must comply with quality management systems standards like ISO 13485, which includes management controls, product planning, and quality process evaluation.

- **Risk management**: Systems in regulated industries must comply with risk management standards, such as ISO 14971, which includes risk analysis, control, and management processes.

- **Environmental standards**: Systems must be designed to perform within certain environmental conditions, such as temperature ranges or energy consumption levels, to comply with industry or local regulations.

As explained above, compliance requirements are critical for avoiding legal issues, protecting user data, and ensuring that the system operates within the legal and regulatory framework of its intended use.

Defining attributes related to system performance

As stated earlier, during the requirements analysis phase, when defining performance properties as NFRs for a project, we would have to propose clear, measurable definitions in order to be able to follow, test, and verify whether our implementation fulfills them. It is also important for stakeholders to fully understand what the requirements are and what the achievable goals are. Knowledge is power, communication is crucial for understanding, and understanding is important for acceptance, support, and collaboration, as all the above get translated into money in the form of a budget. Also, as we are dealing with an iterative lifecycle process, new or changed requirements may be added over time.

To identify quality specifications related to performance, in order to turn into clear system requirements, we could list and manage them from a few angles: the user's perspective, system objectives, and various prioritizations.

Attributes related to system performance are typically as follows:

- **Response time or latency**: The time it takes for the system to respond to a user's request. This is often measured in milliseconds and is critical for systems where timely responses are important, such as real-time applications or interactive web services. This measurement can depend on processing latency, network latency, or the efficiency of our component or service.

  When collecting and analyzing large bulks of such measurements, it is also important to determine how we process all the data and what conclusions we can make of it. Some statistical methods, such as calculating the average or median latency may come in handy, although they may be unreliable, misinformative and misleading (mind you the old story about the statistician who drowned in a lake with an average depth of one meter).

  o Rather than using such middle-based values, a different common strategy is to mark the worst-case scenarios on a specific percentile of the measurements. For example, consider that we have measured the response time of 1000 requests. We sort the results from the best (fastest) response to the worst (slowest) and find the 90th percentile point. 90% of 1000 is 900. Hence, we inspect the 900th item in our sorted list. Since the results are sorted, the measurement in the 900th place represents the worst of 90% of our results. In this example, if the 900th measurement is of 10 milliseconds, we can say that 90% of all our response times are of 10 milliseconds or faster. This puts a pretty good cap on what our measured service is capable of.

  o With this method, the higher the percentile, the better, of course, as we consider a larger portion of our collected measurements, and we know that all of them, to that percentile point, are as bad as that number or better. It is popular to use the 90th, 95th, and 99th percentiles (commonly known as p90, p95, and p99, respectively). It is also not uncommon to go even as high as 99.99% to prove that the vast majority of requests are handled by a certain measure or better.

- **Throughput**: The number of transactions, requests, or operations that the system can process per unit of time. This metric is important for systems that handle a high volume of requests, such as e-commerce platforms or data processing systems. Throughput relates to many kinds of measurements, basically of volume of work over time. This could be, for example, the number of hits per second, the number of transactions per second, the number of actions per minute, the data consumed (such as database queries) per minute, etc.

- **Load time**: The time it takes for a user to load a page or complete a task within the system. This is particularly important for web applications and user interfaces.

The user's perspective

One way to define our performance attributes is to inspect the user's perspective. By identifying and addressing user scenarios and critical paths, we identify how we expect the user interaction with the system to look; that way, we can map attributes such as response times, latencies, and page load times. We can understand and use expectations upfront with research and surveys to understand the thresholds and expectations of system responsiveness. Especially scenarios that we identify as critical, commonly used tasks, or features we consider essential or basic.

Based on our understanding of the user's expectations and critical paths, we can fill in numbers that complete our requirements into clear, measurable metrics. Here are some examples:

- All web pages must load within 3 seconds to ensure a smooth and responsive user experience.

- The application's initial page load should not exceed 4 seconds to engage users quickly and minimize bounce rates.

- The search functionality should return results to the user within 1 second of submitting a search query.

- Interactive features, such as dropdown menus and form validations, must respond to user input instantaneously, aiming for a response time of less than 0.5 seconds.

- In the mobile application, all interactions and transitions between screens should have a response time of less than 1.5 seconds to maintain a seamless user experience.

    All images and media files should be optimized to ensure that they do not contribute significantly to page load times. Aim for an average load time of 2 seconds for media content.

- Some requirements may be specific for the implementation, which would help achieve the goal. For example: implement a caching mechanism to reduce load times for frequently accessed content. Cacheable elements should load within 1 second for subsequent visits.

The system's perspective

On the other side of the screen, lies our system. Researching system objectives involves comprehensive understanding of our application, technical constraints and business goals.

We should begin by understanding the business goals of our project and the key objectives that we need to address. Those may also yield from regulatory and compliance requirements or **Service license agreements (SLAs)**. We may also collaborate with stakeholders, who are business owners, product managers, and end-users. Eventually, we would have to align all those expectations and understand the business objectives. Another point of view is in relation to competitors, to run benchmarks and see what users are used to, and what they expect from similar applications. A popular instance, with over 1 billion users who are accustomed to *Facebook's* pseudo-instantaneous response times, no matter where they are, how many friends, pages, or groups they are connected with, it would be hard to imagine how they would accept a similar product with a lower performance experience. Users of online shops are known to leave the site and abandon their shopping cart if the site does not respond in a timely manner. Those are important metrics.

Apart from the user's perspective, understanding the system's perspective, we can also infer metrics such as latency and throughput. Those may look something like these:

- To maintain real-time data synchronization, the system must ensure that API requests to external services have a latency of no more than 100 milliseconds.
- The system should support a minimum API throughput of 1,000 requests per second to accommodate concurrent user interactions and third-party integrations.
- The system must process a minimum of 500 transactions per minute to meet the demands of peak usage periods and ensure efficient handling of transactional data.
- The system must support a minimum of 5,000 concurrent users, ensuring that the throughput remains consistent even under high user loads.
- Database queries, including both read and write operations, should have a maximum latency of 50 milliseconds to ensure efficient data retrieval and storage.
- For globally distributed users, the system must maintain low latency, with a goal of less than 200 milliseconds for data retrieval and application responsiveness.
- The system should support a minimum data ingestion throughput of 100,000 records per hour to efficiently handle data input from various sources.
- The system must support file uploads with a throughput of 2 megabytes per second to facilitate the quick and efficient transfer of large files.
- Ensure that the system can efficiently utilize network bandwidth, achieving a throughput of 100 megabits per second to prevent bottlenecks in data transfer.

NFR template

There are some common template documents in which NFRs are listed and defined in a formal, clear way. A standard NFR template typically includes several key sections to comprehensively capture and document the system's requirements. While the specific details may vary based on organizational preferences and project needs, there are common sections found in an NFR template. Some sections may be changed, omitted, or added, of course.

This template structure provides a systematic approach to document NFRs, making it easier for development teams, stakeholders, and other project participants to understand and work towards achieving the defined objectives. The specific details within each section can be tailored based on the project's unique needs and requirements.

Introduction and overview

In the introduction and overview section, we learn basic information about the product, its purpose, and its objectives. This provides a soft landing into the document, of the type that any formal technical document can benefit from, to ease the readers into the topic. Including, but not limited to:

- Overview of the document's purpose, scope, and intended audience.
- Explanation of the importance of NFRs in shaping the overall system architecture and performance.

Stakeholders

It is always important to know who the stakeholders involved in the project are. Relevant managers, leads, directors, owners, investors, etc. In the stakeholders' section, we would include the following:

- Identification of stakeholders who have a vested interest in the non-functional aspects of the system
- A description of how each stakeholder's concerns relate to NFRs. Those are always good to note for the sake of clarity and transparency.

Definitions and acronyms

This is also an integral part of many technical documents to set the records straight on what's what. Here we provide:

- A list of terms, definitions, and acronyms used throughout the document to ensure clarity and consistency.
- A clear definition of each is to be used as a glossary.

System overview

For contextual information that provides a foundation for understanding the NFRs, we give a brief overview of our system:

- A brief description of the system's architecture.
- A list and a short explanation for each of the system's components.
- Key functionalities and purposes of our system as a whole and each relevant component.

Non-functional requirements

Categorization of NFRs based on different aspects in the form of a list, such as:

- Performance

- Reliability
- Security
- Usability

Each requirement may be assigned a unique identifier for easy reference.

Requirement sections

This section is a template that is duplicated, repeated, and filled out for each requirement. Its content is as follows:

For each requirement group (e.g., Performance), we dedicate a section that lists the actual requirements and specifications. Potentially in the form of a table, like so:

ID# <arbitrary requirement id>, <Requirement title>	
Scenario	Here we describe the addressed scenario of the requirement. That is, what is the case we are addressing, as a background to this requirement.
Requirement	The actual NFR, in plain words: what the expected behavior is.
Constraints	Additional constraints, which may have to be taken into account
Validation method	A description of how we test and verify that this requirement is fulfilled and followed.
Notes	Any relevant notes, additional information, reference cases, studies, details.

Table 3.1: Details of a system requirement

Dependencies

A list of external dependencies or constraints that may impact the fulfillment of our NFRs.

Approval and sign-off

A space for stakeholders to review, approve, and sign off on the NFRs document.

Guidelines for defining NFRs

Defining NFRs can be a complex task, but following guidelines can help ensure that they are clear, measurable, and aligned with the goals of the project. Here are some such guidelines:

- **Use SMART criteria**: As stated a number of times, we need to specify each requirement in measurable terms clearly. We should ensure that each requirement is **Specific, Measurable, Achievable, Relevant, and Time-bound (SMART)**. This helps create well-defined and achievable objectives. It is best to avoid vague language and use quantifiable metrics whenever possible. For example, instead of saying that the system should be fast, specify a response time target like **the system should respond to user actions within 2 seconds**.

- **Use verifiable language**: Use language that is verifiable and testable. Clearly state how each requirement will be validated or tested during development or after deployment.

- **Align with business objectives**: We should ensure that each NFR aligns with the project's overall business goals and objectives. Consider how non-functional aspects contribute to the system's success.

- **Prioritize requirements**: Prioritize NFRs based on their impact on the overall success of the project. Identify critical requirements that directly contribute to user satisfaction and the achievement of business objectives.

- **Balance conflicting requirements**: We need to acknowledge that certain NFRs may conflict with each other. A proper evaluation should help us find a balance that meets the overall needs of the project. For instance, optimizing for one aspect of performance may impact resource utilization.

- **Include quality attributes**: When defining NFRs, we should consider various quality attributes, such as reliability, scalability, maintainability, and availability. These attributes contribute to the system's overall robustness.

- **Define thresholds and tolerances**: We need to specify acceptable thresholds and tolerances for each requirement. Clearly articulate what constitutes acceptable performance or security levels and identify the limits that should not be exceeded.

- **Document rationale**: When defining a NFR, it is always a good idea to provide a rationale for each, in which we explain why a particular requirement is essential for the success of the project, linking it back to business goals and user needs.

By following these guidelines, you can create NFRs that are comprehensive, well-defined, and aligned with the broader objectives of the project. Effective NFRs contribute to the successful development and deployment of a system that meets the needs of both stakeholders and end-users.

Managing NFRs through the development lifecycle

As the project evolves, we need to integrate the evolution of NFRs throughout the development lifecycle. This involves a systematic approach to ensure that these requirements are considered, validated, and addressed at every stage of the project. Here is a comprehensive approach to managing NFRs throughout the development lifecycle:

- **Initiation phase**: At this point, we need to identify and involve key stakeholders, including business owners, product managers, developers, and quality assurance teams, from the beginning of the project. We need to establish a clear understanding of business goals and user expectations to inform the definition of NFRs.

- **Requirements phase**: NFRs are part of the requirements analysis process. At this point, we need to collaborate with stakeholders to define and prioritize non-functional aspects, such as performance, security, and usability.

  A good practice is to use SMART criteria for requirement definitions. We can refine and clarify requirements later as needed.

- **Design phase**: During the design phase, we need to create design specifications that explicitly address NFRs, such as architectural choices for scalability or security mechanisms.

- **Incorporate into user stories**: When planning the sprint, we break down NFRs into actionable tasks and incorporate them into user stories or sprint planning. We will also ensure that development tasks include considerations for meeting the requirements, such as optimizing code for performance or implementing security measures.

- **Development and testing**: We implement continuous monitoring during development to identify potential issues related to NFRs early in the process and according to need and requirements definition. We will conduct regular performance testing, security testing, and usability testing to validate requirements against defined criteria.

  It is better to leverage automated testing tools to validate NFRs consistently. We establish automated test cases for performance, security, and other non-functional aspects. Then, we need to analyze test results and address and report any deviations from the defined requirements.

- **Code review and quality assurance**: During the code review process, we ensure that the code adheres to performance optimization techniques, security best practices, and other relevant requirements. We can also implement static code analysis tools to catch potential issues early.

- **Documentation phase**: It is good to clearly document how requirements have been addressed in the final system and include details on performance optimizations, security measures, and other considerations.

  We may also need to provide training to operational teams on monitoring and maintaining the system according to the requirements.

- **Deployment phase**: In the deployment phase, we want to monitor the system's performance, security, and other NFRs in the live environment. We can implement continuous deployment practices to quickly address any issues that may arise post-deployment.

- **Post-deployment and maintenance**: After the application is deployed and is up and running, a feedback loop with end-users may be set up to gather insights into the actual performance and user experience. This feedback can be used to inform and trigger ongoing improvements. We can also continue monitoring the system's performance and adjust based on evolving usage patterns.

- **Post-implementation review**: Another type of review we can conduct is a post-implementation review to evaluate how well requirements have been met and identify areas for improvement. We will use insights from the review to refine and update NFRs for future projects.

- **Documentation and knowledge transfer**: Documentation and knowledge transfer are crucial features of any project of practically any size. This is also relevant for NFRs. We can update the documentation to reflect any changes or improvements made in response to post-implementation feedback.

  This also ensures that knowledge about NFRs and their management is transferred to relevant teams for ongoing maintenance and support.

NFR tracing and management in GitLab

GitLab (in many features, pretty similar to its competitor, GitHub) is a rich DevOps platform on which software can be developed (with source and version control, on an elaborate server based on Git) and operated, with a wide set of online tools. It provides tools to support most stages of the software development lifecycle, managing it in code repositories (either publicly available or private), which are grouped by organizations. Some of the tools are free, and some are paid. Most features are also accessible through APIs for an even higher meta-automation.

- **Planning**: Some of the features include managing tasks and open issues, building custom documentation (for example, a Wiki section), and hosting online web pages with a serverless static HTML (or markdown) hosting system called GitLab Pages (similar to GitHub Pages). This system also supports static site generators, such as the popular **Jekyll** and **Hugo**.

- **Creating**: At the core of GitLab (and GitHub) lies Git as a distributed source control mechanism. GitLab supports all features of Git, including complex operations of code repositories, branching, forking, stashing, collaboration through push and pull requests (and integrated discussions on them) with approval workflows and rules, relating commits and pull-requests to work items, security features, such as working through **Secure Shell** (**SSH**) and digital signatures with certificates, and even direct online web-based code editing tools.

- **Testing, deploying, and integrating [Continuous Integration (CI)]**: GitLab (again, much like GitHub) provides a strong mechanism that is easy to work with and allows building automated, elaborate pipelines. Those can be triggered on certain events, schedules, or manually, and we can almost do anything we like by utilizing containers, which can host any platform and tools in order to run tests or automate any required procedures. Sensitive information is kept in secure secrets, and not available directly in the code or in the pipeline configuration.

- **Packaging and deploying [Continuous Delivery (CD)]**: Integration with modern tools and package managers, such as npm, Webpack, Python PyPI, .NET NuGet, etc., allows building, transcoding, and delivering ready packages. Those can be later deployed (again with the wide automated pipeline system) or hosting a built-fronted site on GitLab pages. This is also integrated with version control of the code, features/issues, and documentation, allowing a bird-eye view of status and encapsulating the progress of every work item, but also rolling back in case of trouble.

- **Monitoring**: It is provided by a set of advanced tools (most of which are paid), although this mostly relates to following up on reported incidents and issues rather than actively monitoring a deployed project in terms of performance, uptime, or crashes. The tools here are mostly error tracking and escalations between the different users.

All in all, quite a big piece of extremely useful and powerful services for any software development individual, or team, which is mostly free.

Plugging requirements management into the GitLab cycle is also possible through the given tools, although the options of CD and monitoring limit us from having a truly real-time continuous follow-up on how the system runs (we can, however, for example, build a periodically scheduled pipeline to test the state and responsiveness of our live environment).

As part of the project features, GitLab's planning section allows the creation of a list of requirements, each containing several useful fields. Requirements can also be imported into the system through the GitLab API or from a CSV file (or exported to a CSV file when needed).

Each requirement can be tracked in terms of status, and users who created it, closed it, reopened it, etc.

Executing tests can set and update the status of a requirement if it is satisfied correctly or must be reopened. To follow up, here again, we can update the requirement status through the API (for example, if a test is being executed outside of GitLab) or through a pipeline (for example, if we push a code change into a work branch, we automatically trigger a pipeline which builds, deploys and run tests. If the requirement is satisfied – for example, response time is sufficiently good, the pipeline can update the status of the requirement in the project accordingly).

All in all, it does not provide 100% end-to-end coverage of the entire SDLC and requirements management, but it covers a good chunk of it, handled online, with mostly free features. It is extremely useful.

Conclusion

In this chapter, we examined functional requirements and NFRs, specifically non-functional ones related to performance, to ensure they are well defined, easy to follow, test, and evaluate.

In the next chapter, we will discuss following up on those requirements and how we would want to keep track and predict whether our system can anticipate matching loads. We will look at different ways we can model and predict future loads, in order to keep up with our requirements, and make sure we fulfill them under any conditions.

Let us conclude this chapter with a side anecdote of an old story about a developer of a business application who was going through the list of requirements and asked: *it says our system should be able to serve 100 concurrent user sessions, but it would be better to plan ahead and ensure it does not crash with a load of 1000 concurrent user sessions.* The business development manager laughed and said, *how in the world are we ever going to find 1000 users?*

Key learnings

In this chapter, we examined NFRs in general and performance as part of them.

- We looked at functional requirements vs. NFRs.
- We discussed the different types of NFRs, explaining their abstract nature and looking at examples of what they may actually look like. The types covered were performance, scalability, security, usability, reliability, maintainability, portability, and compliance.
- We learned how we can build and define metric attributes, which help us define performance requirements.
- We defined what the structure of an NFR document should contain.
- We listed some guidelines for properly defining NFRs.
- We looked at different phases of the lifecycle and saw how we could address NFRs as part of them.
- We discussed tracing and managing requirements as part of the software development lifecycle using GitLab, a powerful online management platform.

Join our book's Discord space

Join the book's Discord Workspace for Latest updates, Offers, Tech happenings around the world, New Release and Sessions with the Authors:

https://discord.bpbonline.com

CHAPTER 4
Workload Modeling and Projection

Introduction

In the previous chapters, we introduced performance engineering, looked at how it integrates with the software development process, and how we define the requirements in our projects.

In this chapter, we take it a step further, trying to ensure that our system can live up to its promised performance levels by applying different predictions/projections for it with various methods and models.

Never underestimate the power of prediction. In an episode of *Laugh-In*, a comedy show in the *United States* in the late 1960s, a joke was made, predicting the outlandish idea that the famous actor *Ronald Reagan* (governor of the state of *California* at the time) would become the US president in 1988. The prediction, considered so ridiculously funny, was met with so much laughter that the announcer had to pause the show. 20 years later, in 1988, *Ronald Reagan* indeed became the president of the *USA* (actually elected for two terms, between 1981 and 1989). Retro-jokes about the scenario of him being elected made appearances in other popular entertainment, like the film *Back to the Future*. It is always good to have substantial predictions based on educated data in order to know what to expect. This is especially important when we are building software to serve our business, and money is on the line.

Structure

This chapter contains the following topics:

- Identifying use cases in a system
- Defining key business flows and users of a system
- Identifying workloads
- Usage patterns based on demand and market study
- Trend analysis
- Pitfalls in performance measurement and projections
- Modeling approaches for varying conditions
- Projection algorithms for business growth and demand
- Performance test planning

Objectives

As with the other topics covered in this book, analysis of use-cases and metric tracking are big topics, parts of wider professional fields, such as business analysis, system engineering, requirements engineering, and data science. The goal of this chapter is to sufficiently cover the relevant parts of those subjects for the reader to be aware of them and understand what they are in the context of performance engineering. We will Learn about: use cases, what they are, and how to identify them in a system, business flows and key business flows, and how proper analysis helps us identify typical users in our system. We will also explore how to identify system loads in order to address them, usage patterns, and how they are identified.

Identifying use cases in a system

In this section, we will look at formally defining use cases in a system. We will first understand what use cases are, how we define and map them, and see a few methods that can help us achieve that.

Understanding use cases

A business use-case is a potential usage scenario, in our context: usage of software, describing either how the software behaves to fulfill some need (i.e., what is the *use* of the software?) or how a system interacts with a user (i.e., what the analyzed *case* of the software *usage* is?) and responds to them. Usually, a use case consists of a list of steps, each describing an operation between a user (officially referred to as a **role** or an **actor**, be it a human or another system) and our system, in order to achieve a certain goal.

A simplified example for a use case may be something like:

- **Use-case:** Send a support request
- **Actor:** A registered user
- **Preconditions:** The user is logged into the system
- **Scope:** Backend of the site
- **Flow:** The order of actions taken to follow this use case is as follows:
    1. The user clicks the **Contact support** button on the navbar.
    2. The system opens a modal dialog with a text area for incident details, and fields for date, time, optional file attachments, severity, and a **Send** button.
    3. The user fills the incident fields to their satisfaction, then clicks the **Send** button.
    4. The request is sent, a confirmation message is displayed on the screen, or an error message, in case there was an error sending the report.

There are additional formalities and optional fields in a proper use-case, depending on its complexity, and additional ways to illustrate it, including various formats of visual diagrams grouped under the collective name **System Modeling Language (SysML)**.

SysML diagrams portray different aspects of the system. They include, but may not be limited to, the following:

- Activity diagrams (fancy flow charts)
- Sequence diagrams (showing how one action leads to the next in progression)
- State-machine diagrams (showing which states a system can be in and which state can lead to which)
- Use-case diagrams (basically showing which actor interacts with which use-case)
- Block-definition diagrams (showing parts of the system and how they relate)

Examples: On the left, holding a bouquet of sideways balloons: a simple use-case diagram listing three typical use-cases per specific actor (this diagram maps actors to their relevant use-cases).

On the right, the sketch that resembles a *Donkey Kong* level is a sequence diagram showing the flow of actions, components, and times (the following figure shows the sequence of operations flow between parts of the system).

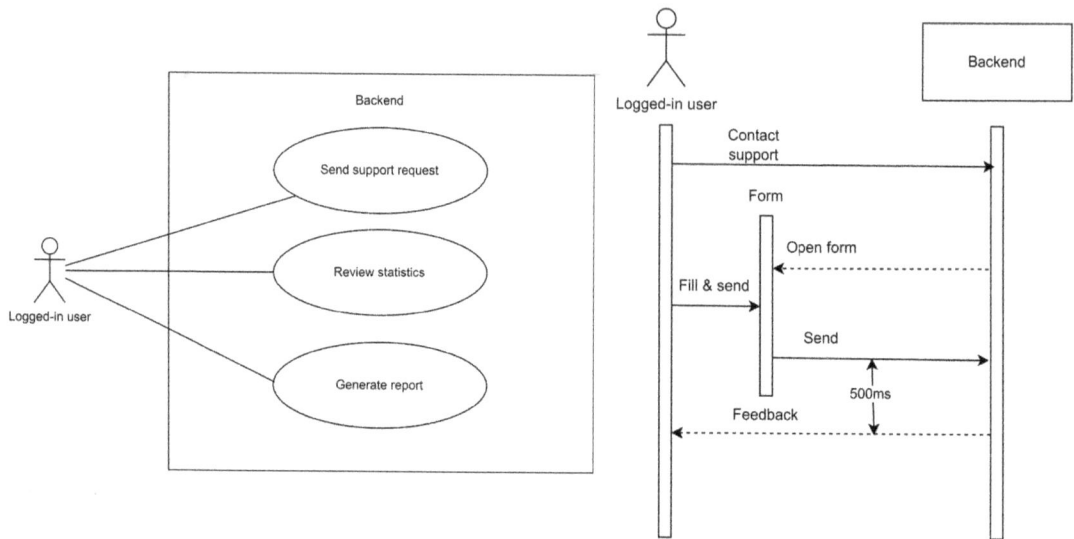

Figure 4.1: A use-case diagram (left) and a sequence diagram (right)

Complex systems handle many objects, functions, features, and scenarios. The tricky part when building the analysis is to identify and map all the use cases, or at least as many of the relevant ones as possible.

Identifying use cases

There are a few common techniques for identifying use cases in a system. In many cases, in order to get a good result, more than one of them is used. Other techniques may be considered, too. I am listing here a couple of the common ones.

The coffee break method

Right from the title, this seems like a good idea, with a minor potential for caffeine addiction. However, this is surely the most informal non-standard technique in use case analysis or system design. The idea behind this method is to take a short break from the main task of identifying use cases, perhaps to grab a coffee or take a walk, and then come back to the task with fresh ideas and perspectives. This approach can help prevent burnout and maintain creativity during the use case identification process. Additionally, once the analyst has identified a whole use case, they should not feel guilty about taking a break. It goes something like this:

1. Start identifying use cases based on your current knowledge and observations.

2. When you feel like you are stuck or need a break, take a short coffee break.

3. After the break, revisit the use cases you were working on. You might find that you are able to see them from a different perspective, leading to new insights or discoveries.

4. Continue this process until you feel confident that you have identified all the necessary use cases for the system.

A point to note here is that such a method can be useful for any brainstormed/creative process, which requires analysis and thought, such as trying to find a solution to a bug or an issue with the software.

Despite the fact that this practice may be considered less serious or formal, keep in mind that the goal of use case identification is to ensure that the system meets the needs of its users and provides value in its intended context. Hence, any technique that helps achieve this goal can be considered effective.

The CRUD method

The acronym CRUD is known to pretty much anyone who has worked on a functional system. It is short for Create, Read, Update, and Delete, the four standard basic actions one can perform on a data element in a system. The idea of this technique is to be systematic (pun not intended): first, identify all the data elements the system handles, list them, attach the four base operations to each, and each (when relevant) yields a use case.

For example, if there is a part of the system that handles orders, we can create this list:

Entity	Operation	Use-case
Order	Create	Create a new order
	Read (Get)	Get a list of orders Get order details Search for an order
	Update	Update order details
	Delete	Delete an order

Table 4.1: CRUD actions for an Order object

Just with this simple list, we have already identified and listed six use cases to add to our stash:

- Create a new order
- Get a list of orders
- Get order details
- Search for an order
- Update order details
- Delete an order

The systematic methodic scan of use cases continues in a similar manner.

Event decomposition method

This technique tackles the use-case identification from a different direction: start by imagining the system as an opaque black box that has to respond to certain events. Hence, first, we identify which events the system should handle, both externally and internally. This is done by the power of thought and brainstorming with relevant stakeholders, business owners, customers, analysts, and anyone deemed relevant.

For example, a user from outside the system can manage their delivery addresses:

- Create a delivery address (system use-case: save address details)
- View details of an address (system use-case: get an address)
- Search addresses (system use-case: get addresses)
- Update an address (system use-case: save address details)
- Delete an address (system use-case: delete an address)

The system, too, can have its internally triggered events, such as:

- Scheduled delivery notifications (system use-case: send notifications)
- Scheduled delivery of newsletters & marketing (system use-case: send newsletter)
- Scheduled creation of reports (system use-case: generate report)

This way, we collect use cases from different angles of the system by analyzing potential events.

Inferring real use-cases

Other techniques involve inferring information from different sources and sometimes require the system to be already usable. Actors/users can be actual users or test users. This gives a glimpse into how people *actually* use the system and provides real-world scenarios. For example:

- **Interview:** This technique involves interviewing users of the existing system. During the interview, the analyst asks open questions initially to understand behavior at a high level, and then more specific, closed questions to get more details. The interview can also involve asking about activities that are undertaken to identify use cases and who is responsible for identifying the actors.
- **Observation:** This technique involves observing the users. By watching how users interact with the system, analysts can gain insights into the actions they need to perform and the goals they are trying to achieve.
- **Analysis of documentation**: This technique involves reviewing existing documentation such as scope documents, regulatory documentation, marketing material, and training material/operational manuals for the existing system. These documents often contain valuable information about the system's capabilities and the actions that users need to perform.

Any of the methods listed previously result in collected use cases. As mentioned, usually, a combination of more than one method is common practice, as long as the **coffee break** method is included, in order to take a rest every now and then.

Defining key business flows and users of a system

As a base step of measuring, projecting and strategizing usage of our system, we would have to first understand who our users are, and how they use our system. In this section we will discuss mapping our main intended interaction flows, and how we plan for our users to realize them.

Key business flows

Taking a higher-view look at a system, we look at the value/profit of it all and what makes it. Key business flows are essential sequences of operations that a business performs to generate value. These flows are typically operational processes that significantly impact the business's customers, employees, and overall performance. They answer the question: *How does our business generate value?*

Typically, key business flows fall within the following categories:

- **Developing vision and strategy**: This includes setting the direction of the business, determining its goals, and formulating strategies to achieve these goals.
- **Developing and managing products and services**: This involves designing, creating, and managing the products or services that the business offers to its customers.
- **Marketing and selling products and services**: This includes promoting the products or services to potential customers, attracting new customers, and retaining existing ones.
- **Delivering services**: This involves providing the services that the business offers to its customers.
- **Managing customer service**: This includes handling customer inquiries, complaints, and feedback to ensure customer satisfaction and loyalty.

These key business flows are not universal or set in stone; they are unique to each organization. Identifying them helps businesses understand where to focus their investments and energy, and allows them to identify areas of strength and weakness that need improvement.

Defining key business flows of a system involves understanding the core processes that the system performs to deliver its value proposition. These flows are the sequences of activities that a system goes through to achieve its purpose. Here are some methods to identify key business flows:

- **Business process modeling**: It involves creating a visual representation of the flow of business activities or functions within a system. It helps to document and understand the current flow of activities to identify improvements and enhancements for faster accomplishment of tasks.

- **Business process mapping**: It is a procedure to document, clarify, and break down process sequences into logical steps. The mapping can be done in a written format or visualized using flow charts. This technique can help identify the main functions of the system and how they interact with each other.

By applying such techniques, one can effectively define the key business flows of a system, helping to ensure that the system meets the needs of its intended users and supports the organization's business processes.

User analysis

Another point of view we would want to take on our system is the user's. To know how to make the most of our software, we need to understand who our users are and how they are expected to use it. Rather than asking, *who are the users?* we distinguish users by what they are expected to do.

As we plan the system and the idea of how it would be used, we often talk about **user flows**, or **user journeys**. This typically means a detailed representation of the specific steps in a path or process that a user takes to complete a given task in our system (e.g., signing into an app).

User flows can be represented verbally as a list of steps or by flow diagrams. An overly simplified diagram can look something like *Figure 4.2*. It shows how a user passes from the products page to the cart, given an option to continue to check out (which would lead to the check-out flow), or go back to see more products.

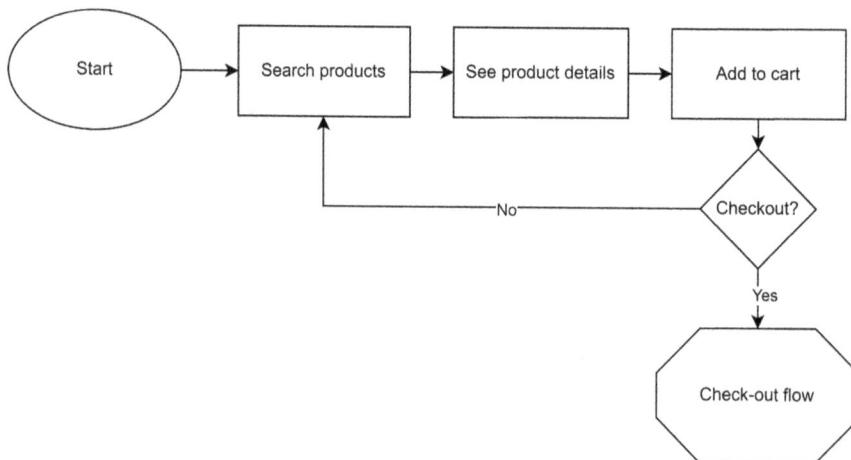

Figure 4.2: Product browsing user flow diagram

Once we gather and understand the user flows, their analysis can be a powerful tool for categorizing users based on their behavior and needs. With this analysis, we can categorize different typical users of our systems and understand their needs and expectations. Here are some of the ways in which this can be achieved:

- **Segmentation-based user flows**: One way to categorize users is by segmenting user flows based on cohorts. For example, you might have different user flows for regular users, new users, paying users, and so on. Each of these cohorts might require different actions or have different needs, so segmenting the user flows can help us understand and effectively cater to these different groups.

- **Identifying friction points**: User flow analysis can help identify areas where users encounter friction or difficulty. These friction points can indicate areas where the system may not effectively meet the needs of certain user groups. Categorizing users based on these friction points can help prioritize improvements and tailor solutions to address these specific needs.

- **Monitoring behavior**: User flow analysis allows monitoring user behavior and track changes over time. This can help us identify patterns and trends among different user groups. For example, we may notice that certain groups of users frequently abandon the system after reaching a certain point, indicating a problem area that requires our attention.

- **Optimizing user experience**: By understanding the user flows and identifying areas of friction, we can optimize the user experience for each group. This might involve simplifying complex processes, improving navigation, or personalizing content to better suit the needs and preferences of each user group.

Identifying workloads

Another aspect we may want to look into, both in advance and after the system stands, in relation to planning for performance development, is loads on the system. Identifying and predicting loads of a system is crucial for ensuring optimal performance and scalability. Loads can refer to the amount of work or demand placed on a system, caused either by an increased number of users interacting or anything that triggers heavier processing, causing increases in CPU and memory usage, network bandwidth, disk space, etc. There can be different ways to predict and measure loads. Some include, but are not limited to:

- **Performance monitoring:** We use monitoring tools to track the current load on the system. These tools can provide real-time data on resource usage, such as CPU utilization, memory usage, network traffic, disk activity, etc. Regularly collecting this data can help identify patterns and trends in system load. Tools such as *Prometheus* (for data collection) + *Grafana* (to produce insightful, informative dashboards) may give a good view of what is going on, and a lot can be learned from that.

  We will discuss performance monitoring techniques in greater detail in *Chapter 8, Designing Performance Monitoring*.

- **Capacity planning (load planning)**: Based on the measured load, we can plan for future capacity. This involves estimating the expected growth in our system's usage and planning for it accordingly. This could involve upgrading hardware, optimizing software, or scaling infrastructure.

  Once we have defined our performance objectives, monitored and measured our workload, and identified bottlenecks, we can create and implement a capacity management plan. The goal of this plan is to meet or exceed our performance objectives (especially during peak usage periods) and to allow for future workload increases. To achieve this, we implement a base capacity plan and then continuously monitor the performance metrics and adjust accordingly. This may include changing hardware specs, number of machines, database configurations and other pieces of the system.

- **Load testing**: It is the classic and a fundamental part of performance engineering. This consists of simulating high levels of traffic or workload on the system, to measure how it handles stress and to identify bottlenecks or performance issues. Load testing can provide valuable insights into how the system behaves under heavy loads and can help us predict future loads.

  We will discuss different load tests and review examples of measurement tools usage in *Chapter 12, Performance Benchmarking*.

- **Trend analysis**: Looking into the future and guesstimating is good, but looking back may also produce valuable results. Analysis of historical load data may help identify trends and patterns. For example, if we notice that the system's load increases every weekday or on specific days, hours, or holidays, we can use this information to anticipate future loads and plan accordingly.

- **Using predictive models**: As another valuable insight from past data, advanced techniques such as machine learning can be used to predict future loads based on historical data. These models can consider factors like time of day, day of the week, season, etc., and use this information to predict future loads.

We will discuss trend analysis further and show examples of using predictive models in *Chapter 14, Performance Behavioral Correlation*.

By identifying and predicting loads, we can ensure that the system is always ready to handle its demands, providing a smooth and efficient service to its users.

Commercial cloud environments today provide automation of system scaling, both up and down, either horizontally or vertically, as an immediate response to load changes, according to predefined rules. This is in order to save on resources, optimize performance, and always be ready for trend changes with minimum worries and intervention.

In the coming sections, we will look at different ways to identify loads by different methods of analyzing market trends and statistical data.

Usage patterns based on demand and market study

Analyzing patterns of actual monitored usage and/or relying on market studies yields insight into regular fluctuations in demand for a product or service over time. These fluctuations can be caused by a variety of factors, such as seasonality, economic cycles, and trends. Here are some steps to identify and define usage patterns:

1. **Data collection**: Collecting historical demand data, customer surveys, and market research. These data sources can provide valuable insights into the demand patterns of our product or service.

2. **Identifying patterns over time**: Look for patterns in the collected data over a period of time. This can help us understand how demand has fluctuated and identify any recurring patterns. Refer to the *Trend analysis* section.

3. **Considering different types of demand patterns**: There are several types of demand patterns, including seasonal, cyclical, trended, and random. We would need to identify which type (or types) apply to our product or service. For example, if the product is seasonal, we may see higher demand during certain seasons and lower demand at other times.

4. **Applying market studies**: Using market studies to identify external factors that might influence demand for our product or service. Such factors could include economic conditions, market trends, competitive pressures, and consumer preferences.

5. **Use demand patterns to inform decisions**: Once we have identified patterns in demand, we incorporate them into our business decisions. For example, we might decide to adjust our inventory levels based on predicted demand, set prices that align with demand patterns, or target marketing campaigns to coincide with periods of high demand.

Equally important, and to the point of our main topic, if we predict higher demand based on those patterns, we can estimate whether our resources are sufficient in order to address it with acceptable performance metrics or to increase/scale our resources accordingly in advance.

Trend analysis

Trend analysis is a statistical technique used to identify patterns in data over time. In the context of system use and load, this technique can provide valuable insights into how usage and load patterns evolve over time. By recognizing these patterns, we can try to understand why these variations occur. For example, if usage tends to increase on Mondays, we might predict that usage will also increase on future Mondays. Similarly, if load tends to peak at certain times, we might predict that load will also peak at these times in the future.

Moreover, by comparing the observed trends to the expected trends, we can identify any discrepancies. These discrepancies can indicate problems, such as unexpected peaks in load or decreases in usage. At the same time, any trends that deviate from the norm can indicate opportunities for improvement, such as reducing load during off-peak hours or increasing capacity to handle increased usage.

Similar to what we pointed out in the previous section, about identifying demand trends and inquiring market studies, once we have identified the trends in usage and load and any potential problems or opportunities, we can use this information to inform our decision-making. For example, we may decide to allocate more resources to handle increased load during peak times, or to investigate why usage is decreasing during certain times.

One example of the use of trend analysis is in the retail sector, where trend analysis can help identify changes in consumer behavior and market dynamics. For instance, a sudden drop in sales during a specific month could indicate a shift in consumer preferences or a change in the market environment. This information can help retailers adjust their strategies and stay competitive. Usage trends can be identified using both statistical methods and machine learning techniques.

Statistical methods involve analyzing historical data to identify patterns and trends. This could involve using simple visual analysis, such as plotting data over time and looking for consistent patterns or anomalies. For example, we may notice that usage increases on certain days of the week or at certain times of the day. More advanced statistical methods might involve using regression models or time series analysis to predict future usage trends based on past data.

Machine learning techniques can automate and refine the process of identifying data trends. Machine learning algorithms can learn from large amounts of data and automatically identify patterns, trends, and correlations that may not be apparent from manual analysis. For example, machine learning can be used to predict future usage trends based on past data, considering factors like seasonality, holidays, and other variables that might influence usage.

One of the advantages of using machine learning for trend analysis is that it can provide quick, objective, and up-to-date overviews of the latest trends. Machine learning algorithms can analyze large volumes of data in real time, providing researchers with the latest information and insights as they emerge. This can help them stay up-to-date with the latest developments in their field and make more informed decisions about their research and innovation strategies.

Pitfalls in performance measurement and projections

Software performance measurement and projections can be a complex task, and there are several pitfalls that teams often encounter. Some of these include:

- **Misalignment with organizational goals**: One of the most common pitfalls is a misalignment between performance models and organizational goals. It is crucial for performance models to be designed in a way that complements the overarching objectives of the organization. This means verifying that the metrics being tracked are relevant and contribute to the overall success of the organization. If not, failure to align performance models with organizational goals can lead to misguided efforts and wasted resources.

- **Overemphasis on quantitative metrics**: While quantitative metrics play a crucial role in performance evaluation, overemphasizing them can be detrimental. Organizations that solely focus on numerical data may overlook important qualitative aspects such as employee engagement, innovation, and customer satisfaction. A balanced approach that incorporates both quantitative and qualitative measures is crucial for a holistic performance evaluation.

- **Poor data quality**: The quality of the data used in performance measurements and projections can greatly affect the accuracy of the results. Poor data quality can lead to inaccurate predictions and misleading conclusions. Ensuring that the data used is accurate, reliable, and representative of the population being studied is therefore crucial.

- **Failure to adjust for external factors**: External factors such as changes in technology, market conditions, or competition can significantly impact software performance. If these factors are not properly accounted for in performance measurements and projections, it can lead to inaccurate predictions and decisions.

To overcome these pitfalls, it is important to align performance models with organizational objectives, balance the use of quantitative and qualitative metrics, ensure data quality, and adjust for external factors. Additionally, regular reviews and adjustments based on changes in the organization or the environment can help maintain alignment and accuracy.

Modeling approaches for varying conditions

Modeling for different load and time conditions is a crucial aspect of system design and performance analysis. It involves creating mathematical representations of a system's behavior under different conditions, which can then be used to predict how the system will perform under those conditions.

Here are some techniques for modeling system behavior under different load and time conditions:

- **Static vs. dynamic models**: Load models can be classified into static and dynamic models. Static models assume that the system's load is constant over time, while dynamic models consider changes in load over time. The choice between static and dynamic models depends on whether the system's load varies significantly over time.

- **Measurement-based vs. component-based**: Two types of approaches can be used to identify model parameters: measurement-based and component-based. Measurement-based approaches involve collecting data about the system's actual behavior and using this data to estimate the model parameters. Component-based approaches involve breaking down the system into its individual components and modeling each component separately.

- **Artificial neural networks**: **Artificial neural networks (ANNs)** can be used to create complex models that can capture the nonlinear relationships between input and output variables. ANNs can be trained on historical data to predict future system behavior under different load and time conditions.

- **Bayesian estimation**: Bayesian estimation can be used to update the model parameters based on new data. This approach can provide a probabilistic framework for modeling system behavior under different load and time conditions. In simple words, Bayesian estimation involves making a data estimate, based on various factors, then update those estimations with observations, which either reinforce or weaken them.

These techniques allow for a comprehensive understanding of system behavior under different load and time conditions, enabling more accurate predictions and better system design.

Projection algorithms for business growth and demand

Demand forecasting plays a crucial role in the success of any business. By accurately predicting customer demand, businesses can not only plan in order to accommodate the performance requirements, but also to optimize inventory, production, customer satisfaction, pricing and many other business properties. Without demand forecasting, businesses may face numerous challenges, such as lost sales opportunities, excessive inventory costs, and inefficient resource allocation.

Forecasting algorithms can be broadly categorized into several types, including statistical models, machine learning models, and hybrid models that combine both approaches. Each algorithm has its strengths and weaknesses and is suitable for different types of data and forecasting scenarios.

Machine learning algorithms can help forecast demand and load by analyzing historical sales data and incorporating external factors such as economic indicators, weather data, or social media trends. Machine learning algorithms can generate more accurate sales forecasts. These forecasts can provide valuable insights for adjusting the system to be able to handle the load changes. Forecasting in this context is generally divided into forecasting demand and forecasting growth:

- **Growth forecasting**: This involves predicting the overall increase in system usage, user base, or data volume over a given period. It helps businesses understand the scale of growth they are expecting, which can influence decisions around system scalability, infrastructure upgrades, and resource allocation. Accurate growth forecasting can enable businesses to prepare for increased demand, avoid overprovisioning resources, and ensure that their systems are capable of supporting the expected growth.

- **Demand forecasting**: This involves predicting the specific demand for a system's resources or services at a given time. It involves analyzing historical data, market trends, and consumer behavior to estimate future demand for a product or service. By identifying patterns and fluctuations, businesses can anticipate potential surges or dips in demand, enabling them to adjust production, inventory, and marketing strategies accordingly. This approach provides a broader perspective, helping companies stay agile in a rapidly changing marketplace.

While both growth and demand forecasting aim to predict future conditions, they serve different purposes and require different methodologies. Growth forecasting is more about the overall scale of growth, while demand forecasting is more about the specific demand for resources or services at a given time. Both are crucial for performance engineering, as they can help businesses anticipate future system loads, plan for capacity needs, and optimize system performance.

Two popular growth forecasting algorithms are the **generalized linear model** (**GLM**) and **XGBoost**, as discussed.

GLM is an extension of traditional statistics linear regression models, which allows for a broader range of response types, making it more flexible. It compares the effects of multiple variables on continuous variables before drawing from an array of different distributions to find the best-fit model.

The advantage of this algorithm is its quick training time. The response variable can have any form of exponential distribution type. The GLM is also able to deal with categorical predictors while being relatively straightforward to interpret. On top of this, it provides a clear understanding of how each of the predictors is influencing the outcome and is fairly resistant to overfitting. However, it requires relatively large data sets and is susceptible to outliers.

Simply speaking, GLM typically tries to find a linear trend, as close as possible to the collected data. The shortest way to intuitively explain how it works is by showing a simple diagram, such as this one:

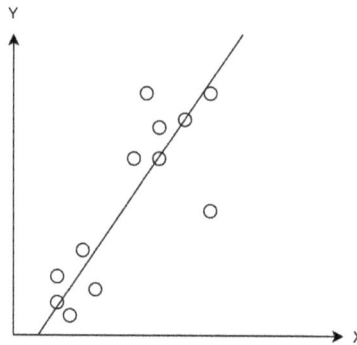

Figure 4.3: Generalized linear modeling of results in a graph

eXtreme Gradient Boost (**XGBoost**) is a gradient-boosting algorithm that can be used for solving different machine learning issues, such as classification and regression. It is also one of the most used algorithms for forecasting. A boosting algorithm is an ensemble algorithm of decision trees that increases the complexity of models that suffer from high bias. That means it is constructed of multiple learning algorithms to achieve better results. XGBoost is an implementation of the Gradient Boosting algorithm under the open-source software library. It's focused on the computation speed and model performance. This library has the ability to distribute model training to generate faster, more accurate results.

Simplifying the idea of XGBoost, following and enhancing gradient areas of data, i.e., where the data is more crowded and tighter, being able to learn the data, and building predictions based on trends. As mentioned, it has many uses, including, for example, forecasting, to recognize and classify textual characters.

Performance test planning

Predicting, expecting, and planning for load changes is one side of the equation. The other side is to ensure our software is ready to handle the anticipated load and to be prepared for this in advance. Performance test planning is crucial for achieving just this. It is the process of defining a road map for conducting successful performance testing.

We have brought this up more than once, but this is one of the important phases of the performance test life cycle where a performance tester prepares an approach to test a system or an application. A detailed test plan will outline all the relevant information about the system, and relevant details of what we are planning to test, why and how, and what we would like the test results to be, according to SLAs, KPIs and NFRs. The outcome of the process is a documented test plan.

The details in a performance test plan may vary, of course, just like any other aspect, depending on the project, the requirements, and what we actually plan to test. Some of the headings that are to be detailed in a performance test plan may be:

- **Overview of the project**: The purpose of the project, users, and any other relevant details to present it.

- **Project architecture**: In order to plan for any testing, we should outline the project's architecture —how it is built, with which technologies, how the components are laid out, how they interact, and what their output is. References to existing architectural documents can be handy here too.

- **Requirements, and more specifically, performance test requirements**: This is an important part where we would list our business nonfunctional requirements. If there are special justifications for those NFRs, this section would be a good place to include them. This is where we explain what we expect from our system and why.

- **NFRs vs NFTs**: Next, we could put a matrix, outlining the list of relevant nonfunctional requirements on one axis, and a list of nonfunctional test cases on the other axis.

  This way, we can mark and see which test cases cover which performance requirements. It also gives a quick visualization of what is covered and what is not (if anything).

- **Performance tests approach**: This section outlines a high-level performance testing approach: how we categorize tests (different load tests, stress tests, soak tests, etc.), which metrics each test addresses, and the pass/fail criteria. It also explains what tools will be used for each test or for continuous monitoring.

- **Detailed performance tests**: Here, we can list the actual steps that each test includes (e.g., go to the homepage | login | search for a product | select a product | add to cart | go to the payment page | logout) as well as expected performance metrics wherever they are relevant.

- **Monitoring metrics**: Planning for continuous monitoring is also part of the plan. We can include which metrics we intend to monitor, how and when, and what we expect the result to be in different scenarios of load.

- **Performance test data plan and preparation**: This includes a summary of the test data that will be needed during the performance test phase. Details of what type of data and how much test data will be needed for all the in-scope business flows.

  Also, include how the test is generated, or where it should be extracted/cloned from.

- **Test environment details**: A description of the test runtime environment is important, listing the hardware details, services, clusters, and any relevant information. Planning to test or monitor multiple environments, we may put a detailed comparison list of them.

- **Assumptions, constraints, risks, dependencies**: It is also known as **Risk, Assumption, Issue, and Dependency (RAID)**. It is more about knowing what to expect and what not to expect.

  - Assumptions are important in order to avoid confusion. Any relevant assumptions about the software's stability, code versioning, environment status, active services, licensing, test data should be outlined.

  - Constraints, which are important for people to know, better be listed too. For example, emphasize the differences between the test environment and the production environment, in terms of resources, licenses, or any other aspect.

  - Risks should be documented concerning the test schedule, release software, dependencies, tools, test approach, test environment, and other items pertaining to the performance test. For example, run functional tests both before and after performance enhancements are put in place, in order to mitigate regression, which is a risk.

  - Dependencies should be documented concerning the latest build, test data, schedule, required tools' installation, test environment and other items pertaining to the performance tests.

Conclusion

In this chapter, we talked about how to be prepared for rainy performance days. The art of predicting and projecting loads touches many wide fields, from requirements engineering through market studies to machine learning. This chapter was less technical in nature but covered side-topics from those aforementioned areas and gave just a quick crash list of common important aspects to keep in mind. Those who wish to understand those topics more deeply may encounter an ocean of endless knowledge.

In the next chapter, we will return to more technical discussions about modeling our project for performance, by looking at high-performance design patterns in code and in data.

Key learnings

As mentioned, a number of times, this chapter contains many topics, tackling the subject of workload modeling and projection, by giving just a taste and a brief explanation of each, due to the size and depth of each topic.

- We learned what use cases are and how they are detailed and charted.
- We learned about different methods to help us identify use cases in a system.
- We learned what key business flows are and how they are defined.
- We learned how we identify users of different roles in our system.

- We learned how we identify workloads in a system by monitoring, testing, and analysis.
- We learned how usage patterns are analyzed and inferred.
- We talked about data trend analysis with statistics and machine learning.
- We learned about common pitfalls that may be encountered when measuring and projecting performance.
- We learned about different data modeling approaches for different load and time.
- We learned about common projection algorithms for forecasting demand and growth.
- We learned about performance test planning and what information we may want to detail in such a planning document.

Join our book's Discord space

Join the book's Discord Workspace for Latest updates, Offers, Tech happenings around the world, New Release and Sessions with the Authors:

https://discord.bpbonline.com

CHAPTER 5

High Performance Design Patterns

Introduction

Performance engineering is a topic of many angles, since there are various strategies for optimizing software's execution runtime. Some include utilizing the hardware to the fullest or maximizing and scaling resources. Producing an optimal solution architecture is also a good way to ensure implementation takes advantage of proper practices and efficiency.

Software architecture is the high-level design and organization of a software system that serves as a blueprint for constructing and maintaining scalable, reliable, and efficient applications. It encompasses the arrangement of components, the interactions between them, and the overall structure that guides the development and evolution of the software. Software architecture decisions profoundly impact the system's performance, maintainability, and adaptability, influencing how components collaborate and ensuring that the system aligns with functional and non-functional requirements.

As part of good design and architecture, design patterns are reusable, proven solutions to common problems encountered in software design. They provide templates for solving recurring challenges, offering a shared vocabulary and set of best practices within the software development community. These patterns encapsulate successful design principles and promote modular, flexible, and maintainable code. Design patterns address specific issues such as object creation, structural composition, and behavioral interactions in a systematic and organized manner.

In this chapter, we will discuss software and solution architecture. We will review some popular software design principles and patterns, both at the infrastructural and solution levels. We will learn what they are, why they are good, and how to use them properly.

Structure

This chapter contains the following topics:

- Different types of software architecture
- Design principles
- Hidden aspects of running software on virtual machines vs. containers
- Legacy monolithic architecture vs. microservices
- Design patterns for performance
- Design patterns for scalability
- Design patterns for high-availability
- Dynamically scalable architectures
- Cloud-native designs
- Highly scalable datastores

Objectives

As with other chapters in this book, the worlds of architecture and design patterns are huge, with entire books and certification programs associated with them, and cannot be covered in a single chapter. The aim of this chapter is to give an overview of software and solution architecture, how it has evolved over the years with the evolution of technology, and demonstrate some popular design patterns, how they work, and how they are beneficial for building a solid, performant, scalable, complex, and modern system.

Different types of software architectures

As mentioned in the introduction, the craft of software architecture provides the foundational structure for designing and organizing complex software systems, offering a scheme that dictates how various components interact and collaborate.

Throughout history, various architectural styles and paradigms have evolved to address the challenges posed by increasing software complexity, changing computing environments, and the growing demands of modern applications. The field continues to evolve with ongoing advancements in technology and the ever-changing landscape of software development.

A brief history of software complexity and architecture

Much like the growth of computing, namely software applications, programming languages, paradigms, libraries and frameworks, infrastructures, and computers themselves, software architecture has also grown and evolved over the years.

Starting from the early mainframe days during the 1950s-1960s, the usage of digital computers and their applications was still being explored. Software was mostly built for small and focused solutions, trying to make use of computers and understand what they can do for us. Software architecture was not exactly present, or at least not recognized. Programs were mostly in sequential blocks of code, and computers were mostly centrally controlled and triggered by slim terminals. The blocky sequences code for those early programs may be referred to as **monolithic architecture**, although this was not an aware design decision (modern code **monoliths** are commonly more complex than that; more about that later).

Programs started growing during the 1970s and 1980s, and with the rise of personal computers, more software was built for a larger diversity of needs, from spreadsheets to word processing and computer games. Applications started to become bigger and more complex. This yielded in more structured programming paradigms, also referred to as functional or procedural programming. Structuring and breaking down software into manageable pieces laid the foundation for future architectural concepts.

Towards the 1990s, began the rise of **object-oriented programming** (**OOP**) and **object-oriented design** (**OOD**). The C programming language had already been around since 1972 (and earlier variants such as B and BCPL much before that), but in 1985 C++ appeared, one of the most popular and important programming languages in the world, with a wide range of applications in many different industries. It is not the only object-oriented language, but it is surely the most important one, as it is compiled into independent executable binaries. It is cross-platform (although unlike languages such as Python, which depends on an interpreter runtime that makes the code indirectly compatible with any operating system, C++ code stands alone and interacts closely with the processor and the operating system, hence needs to be adjusted to the operating system, and built with an appropriate compiler, to make an executable with the right type and structure, you can still say C++ is cross-platform, as it has compilers for all operating systems), it is efficient and fast (as it executes **closer to the bare metal**), and its code syntax is fairly easy (and has affected modern languages, such as Java, JavaScript, C#, Rust, Go, and many others). This syntax actually comes from C++'s parent language, C (and often referred to as **the C-family programming languages**), but it is C++ that brought the cross-platform, strong, fast, native binaries, convenient syntax, together with the super-powers of proper OOP, by providing powerful abstraction tools, such as classes, access specifiers, abstract classes (which act as skeleton interfaces) and templates (which act as generics in other languages).

The adoption of OOP introduced the concept of objects and classes, promoting modularity, encapsulation, and reuse. Design patterns started to emerge as reusable solutions to common design problems. When mentioning software design patterns, object-oriented solution blueprints, based on inheritance and abstraction tricks, are most commonly the ones referred to.

With the proliferation of networking, distributed systems, and the Internet in the 1990s came the rise of **client-server architecture**. In short, middleware technologies facilitated communication between distributed components. This means that software components became more modular and broken into functional components: user interface, or just code modules as multiple *clients* invoking the data requests, a separately executing *server* that handles the requests and issues responses as needed (and mostly hosted on a different computer), a separate (or not separate) database and/or managed files to hold all the collected and processed data. There may be other components of the system on other computers out there, but this is a pretty common, versatile setup. The term **middleware** refers to virtual *layers* of handling of data by code components (for example, when the server receives a request from a client, the sent request data first passes through a middleware that checks for user authentication details in order to ensure that the user even has sufficient permissions to execute the action. Otherwise, an error code is sent back, then to a middleware that takes the user-submitted data, parses it, analyzes it, and then a middleware that processes the data according to the requester's need.

In the late 1990s and early 2000s, the client-server architecture was extended to what is known as **service-oriented architecture (SOA)**. Taking the client-server model to the next level, emphasizing the use of services that communicate over well-defined interfaces. Rather than arbitrary communications between a client and a server (sending whatever information in whatever format), standards emerged, powered by (but not just) XML, such as SOAP and WSDL. Services run on protocols such as HTTP/S (hence, the services are sometimes referred to as *web services*), but there are other implementations, such as message queuing protocols (e.g., AMQP, MQTT), **Java Message Service (JMS)**, WebSockets, and **remote procedure call (RPC)** protocols (e.g., XML-RPC, JSON-RPC).

The main point is that SOA is an architectural style that can use various protocols depending on the system's requirements. It emphasizes the creation of modular, loosely coupled services that communicate with each other over well-defined interfaces.

Moving into the 2000s, the massive growth of the internet and web applications, prompted the development of web-based architectures. The mid-2000s saw the emergence of microservices architecture, emphasizing small, independent services that could be developed, deployed, and scaled individually.

This takes the client-server and SOA to the next level (although reducing the standards of communication protocols to mostly HTTP/S) by making communications flow everywhere between individual independently developed services. Each can act both as a client or a server, but with reduced, focused purpose and functionality, which increases the efficiency and modularity of the software system as a whole.

In contrast to the modularity of object-oriented projects or breaking the software into microservices, some applications today are designed and built with a **monolithic architecture**. That is a traditional software design model, where the entire application is developed as a single, indivisible unit. In a monolithic architecture, all the components and functions of the application are tightly integrated and interdependent. This has some limitations, such as a lack of technology stack flexibility (with microservices, each microservice can be developed completely independently, with a completely different technology, which may be more suitable for it), tight coupling and dependency between components, and problematic scalability (in order to scale to more servers, the entire application must be deployed on each one).

On the other hand, for simple applications, sometimes a monolith is considered a solution, as building, managing, and deploying multiple microservices adds a great deal of complexity to a project at many levels.

There is no cloud; it is just someone else's computer.

From the 2010s and on, we witnessed the rise of **cloud computing** and **containerization**. Cloud computing became a dominant force, enabling scalable and flexible architectures at levels and sizes we had not seen before. Cloud infrastructure is unprecedentedly powerful for scalability and elasticity, resource virtualization (allowing spinning up, or tearing down, powerful virtual machines for any purpose at any given time, according to any needs. This is also extremely effective in terms of cost and global reach. If the company is in Sweden but needs to reinforce servers in *North America*, those can be created and become productive within minutes). Pushing microservices to the next level by making their deployment native and easy, also fluently supported by automation and continuous integration/continuous delivery tools, the cloud provides powerful platforms, as well as additional managed services, which are built into the platform, and provided **as a service**, i.e., running and served on the cloud provider's computers, and accessible as a service without the need for much intervention or management. Services such as **databases (DBaaS)**, **messaging queues (MQaaS)**, **caching (CaaS)**, and many others are commonly provided as <something>aaS.

Additionally, containerization technologies like **Docker**, which have become popular in recent years, have further facilitated the deployment of microservices, enhancing portability and scalability. They allow easy deployment of software in a configured environment with the help of a thin layer of virtualization, providing all the necessary configuration, dependencies, and additional tools the software may need to operate properly.

Even further, complex orchestration tools, such as Kubernetes, allow managing multiple containers in clusters with powerful automation and management of redundancy, load balancing, fallbacks, rollbacks, inter-networking, and inter-storage. They also connect natively to cloud environments and help run complex; large-scale projects based on microservices.

Additional complementary tools, such as *Terraform* (which ensures all the required resources are created, on any cloud provider, in correspondence to a simple configuration file) or *ArgoCD* (which gives powerful, yet easy to use, tools for managing deployment of multiple microservices in Kubernetes clusters), power the operations/DevOps teams, giving a strong hand for orchestrating the widest, biggest, most complex, most elaborate cloud-based projects.

Architectural trends

Predicting future trends in software architecture involves some degree of speculation but based on the current technological landscape and emerging developments, several trends are likely to shape the future of software architecture. Here are some of them, with a very brief description of each:

- **Microservices evolution and continued cloud-native adoption**: Microservices architecture is expected to continue evolving, with an increased focus on addressing challenges such as service communication, data consistency, and observability. Technologies and best practices for managing microservices at scale will likely become more sophisticated.

  Cloud-native principles, including containerization and DevOps practices, will continue to be integral to modern software architectures. Organizations are expected to increasingly leverage cloud services for scalability, flexibility, and resource efficiency.

- **Serverless and Function as a Service**: Serverless computing and **Function as a Service (FaaS)** are gaining popularity, allowing developers to focus on writing functions without managing the underlying infrastructure. The trend towards event-driven architectures and the serverless paradigm is likely to persist.

- **Edge computing**: With the rise of IoT and the need for low-latency applications, edge computing is becoming more prevalent. Future software architectures may need to consider distributed computing at the edge to process data closer to the source.

- **Event-driven architectures**: Event-driven architectures are expected to play a more significant role, especially in systems requiring real-time processing. Technologies supporting event sourcing, event streaming, and asynchronous communication will continue to advance.

- **AI and machine learning integration**: Integrating AI and machine learning capabilities into software architectures is anticipated to become more commonplace. Architectures will need to support the deployment and management of AI models, real-time inference, and data pipelines for training.

- **Blockchain and distributed ledger technologies**: As blockchain and distributed ledger technologies mature, they may find broader applications beyond cryptocurrencies. Future software architectures may incorporate decentralized and trustless systems for enhanced security and transparency.

- **Quantum computing impact**: While quantum computing is in its early stages, its eventual development could have a profound impact on software architectures. New algorithms and architectural patterns may emerge to leverage the unique capabilities of quantum computers.

- **Immutable infrastructure**: The concept of immutable infrastructure, where infrastructure components are replaced rather than updated, is likely to gain more traction. This approach enhances reliability, security, and the ability to roll back changes.

- **Human augmentation**: As technologies like **augmented reality** (**AR**) and **virtual reality** (**VR**) advance, software architectures may need to consider human augmentation aspects. This includes designing systems that seamlessly integrate with augmented experiences.

Design principles

Some common good-practice basic software design principles were listed in *Chapter 1, Introduction to Performance Engineering*. Such principles usually take advantage of object-oriented features of a programming language, such as abstraction, encapsulation, inheritance, and polymorphism. These principles play significant role in designing powerful reusable software design patterns.

As much as writing code is a common craft that many people have mastered, software and code are still logically counterintuitive to many. Core common software challenges repeat over and over again on many different projects, and as there is no need to reinvent the wheel, following proven, well-structured solution principles and patterns save time and ensures building a strong application that is much more secure, performant, scalable, and relatively easy to modify, extend, and maintain.

We will repeat some of the notes from *Chapter 1, Introduction to Performance Engineering* and add a little bit of information about their importance.

Abstraction

A central principle in good practices of software and OOD. Software abstraction refers to the process of simplifying complex systems by representing high-level concepts and hiding unnecessary details, allowing developers and users to interact with the system at a more manageable and conceptual level. Abstraction is a fundamental principle in software engineering that helps in understanding, designing, and building complex systems by focusing on essential features while suppressing unnecessary intricacies.

Abstraction allows for the creation of more manageable and understandable systems by breaking them down into simpler, more abstract components. Popular design patterns heavily rely on abstraction to achieve various goals, such as flexibility, reusability, and maintainability. Some of the most commonly used design patterns that utilize abstraction are the factory pattern, the adapter pattern, the decorator pattern, the observer pattern, and the singleton pattern (probably the most famous design pattern of all. It does rely on abstraction, although it might not be immediately apparent due to its straightforward implementation).

SOLID principles

We have listed the 5 SOLID principles in *Chapter 1, Introduction to Performance Engineering*. I will add here that these principles provide a set of guidelines to create software that is easy to understand, maintain, and extend.

They encourage developers to design classes and modules that have a single responsibility, can be extended without modifying existing code, and are interchangeable without affecting the system's behavior. By promoting a modular and flexible design, SOLID principles help in building software that is resilient to change, scalable, and less prone to errors. The principles also emphasize the importance of dependency management, abstraction, and encapsulation, ensuring that components are loosely coupled and can be easily replaced or extended. In simpler terms, SOLID principles guide developers to create software that is like a well-organized toolbox, where each tool has a specific purpose, is easy to use, and can be swapped out or added without messing up the entire toolkit.

KISS and DRY

Again, both reviewed briefly in *Chapter 1, Introduction to Performance Engineering,* the **keep it simple, stupid!** (**KISS**) and **don't repeat yourself** (**DRY**) principles are all about avoiding complications.

KISS encourages simplicity in design, advising developers to avoid unnecessary complexity and keep things as straightforward as possible. This simplicity makes the software easier to understand, maintain, and troubleshoot.

On the other hand, DRY emphasizes the importance of avoiding code duplication. Instead of repeating the same code in multiple places, developers are encouraged to create reusable components or functions, reducing redundancy and making updates or fixes easier to implement consistently.

Together, KISS and DRY promote clarity and efficiency, ensuring that the codebase remains clean, concise, and easy to work with throughout the development process. In simpler terms, these principles encourage developers to keep things simple and avoid unnecessary repetition, making their code more effective and maintainable.

Decoupling

An important aspect, which is good to keep in mind when designing a software solution, the software principle of decoupling is like organizing a team of people where everyone works independently without knowing too much about what others are doing.

In software, it means keeping different parts of the code separate and not relying too much on how one part is implemented when working on another. This way, if you need to change or update one piece, it would not have a big impact on the rest of the code. It is like playing with building blocks; each block is its own thing, and you can change one block without affecting the others. Decoupling helps make software more flexible and easier to maintain because you can work on different parts without worrying too much about how they are connected.

Law of least astonishment

There are many other software design practices and principles, more than this book can contain. We will conclude this short list by mentioning just one more: the law of least astonishment, which is good also in other aspects of life, not just in software engineering.

According to this principle, we should design components and systems to behave in a way that is least surprising to users or developers. Avoid unexpected behaviors that could lead to confusion or errors.

As a personal anecdote, when I was getting into Windows application development, sometime during the 1990s, I remember going through books that explained how to use tools like Visual Basic or Visual C++ (which later evolved into Visual Studio) in order to build native Windows applications. One of the first tips, which was repeated in every book, tutorial, and article, was to reuse the tools, icons, and structures that Microsoft had already built into their frameworks in order to build a familiar user interface, which many users would already find intuitive and known, rather than starting to invent a completely new, innovative, avant-garde, unknown design.

The law of least astonishment is akin to crafting a user experience that feels like a familiar and friendly conversation. It is about creating software behavior that aligns with users' expectations, minimizing surprises, and avoiding unnecessary confusion. Just as a well-designed door opens with a handle in a way you intuitively understand, software should operate in a manner that feels natural and logical to users. There are many online videos showing how people try to open a Tesla car door, not managing to figure out where the handle is tucked and how to simply get the door opened. This principle encourages developers to design interfaces, functions, and interactions that follow common conventions, ensuring that users are pleasantly guided through the digital landscape rather than encountering unexpected twists and turns. In essence, it is like offering users a well-marked path in a forest, where each step feels just right and leaves them pleasantly unastonished.

It may also be a proper opportunity, as part of this principle and of good coding practices in general, to write code with variable and function names that are clear, make sense, and are understandable and do what they say they do.

Along with KISS and DRY, this would help our code tremendously by making it simple, understandable, and thus maintainable.

Hidden aspects of running software on virtual machines vs. containers

Software virtualization is a technology that allows the creation of simulated environments, abstracting physical hardware and allowing multiple operating systems or applications to run on a single physical computer simultaneously. The software running inside the virtual environment is not aware it is running inside a simulated machine. With that, we can run multiple virtual operating systems (a.k.a. guests) on a single physical machine (host).

A **virtual machine** simulates an entire computer and all the hardware components and peripherals, allowing any matching operating system and software to run natively in its environment. The guest's hardware is fully simulated in software, and the guest's operating system does not have to match the host's (e.g., a Linux virtual machine can run inside a Windows computer, and a MacOS can run on a virtual Apple Mac guest inside a Windows or Linux PC).

In contrast to virtual machines, **software containers** are lightweight, portable, and efficient units for packaging, distributing, and running applications. Containers are a leaner solution, encapsulating an application along with its dependencies and runtime environment, ensuring consistency across different environments. Unlike virtual machines, containers share the host operating system's kernel and provide only the required dependencies in terms of software (they do not run a full operating system on an entirely simulated system). Another difference is that since a virtual machine simulates an entire computer, it can run multiple applications, software services, and other components. A container is usually dedicated to a single purpose: to run a single service or a single application. This leads to faster startup times and reduced resource overhead. Containerization technologies, such as Docker, have become integral to modern software development practices, offering seamless deployment, scalability, and ease of management. Containers facilitate a microservices architecture, enabling developers to build, deploy, and scale applications more efficiently while ensuring consistent behavior from development to production environments.

Cloud platforms provide infrastructure for both virtual machines [either as a bare **infrastructure-as-a-service (IaaS)**, literally using someone else's computer, onto which virtual machines can be created and attached, or as **platform-as-a-service (PaaS)**, where a managed virtual machine is created, built, and started, used as an independent computer, upon need and request], and for deployment of containers and clusters.

Obviously, the two virtualization solutions are not the same in size, robustness, resource utilization, performance, and flexibility. Here are some aspects to keep in mind:

	Virtual machine	Container
Architecture	VMs operate with full virtualization, including their own operating system and hypervisor layer. Each VM runs a separate guest operating system, leading to a heavier footprint.	Containers share the host operating system's kernel; hence they are more lightweight and efficient. They encapsulate single applications and their dependencies, providing isolation without the need for a full operating system per container.
Isolation	VMs provide stronger isolation since each VM has its own operating system, leading to a higher level of security and independence.	Containers share the host's OS kernel, offering a level of isolation suitable for most applications. However, they may not provide the same level of isolation as VMs.
Resource overhead	VMs have higher resource overhead as they include a complete guest operating system. This can lead to slower startup times and increased resource consumption.	Containers have lower resource overhead because they do not include a full operating system. They share the host OS kernel, resulting in faster startup times and efficient resource utilization.
Portability	VMs are less portable due to their larger size and dependence on specific hypervisors. Moving VMs between different environments may require more configuration.	Containers are highly portable and can run consistently across different environments if the host OS supports the container runtime. They encapsulate everything needed to run an application.
Scaling	VMs can scale horizontally, but each VM requires more resources, making vertical scaling (increasing resources for a single VM) a more common approach.	Containers are designed for horizontal scaling, where multiple instances of a containerized application can run simultaneously. This is achieved easily through container orchestration tools.
Resource utilization	VMs have higher resource utilization because each VM includes its own operating system, resulting in more significant memory and storage requirements.	Containers are more resource efficient as they share the host OS kernel and do not duplicate the underlying OS components.
Deployment speed	VMs generally have longer startup times because they need to boot a complete operating system.	Containers have faster deployment times due to their lightweight nature. They can start quickly, making them suitable for dynamic and scalable environments.

Table 5.1: Virtual machines vs. containers

Legacy monolithic architecture vs. microservices

As previously discussed in the section: *A brief history of software complexity and architecture*, writing a monolithic application as a single unit of code is considered more traditional, at times old-fashioned, in comparison to a microservices architecture, as nowadays microservices are all the rage. There are distinct differences between the two approaches, and at times, it may be preferable to write monolithic code.

In a monolithic architecture, the entire application is conceived as a single, unified entity, with all modules and components tightly interconnected within a shared codebase and often sharing a common database. While monoliths simplify development and deployment, as changes can be made within the same codebase, they can encounter challenges as the application scales. Scaling, updates, and maintenance may become cumbersome, and any modification to one part of the application may require redeployment of the entire monolith.

On the contrary, microservices architecture breaks down the application into smaller, independent services, each encapsulating a specific business capability. These services communicate with each other through well-defined APIs, and each service can be developed, deployed, and scaled independently. Microservices offer enhanced scalability, agility, and fault isolation, making them well-suited for large, dynamic systems and distributed development teams. However, the transition to microservices introduces complexities related to service communication, data consistency, and overall system orchestration. The decision between monolithic and microservices architecture hinges on factors such as the project's size, complexity, development team structure, and the need for flexibility in scaling and updating specific functionalities. Each architecture comes with its set of trade-offs, and the choice depends on the unique requirements and goals of the software project at hand.

This reminds me of the difference between virtual machines, which come as a **monolith**, a whole virtual computer with its operating system, services, and preinstalled applications, and containers, which are lean, compact virtual units that run single-purpose wrappers that provide the application with just what it needs to execute. Both architectures have their advantages and challenges, and the choice depends on factors such as project size, development team structure, scalability requirements, and the need for flexibility in updating and deploying specific functionalities. It is fair to say that one architecture's advantages are the other's disadvantages, and vice versa.

Here are a few points of comparison:

	Monolith	Microservices
Complexity	Developing and deploying a monolithic application can be simpler because there is only one codebase to manage.	Managing multiple services can be more complex than managing a single monolithic application.
Efficiency	Since all components are tightly integrated, communication between them is fast and straightforward.	Communication between services can introduce latency, which might affect the application's performance.
Cost	Since there is only one codebase and virtually one application to manage, the initial development and maintenance costs are generally lower. Deployment or scaling can be more straightforward and less expensive, as you scale the entire application as a unit.	Initial development cost can be higher due to the need to develop, test, and deploy multiple services. Maintenance costs can be higher because each service needs to be managed and updated separately. Deployment and scaling individual services can be more efficient and cost-effective but requires planning and management to ensure services are scaled appropriately. Additionally, microservices often require more complex infrastructure to manage, which can increase costs. This includes the need for container orchestration systems (such as Kubernetes), service discovery, and potentially more servers or cloud resources.
Security and compliance	A single application with its security, compliance and other non-functional requirements is easier to build and manage.	Managing security and compliance across multiple services can be more complex and costly.
Flexibility	Adding new features or making changes can be challenging because it requires modifying the entire application.	It is easier to update or modify a service without affecting the entire application.
Technology diversity	All components share the same code and solution; Hence they should all adhere to one technology stack.	Each service can be developed using the technology stack that best suits its needs.

Table 5.2: Monoliths vs. microservices

Design patterns for performance

Performance-oriented design patterns focus on optimizing the performance of applications. They address common performance bottlenecks and challenges, such as memory usage, execution speed, and resource management. By keeping those patterns in mind, and applying them, developers can significantly improve the efficiency and responsiveness of their applications.

In this section, we will review a few of those patterns of solution and architecture and explain how they work and what impact they have on performance. In the examples to come, we show how such patterns help us handle data more efficiently.

Cache aside

Caching is a common technique, widely used in different areas, localized or complex software solutions, browsers, or as a coding technique to improve performance. In this section, we will discuss **cache** and the **cache aside** pattern.

About caching

The idea in caching is to store a copy of data in some form of alternative accessible location, which is a smaller and faster storage system, so that subsequent requests for the same data can be served more quickly (instead of bothering the database every time, for example).

Caching can occur at various levels within a system, such as in-memory cache, where data is stored in the system's RAM, or at a higher level, such as on a **content delivery network** (**CDN**), where copies of web content are stored in servers closer to the end-user geographically. Many times, dedicated CaaS servers, which are specialized for this purpose, are allocated; for example, Redis is a common server. Caching is widely employed in applications, databases, web browsers, and various other systems to reduce latency, minimize data retrieval costs, and enhance overall system efficiency.

In general, the cache is stored in a simple structure of hash-tables (or key-value pairs), which allows fetching data by a given key very quickly. The data in the cache should correspond to the application's data at the same time, hence there are a few aspects to keep in mind when managing cached data:

- Cache is mostly stored on fast medium (in RAM, or SSDs, on servers dedicated for this task). The idea is to have fast readings.
- However, the cache does not replace the database. Caches have limited space, and a policy of rotating the data in the cache needs to be implemented. The cache is more **expensive** and limited in space, but it is fast. With a proper strategy, it can save a lot of time.
- It is possible to consider preloading data into the cache in advance (**warm-up**).

- It is important to consider when cached data expires and is automatically removed [**Time To Live (TTL)**].
- It is important to consider the strategy of freeing data from the cache in order to free space for other data (eviction).

Given this toolset, there are a few common caching strategies. Which one to use depends on factors such as the size of the data, how often it changes, how many clients read it, the scale of the system, etc.

Cache aside

The **cache aside** pattern is one of those caching strategies. It is good for read-heavy situations (where the system requires significantly more read operations than writes to the database. That is, the frequently accessed data does not get updated often but is read more).

In contrast to common caching patterns (e.g., **Read through** or **Write through**, which rely on features of the cache server), **cache aside** puts the management and control over the cache in the hands of the application. The algorithm is pretty simple:

The app needs to get some data. The flow of operations is as follows and can be followed by the numbered items in *Figure 5.1*.

1. The app gets the cache key and checks if the data is stored in the cache. If the data is in the cache, it fetches it from there, and returns.
2. If the data is not in the cache, it fetches the data from the database.
3. Later, update the cache asynchronously when possible.

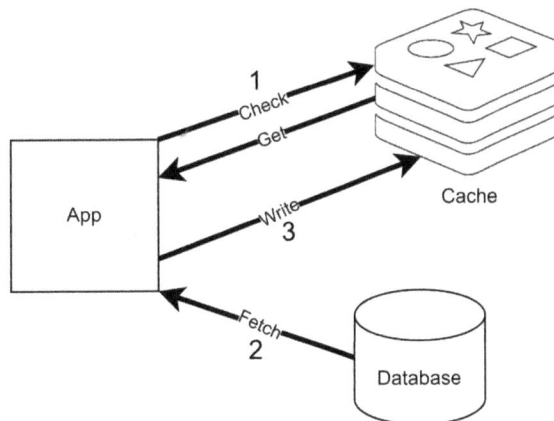

Figure 5.1: Cache aside flow of operations

This strategy has some performance advantages, especially in cases where the data does not get frequent updates but needs to be retrieved many times. Also, updating the cache is done asynchronously and does not interfere with the application's runtime process.

Example: Consider the following scenario as an example:

- Suppose the following:
    - Reading from the cache takes 5 milliseconds.
    - Reading from the database takes 35 milliseconds.
    - We plan the cache in a way that 95% of the time, the data we need is in the cache.
- Then, if we query the cache, and the data is there, we have a latency of 5 milliseconds.
- If we query the cache and the data is not there, we will have a latency of 5ms (to check the cache) + 35 milliseconds (to get the data from the database.
- Our average data query latency in milliseconds will be:
- An average query time of *6.5 milliseconds* is significantly better than database reads of *35 milliseconds*.

Additional considerations

As previously mentioned, we would need to keep in mind the freshness of the cached data (for example, let an item in the cache automatically expire after 5 minutes) and also a strategy for what happens when we try to store an item in the cache, but the cache is full (for example, evacuate items from the cache, if they are the oldest, or if they are the least recently used ones, or if they are the easiest to retrieve from the database, in order to make space). These decisions need to be taken depending on the actual project and data considerations (for example, we may decide that certain items are not to be evacuated, even though they are the oldest in the cache, as they are more important, or if retrieving them again from the database is significantly more costly).

One last aspect to consider is the active invalidation of cached data once it is updated in the database. We would need the database (or the part of the application that updates the item in the database) to invalidate or evacuate the corresponding cached item in order to keep the data integrity.

Command query responsibility segregation

Command query responsibility segregation (**CQRS**), is another architectural pattern that helps optimize handling data in our system.

A classic layered system architecture may look something like this:

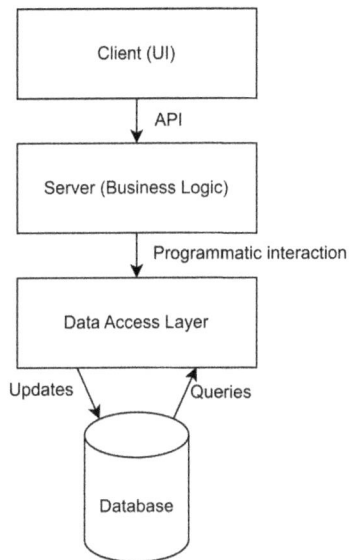

Figure 5.2: Blocks of a typical layered system architecture

The blocks depicted in *Figure 5.2* conduct the following typical flow:

- A client (for example, UI) sends a request to the server through an API.
- The server supports functionality such as data validation and business logic operations. It interacts with the data layer.
- The data layer is an abstraction module that is responsible for interacting with the database.
- The data layer performs CRUD operations against the database, such as querying (reading) data or updating (creating, modifying, or deleting) records.

To improve this model's data access to get better performance, many times, there are elementary differences between reading and writing data in terms of volumes and load (in many systems, data is more frequently read than updated). The CQRS pattern proposes the following:

- The term **queries** refers to data retrieval (the R in CRUD).
- Other operations (C, U, D in CRUD) are referred to as **commands**.
- CQRS suggests that we segregate the system's responsibilities of running commands from those running queries. Hence, the name CQRS.

The segregation of responsibility may extend not just by splitting the application data models to **read** (query) and **write** (command) but even by splitting the database into 2 (or more) separate ones. Splitting the database is not mandatory. In fact, CQRS is a pretty flexible pattern. The idea is to mainly segregate the logic of the operations between commands and queries so that they can grow and live independently. Data gets updated in the **write database** and then gets synced to update the **read database**. Once data is updated on the **write database**, it gets synced into the **read database**.

Other layers (client, server + business logic) may also be split in two accordingly, if this is deemed to be profitable. For this example, we split only the parts that CQRS requires to be split: the model (data access layer), and the database itself. Look at the following figure:

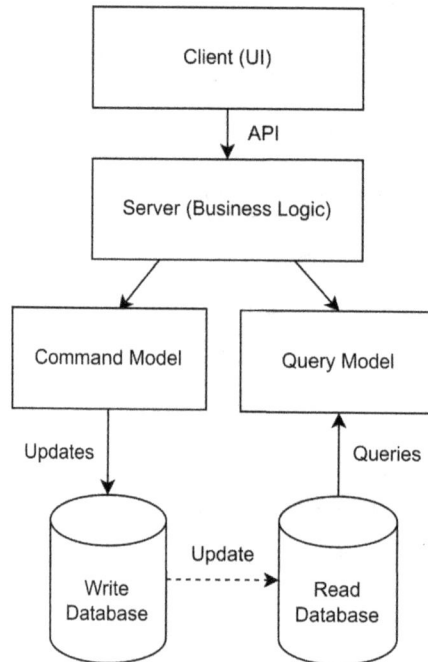

Figure 5.3: A typical CQRS flow

The following is why we should split reading and writing data in the first place:

- We reduce the load on the database, and the data access layer, by splitting the interactions into 2 unrelated ones.

- CQRS allows optimizing read and write operations independently, which can lead to improved performance. Read-optimized models can be tailored for efficient querying (for example, complicated views can be pre-generated), while write models can focus on handling commands.

- Furthermore, they do not even have to be of the same database type. We could write to a Microsoft SQL Server, while we read data from a NoSQL server, such as MongoDB, if we want to.

- Databases can scale independently. If we have heavy load of data reading, we can scale the **read database** only.

Queue-based throttling

The **queue-based throttling** pattern (also known as **queue-based load leveling** pattern) is a design pattern used to control the rate at which tasks are processed.

This pattern is particularly useful in scenarios where the processing of tasks needs to be limited to prevent the overloading of resources or to ensure fair distribution of resources among different tasks or users. The core idea behind this pattern is to use a queue to manage the tasks that need to be processed. The tasks are added to the queue, and a separate process or thread continuously removes tasks from the queue and processes them at a controlled rate.

In case of uneven, high, unstable demand to push tasks directly for the application (or service) to handle, which may overwhelm the system with a high volume of requests, we let the system handle them in an orderly fashion and without high peaks and bursts (hence the **throttling** or **leveling**). It may be that the service can handle more than one request at a time, but it is up to its implementation to pull the tasks out of the queue according to its availability and capacity to handle them.

Schematically, it looks something like this: instead of interacting directly with the service, the clients who make the request push it into a message queue. The service then dequeues them one at a time in the order in which they were pushed, thus throttling the execution and not crashing, as shown in the following figure:

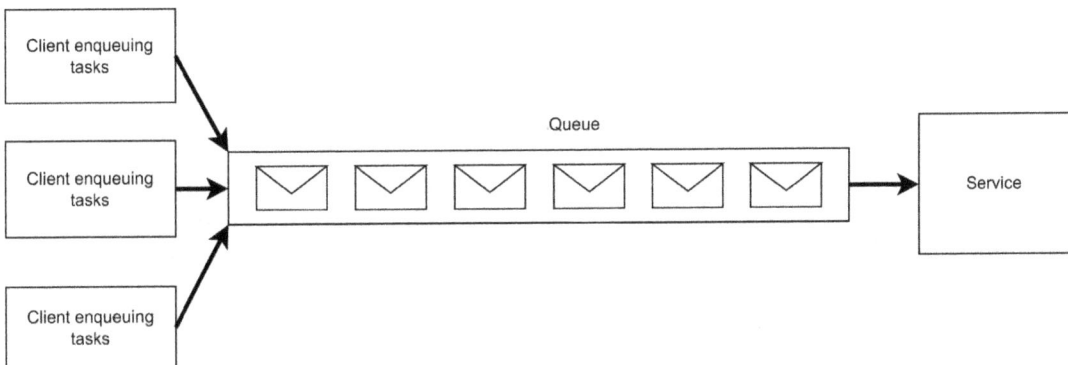

Figure 5.4: Queue-based throttling

This pattern is useful to any application that uses services that are subject to overloading. This pattern is not useful if the application expects a response from the service with minimal latency. In terms of performance, it helps keep things steady, alive, and efficient, rather than fast (as the service can only handle so much anyway).

A few points to consider here are: Message queues are a one-way communication mechanism. If a task expects a reply from a service, it might be necessary to implement a mechanism that the service can use to send a response, either through asynchronous messaging, calling back a function on the client, or a different message queue.

Sharding

Sharding is a commonly used optimization technique for scaling large maximizing databases and keeping high performance, though it needs to be used carefully.

The need for data sharding

Nowadays, databases are made to handle huge amounts of data (and growing), which, at some point, takes its toll on performance. **Sharding** is a method used to improve the performance, scalability, availability, and manageability of large-scale databases.

If we run a database that starts pushing its limits, one way to maintain high performance is to scale up (vertically): upgrade the hardware (be it physical hardware or virtual), but hardware can only be upgraded to a limit, and hardware upgrades are also quite costly.

Another option is to scale out (horizontally) by adding more computers. This will handle and distribute the workload, but then what do we do with all the data? Replicating the entire database across scaled machines is not a good idea, as each of them will become the complete, heavy, large database from which we started. It is also possible to dedicate servers to run as read replicas; that is, they contain all the data, optimized as much as possible specifically for reading, in order to increase the performance of data retrieval. Still, this way, each replica should contain the entire database. Another point in such cases is that read replicas need to be updated by the master database whenever a data record gets updated, but this may not be immediate enough, which leads to inconsistencies in the data across the replicas. This is called **eventual consistency**.

Enter sharding

Another way to handle heavy databases, is to split them into smaller databases, which is called **sharding**. Sharding splits the database into smaller databases, each shard runs on a separate server, has the same structure and relations of the original database, but records are split between the shards.

In the following example figure, we can see how the first three records are moved to shard 1, and the last two records are moved to shard 2:

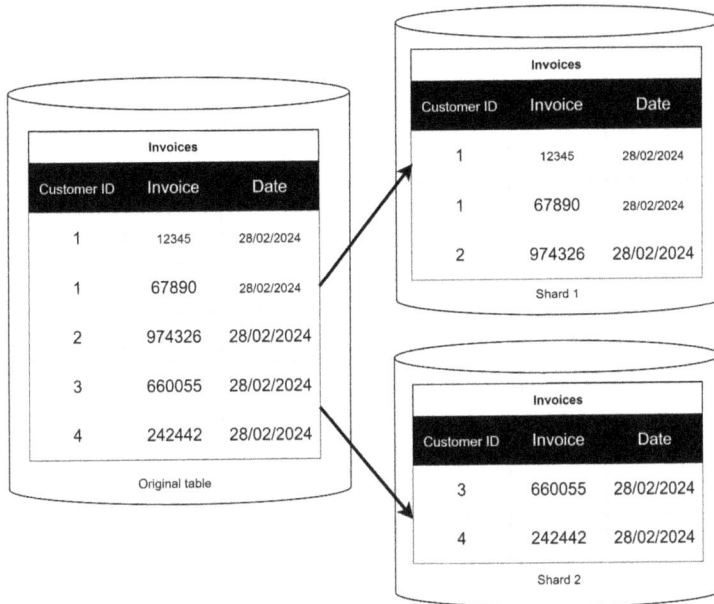

Figure 5.5: Horizontal split (sharding) of the data.

Now, we have two small-volume databases instead of one.

Sharding is a private case of general data split techniques under the common name partitioning (more about partitioning techniques ahead). As can be seen in the diagram, we cut the table by rows. This is referred to as **horizontal partitioning** (or horizontal sharding), but data may be partitioned by columns too, which would be referred to as **vertical partitioning**.

Challenges of sharding

Since our data now spans multiple databases, once we run a query to fetch data, we would need to know which database the records are in.

Consider *Figure 5.5*, we can see that the records for customers with IDs 1 and 2 are moved to shard 1, and records for customers with IDs 3 and 4 are moved to shard 2. If we wish to get the records for customer 3, we would have to somehow know to look for them in shard 2.

The solution is to have some sort of hashing algorithm that can calculate and produce the right shard for each record by an identifier, normally referred to as a **shard key** (for example, use a calculated hash based on the customer ID). That way, we use the algorithm to realize where to move the records to and, later, where to fetch them from. This logic can be implemented in a separate routing software component, whose job is to dictate which records are on which shard.

Some of the advantages of sharding are:

- **Scalability**: Sharding scales our database horizontally into multiple databases. The shards of the original database can also be sharded, in turn, into smaller pieces. They can also be replicated in case we need to reinforce access to specific shards.

- **Availability**: With an entire database in one place, all the data goes down in case of a malfunction. With shards, we can retain the availability of at least some of the data if just one shard crashes.

Sharding also brings some challenges with it. For example:

- Sharding comes with complexity. We would need to devise a deterministic way to calculate on which shard each record is located.

- Once our data is split and spans different servers, running complex queries or analytics that run through more than one shard may be challenging.

Note: Implementing sharding is complex, but some databases, such as MongoDB, Cassandra, and Microsoft Azure CosmosDB support sharding as a feature out of the box. Thus, relieving the engineers from the challenges of manually implementing and managing the sharding.

Design patterns for scalability

In this section, we will look at a few more basic architectural patterns that can help enhance the performance. Some are related directly to scalable setups, and some indirectly.

Lazy loading

Lazy loading is an optimization pattern where data is loaded on demand rather than loading everything upfront. This minimizes the data pulled in advance, reduces traffic and, improves efficiency, reduces resource consumption, and enhances performance by loading only the essential data when it is needed.

Lazy loading is often associated with scaling in the context of web applications, databases, and other systems where efficient resource utilization is crucial for handling increased workloads.

Listed as follows are some real-world examples of how the importance and standardization of lazy-loading gets it implemented in different scenarios, to the point of being a native feature, baked into the development and runtime frameworks:

- Lazy loading is a common practice on web applications, as web pages may take time to fetch and load all their information and images. Web traffic is expensive, and large web pages may not only be fetched slowly from the server but also take time to get loaded and displayed properly on the client's browser. So much so that some frameworks (like next.js) and browsers (like Firefox) already natively support lazy loading features. For example, we can add the **loading="lazy"** attribute to an image tag like so: `<img src="images/book.png" loading"lazy" />`

This will make the image load only when it's visible on the page in the browser's viewport. Other parts of the page may be loaded first, but in order not to get slowed down by images, they get dynamically fetched from the server and loaded later.

- Similarly, with frontend frameworks such as React, which use modular UI components to build single-page web applications, the components often display data that is fetched from the server. Built-in functionality allows data to be loaded from the server only when the component is visible in the browser.

- Without using complex frontend frameworks, web pages using *vanilla* JavaScript often use XMLHTTP calls to post or get data from the server, only when needed. This requires a thought and an architecting process in order to optimize the page to load only what is needed, when it is needed.

- Another example is that in Python, we can import pip modules dynamically, only when they are needed, using the **importlib** library.

- Another common example from websites is any kind of paging or infinite scrolling. Many sites, when displaying large amounts of data (e.g., Google search results, Gmail messages, an online shop list of products), will show them on pages. Going through a large number of results loads them one page at a time. A more modern variant of paging through is the **infinite scroll**. Rather than having to click on the next page link, once the user scrolls down to the end of the results page, the next results get loaded below so that the user can just keep scrolling down indefinitely. Both paging and infinite scrolling have their own advantages and disadvantages in terms of user experience, but in terms of performance, they have the same effect: lazy loading.

Partitioning

In the previous section, we reviewed sharding as a strategy to split databases to improve the performance of big data storage was mentioned. Sharding is one form option of database partitioning, that is, splitting the data one way or another. However, there are other partitioning strategies, each with its considerations, advantages, and disadvantages. Regardless of the partitioning used, it is up to the DBA / architect to devise the strategy and the data management. From the application's perspective, this should not matter: getting the data means getting the data, regardless of how and where it is partitioned and what the method of fetching the right data is.

Partitioning, being a general term, is sometimes understood and referred to differently. Sharding is described as horizontal partitioning (by rows), but also when the partitioning splits the data across multiple servers. Partitioning, as a general term, may refer to all forms of database slicing. There should always be a unique partitioning key, which maps a partitioned data record to the right place (both when selecting and when adding new data).

Horizontal partitioning

It is also known as sharding. As already described earlier, it cuts the data by splitting rows and placing them on separate databases that share the same schema. We have already mentioned the advantages of horizontal partitioning, which mainly include:

- Scalability by splitting the data across lighter, smaller servers.
- Availability, as this increases the chances of at least some of the data to be available.

However, it may have some challenges, such as:

- Complex queries and joins may be more difficult across partitions.
- Uneven partitioning of the data. We would need to plan well how we define the partitioning key in order to distribute the data evenly across partitions.
- Transactions across partitions may be complicated to manage and ensure.

Vertical partitioning

In contrast to horizontal sharding, vertical partitioning splits tables by dividing the columns. That is, different partitions are parts of one table, but now have different schemas. It is for the DBA to decide and plan such a strategy, but vertical partitioning is useful when different columns have varying access patterns or when some columns are more frequently accessed than others. Still, we would need to use a unique identifier partitioning key to relate records across partitions.

The advantages of vertical partitioning are:

- High performance and efficient data retrieval, in the case the partitioning is planned well, and we consider specific column queries. Planned properly, specific queries will return records from as few as possible partitions.
- Simple schema management. Unlike horizontal partitioning, in which when we need to change the table's schema and add a column, we would have to add it in every partition, here we update only one partition.

Of course, vertical partitioning comes with its own challenges:

- **Query complexity**: Any partitioning brings query complexity with it. With careful planning, we will minimize this impact, but for some queries, this will still be unavoidable.
- **Complex scalability**: Changes to the database schema may affect column partitioning, hence we may need to plan and re-partition the tables, if their structure changes and breaks the partitions balance.

Let us look at the following figure:

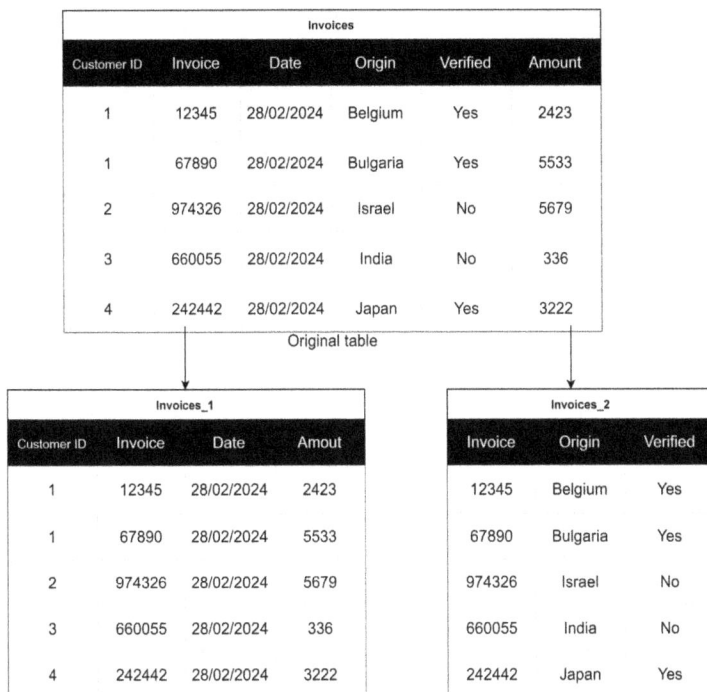

Invoices

Customer ID	Invoice	Date	Origin	Verified	Amount
1	12345	28/02/2024	Belgium	Yes	2423
1	67890	28/02/2024	Bulgaria	Yes	5533
2	974326	28/02/2024	Israel	No	5679
3	660055	28/02/2024	India	No	336
4	242442	28/02/2024	Japan	Yes	3222

Original table

Invoices_1

Customer ID	Invoice	Date	Amout
1	12345	28/02/2024	2423
1	67890	28/02/2024	5533
2	974326	28/02/2024	5679
3	660055	28/02/2024	336
4	242442	28/02/2024	3222

Invoices_2

Invoice	Origin	Verified
12345	Belgium	Yes
67890	Bulgaria	Yes
974326	Israel	No
660055	India	No
242442	Japan	Yes

Figure 5.6: Horizontal split (sharding) of the data

Defining a partitioning key

There are a few common methods to define the keys by which the data gets split (by default, this relates to horizontal partitioning, but may also refer to vertical). They can be considered according to the nature of the data and the type of partitioning we are trying to implement. Some of which are:

- **Hash partitioning:** Uses a calculated hash to split the data.
- **Range partitioning**: Cuts the data into ranges (alphabetically, by dates, or any other rule).
- **Round-robin partitioning:** Distributes the data evenly in a cyclic manner.

Load balancing

Load balancing is an important concept in scalable apps. The idea is to distribute network traffic evenly across a number of servers or services. The load balancer is a device (or a virtual device) whose job is to handle the load. Load balancing is a scalability pattern, which is also a form of server redundancy: the purpose of the server duplication is not just to balance the load but also to act as a backup responsive server in case one of the duplicates misbehaves. We will read more about redundancy patterns ahead.

The common reason to scale out a system, a server, or a service into multiple duplicates is expectations of a heavy workload and a large number of requests, which may overwhelm, block, or crash the system. However, each server has a different endpoint address. With load balancing, clients connect to the service through a single endpoint. Instead of directing to a single server, a load balancer is put at the central point of contact, receives all the requests, and directs each one to the designated server, as shown in the following figure:

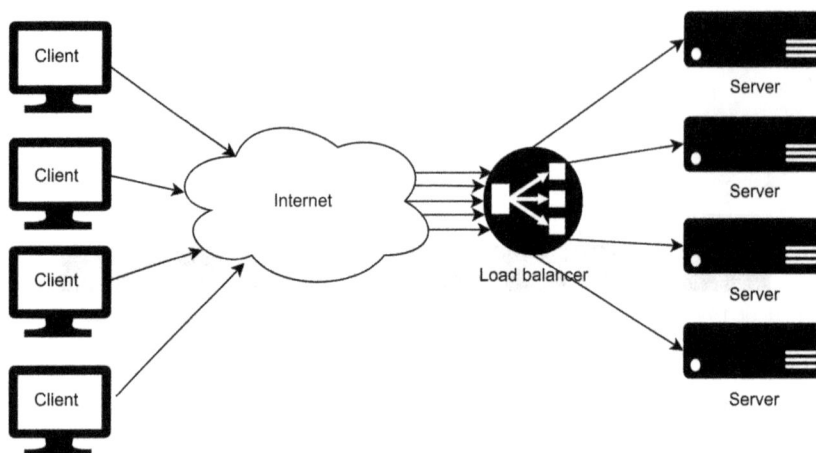

Figure 5.7: Load balancing multiple client requests to multiple scaled servers

By efficiently distributing the workload, load balancing helps optimize resource use, minimize response time, and prevent any single point of failure from causing significant downtime.

This is achieved through various algorithms and methods, such as round-robin, least connections, and IP hash, which determine how incoming requests are distributed among the servers in the pool. Load balancing can be implemented in hardware, software, or a combination of both, and it plays a crucial role in maintaining high availability and reliability in large-scale, high-traffic environments.

Asynchrony

Asynchrony is a programming concept that allows operations to execute independently of the main program flow. This means that an operation can start, and the program can continue to execute other tasks without waiting for the operation to complete. Asynchrony is particularly useful in scenarios where operations are time-consuming, such as network requests, file I/O, or any operation that involves waiting for external resources. By executing these operations asynchronously, the program can remain responsive and continue processing other tasks, leading to better performance and user experience.

In many programming languages, asynchrony is implemented using callbacks, promises, futures, or async/await syntax. These mechanisms allow developers to write code that looks synchronous but executes asynchronously, making it easier to manage complex operations without blocking the main thread. Here is a simple code example for issuing an asynchronous web request in Python:

```
import aiohttp
import asyncio


async def fetch(session, url):
    async with session.get(url) as response:
        return await response.text()


async def main():
    async with aiohttp.ClientSession() as session:
        html = await fetch(session, 'http://python.org')
        print(html)


if __name__ == '__main__':
    asyncio.run(main())
```

In the above example:

- `fetch` is an asynchronous function that takes an **aiohttp.ClientSession** and a URL as arguments. It uses the session to make a GET request to the specified URL and returns the response text.

- `main` is another asynchronous function that creates an **aiohttp.ClientSession** and uses it to fetch the content of **'http://python.org'**. It then prints the fetched content.

- **asyncio.run(main())** is used to run the main coroutine. This is the entry point for the asynchronous program.

- This example demonstrates how to perform a simple asynchronous web request in Python. The **aiohttp** library provides a powerful and flexible way to handle asynchronous HTTP requests, making it easier to build high-performance web applications.

Design patterns for high-availability

As part of our high-performance system, in this section, we will look at some design patterns to help us ensure that it is always available to users.

Circuit breaker

Circuit breaker is a design pattern used in modern software development to prevent a software system from repeatedly trying to execute an operation that's likely to fail. This pattern is particularly useful with microservices and distributed systems, where a failure in one component can cascade and affect other components, leading to a system-wide failure.

Somewhat like the physical electric circuit breaker, aimed to keep the home electric system healthy, it is normally transparent and non-intrusive, but as a precaution, it can also completely switch the power off in case of a dangerous malfunction, the circuit-breaker pattern helps monitor the health of a service, and keeping the system from turning unexpected failures into catastrophic crashes. The **circuit breaker** pattern uses an intermediate server (the circuit breaker), acting as a reverse proxy to the actual server/ service.

In normal conditions, the circuit is closed i.e., requests come from the client to the intermediate circuit breaker and get forwarded to the destination server. Responses find their way back to the originating client. The circuit breaker is transparent and not interrupting the flow. *Figure 5.8* depicts a closed circuit:

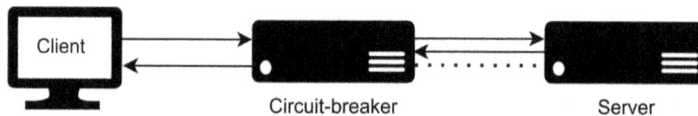

Figure 5.8: A closed circuit

However, the circuit breaker has another function, on top of acting as a transparent reverse-proxy server (marked with the dotted line in the figure above): it continuously checks the destination server's availability and response, acting as a guard for when the calls fail.

In case of any detected malfunction, response timeout, or server error, the circuit breaker breaks the connection and opens the circuit. That way, the clients still get an immediate response and are notified that the server is currently unavailable. This is shown in *Figure 5.9*:

Figure 5.9: An open circuit due to a failed server

While the destination server is down, one option is to use a **fallback server** and/or cached responses to keep the data flow going, as shown in *Figure 5.10*:

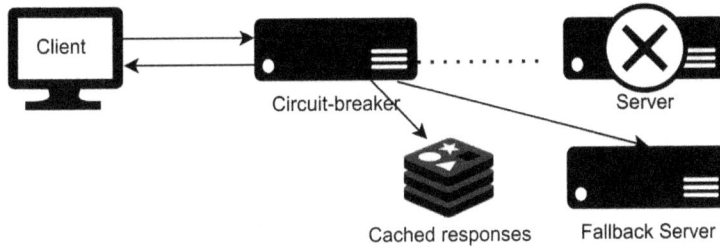

Figure 510: *The circuit breaker detects and takes action for the failed server*

Another option in case of server error is to maintain the circuit breaker in a half-open state: allowing some of the requests to pass through, and check if they respond properly. That way, if the destination server becomes active again, the client gets the response appropriately, and the circuit gets closed again. There are various strategies for which requests to block and which ones to let pass, while the circuit is half-open.

Redundancy

A key principle in a highly available system lies in identifying and addressing single points of failure, which refers to any part whose failure will result in a total system shutdown. Each production server of a complex system, whose availability depends on multiple factors, including hardware, software, and communication links, is a potential point of failure.

The redundancy design pattern is a strategy employed in system architecture to enhance reliability and fault tolerance by incorporating duplicate or redundant components. This pattern aims to mitigate the impact of potential failures or faults within a system by maintaining multiple instances of critical components. Redundancy can be applied at various levels, including hardware, software, and network infrastructure. By introducing redundancy, the system becomes more resilient to hardware failures, network issues, or unexpected outages, ensuring continuous operation and minimizing disruptions. While redundancy adds complexity and cost to a system, the increased reliability and availability are often deemed essential for critical applications and services that require high levels of uptime and dependability.

We have already looked at load balancing as a potential implementation of redundancy, and how it is managed. Load balancing is sometimes referred to as an **active-active redundancy**: meaning, all server duplicates are equally active in maintaining the service at all times.

An alternative is sometimes **active-passive redundancy**, as depicted in *Figure 5.11*. One server is active as the main server, while the backup (fallback) server remains inactive until the main server fails. This is not a very economic implementation, as we have to put up 2 production servers, while keeping one of them inactive most of the time, while we could load-balance both, be more efficient and performant, and reduce load.

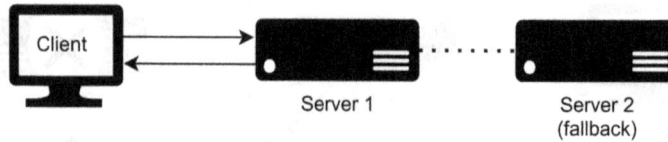

Figure 5.11: *A fallback redundancy server*

A third approach for redundancy handling is a hybrid between both load balancing and active-passive redundancy. This pattern is referred to as **N+1 redundancy**. With this pattern, we keep a **number (N)** of servers behind a load balancer but also keep an additional fallback server (+1) dormant, standing by to become active in case one of the active servers fails. Something like in *Figure 5.12*:

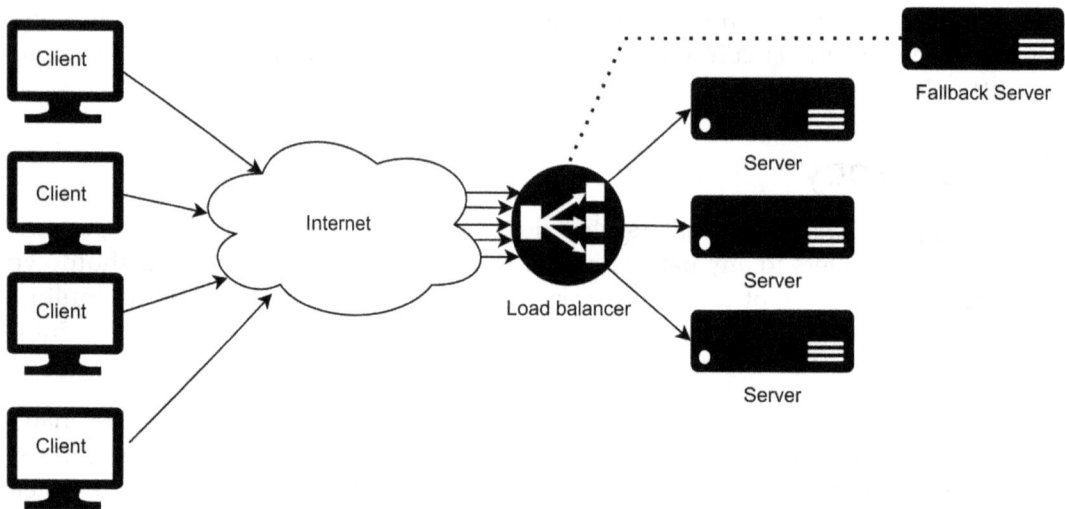

Figure 5.12: *N+1 redundancy scheme*

Decoupling

Decoupling is another important design principle that emphasizes reducing interdependencies between different components or modules in a system, promoting flexibility, maintainability, and scalability. The goal is to create a more modular and loosely coupled architecture where changes to one component have minimal impact on others. This pattern particularly benefits large and complex systems, promoting easier maintenance, testing, and extensibility. Here are a few key aspects of decoupling:

- **Independence** among system components, allowing them to be modified and evolve independently. This is crucial for parallel development efforts and ensures that changes in one module don't adversely affect others.

  Components should not know much about each other. They interact through well-defined interfaces or contracts, reducing the ripple effect of changes.

- Decoupling often involves creating **abstraction layers** that shield components from the internal details of one another. Abstraction promotes a higher level of encapsulation and simplifies the interactions between components.
- With complex systems and **microservices**, decoupling is often a foundational principle. Microservices are designed to be independently deployable and scalable, with each service operating as a loosely coupled, independent unit.

Keeping a good level of decoupling increases modifiability, testability, scalability, and maintainability. Of course, it is important to remember that it also increases complexity, and in a small system, may be an overkill which actually makes the system more difficult to maintain.

As always, balance is the key, and it is up to the architects and developers to decide how decoupled and how complex they let the system be.

Examples which demonstrate why decoupling is important, as well as the consequences of not implementing it properly, will be given in the next chapter, *Chapter 6, Performance Antipatterns*.

Dynamically scalable architectures

Today's cloud and virtual environments offer great control over the architecture of big distributed systems. While running a complex system architecture on-premise may be a hassle, and system upgrades require management of hardware, which may or may not be available, today's modern cloud service providers allow performing infrastructure architecture changes easily and economically. If we require more resources, hardware, appliances, clusters, redundant servers, databases, load balancers, storage devices, cache servers, etc., we can achieve that by a simple change in a configuration file, or even better: automatically dynamically allocated (both for increasing resources when needed, and decreasing resources when not needed anymore) within seconds.

Dynamic scalability architecture is a model based on a system of predefined scaling conditions that trigger the dynamic allocation of IT resources from resource pools. Dynamic allocation enables variable utilization as dictated by usage demand fluctuations since unnecessary resources are efficiently reclaimed without requiring manual interaction.

An automated scaling listener is configured with workload thresholds that dictate when new resources need to be added to the workload processing. This mechanism can be provided with logic that determines how many additional resources can be dynamically provided, based on the terms of a given cloud consumer's provisioning contract.

Dynamic scaling works both vertically, scaling resources up (upgrading existing machines and virtual machines) or down (downgrading them), and horizontally, scaling resources out (provisioning new machines/resources) and in (tearing them down).

Building an effective dynamic scaling architecture is up to the performance and infrastructure architects, working on defining the system's resources, designing the architecture with the right load monitors, and defining which resources are to be automatically scaled, and in which conditions.

Cloud-native designs

As we have discussed, modern infrastructure is governed and supported by cloud environments, which are becoming more dominant. This gives a great deal of power, scalability, agility, and control, but with great power comes great responsibility and complex, demanding architectures.

To adapt our systems to the modern landscape, we would have to consider and design our solutions to maximize efficiency in a cloud environment. Cloud-based design allows easy implementation of patterns such as CQRS, dynamic scaling, using microservices, containers, clusters, and automation. Infinite potential for growth of both data and components, allowing data and systems to expand tremendously. With the right DevOps and architects, a powerful resilient efficient performant system can be built.

Some principles of cloud-native design are:

- **Design for automation**: Creating automatic processes for deployment, scaling, repair, redundancy, building declarative configuration-based infrastructure, and producing monitoring, logging, and events to help keep the environment running and adapt to load, crashes, and other changes.

- **Decouple:** Cloud environments give great freedom in terms of technologies, programming languages, tools, hosting, clustering, and virtualization. This allows components to be independent and built in a way that is optimized for them. Communications are based on REST APIs, giving flexibility between components, regardless of how they were built.

- **Decoupling is effective for microservices architecture**: Cloud-native applications are often built using a microservices architecture, where the application is broken down into smaller, independent services. These microservices can be developed, deployed, and scaled independently, allowing for greater flexibility and agility in development and operations.

- **Security**: Given that cloud-native applications are often exposed to the internet, implementing robust security measures is critical. This includes adopting a defense-in-depth approach, securing communication between services, and implementing strong access controls and authentication mechanisms.

We will discuss cloud native strategies and considerations further in *Chapter 7, Performance in the Clouds*.

Highly scalable datastores

Apart from building cloud native applications, planning for them to be resilient, scalable, agnostic, decoupled, and distributed, we would have to consider the scalability of our datastores. Those were covered a bit in the previous sections about sharding and partitioning, and the mentions of database replicas, which are redundant copies of our database.

In any case, highly scalable data stores are essential for managing the increasing volumes of data and ensuring that applications can handle growing workloads efficiently. To recap on a few principles:

- **Partitioning and sharding** as mentioned, are crucial strategies for improving performance and scalability. Partitioning divides a dataset into logical subsets based on a defined criterion, such as ranges of values, date ranges, or geographic locations, which can help in improving query performance. Sharding, a specific type of partitioning, involves distributing data across multiple servers, each responsible for a specific shard or partition. This approach is commonly used in distributed database systems, particularly NoSQL databases, to achieve horizontal scalability.

- **Database choices** between relational, NoSQL, and NewSQL databases play a significant role in scalability. NoSQL databases (such as MongoDB, DynamoDB, or Cassandra) offer more flexibility and are better suited for handling unstructured or semi-structured data, making them ideal for scalable architectures. NewSQL databases (such as CockroachDB, Google Spanner, or the open-source TiDB, also known as TitaniumDB) aim to combine the best of both worlds, offering the scalability and performance benefits of NoSQL while maintaining the **Atomicity, Consistency, Isolation, Durability** (**ACID**) properties of traditional relational databases.

- **CQRS** will divide reading from writing, split the datastore into multiple nodes, and smartly divide operations.

Conclusion

In this chapter, we took a comprehensive look at design patterns, modern software architectures, cloud and scalability, and virtualization, and looked deeper into a variety of design patterns, aiming for improved performance, scalability, and availability.

In the next chapter, we will explore the world of anti-patterns: common design habits that may actually harm more than help.

Key learnings

- We reviewed the evolution of software architecture over the years, alongside the evolution of applications and software.

- We briefly looked at future trends in the world of system design and architecture.

- We explained what design patterns are, and some basic principles of system design: abstraction, SOLID, KISS, DRY, decoupling and the law of least astonishment.

- We looked into virtualization solutions, such as virtual machines and containers, and the differences between them.

- We looked at monolithic system architecture versus the more modern microservices.

- We looked in detail at some design patterns and principles aimed (not just) at performance: cache aside, CQRS, queue-based throttling, and database sharding.

- We looked in detail at some design patterns and principles aimed (not just) at scalability: lazy loading, data partitioning, load balancing, and asynchrony.

- We looked in detail at some design patterns and principles aimed (not just) at high availability: circuit breaker, redundancy, and decoupling.

- We discussed dynamic scaling architecture.

- We discussed considerations of system designs aimed at cloud environments.

- We briefly discussed the principles of high scalability of datastores.

Join our book's Discord space

Join the book's Discord Workspace for Latest updates, Offers, Tech happenings around the world, New Release and Sessions with the Authors:

https://discord.bpbonline.com

CHAPTER 6
Performance Antipatterns

Introduction

Much like design patterns, which are considered useful, architectural solution templates included in the arsenal of many architects' good-practice lists, it may be beneficial to familiarize with the opposite world. Antipatterns are common design pitfalls as they usually bring negative, rather than positive, results. In this chapter, we discuss antipatterns, as well as a selection of common ones, see how and why they are used, and the impact they have on performance.

Structure

In this chapter, we will cover the following topics:

- Introduction to antipatterns
- Performance antipatterns overview
- God object antipattern
- Tight coupling antipattern
- Premature optimization antipattern
- Blob antipattern
- Chatty communication antipattern

- Global interpreter lock antipattern
- Busy waiting antipattern
- Refactoring and optimizing performance antipatterns
- Common pitfalls and best practices

Objectives

Learning about patterns and antipatterns is an entirely wide subject, which covers programming patterns, architectural patterns, and even runtime-related patterns (as we will see with the global interpreter lock example later). In this chapter, we will look at a handful of common bad practices and antipatterns and discuss them in detail. The objective is to learn to be aware of their existence as a precursor for those who wish to explore further into the subject.

Introduction to antipatterns

Patterns are commonly repeated templates that provide blueprints for solving common problems in software development. Patterns are many times implemented and repeated, but that does not mean that all patterns are silver-bullet solutions to all problems. Sometimes, a popular pattern of work may actually introduce more problems than solve them. In the previous chapter, we looked at some common design patterns, which help ensure that systems are scalable, maintainable, and adhere to best practices.

On the flip side of useful design patterns are antipatterns: popular design or implementation practices that may initially seem like solutions but, in reality, do the opposite: hinder system performance and impede maintainability.

Antipatterns represent counterproductive approaches or pitfalls that can lead to unintended consequences. Recognizing and understanding antipatterns is crucial for developers and teams as it enables them to identify and avoid potential pitfalls, ensuring the creation of more robust, maintainable, and scalable software systems. By addressing antipatterns early in the development process, teams can enhance the overall quality of their code and contribute to the long-term success of the software project.

The concept of antipatterns in software development emerged in the early 1990s as a way to describe common pitfalls and poor practices that developers may unknowingly fall into when designing or implementing software systems. The term **antipattern** was coined by *Andrew Koenig* in his paper titled *Patterns and Antipatterns* presented at the *Pattern Languages of Programming Conference* in 1995. The paper explored the idea that, just as there are design patterns that encapsulate best practices, there are also recurring bad practices that can hinder software development.

In 1998, four authors, *William Brown, Raphael Malveau, Hays McCormick,* and *Thomas Mowbray,* published the book *AntiPatterns: Refactoring Software, Architectures, and Projects in Crisis*, which is considered a seminal work in the field of antipatterns and provides detailed insights into various common pitfalls and their potential solutions. The term gained popularity and became widely accepted in the software engineering community.

Since then, the concept of antipatterns has evolved, with numerous examples documented in literature and discussed within the software development community. Antipatterns are categorized into different types, including design antipatterns, architectural antipatterns, project management antipatterns, and more, each addressing specific aspects of software development where mistakes and pitfalls commonly occur.

Performance antipatterns overview

Much like patterns, antipatterns may have an effect on different aspects of a software project. The difference is that antipatterns have a negative, rather than positive, effect. One such aspect is performance, which can lead to inefficiencies, decreased system responsiveness, and resource wastage. They basically do the opposite of what good practice patterns do. Rather than save on resources and work efficiently, the software becomes wasteful and not minding its misbehavior.

As we will see in the patterns listed in detail in this chapter, not only do solutions that use antipatterns still provide a working solution, but those patterns were developed for a reason, for which they are good, but misusing them or overusing them may present issues.

Some symptoms may include:

- **Overuse of resource-intensive operations:** Performing operations with high resource demands, such as excessive database queries or complex computations, without proper optimization, can lead to bottlenecks and reduced system performance.

- **Eager-loading of resources:** We mentioned lazy-loading in the previous chapter, as a good way to minimize calls and costly data traffic. Eager-loading does the opposite: loading or initializing resources and data prematurely, even if they are not needed. That can result in unnecessary resource consumption and increased startup times.

- **Memory leaks:** Yes, they still exist. In languages like C and C++, where each memory allocation and deallocation is performed by manual operations, memory leaks are common bugs. Modern frameworks, like Java and the .NET framework, provide built-in features for garbage collection to free and automatically deallocate any used memory resources. This renders memory leaks rarer but not extinct. They still happen in all sorts of scenarios, like interacting with external libraries (which are implemented in lower-level languages) and not releasing resources properly. Failure to release unused objects or memory can lead to memory leaks, gradually depleting system resources, and affecting overall performance.

- **Blocking the main thread:** We mentioned asynchrony in the previous chapter, aimed to keep the app running while performing background operations. Time-consuming or blocking operations on the main thread can result in unresponsive user interfaces in applications, negatively impacting user experience.

- **Inefficient database queries:** Poorly optimized or excessive database queries, including unnecessary joins or fetching of redundant data, can strain the database and lead to increased response times.

- **Inefficient algorithmic choices:** Choosing inefficient algorithms for common operations, such as sorting or searching, can result in suboptimal performance and resource utilization.

- **Deadlocks:** As per the last three items, the bad implementation of multi threads, queries, or algorithms may eventually cause deadlocks, which is a state where two or more processes are unable to proceed because each is waiting for the other to release a resource, resulting in a mutually blocking scenario. In simple words, it is a stuck system.

In the following sections, we will look at a few concrete antipatterns in detail.

God object antipattern

In previous chapters, we mentioned more than once the importance of solid software design practices (repeating examples of solid practices are the SOLID principles). In summary, we want to keep our modules and classes lean, on a need-to-know basis, to keep their functionality concise, understandable, and purposeful. Having a single responsibility helps classes be easy to understand, maintainable, testable, replaceable, and scalable.

The God object (also known as the **all-knowing class**) is a good method to achieve the exact opposite. It is not much of a pattern; as much as it is a bad practice, it is the result of giving a data module too much knowledge, information, and responsibility. An inexperienced developer may think centralization is a good idea, as it is easy to have control over the data and have everything their class needs at their fingertips, but we have learned previously, and many software architects and developers learned the hard way, centralized control of a module or class is a bad idea and breaks the basic design principles of good practice of software engineering.

Here is a Python example of an Employee skeleton class that *knows too much*:

```python
class Employee:
    def __init__(self, id, fn, jt, ln, ad, ct, pc, t1, t2, t3, sl, cc) -> None:
        self.id = id
        self.first_name = fn
        self.last_name = ln
        self.job_title = jt
```

```
        self.home_address = ad
        self.home_city = ct
        self.home_postcode = pc
        self.active_task1 = t1
        self.active_task2 = t2
        self.active_task3 = t3
        self.salary = sl
        self.company_car = cc

    def calculateSalaryTax(self):
        return self.salary * 0.1 #in Bulgaria
```

Another term that often gets attributed to a *jack of all trades* piece of code is that it has low cohesion. Cohesion of code is how focused a portion of code is on a unified purpose.

The code example above is a bit extreme. Let us understand what is wrong here:

- The properties of the Employee class manage the employees, names, addresses, work tasks, salary, and company car, and even has a method to calculate tax. We could add other fields and methods, but the more we add, it would make the implementation more grotesque and unusable.

- If anything changes with active tasks, the employee has more than one address to manage, or there are any changes in salary or tax handling, we would have to modify the employee's class. If we scale, all these properties and handlers, which should be external to the employee entity as they are general characteristics and require a completely separate modular implementation, will go with our cumbersome, oversized class.

- We are breaking the SOLID principles. Giving too much responsibility, bloating the class, and making it very difficult to maintain, extend, test, and scale. Tracking performance and applying complex measures of security on different parts become also very difficult.

Generally, we have been mentioning principles such as SOLID throughout the book, but in many cases, rather than trying to analyze how a code adheres to those principles, it is easier to immediately tell, at a glance, if it has low cohesion if you see too many areas it is trying to dominate.

Tight coupling antipattern

After kicking the bad habit of granting too much power to a single God class, one may think about breaking the modules into smaller pieces, which is definitely the right decision for any project we plan to ever edit, modify, extend, debug, scale, or fix. The bottom line is that modularization is a good practice in any project, except if the project is a single function, and even then, one should question the structure and be in the mindset to keep it compact and concise.

However, splitting code should also be done right. Keeping too strong interconnections and interdependencies between modules could get to the point where it would be as if we had not split them at all. Of course, semantically, we do split the code into different classes, but if they are too tightly coupled to one another, they would still make tasks such as extending, modifying, scaling, or maintaining difficult.

Of course, our code represents one of many parts in a complex system; hence, they are inevitably related, but making the parts communicate directly with one another and knowing each other too much is what we call **tight coupling**.

From the previous example, we can observe in the code sample as follows:

- We have removed a lot of data from the **Employee** class, trying to keep it to a minimum, holding just direct information about the employee.

  We could go further and create an inheritance of **Employee** from a base class representing a person in the system (call it, for example, **Person**), as the system may manage various types of **Person**s. However, for the sake of simplicity, let us keep **Employee** as the only person type in our system, and no inheritance involved.

- The **calculateSalaryTax** method is now moved to a separate class. The Employee still has a method to calculate tax, but the actual implementation of **calculateSalaryTax** is actually delegated to a new class, **TaxCalculator**.

  This is great because we have a separation of responsibility and authority. The **Employee** class manages the employee details and does not care about the details of salary calculation (if the employee happens to be an accountant, they would probably do care, but in terms of code separation, we have two separate roles/responsibilities).

```
# A helper class to calculate salary tax
class TaxCalculator:
    def calculateTax (self, salary):
        return salary * 0.1 # For Bulgaria


# Represents a company employee
class Employee:
    def __init__(self, id, fn, ln, jt, sl) -> None:
        self.id = id
        self.first_name = fn
        self.last_name = ln
```

```
        self.job_title = jt
        self.salary = sl


    def calculateSalaryTax(self):
        calculator = TaxCalculator()
        return calculator.calculateTax (self.salary)


# Example:
alon = Employee(1234, "Alon", "Rotem", "Software whisperer", 1000)
print(f"{alon.first_name}'s tax is {alon.calculateSalaryTax()}")
```

The output will be:

```
Alon's tax is 100.0
```

We have now presented a **tight coupling** between the **Employee** and the **TaxCalculator**. The **Employee** creates a concrete instance of the actual **TaxCalculator** class and calls its specific **calculateSalaryTax** method. In essence, we can represent this relation like this:

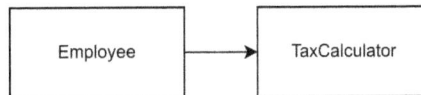

Figure 6.1: Tightly coupled relation

We have created **dependency**. If the **TaxCalculator** changes its behavior its methods, or suppose we want to use a different type of tax calculator, we would need substantial changes in the Employee implementation too. For example, suppose managers have special tax conditions, and a new type of calculator is required for them due to some special cases. We would now have something like this:

```
# A helper class to calculate salary tax
class TaxCalculator:
    def calculateTax (self, salary):
        return salary * 0.1 # For Bulgaria


# A helper to calculate salary tax for managers!
class ManagerTaxCalculator:
    def calculateTax (self, salary):
        return salary * 0.05 # Managers pay less tax


# Represents a company employee
class Employee:
```

```python
    def __init__(self, id, fn, ln, jt, sl) -> None:
        self.id = id
        self.first_name = fn
        self.last_name = ln
        self.job_title = jt
        self.salary = sl

    def calculateSalaryTax(self):
        if(self.job_title == "Manager"):
            calculator = ManagerTaxCalculator()
        else:
            calculator = TaxCalculator()
        return calculator.calculateTax (self.salary)

# Example
alon = Employee(1234, "Alon", "Rotem", "Software whisperer", 1000)
zaphod = Employee(5678, "Zaphod", "Beeblebrox", "Manager", 6000)

print(f"{alon.first_name}'s tax is {alon.calculateSalaryTax()}")
print(f"{zaphod.first_name}'s tax is {zaphod.calculateSalaryTax()}")
```

Output:

Alon's tax is 100.0

Zaphod's tax is 300.0

Notice the following:

- We have two calculators: **TaxCalculator** and **ManagerTaxCalculator**.
- The **Employee** now must intimately **know** both. It still creates a concrete instance and calls a concrete method.

Coupling got even tighter, as the **Employee** now has to handle a couple (pun intended) of classes.

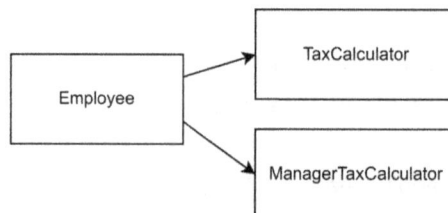

Figure 6.2: Double tightly coupled relation

It is not impossible to see how this can escalate further.

The solution to tight coupling is loose coupling. Connect entities indirectly. Instead of classes knowing too much about each other, we establish abstract interfaces.

A small anecdote here: as the examples in this book are mostly Python-based, it is good to note that there are debates about whether or not interfaces are necessary to be implemented in Python, as it supports strong inheritance features, and a rather unique implementation of dynamic typing, referred to as *duck-typing*: automagically mapping supported functions to supported objects (*"If it walks like a duck and it quacks like a duck, then it must be a duck"*). See how in the above example, the `calculateSalaryTax` method uses the `calculator` object, which can agnostically be either `TaxCalculator` or `ManagerTaxCalculator`. For whichever object that was instantiated eventually, the `calculateTax` is called. However, even in Python and any other language that supports it, it is not a bad practice to reduce coupling by using interfaces.

Interfaces are strong, binding contracts. They provide expectations but not implementations. Once the **Employee** class uses an interface rather than an actual class, it knows what methods are supported and does not care which actual object is being used. On the other hand, any class that implements the **ITaxCalculator** interface knows which methods are expected to be included. Nobody knows anybody, but everybody knows the rules and follows the contract.

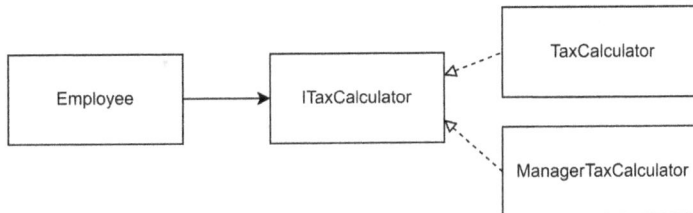

Figure 6.3: Loosely coupled 3-way relationship

This way, we can change the **TaxCalculators** or add new ones. They just have to keep following the interface as a contract, so no **breaking changes** occur.

The solution may look something like this:

```
from abc import ABC, abstractmethod

# A binding interface
class ITaxCalculator(ABC):
    @abstractmethod
    def calculateTax(self, salary):
        pass
```

```python
# A helper class to calculate salary tax
class TaxCalculator(ITaxCalculator):
    def calculateTax (self, salary):
        return salary * 0.1 # For Bulgaria

# A helper to calculate salary tax for managers!
class ManagerTaxCalculator(ITaxCalculator):
    def calculateTax (self, salary):
        return salary * 0.05

# Represents a company employee
class Employee:
    def __init__(self, id, fn, ln, jt, sl) -> None:
        self.id = id
        self.first_name = fn
        self.last_name = ln
        self.job_title = jt
        self.salary = sl

    def calculateSalaryTax(self, calculator:ItaxCalculator):
        return calculator.calculateTax (self.salary)


# Example
alon = Employee(1234, "Alon", "Rotem", "Software whisperer", 1000)
zaphod = Employee(5678, "Zaphod", "Beeblebrox", "Manager", 6000)

calc = TaxCalculator()
manager_calc = ManagerTaxCalculator()

print(f"{alon.first_name}'s tax is {alon.calculateSalaryTax(calc)}")
print(f"{zaphod.first_name}'s tax is {zaphod.calculateSalaryTax(manager_calc)}")
```

Output:

Alon's tax is 100.0

Zaphod's tax is 300.0

Notice that now, in the example, we have separate objects for employees and calculators. The **Employee** method **calculateSalaryTax** only knows it expects a calculator that follows the **ITaxCalculator** interface, which is defined as an **abstract base class** (**ABC**) with an empty abstract method **calculateTax**, to be implemented by every relevant class. We pretty much inject the right calculator into the implementation that uses it. It doesn't get much more loosely coupled than that.

Premature optimization antipattern

In the previous two sections, we reviewed a common thought process of a seasoned developer or architect: make the code more efficient by increasing cohesion and modularizing while reducing coupling among components. Observing these patterns and including them in the development process mindset becomes more natural over time. This book talks about effectiveness and efficiency as attributes of enhanced software performance, but there is a pitfall to resist the urge to optimize at all costs and at any time.

The root of all evil

Optimizing, as stated above, in terms of keeping good practices and principles such as SOLID and modularization are mostly good. Optimization and analysis take effort and time. Premature optimization is all about rushing into over-optimizing the project without knowing or assessing the actual need to apply it before it is decided that the optimization measure is necessary. *Premature* is the keyword here.

It is important, while advocating optimization and good practices, clean code, and effective design patterns, to also mention antipatterns but also mention the other side of optimization: optimizing code for maintainability and scalability is not always the most effective for performance. In fact, it has been shown and proven many times that code optimization lowers performance optimization, especially in complex compiled languages, such as C++, where *clean* code with proper abstractions, virtual functions, polymorphism, and encapsulation (core properties of proper object-oriented design), results in inefficient compiled implementation, over-complicated virtual function pointers and other in-memory constructs, while *dirty, messy* code where implementation is not sophisticated, and just sticks to the functionality (for example with simple if-else/switch blocks, rather than abstract polymorphism), may work much faster by significant orders of magnitude.

A classic quote that cannot be left out when mentioning premature optimization is by *Donald Knuth*, one of the founding fathers of computer science, who published the series of books titled *The Art of Computer Programming*, consisting of 4 volumes, published between 1968 and 2019 (indeed, work on this series of books took more than 50 years, and additional extensions to volume 4, and new volumes 5 – 7 are pending publication at the time this book is being written). Those books represent the central pillar of computer programming and are considered some of the most important computer science foundation books of all time. A famous quote, usually wrongly attributed to those books, while in fact it was published by *Donald Knuth* in a 1974 academic paper for *Stanford University*, named *Structured Programming with go to Statements* states:

There is no doubt that the grail of efficiency leads to abuse. Programmers waste enormous amounts of time thinking about, or worrying about, the speed of noncritical parts of their programs, and these attempts at efficiency actually have a strong negative impact when debugging and maintenance are considered. We should forget about small efficiencies, say about 97% of the time: premature optimization is the root of all evil.

Prioritize performance optimizations properly

Considering the famous quote from *Donald Knuth*, we should not forget about performance, but learn to prioritize performance optimizations properly.

Efficient software development is a fine balance between 3 properties:

- **Performance**: How fast your software runs.
- **Velocity**: How fast you can build your software.
- **Adaptability**: How easy it is to make changes, adapt, port, deploy, and modify your software.

Look at the following figure:

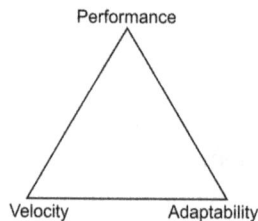

Figure 6.4: Trade-off properties of efficient development

In many cases, inclining towards one comes at the expense of the others. It takes more effort and more time (less velocity) to build a high-performance app. Making it performant usually means also making it more specific, and less adaptable, and vice versa.

There are considerations to make the software as performant as possible, if that's a core requirement. In some cases, we would want the software to be out and released as fast as possible (high velocity), or we would want to be able to quickly and easily add features (adaptability).

The pitfall of premature optimization is about evaluating performance when it is relevant, yet usually by nitpicking the code, with thoughts about cleaner code, design patterns, or prior knowledge about the efficiency of libraries or language features. For example, one may argue that in Python, using the string `join` method,

```
result = ''.join(['a', 'b', 'c'])
```

It is more performant than using the + concatenation operator:

```
result = 'a' + 'b' + 'c'
```

At least, that is what a seasoned senior developer may claim. So, using the **+** operator may not pass the code review, with a comment to use the **join** method, as it is more performant. This is an excellent example of nitpicking and unnecessary, premature optimization. Even though technically, the senior engineer's observation and considerations in this example are correct, it is also important to take into account:

- Whether it is really proven to be significantly more performant, in our case.
- The effect it would have on our application.

Of course, to prove effectiveness, we would have to do some research on the differences between + and join, run some benchmarks, and see if it is really worth the optimization. Or we can just blindly accept the optimization and not deal with it. As *Donald Knut* correctly observed, such nitpicks can take a great deal of time and effort, which is, in many cases, utterly unnecessary. This is sometimes referred to as **micro-performance**.

Facebook was initially written by *Mark Zuckerberg* in the questionable, awkward, inefficient, inconsistent language called PHP, which in its original form is not very appreciated by many developers. However, it is good enough for relatively quick, concise, focused web projects, which is why it works well as the backend of the world's most popular content management system, *WordPress*. However, PHP has many drawbacks compared to highly scalable, modern, performant languages. Facebook runs on specifically tailored virtual machines called **HipHop Virtual Machines** (**HHVM**), and later, they engineered a PHP to C++ compiler called **HPHPc** (*HipHop for PHP*), as compiled C++ server-side code is immeasurably more performant than the clumsy interpreted PHP. Later, in 2014, they built a new dialect of PHP called **Hack** (or **Hacklang**), which was specially designed to run with high performance on HHVM. Hack is compatible with PHP but has more features and type restrictions. It was a specially tailored solution, and it is still being used by *Facebook* to this day.

We may argue that it would have been better if Facebook had been developed in more performant languages (such as C or C++) from the beginning, but in reality, such a decision may not have had a positive effect, since, in the beginning, velocity was the main priority: to build and release Facebook quickly. Only later, when engineers decided performance was insufficient, they came up with solutions.

Even if performance is an important non-functional feature of our application, we should still first build the app, with minimum nitpicking on micro-performance. Then, we can measure performance, optimize it as much as possible, and verify with measurements. A good progression might be as follows:

- Research and consider using the right data structures.
- Research and consider using the right algorithms.

- Run profiling to discover bottlenecks.
- Optimize upon need after assessing, measuring, and profiling.

Do not fall into micro-optimizations or rush into premature optimizations. The right data structures and algorithms may have a profound effect on our software, but nitpicking about using a **StringBuilder**, a **join** or a **+** operator, lists or sets, enumerators or plain loops, or over-cleaning the code, may take too much of our time, and result in negligible improvements nobody will ever appreciate.

Blob antipattern

Do not confuse the blob antipattern with the BLOB database data type (which represents a Binary Large Object for storing large binary data, such as images or other binary files, encoded into a database table column). Also, do not confuse the blob antipattern with the **God** object antipattern. They are both related but not completely similar.

The word **blob** (originating from Middle English from the 14th century) refers to an amorphous mass, especially of a liquid or semisolid (jelly-like) substance that clumps and groups together without a definite shape.

The **God** class, which may or may not be too big, violates the single responsibility principle of design and grants a class too much responsibility. Blob, on the other hand, refers to a class or module that keeps getting extended and growing, making it too big to maintain. Much like the original meaning of the word **blob**, the blob antipattern describes a formless, amorphous mass mess of code. It tends to accumulate various methods and attributes, making it difficult to understand, maintain, and extend, violating the principles of modularity and separation of concerns.

Blob is metaphorically that drawer of junk where you accumulate all kinds of things you may or may not need (every technical person has at least one), which keeps becoming more crowded and cluttered as more stuff is thrown into it until it is a complete shapeless mess (although the owner of the drawer can surely find anything they are looking for). The blob class is that drawer into which we throw everything we cannot find a better place for.

As a simple example, take a look at this class:

```python
class ListManager:
    def __init__(self):
        self.data = []

    def add_item(self, item):
        self.data.append(item)
```

```python
    def remove_item(self, item):
        if item in self.data:
            self.data.remove(item)

    def calculate_average(self):
        if len(self.data) == 0:
            return 0
        total = sum(self.data)
        return total / len(self.data)

    def display_data(self):
        for item in self.data:
            print(item)

    def save_to_file(self, filename):
        with open(filename, 'w') as file:
            for item in self.data:
                file.write(str(item) + '\n')

    def load_from_file(self, filename):
        with open(filename, 'r') as file:
            for line in file:
                self.data.append(float(line.strip()))
```

In this example, the **ListManager** class has multiple methods responsible for various tasks, such as adding and removing items from a list, calculating averages, displaying data, and saving/ loading data to and from a file. While each method performs a specific task, the class as a whole is taking on too many responsibilities, violating the principle of single responsibility and leading to a lack of cohesion.

To address the blob antipattern, the class should be refactored to separate concerns and promote better modularity and encapsulation. For instance, functionality related to file I/O could be encapsulated in a separate class, and methods with related functionality could be grouped together into smaller, more focused classes or modules.

Chatty communication antipattern

Chatty communication antipattern, also known as **chatty API** or **chatty I/O**, this antipattern has a direct impact on application performance. As the name implies, we are talking here about excessive, unnecessary communication. API calls and data transmissions are costly. Depending on the infrastructure and conditions (e.g., across different continents), network requests and communications come with their overhead and can be quite a bottleneck. In any case, any operation that has to go through a network will be slower than operations taking place locally on the machine, by definition. A chatty communication is one that is active much more than necessary. It means we inefficiently keep making too many little calls over the network for specific, bulky operations of a badly designed API.

A common example may be of an API that returns user profile information. In a good scenario, we could make a single request to get a single JSON string with all the user's data (or all relevant user data). A performance-aware architect may want to make the requests smaller and lighter, allowing greater granularity of requesting just the required field every time, as lazy-loaded data. However, if, in most cases, we will need a large number of fields, instead of bundling them into a single request (textual JSON is mostly lightweight anyway), what we end up with is a series of too many little requests fetching a single field every time.

The following code demonstrates what such an implementation might look like. For the sake of the example, the data is stored in an array of objects, and not in a database, and there is a generic method called **get_property**, which gets a user ID, and a property to retrieve, and returns the property of the user. Instead of getting the user object in one call, we need to invoke a separate request to get each property. That gets the API to be way too chatty.

```python
from flask import Flask, request, jsonify


app = Flask(__name__)
# Sample data array of users
users = [
    {
        "id": 1,
        "name": "Alon Rotem",
        "gender": "M",
        "birth_year": 1973,
        "role": "Software engineer"
    }
]


# General method to get a user's property by ID
def get_property(user_id, property_name):
```

```
    user = next((user for user in users if user['id'] == user_id), None)
    if user:
        return jsonify({ "id": user_id, property_name: user[property_name] })
    return jsonify({"message": "User not found"}), 404


# GET a specific user's name
@app.route('/user/name<int:user_id>', methods=['GET'])
def get_user_name(user_id):
    return get_property(user_id, "name")


# GET a specific user's gender
@app.route('/user/gender<int:user_id>', methods=['GET'])
def get_user_name(user_id):
    return get_property(user_id, "gender")


# GET a specific user's birth year
@app.route('/user/birth_year<int:user_id>', methods=['GET'])
def get_user_name(user_id):
    return get_property(user_id, "birth_year")


# GET a specific user's birth year
@app.route('/user/birth_year<int:user_id>', methods=['GET'])
def get_user_name(user_id):
    return get_property(user_id, "birth_year")


# GET a specific user's role
@app.route('/user/role/<int:user_id>', methods=['GET'])
def get_user_name(user_id):
    return get_property(user_id, "role")


# ... more profile property fetching API functions here

if __name__ == '__main__':
    app.run(debug=True)
```

This is just an overly granular, badly designed, chatty API.

Global interpreter lock antipattern

It is not a design pattern nor an antipattern per se, at least not in the developer's realm, but the **global interpreter lock (GIL)** is a feature baked into the way Python works as a language. There are other languages that include GIL, but they are rare. GIL is mostly attributed to Python, maybe because of its popularity as a language, in comparison to other languages, such as **Ruby**.

Python and CPython

Many people know about Python, but not as many have heard the term **CPython**, and many who have, confuse between the two. Let us understand both of these terms.

Python is a popular programming language. It has been around since 1991, and its name is a tribute to the legendary British comical group, *Monty Python*. Defining a programming language includes its syntax, principles, and rules, and a set of build and runtime tools, which help turn the programmer's idea into a running executable.

Python is an interpreted language, meaning that in order to execute a Python program, we need to run the source code through an interpreter, which reads and executes what it finds. Normally, a Python interpreter will be an executable binary, invoked with the command **python**, followed by a command-line argument, referencing the source code file.

Knowing the programming language specifications, anyone can build a compatible Python interpreter in any language, and indeed, there are several implementations of Python out there: **Jython** (which is a Python interpreter built in Java, to execute on a Java virtual machine), **IronPython** (which is a Python interpreter built in C#, to integrate Python runtime into the Microsoft .NET framework), but the most popular Python implementation, by far, is **CPython**. It is a Python interpreter written in C, as the name implies, and it is the interpreter we get, when we download and install Python from the main website, at *python.org*.

CPython has the implementation of the GIL baked into it, although due to GIL's disadvantages, a post of the Python Steering Council on the **official Python Enhancement Proposals (PEPs)** list at *python.org* from January 2023 proposes to remove the GIL or at least add an option to switch it off.

Although GIL is mostly attributed to Python, that is, CPython, as other implementations such as Jython do not include GIL, there are other occurrences of GIL **in the wild**. Similarly, to the relation between Python, as a language, and CPython as an implementation of it, the main implementation of the Ruby language, called **CRuby** (also known as MRI: Matz's Ruby Interpreter – Matz being short for *Yukihiro Matsumoto*, the founder of the Ruby language), also includes a GIL.

Disadvantages of GIL

So far, we have understood **where** the GIL comes from, but not **what** it is, and why it is mentioned in this section as something that may have a negative effect on our project.

As explained, Python is an interpreted language. In order to execute Python code, we need it to go through a preinstalled interpreter (hence the *Global Interpreter*, in *Global Interpreter Lock*). As with many other computer language implementations, running over modern hardware and modern operating systems (Python is platform independent and OS agnostic in that sense), our Python program can spawn multiple threads to run in parallel. However, all thread requests pass through the same single global interpreter.

The GIL allows synchronizing Python threads in a very basic way: letting just one thread be active in the interpreter at a time. This creates mutual exclusion of threads, so that no two threads can access shared Python objects at once, which makes multithreaded Python thread-safe.

Thread safety is a common topic of multithreaded programming and relates to regulating access of multiple threads to shared resources, a situation which may create **race conditions** (that is, when more than one thread tries to modify an object at once, letting the other threads wait on it, or creating data discrepancies upon reading/writing due to multiple access). There are numerous techniques to regulate threads and make a code thread-safe, namely, to consider the scenario where more than one thread calls the same method, or tries to access the same shared object at the same time. Access should be streamlined and controlled to ensure data integrity and proper access. One technique is to use an **atomic operation** (one that cannot be interrupted nor split), and to atomize an operation by using a lock object (such as a **mutex**, which refers to *mutual exclusion* of operations), which locking and unlocking is considered atomic (in the eyes of the interpreter or compiler), and any other threads are bound to wait until the mutex is unlocked, before they can access the same code or resource.

In the case of GIL, there is a controlled streamline of operations, which eliminates race conditions and elevates thread safety. The Python global interpreter uses its own lock (hence the L, in GIL), and whatever thread is trying to execute, it must first wait for the lock to be released. That is: only one thread can really execute an interpreter's instruction at a time.

Suppose we have two threads trying to read/write from the same memory resource or file. The first goes through the interpreter (acquiring the lock, then releasing it when done), the 2nd thread awaits until the lock is released, before it can access the same resource. The GIL is a simple and effective solution to thread safety in the Python interpreter, but it has the major downside that full multithreading is not supported by Python.

Other multithreaded languages, such as C++ or C#, which are not bound to an interpreter but operate on the main processor (once compiled into binary code), can do whatever they want, but it is up to the developer to consider and implement the thread-safety of multithreaded code. With GIL-enabled languages, there is a limiting mechanism that streamlines the threads into linear, serial, and sequential operations. This makes Python more thread-safe but also more controlled and more limited. Junior Python developers who encounter multithreading in Python are many times frustrated with how Python threads behave in a counterintuitive way, and limited performance, as threads are handled one at a time, which harms Python's reputation as a multithreading language.

It does not mean that things do not run in parallel in Python. For example, suppose we have a UI thread and a web-request parallel thread. The interpreter, with the help of GIL, runs them one at a time while the web-request thread awaits its response. The UI keeps running, but the interpreter alternates back and forth (between running the UI and waiting for the web response), and executes one thread at any given time. The threads DO run in parallel, but the interpreter switches from one thread to the other to inspect input/output in a serial manner.

This is definitely an aspect of GIL-enabled languages that not everyone is aware of. One last point to note is that Python does support real multithreading through multiprocessing. That is, running more than one instance of the app at a time, but this may be cumbersome and inefficient.

Busy waiting antipattern

In the context of performance, we mention terms like lazy loading to save on resources and traffic. There is also a famous quote attributed to Microsoft's founder, *Bill Gates: I choose a lazy person to do a hard job. Because a lazy person will find an easy way to do it.* A form of laziness may also be interpreted as: as long as there is no work to be done yet, do not do anything.

Busy waiting, also known as **spinning** or **busy looping**, is when a process or thread continuously checks for a condition in a tight loop without yielding processor time to other tasks. Rather than waiting for an event to be triggered, a callback function to be invoked, a message to be received from a queue, or any other means to get notified when it is ok to move on, busy waiting keeps being busy, and looping through keeps the CPU busy, while actually doing nothing.

This approach is characterized by its inefficiency and wasteful consumption of CPU resources, as it continuously consumes CPU cycles even when there is no meaningful work to be done. Busy waiting loops are typically used when waiting for a condition to be met, such as the completion of an asynchronous operation or the availability of a resource. However, this pattern can lead to high CPU utilization, reduced performance, and potential scalability issues, especially in multi-threaded or multi-process environments. This is a classic antipattern, a bad habit and malpractice.

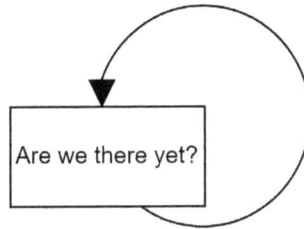

Figure 6.5: An infinite loop of active waiting

Here is an example of what busy waiting may look like:

```
import time

def check_condition():
    # Simulated function to check a condition
    return False

def busy_waiting():
    while not check_condition():
        # Busy waiting loop
        print("Waiting for condition to be met...")
        time.sleep(1)  # Sleep for 1 second before checking again

busy_waiting()
print("Condition met. Continuing...")
```

The only point of light with the **busy_waiting** function is that it sleeps for one second before iterating and checking the status of the condition again. This moderates the excessive activeness of our program. If we comment out that line too, we may get to the point of driving the CPU to 100% just by empty looping pretty quickly.

As previously mentioned, to mitigate busy waiting, it is essential to adopt more efficient and scalable concurrency models, such as event-driven programming, with or without callback functions, asynchronous I/O, or blocking synchronization primitives like condition variables or semaphores. These approaches allow tasks to suspend execution when waiting for a condition to be met, freeing up CPU resources for other tasks and improving overall system performance.

Refactoring and optimizing performance antipatterns

It is not easy to detect performance antipatterns. In many cases, they are disguised as patterns or common practices. It takes a great deal of experience to detect such well-baked-in problems. Even in cases of tight coupling, which is a common, known principle, it is not always easy to detect, as classes span across different files. The more we learn, the more experience we have in identifying and mitigating bad code habits. Following are some tips that may help:

- **Understand common performance antipatterns**: Before diving into the code, it is essential to understand common performance anti-patterns. There are more than the ones listed in this chapter. They include issues like unnecessary object creation, inefficient data structures, improper use of loops, and excessive database queries. Recognizing these patterns is the first step in identifying potential problems in our code.

- **Use UML design diagrams**: It may be helpful to map the code components and see how they relate to each other, which part does what. Thus, we can detect things like duplicate responsibilities, tight couplings, God and blob components etc.

- **Use automated profiling and analysis tools for detection**: Automated tools can help identify performance anti-patterns in our code. For example, static analysis tools can analyze our codebase to detect common issues like inefficient loops, unnecessary object creation, and improper use of data structures. Profiling tools can help detect bottlenecks or overuse of certain code areas. These tools can provide insights into areas of our code that may be causing performance issues.

- **Manual code review**: Not easy, but very important. In addition to automated tools, manual code review is crucial. This involves going through our codebase to identify patterns that could lead to performance issues. For instance, looking for loops that iterate over large collections without optimizing for performance or methods that perform unnecessary computations. Manual review can help catch issues that automated tools might miss, especially in complex or less common patterns.

- **Performance testing and continuous monitoring**: We have already mentioned those tools, as core practices to detect performance issues, both during development and after deployment. As they help identify performance issues of our app modules, they can help us focus our attention on the problematic ones, which may help identify malpractices and antipatterns.

- **Mind premature optimization**: As stated earlier, be aware and beware of losing time on premature or excessive meaningless optimization. The previous bullet points may help focus our attention to detect antipatterns and refactor/ correct/ mitigate them.

Common pitfalls and best practices

Common pitfalls with code performance antipatterns often stem from misunderstanding the nature of performance issues, the misapplication of optimization techniques, and the failure to consider the broader impact of code design on system performance. To keep away from performance antipatterns, it is essential to adopt a proactive approach that involves understanding, identifying, and avoiding those patterns. Here are some best practices based on the provided sources:

- **Regular refactoring**: Keep the codebase clean and organized to prevent it from becoming a **big ball of mud**, which is often the result of several antipatterns. Regular refactoring helps in maintaining code quality and making it easier to identify and fix performance issues.

- **Avoid other antipatterns**: Being aware of and avoiding other common antipatterns can prevent our project from becoming a **big ball of mud**. This includes not just performance antipatterns but also bad programming practices, software architecture issues, and even project management pitfalls.

- **Code reviews, code reviews, and code reviews**: Regular code reviews can help catch signs of a deteriorating codebase, including the presence of antipatterns. These reviews are crucial for managing technical debt and ensuring that the codebase remains maintainable and efficient.

- **Profile first, instead of premature optimizations**: Before diving into optimization, use profiling tools to identify actual performance bottlenecks. Focusing on premature optimization can lead to unnecessary work and potential performance issues. Ensure the application works correctly before optimizing to avoid bad programming practices.

- **Focus on functionality**: Ensure the application works correctly before diving into optimization. This approach helps avoid bad programming practices and ensures that optimizations are targeted and effective.

- **Learn and apply design patterns**: Design patterns provide well-established solutions to common problems in software design. Learning and applying these patterns can help avoid antipatterns and pitfalls that may arise from using certain techniques or technologies. For example, the Singleton pattern can help ensure that only one instance of a class exists, but it can also create problems with testing or concurrency if not used correctly.

- **Stay updated on best practices**: Stay abreast of industry trends and best practices in system design and performance optimization. Attend conferences, webinars, or workshops to learn about new tools, techniques, and methodologies for identifying and avoiding performance antipatterns. This continuous learning helps make informed design decisions that prioritize performance.

Most importantly, keep an open mind with healthy critical thinking and open eyes to look for potential problematic areas.

Conclusion

In this chapter, we looked at some performance antipatterns, saw what they are, why they induce problems, and listed some common practices to help us avoid and prevent them.

In the next chapter, we will understand the complexities and nuances of ensuring optimal performance in the modern landscape of distributed systems.

Key learnings

- We learned the concept of antipatterns, in contrast to good practices and design patterns.
- We looked at some symptoms of performance antipatterns.
- We looked into some common antipatterns in detail.
  - The God object
  - Tight coupling
  - Premature optimization
  - Blob
  - Chatty communication
  - The GIL
  - Busy waiting
- We reviewed tips for detecting, fixing, and optimizing antipatterns and listed best practices for avoiding pitfalls.

Join our book's Discord space

Join the book's Discord Workspace for Latest updates, Offers, Tech happenings around the world, New Release and Sessions with the Authors:

https://discord.bpbonline.com

CHAPTER 7

Performance in the Clouds

Introduction

Cloud platforms appear to be the gospel of modern application development. They offer infinite power, speed, flexibility, storage, and processing power, but great power needs to be used smartly to maximize its potential and avoid common problems.

This chapter discusses the complexities and nuances of ensuring optimal performance in the modern landscape of distributed systems. As organizations transition towards scalable and flexible architectures, understanding the unique challenges and employing effective strategies for performance engineering becomes paramount. This chapter explores some key considerations and methodologies for improving performance in these dynamic environments.

Structure

This chapter contains the following topics:

- Architectural considerations
- Scalability and elasticity
- Microservices performance challenges
- Cloud-native performance optimization
- Data management and storage

Objectives

In this chapter, we will review architectural considerations for building cloud-ready distributed applications. We will look at the biggest advantages of cloud computing: the abundance of ready-made services, scalability and elasticity, and architecting microservice applications. We will also consider potential drawbacks and challenges we may encounter while breaking the monolith and distributing it to a scalable cloud-hosted app.

Architectural considerations

In previous chapters, we have already looked at the evolution of software architecture in reflection of the growth in the demands people have from software, in the hardware capabilities, and availability of environments. In this chapter, we will look closer at the characteristics of cloud-designed software. Modern cloud environments give infinite flexibility and offer an abundance of services out-of-the-box (some at the infrastructure level - **IaaS**: tailored virtual machines or virtual appliances, some at platform level - **PaaS**: preconfigured virtual machines, operating systems and tools, and some at the software level - **SaaS**: usable services easy to plug into and integrate into our solution).

High performance computing

As an extreme current example of distributed computing, we can consider how the power of today's networks and clouds introduces capabilities that were unthinkable before. Combining the computing power of literally thousands of CPU cores across computers, data centers, over countries, and continents results in an unimaginable scale of mega-supercomputers capable of vast volumes of computation. This is referred to as **high performance computing (HPC)**.

In contrast to virtualization, where we take the hardware of one computer and **slice** it into multiple computing units, each running a virtualized operating system independently, with distributed HPC, we do the opposite: we take a number of computers and join them into one single computing entity, dividing the workload between them. This is especially beneficial for large-volume calculations. The more computers that take part, the faster the calculations can go through. HPC refers to the combined work of dedicated supercomputers or large clusters of specialized hardware.

The popular term **supercomputer** is used with liberty and abstraction because it is a relative term, not an absolute one. Supercomputers have evolved over time, but in general, we are talking about a highly capable computer containing multiple cutting-edge processors running in parallel, each with a large number of processing cores, to achieve fast calculations in large volumes. Generally measured by the number of floating-point operation calculations (FLoating OPerationS, shortened as FLOPS) per second. Since 2017, supercomputers have been able to perform over 10^{17} FLOPS, while a typical desktop computer is in the range of 10^{11} to 10^{13} FLOPS, many magnitudes behind. HPC normally refers to the joint powers of multiple supercomputers.

One example commonly associated with high-volume computing is weather forecasting. Weather and climate conditions involve the collection of huge amounts of data, and extrapolating the weather conditions and forecasts takes a lot of calculations. It is a good example of when more computing power translates to immediate results. Contrary to the popular jest, suggesting that a project manager is someone who believes that, through collective effort, nine women can produce a baby in one month, when it comes to pure large volume calculations, more is directly better. We are not talking about high-complexity neural networks of large language models and AI; we are talking about classic statistics and arithmetic. Just loads and loads of it. More CPU cores calculating results in more efficiency and less time: HPC, as the name suggests. For weather forecasts, high performance is important. The three elements of weather prediction are the collection of atmospheric data, building the models and software to calculate the predicted outcomes, and actually running those calculations to get the predicted forecast. To achieve high accuracy, we would need as much as possible of all three elements. There is no use in calculating the forecast for the next 5 days if it takes 5 days to calculate it.

The Swiss National Supercomputing Centre operates cutting-edge HPC systems as an essential service facility for Swiss researchers. In it, the Swiss meteorological institute, *MeteoSwiss* uses the open **weather research and forecasting** (**WRF**) model, operated on a GPU-based supercomputer, with a total of 387,872 Intel E5-2969 v3 cores and 4,888 NVIDIA P100 GPUs, and a total memory of 512 TB. That is RAM memory, not storage.

Distributed computing power does not always have to come from large and capable commercial data centers. In fact, anyone with a computer can harness some of their unused CPU capacity for the greater good. SETI@home (**Search for Extra-Terrestrial Intelligence** (**SETI**)) is a project of *Berkeley SETI Research Center* to analyze radio signals with the aim of searching for signs of extraterrestrial intelligence. Somewhat like weather forecasting, analysis of radio signal patterns takes plain computing power. Between the years 1999 and 2020, this initiative was based on volunteers worldwide who were willing to contribute some of their home computer CPU time (hence the **@home** postfix) for the greater good of detecting the aliens who may be on their way to wipe out humanity. SETI@home distributed their app for free download, and runs in the background, or on screensaver time.

More than 5.2 million participants have taken part in SETI@home, while the original intent was to use just 50,000-100,000 home computers. Combining all the computations performed, results in a total of more than 2 million years of computing time. On September 26, 2001, SETI@home had performed a total of 10^{21} FLOPS, which was later acknowledged by the 2008 edition of the Guinness World Records as the largest computation in history. However, since SETI@home did not involve supercomputers, it is not usually referred to as HPC per se.

One last anecdote regarding supercomputers: they have not always been based on specially built hardware. Sony's PlayStation 3 video game console was released in 2006, with a powerful Nvidia RSX GPU (which was not initially planned to be included, and at the time was quite a powerful GPU). With that, and the fact that it was a very energy-efficient computer, which allowed installation of 3rd party operating systems, such as specially crafted Linux, it was not uncommon to create powerful distributed computing clusters out of interconnected PlayStation 3s. In 2010, the *United States Air Force* needed a new supercomputer to process ultra-high-resolution satellite imagery and work on artificial intelligence research. The computer they needed would have cost around $10 million with off-the-shelf parts. Instead, they bought 1,760 PlayStation 3 consoles, wired them together, and created a supercomputer capable of processing 500 trillion FLOPS, which cost close to 10% of the cost of the traditional supercomputer. The supercomputer was named the *Condor Cluster*. It was in operation for approximately four years before being decommissioned. The main reason for the decommissioning was that *Sony* disabled the *OtherOS* feature in PS3 firmware updates, which allowed the consoles to run 3rd party operating systems. This feature was essential for using the PS3s as part of a computing cluster. Without the ability to run Linux, the consoles could no longer contribute to the cluster's computational tasks. This is one of the most famous unusual PlayStation 3 cluster supercomputers, but not the only one at the time. PlayStation 3 was cheap in relation to their hardware specifications (Sony's strategy was to subsidize the costs of the console and to rely on future game sales); some people were buying them for their included BluRay player, which was considered cheap compared to others on the market.

Advancements in quantum computing

No discussion on high computing power is complete nowadays without mentioning the most recent advancements in quantum computing. It is important to note that quantum computers work completely differently from classic digital computers and are not made for personal use. At least not yet.

With traditional computers, our goal is to run as many calculations as possible in the shortest amount of time, by flipping digital **binary digits** (**bits**), electronically represented by tiny transistors, which are created in an intricate process of growing molecular layers of silicon, acting as microscopic (if we use an electron microscope) deterministic on/off switches (also known as a **Turing machine**). A high-performance computer just means we have many of them, and that they respond **very quickly**, but as many and quick as they may be, they dictate the performance boundaries of our computing system.

Quantum computers go a different route, taking advantage of bizarre quantum phenomena of matter at sub-atomic levels. In a very simplified manner, and without delving too deeply into quantum mechanics, a quantum computer uses **quantum-bits** (**qubit**), pronounced *cue-bit*) instead of traditional bits. Unlike a bit, which acts as a single-state on/off switch, the state of a qubit relies in limbo on quantum properties, such as the spin of an electron, or the polarization of a photon, which exhibit counterintuitive behaviors, like being in more than one state at once, with different probabilities (superposition) or being directly connected to the state of other particles, even if they are at the other end of the galaxy (entanglement). Rather than holding a state of either 0 or 1, like a traditional bit, a qubit holds both 0 and 1 at the same time.

Qubits' behaviors are much more complicated than can be explained here, but their fantastic properties give them huge superiority over traditional bits. One of the most important examples in this context is encryption.

A great part of our modern world's communications, relies on known, tested encryption algorithms, which are mathematically proven to be impossible to break (thus far), unless we check each and every possible key combination, one after the other, known as **brute-force**, which normally would take an exponential amount of computing time. The gigantic, unintuitive magnitude of exponents comes into play here. For example, even though the widely adopted Rijndael algorithm, also known as AES-128 (for 128 bits long encryption keys), has been partially cracked, running a brute-force attack of serially testing keys would still take millions of years on today's hardware, not to mention that 256 bits keys are more common now, raising the estimate of the calculation time to around 200 times the age of the universe (cracking AES-256 is estimated to take 2.29×10^{32} years, while the universe is currently estimated to be just around 1.38×10^{10} years old). The bottom line is that those encryptions are indeed unbreakable. With today's digital computers, that is. A quantum computer with enough qubits in superposition can run through **all possible key combinations** at once, rendering the encryption security useless, and indeed, this is one of the biggest threats quantum computers impose: the day when all encryptions are broken. A mentionable area that would also be affected by the break of all encryptions is cryptocurrencies, such as bitcoin, as they also rely directly on encryptions (hence the **crypto** in **cryptocurrency**).

That singular point in time, where quantum computers surpass the abilities of classic computers, is known as **quantum supremacy**.

For the time being, quantum technology is not there yet, and encryptions are still considered safe, but an important point to note is that there are governments and other, possibly more shady entities, who practice a strategy known as **retrospective decryption** (sometimes referred to as **harvest now, decrypt later**, or **store now, decrypt later** shortened as *SNDL*, sometimes even **steal now, decrypt later**): collecting documents, communication logs, passwords, even though they are opaque and hard-encrypted, and waiting for the day where quantum computers take their supremacy, rendering the harvested information open and transparent. Listening in on communications is easy, and as long as the information collected is nothing more than gibberish or encrypted data, it is safe, that is, as long as we rely on our standard computers.

The advancements of quantum computers sound both fantastic and threatening, and our understanding and research of quantum mechanics progress every day. On the other hand, quantum computers are still incredibly hard to build. If we disregard the subatomic scale we are dealing with and the difficulty of interacting with particles at that level, quantum computers come with great complications when it comes to writing, maintaining, and reading information from qubits. Qubits' states are volatile and fragile; they may easily lose their superposition and collapse into a **classical** single state. This is known as **decoherence**, and it is one of the main difficulties of building a reliable quantum computer. Noise and disturbances in a quantum system are also great challenges, as they introduce errors. Hence, error correction techniques and algorithms should be developed and included too. Other challenges are with the hardware itself, which has to be operated in an isolated nested vacuum container, and at extremely low temperatures, near absolute zero (the zero is in Kelvin degrees, 0°K, which means -273.15°C or -459.67°F, the lowest possible temperature). This isolation from air and temperatures is in order to protect the processor from noise, in the form of atoms in the air, or energy in the form of electromagnetic, or other forms of radiation or heat, which may affect the delicate processes of the qubits. With that, it is also notable that quantum computers come to serve very specific applications and solve specific problems, and not to replace our classic digital computers altogether. They may be good for specific tasks such as breaking encryptions, but they are not planned to replace our standard desktop PCs for playing Doom anytime soon.

Despite the difficulties, the quantum computing race is very much alive. Quantum supremacy has already been claimed at different levels and scales. In October 2019, Google's Sycamore quantum processor was able to perform a task that would have taken the world's most powerful supercomputer at the time 10,000 years to complete, in just 200 seconds. This was published in the scientific journal Nature, in an article named *Quantum supremacy using a programmable superconducting processor*. Sycamore contained 54 qubits (one of them was in fact not working, so it was running on 53 qubits). Some doubts were raised at the time about Google's achievement, for example, by research directors at *IBM*, claiming that *Google* still has a way to go with error correction and other features of their quantum computer.

Google continues its research and development of quantum computers, and in December 2024, announced the release of the Willow quantum processor, with no less than 105 qubits, which, in pictures, looks very much like any other regular CPU chip. According to Google, Willow possesses highly efficient error correction features (for example, by combining multiple physical qubits into one logical qubit) and was reported to be able to perform a computation that would take today's fastest supercomputers 10 septillion years to solve in under five minutes. Ten septillion are 10^{25} years, or 10,000,000,000,000,000,000,000,000 years. This is impressive, but it is estimated that in order to break today's encryptions, we would need roughly another 10 years of development, and 4 million physical qubits. Willow's achievement is so grand that it even sparked a debate among scientists about the fabric of reality itself, and whether or not running qubits in superposition supports the theory of multiple universes (a multiverse).

Hacking and harnessing subatomic particles for a functional quantum computer continues to reach new heights. At the time this chapter was being written, in mid-February 2025, Microsoft announced its own revolutionary quantum chip, named Majorana 1, which at this point sounds like science fiction. According to publications, the Majorana 1 chip uses a completely new type of architecture, taking the quantum computing setup to a whole new level, based on a particle named **Majorana fermion** (or just the **Majorana particle**), which was hypothesized by the Italian physicist *Ettore Majorana* all the way back in 1937 (Technically speaking, a fermion is a subatomic particle, such as an electron, proton, or neutron whose spin quantum number is an odd multiple of ½). Among the Majorana fermion's special qualities is the fact that the particle is also its own anti-particle (unlike an electron vs. a positron): it has the same properties either way. It is inherently resilient to noise, which makes the theoretical Majorana qubit highly sought after for fault-tolerant quantum computing. The Majorana fermion remained theoretical until 2020, although Microsoft claims to have observed it already in 2018 in a study paper that was retracted. The new Majorana 1 chip takes advantage of exotic phenomena in quantum physics called **topological superconductivity**, which is greatly more resilient to noise in comparison to other techniques. Topological properties of a particle are ones that remain stable even if their physical properties change due to noise. Also, rather than relying on a single particle's quantum properties, the topological quantum computer puts together particles to work together, making what is called a **topological qubit**, built in an intricate process of layering literal atoms of material (a nanowire). Majorana particles help protect the integrity and stability of the topological qubits from noise and errors. Microsoft has been researching topological qualities and quantum particles for some time, but the Majorana 1, announced as a working, scalable, capable quantum processor, sent shockwaves throughout the industry.

In any case, the race to quantum computing supremacy is in full throttle, in a way that will dramatically change the performance capabilities of computers and ridicule the capabilities of even the highest supercomputers we have today.

Performance considerations

Since most of the commonly built projects are not based on supercomputers and HPC, we need to take into account the tools we do have at hand. For economy purposes and in order to utilize the cloud to the max, in many cases, we would use a multitenant configuration.

Tenancy and virtualization

Tenancy refers to the amount of separate virtualized machines on a single real-world, hardware-based, metal, cloud computer. Sometimes, we would want to use a dedicated single-tenant environment. That is a whole dedicated computer for our use. This has several advantages, such as isolation from other services, which gives elevated security and resource utilization, as you have the entire machine all to yourself. It may also be more performant, as the computer does not have to support multiple virtualized operating systems and services all at once. On the other hand, single tenancy is expensive, as one tenant must pay the entire rent. Similar to fine whisky, where greater homogeneity, progressing from a multitenant blend to a single malt and ultimately to a single batch or barrel, is associated with higher quality and cost, a mixed multitenant cloud server is inherently less expensive and less tailored in its usage. Therefore, sharing a single computer or resource among multiple users or applications is more common. Hosting more than one virtual machine on the cloud computer and sharing with other such **tenants** is referred to as **multitenancy**.

Running one or more virtual machines is sometimes thought by developers to lead to degraded performance, as we have the overhead of running an entire operating system and a virtual machine on top of it. However, virtualization in the cloud does not necessarily lead to impaired performance, mainly for two reasons: your home computer's hardware is most probably inferior to the beast computer running in the cloud's data center, and virtualization today is a common necessity. So much so that cutting-edge processors support virtualization natively right through the hardware and out of the box, in that setup, they can run a virtual machine while not harming performance at all, as if it is running directly on the hardware with near-zero overhead.

On the other hand, when extreme performance is required from specific I/O operations, the *near-zero* overhead may be significant, in which case we may want to ensure we use a single-tenant dedicated server, not virtualized.

Infinite options

On the bright side, even if we are not talking about extreme HPC and supercomputers, even for the layman architect, building a high-performance solution with today's cloud resources is definitely within reach. The cloud opens an easy route for high scalability. When greater power, RAM, or storage is required, vertical scaling provides a seamless solution. For increased load, additional servers can be allocated and deployed at geographically optimal locations to ensure maximum efficiency and user satisfaction.

Another example is storage. Maybe working with an Amazon S3 bucket as cloud storage is convenient but, in some conditions, fails to fulfill our performance needs. There are infinite options, literally at the palms of our hands. Maybe an NFS mount over high-speed ethernet may work better, or perhaps plain SSH/SFTP mount to a physical drive works better for the case. The point is, again, whatever works better for the case, scenario, configuration, and requirements.

Anything is achievable. In the cloud, even the sky is no longer the limit.

Cloud-native services

The cloud is vast, and it is a versatile, powerful tool. It not only gives us resources such as servers and virtual servers. It is a Swiss knife with a variety of additional services, each for its own purpose. Built-in cloud services vary from one provider to another. **Google's Cloud (GCP)** provides a selection of services, different from **Amazon Web Services (AWS)** and **Microsoft's Azure**. However, many of them provide similar functionality under different names. Those services are on a pay-as-you-go basis, so they are quite economical and paid for only when needed. Using cloud-native, proven, tested, optimized services, offered by the cloud providers may help boost performance, as they are proven, tested, and optimized. Some examples include:

- **Computing services**: Which include virtual machines available at the requested configuration, serverless functions, or bash runners.

- **Storage services**: For storage of files, such as Amazon's S3 or EBS, Azure Blob and Disk storage, and Google's Cloud Store and Filestore.

- **Database services**: For running a database natively in the cloud, including Amazon **Relational Database Service** (**RDS**) or DynamoDB, Azure SQL or Cosmos, and GCP Cloud SQL or Cloud Spanner.

- **Networking services**: For setting up virtual private networks and complex routes, including Amazon **Virtual Private Cloud** (**VPC**) and Route 53 (DNS), Azure Virtual Network, Azure DNS, Azure ExpressRoute, GCP VPC, Cloud DNS, and Cloud VPN.

- **AI/machine learning services**: Including Amazon SageMaker, Rekognition, and Comprehend, Azure Machine Learning, Cognitive Services, and Bot Service, Google Cloud AI Platform, Cloud Vision API, and Cloud Natural Language API.

- **Analytics services**: For tracking multiple statistics, such as Amazon Redshift, EMR (Elastic MapReduce) and Athena, Azure Synapse Analytics, HDInsight, Data Lake Analytics, GCP BigQuery, Dataflow and Dataproc.

- **Security services**: For authentication and identity management, storage of secrets and keys, network firewalls, etc. For example, Amazon AWS **Identity and Access Management** (**IAM**), **Key Management Service** (**KMS**), **Web Application Firewall** (**WAF**), Azure Active Directory, Key Vault, Security Center, GCP IAM, Cloud KMS, and Cloud Armor.

- **Monitoring and management services**, for monitoring applications, logging, and tracing collected data. Such as Amazon CloudWatch, AWS CloudTrail, AWS Config, Azure Monitor, Log Analytics, Policy, GCP Stackdriver Monitoring, Stackdriver Logging, and Stackdriver Trace.

Managed apps

In addition to the hosted cloud services, there are also managed apps we can leverage to our benefit. Managed apps, particularly in the context of cloud computing, refer to applications that are managed by a third party, often a cloud service provider. These managed apps are designed to be easy for consumers to deploy and operate, offering cloud solutions that abstract away the complexities of managing the underlying infrastructure. This approach allows users to focus on the application's functionality rather than the technical aspects of deployment, scaling, and maintenance. They can be easily deployed, from a dedicated marketplace or repository, or already run natively in our cloud environment, and interacted with as SaaS. Those include, for example, Azure AI services, Amazon QuickSight (for business intelligence), or Google's AI/ML services.

Application architectural considerations

Optimizing the application for the cloud means using the advantages the cloud gives us. Designing the app properly would also help optimize performance. Designing a dynamic app, which can grow and scale on need, can help increase throughput upon need. The cloud framework provides agility, scalability, cost optimization, security, sustainability, and reliability. To help maintain and keep our app up to date, we can use a selection of automation tools, also embedded into the cloud environments. To conclude, some base principles:

- **Modularity**: Microservices architecture and loosely coupled components will make scalability, maintenance, and continuous deployment easier.

- **Resilience**: Fault-tolerant design patterns such as load balancing, replication, and automated failover will ensure minimal service disruption.

- **Automation:** Leverage tools, workflows, and orchestration frameworks to streamline provisioning, deployment, configuration, and management of cloud resources.

- **Data**: Use proper data storage and management strategies, including replication, backup, archival, and efficient retrieval mechanisms.

- **Monitoring**: Comprehensive monitoring and observability practices will help gain insights into system performance, resource utilization, and potential bottlenecks. Utilize logging, metrics, and distributed tracing for proactive issue identification and resolution.

- **Built-in services**: Using the built-in services can help accelerate the use of good practices and optimize common patterns and tools.

The 12-factor principle of a modern app

Drafted in 2011, the 12-factor app principle is a base set of rules and best practices for building a modern application (mostly aimed at services, but those principles are useful for any app). They should be known and followed by every developer, but, in fact, this knowledge is not commonly spread. Well, most of the included principles actually are known to many developers, though those developers are not aware that they are following (or not following) the 12-factor app principle. It is not a bad idea to follow the list and apply the following 12 principles to any cloud-based service. They help our app remain neutral wherever we run it. This may save a lot of unnecessary work and ensure our application is optimized for multiple environments, efficient deployment, resilience, scalability, and smooth performance.

Following this methodology, the 12 factors of the modern app are:

- **Codebase**: Keep your app in **one** version-controlled repository. The code should be environment-agnostic and may be deployed in different runtime environments (e.g., development environment, test environment, production environment, etc.).

- **Dependencies**: Do not rely on globally installed dependencies, and do not assume they are natively there. Create a configuration list of dependencies that your app requires. That way, you can always make sure all the necessary dependencies and packages are there. In Python, it is in the `requirements.txt` file. In JavaScript/Node, they are in the `package.json` file. It is also good to work in an isolated virtual environment (Python intrinsically provides this option) so we can always ensure the environment is set up properly and has everything it needs to run the app.

- **Config**: Do not use properties and variables, such as ports and addresses or debug settings, which are specific to a runtime environment, in your code. Instead, build a dynamic configuration file to hold them. That way, the app can easily adjust to any new environment.

- **Backing services**: Any service that is external to the app (notification service, database) should be kept loosely coupled with the app as much as possible. That way, one service may be interchangeable with another, without affecting the code, provided that the API is compatible. Or if, for example, a database fails and an admin restores a new instance from the backup, the app should continue normally from that point.

- **Build, release, run**: This factor states that the three stages of the app (**Build**: to convert the code to an executable, compile/transpile, minify; **Release**: apply all configurations, make the app deployment-ready, and deploy it; **Run**: start the app on the server/environment), should be well defined and separated. No code or configuration changes should be allowed on the released app. The release cycle works only in one direction.

- **Process**: Keep the app a stateless process. Any state and data should be stored in a backing service (e.g., database). The app should be able to start at any point, restore its state, and continue running like nothing happened.

- **Port binding**: Differentiate endpoints by specific ports, not addresses. For example, if the app uses a backing service of a PostgreSQL database, and the specific connection uses PostgreSQL's default port, 5432, this should remain the port to connect through, and the server configuration should decide whether to connect to the dev server on the dev environment (which may be something like *dev.myapp.com*), to the test server on the test environment (which may be something like *test.myapp.com*) or to the production server on the live environment (which may be something like *www.myapp.com*). The app is agnostic to where it connects, but the port differentiates the type of service.

- **Concurrency**: Modularize your app into small independent parts (microservices), which can run in parallel without interrupting each other and can scale independently upon need.

- **Disposability**: Make sure the app behaves well when starting up and shutting down. Making sure no open connections, sessions, and processes are cut abruptly, which may lead to discrepancies, errors, and integrity problems.

- **Dev/Prod parity**: Keep all development, staging, and production environments as similar as possible. The app should not care where it is deployed; it should work similarly. Only environment-based configuration variables should differ. Release and deployment procedures should also be as similar as possible.

- **Logs**: Logs are important for keeping track of the application's execution. However, there are input/output standard streams and error streams, which the application should interact with rather than explicitly writing to a log file. Logging utilities interact with the i/o/error streams and aggregate logs separately from the app, and log production should be left to them. The app should not care about that.

- **Admin processes**: Accompanying administrative tasks that the app requires (normally utilities, such as background processing of data) should be kept in source control and packaged with the application. Again, to ensure the integrity and proper work of the app, wherever it is.

Scalability and elasticity

The terms scalability and elasticity are closely related. In this section, we will look into both and understand their uses and advantages.

Scalability

One base concept that is commonly brought up when it comes to cloud infrastructure and performance is scalability. We have already discussed scalability on several occasions. Suppose our service, or microservice, gets to the point where it cannot accommodate the load of requests. We need more power. Either to keep the service alive or just to keep it sufficiently performant. In any case, we would want it to be resilient enough to the load and respond in a timely manner.

As mentioned, we differentiate the two common flavors of scalability:

- **Vertical scaling**: Refers to changing the processing power of an existing server, in order to be able to better match the server performance and capabilities to the runtime requirements (not to waste needless resources, but not to fail to serve when needed). Increasing (scaling up) or decreasing (scaling down) the hardware: processor, RAM, cache, or storage.

- **Horizontal scaling**: Refers to changing the number of servers, to balance the workload and distribute it across several machines. Adding more servers (scaling out) may distribute functionality across multiple computers, data servers, and even geographic locations, while removing servers (scaling in) saves costs when the load is low.

The following figure depicts the difference between vertical and horizontal scaling:

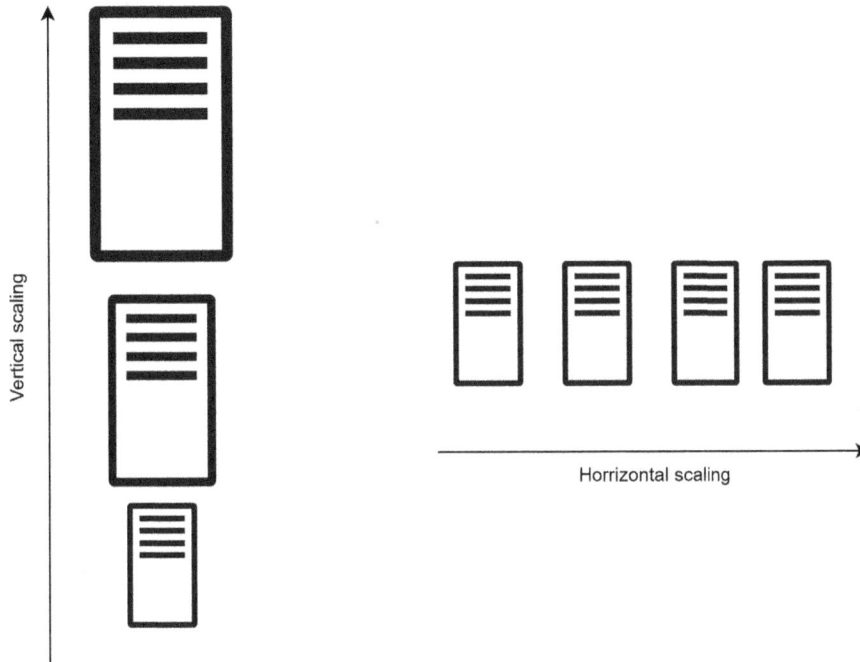

Figure 7.1: *Vertical vs. horizontal scaling*

Unlike running services on pure hardware, where modifying scaling is a cumbersome operation that requires acquiring hardware, modern cloud providers' powerful virtualization infrastructure provides dynamic tools for easy and quick scaling upon need. Of course, this can be achieved on premise as well, with some virtualization work, but not easily nor effectively.

Elasticity

A more powerful server, an upgraded CPU, additional RAM, or expanded storage can be provisioned effortlessly. When server replicas exceed demand and the load decreases, redundant servers can be decommissioned with a single action.

Having said that, it is not uncommon for scaling to be proactive and to try to plan for resource optimization: Scale horizontally or vertically according to predicted workload growth or shrinkage (the decision as to the type of scaling, be it vertically and/or horizontally, is also based on policies, needs, and plans).

Elasticity takes scalability to the next level: make it responsive and automatic. Instead of guessing an increase or decrease in load, based on studies or experience (e.g., increased load of shoppers around Christmas or Easter), make the system automatically and dynamically adjust its resource allocation based on changes in workload or demand.

This could involve automatically scaling up or down the number of servers or resources in response to changes in traffic or usage patterns. Elasticity is typically reactive and involves the system automatically scaling resources in real time without human intervention. Cloud computing platforms often provide elastic services that allow users to scale resources up or down on demand, paying only for the resources they use.

The name implies the ability to change the system flexibly and responsively. For elasticity to work, a few rules and measures should be put in place and operate in sync:

- **Monitoring**: The system continuously monitors various metrics such as CPU usage, memory utilization, network traffic, and application performance in real time.

- **Thresholds and triggers**: The next phase is thresholds and triggers, which are defined based on the monitored metrics. These thresholds indicate when the system should scale resources up or down in response to changes in workload.

- **Scaling policies**: Once we define a threshold and/or rules to trigger scaling, scaling policies, which specify the rules and actions to be taken when certain thresholds are exceeded, get applied. For example, when CPU usage exceeds 80% for a sustained period, scale up the number of compute instances.

- **Automation**: Automation is key to elasticity. When a threshold is crossed, and a trigger is activated, the system automatically triggers the appropriate scaling actions defined in the scaling policies.

- **Resource provisioning**: Depending on the scaling action required (scale up or scale down), the system provisions additional resources (such as virtual servers, storage, or networking) or deallocates resources accordingly.

- **Dynamic scaling**: Elasticity allows for dynamic scaling, meaning that resources are added or removed in real time to match the current workload demand. This ensures that the system can handle fluctuations in traffic and workload efficiently.

- **Feedback loop**: The system continuously evaluates the effectiveness of its scaling actions and adjusts its scaling policies based on feedback and historical performance data. This iterative process helps optimize resource utilization and performance over time.

By leveraging elasticity, organizations can achieve several benefits, including improved performance, better resource utilization, cost optimization, and enhanced reliability and scalability. Elasticity enables cloud-based applications and services to seamlessly adapt to changing demand patterns, ensuring a smooth and responsive user experience while optimizing resource utilization and costs.

Microservices performance challenges

Microservices are not a silver-bullet solution for all modern application implementations, though sometimes they are considered to be. They come with their own considerations and challenges. In this section, we will look at some of them.

With great power comes a great electricity bill

As we read in the intro to this chapter, the cloud is the gospel of modern applications development and architecture, ditching the old rigid local environments, which take great effort to build, configure, equip, maintain, and update.

Alongside this evolution, microservices seem to be all the rage. Microservice architecture is the perfect match for the flexible cloud. They match scaling and elasticity patterns; they help us fine-tune the product distribution, grow some parts, shrink others, balance loads, fix issues and update just one specific piece without interrupting others, and tailor each microservice with the technology that best suits exactly what it is supposed to do. We definitely live in the future of software architecture. This is indeed great power.

However, this is not an invincible silver bullet. Using such powerful tools such as microservices in the cloud requires wise considerations and careful choices, to use the tools properly, optimize performance, and utilize the great power vested upon us. Microservices may become a multiheaded monster, difficult to design, build, deploy, operate, control, tame, and keep in high performance. Here, we will look at some common challenges in such setups and see what we may wish to consider and avoid.

Communication issues

Microservices break our application into small pieces and then runs them all separately. Communications are either via direct calls to APIs, or through messaging queues. In whichever way, intercommunications between services go through network protocols. This, of course, adds a significant overhead to pay.

Communicating over the network may introduce **latency** compared to in-process communication within a monolithic application. The overhead of network communication, especially in distributed environments, can impact overall system performance.

As the number of microservices increases, so does the complexity of service-to-service communication. Each interaction between microservices introduces **overhead** such as serialization/deserialization, network latency, and protocol processing. The bigger and more distributed our project grows, the slower the communication may become. Taking this factor into account may help mitigate potential performance issues. Grouping services geographically, clustering closely related ones, sharding data, and caching data (on clients and/or on servers), all these techniques, used smartly, can help reduce latency and unnecessary communications between microservices calling each other.

One more point to the overhead of communications, is that the microservices do not necessarily speak the same language. This relates to a programming language (as each can be built with the technology that is optimal for its needs. A Java microservice can easily communicate with a JavaScript microservice. Despite the similarity in the name, it is known that the difference between Java and JavaScript is analogous to the difference between car and carpet or ham and hamster). However, each is built with a different set of APIs and data needs. Some consume XML, others consume binary streams, while others require JSON. The means of communication also differ. Some microservices expose REST endpoints, while others work with gRPC. Data translations are to be added between services, adding to the complexity of APIs and data structures. One option is to build translators that flatten the communication differences, but this also costs development time, potential risk of discrepancies and mismatches of breaking changes, and, of course, runtime CPU clock ticks, which cost money and time (performance, as well as more money, as it is known that time is money).

Growing complexity of breaking the monolith

Breaking a monolith into microservices means taking one big, complex project with all its functional and non-functional requirements, such as security in the form of authentication, authorization, encryption, data considerations, communications, cache management, etc., and breaking it down into multiple complex projects, each of which with all its functional and non-functional requirements, such as security in the form of authentication, authorization, encryption, data considerations, communications, cache management, etc.

With increasing our projects' friction points, we would have to consider the increased complexity. It may come as an advantage; for example, if we have performance issues, we may be able, with proper analysis, to pinpoint and isolate the misbehaving microservice and focus on increasing it, but this comes with the price of complexity or designing, building, deploying and managing it all. If we consider performance, we would have to think about which microservices are to be deployed where, when and how, how and when they should scale, and which of them are more crucial and/or sensitive.

Integration overhead and dependency hell

Microservices are developed independently and deployed inside isolated containers. At runtime, all the isolated and independent microservices must communicate with each other. That means more integration of RESTful endpoints and standardized JSON or XML exchanges.

Managing the interdependencies between microservices is a major struggle. RESTful endpoints are exceptionally fragile. Changes to one component can produce unintended consequences for another.

In a monolithic application, components interact directly through function invocations. There is no need for a common data exchange format or RESTful APIs. Furthermore, all interactions are type-checked and validated at compile time.

Cloud-native performance optimization

In this section, we will look at some considerations to bear in mind, for optimizing our cloud-ready and cloud-native application.

Fine orchestration

As mentioned earlier, the cloud gives us an abundance of infrastructure and tools and great power at the tips of our fingers, be it computing power, storage, database, or networking. The tricky part is to make smart use of it all. It is easy to shoot in all directions, but using this power requires expertise, delicate tuning, and orchestration. The cloud, with all its power, is naturally a good place to host our live production system. Therefore, we need to be extra careful considering budgets and performance optimization. It is also a balance of what we can spend and what we can get. Given enough resources, we can easily harness a supercomputer, or a high-performance computing cluster of supercomputers, although people may suggest it is a slight overkill for a small commerce website. An easier transition would be using the cloud for provisioning virtual machines to host whatever we want, but that, too, may be an overkill, as there are offered services that make the work lighter, simpler, faster, and cheaper. In any case, almost everything is possible when you have infinite money.

Migrating to the cloud

Also, as good as **the cloud** may be, the transition to the cloud is not always so straightforward. It may be easy for a startup with an idea, to hire a couple of cloud-platform experts, and build their solution cloud-ready from the ground up, from day one. That is, building a cloud-native solution right from its high-level design, using as many of the available tools as possible.

For older, bigger, more cumbersome organizations with established applications, their large data, and well-established (and usually pretty strict) requirements of security, privacy, and regulatory restrictions, things may not be so simple. Organizations such as financial or regulatory institutions may have a much harder time making the transition to the cloud, or at least making the complete transition. Unintuitively, such organizations may also be stricter on budget planning and would be more careful about spending money on such big moves. Besides, as mentioned, a smart migration to the cloud is not a plain **lift & shift** (as in, take what we've got and run it on a cloud-provisioned virtual machine), but instead, a calculated, orchestrated, planned migration.

Cloud-native apps

Making our app cloud-native and cloud-optimized requires knowing what we use. As listed in the above section, *Cloud native services*. We have many types of tools at our disposal. In the following segments, we will list some advantages we can take, using the right tools in the right place, and how we can benefit from them.

Proper architecture and usage of the cloud-provided building blocks would make our app cloud-native (although it may easily become **cloud-dependent** and not easy to migrate from the cloud to a locally hosted app. Migrating from one cloud provider to another may also be an issue, as cloud services differ in capabilities, APIs, CLIs, and tools between the different providers.

The Cloud Native Computing Foundation

Since we are talking about *cloud-native*, it is worth mentioning the **Cloud Native Computing Foundation** (**CNCF**), which not many people are aware of.

As part of the **Linux Project** (a non-profit organization established in the year 2000 to support Linux development and open-source software), the CNCF was established in 2015, with members from companies such as *Google, Red Hat, Intel, Cisco, IBM, Docker,* and *VMware,* in order to develop and promote tools for containerization and cloud-native support for distributed applications. Now, with more than 450 members, the CNCF has developed and supported many important projects in the microservices containerization world (all of which are free and open source, of course, by various licenses), probably **Kubernetes** being the most well-known, but also other known fundamental tools. To mention a few widely used ones:

containerd, **Helm**, **Prometheus**, **gRPC**, and **OpenTelemetry**, which we will look at in the next chapter.

Computing performance optimization

Cloud environments provide us with tools to enhance our computing power and/or smartly distribute, minimize, optimize, and use it. Here are some of the techniques and tools we can use:

- **Workload distribution**: Breaking the app into microservices, as mentioned earlier. It is useful to architect them with good practices, such as single responsibility. This helps later, when we want to scale a service; we can be precise on which part of the system we'd want to scale, according to their criticality and workload.

  Using virtualization containers, which are also natively supported by cloud environments, both with single-container configuration, and complex clusters (such as Kubernetes), takes our microservices one step forward, as we do not need to run microservices on provisioned servers or virtual machines; we can use the cloud-power of native support of containers, and run them in a lean, more effective configuration, keeping our application lightweight, maintainable, performant and flexibly scalable.

- **Computing optimization**: As mentioned earlier, we are presented with a variety of computing tools, including straightforward computing power; we would have to consider if we want to use a cloud-based computer (be it a physical machine or a virtual machine). This translates to plain hardware. CPU, caching, RAM, storage, networking (and additional perks such as GPU). Depending on our needs, we would have to match the computer we are utilizing to the task. For example, machine learning may require a beast processor and sufficient RAM, and some network-savvy apps may require enhanced networking, and potentially strong enough hardware to handle multiple connections. For heavy file operations, we would want a fast SSD-based storage.

All in all, the choice of how to configure our computing unit to suit our performance needs is in our hands, and the cloud is the limit.

- **Scaling**: As already mentioned in detail, scaling (with or without the assistance of elasticity) allows us to grow (and shrink) our resources. Easy if we are backed up by a cloud provider. This can help us both optimize our app for computing power (vertical scaling) and distributed load and high availability (horizontal scaling). A well-orchestrated scaling may help us achieve a highly optimized, powerful app and is one of the core benefits of cloud-native apps.

- **Serverless**: Rather than running an entire machine (virtual or not), for compact functionality, while having to worry about its hardware and software configuration, operating system, security patches, or runtime environment, serverless computing gives us an easy-to-use tool for fast, lightweight, performant, small-size function execution, without any of the hassle and worries, and without the performance overhead of running an actual server or fully featured microservice. It is an effort to refactor and move small functionalities to serverless, but it may pay off in performance, maintenance, and budget.

Networking performance optimization

In addition to extremely high computing power, cloud providers' data centers are also incredibly well-connected and offer many options for the benefit of our application:

- **Backbone networking**: Unlike our local on-prem server room/data center, large cloud providers come with much greater, more elaborate networking options. To begin with, they are globally distributed in multiple locations on each habitable continent. No matter where we'd want to place our servers or span them over more than one location, it is just a button-click away.

  Unlike our reliance on local internet service providers, these data centers are connected with a backbone network, which is also developed by the cloud providers that are dedicated to their inter-regional communication. This is a great advantage. A wide range of networking tools is also at the disposal of our cloud-native app, such as direct, private, secure connections, tunneling, and VPNs, which allow us to keep our app well-connected, distributed, available, fast, and secure.

- **API gateway caching**: We already mentioned caching in the context of a service, either as a feature of the app or using a shared caching service such as Redis. Cloud providers also provide caching at the API gateway level. That is, since our apps run in a data center, either on a real or virtual machine, API gateways are the network components we use for relaying requests to them. API gateways managed cache is useful for storing cached responses and returning them directly to the caller, without even hitting our service. This gives quite a benefit for high performance and low latency, and they are supported by all major clouds.

- **CDNs**: Using a **Content Delivery Network** (**CDN**) allows returning static resources quickly and efficiently, without querying our services at all. They can be globally distributed and replicated; they can be secured, manage different versions of our assets, such as images, documents, or static HTML, CSS, or JS files, and give a significant performance advantage. Those files do not change often, and major cloud platforms offer CDN services that give really good results as far as content delivery of static data is concerned.

Data management and storage

Another set of cloud-aided tools and techniques for improved performance, this time from the data side, is summarized here. When our application becomes big enough, more distributed, and scalable, as the data grows, we can use some of the cloud-native features in order to keep its performance sharp.

Some techniques to help us better optimize and manage our data include:

- **Replicas and CQRS**: One of the database versions for scalability. Just as we can scale and replicate our services, we can also replicate our databases. Cloud environments allow apps to easily replicate their natively supported databases, either for bi-directional synchronization between all the replicas or by implementing CQRS (A reminder from *Chapter 5, High Performance Design Patterns*, refers to Command query responsibility segregation) to separate read databases from write databases. It all depends on how the architects and DBAs prefer to optimize the app and benefit from it.

- **Partitioning**: Just like distributing the workload of computing modules, as mentioned earlier, partitioning our data may help gain improved performance with large volumes of data. Cloud platforms provide various services as far as the partitioning of the data is concerned. As opposed to the traditional ways, all the partitioning needs are handled by the platform itself once configured. Including this in our cloud-native app makes it easy, resilient, useful, and effective, and it may improve performance dramatically.

- **Caching**: Another tool that is natively supported by cloud providers is caching, which, with proper setup, reduces the number of expensive database calls dramatically. Cloud providers offer support, solutions, and services to host Redis or memcached (and potentially other cache servers) to enhance the performance of the systems. As the name implies, the shared cache is a fast, central, key-value data storage that can serve multiple nodes, rather than creating a cache in software, which serves just the node it runs on. Again, a powerful tool for high performance with minimum effort for our cloud app.

- **Eventual consistency**: Eventual as in relying on events, not *eventual* as in final. Eventual consistency is a mechanism made for performing asynchronous data updates and returning a quick response to the requesting client. It decouples the relationship between the service and the data. In a common scenario, the service that receives the update request performs the database update directly and then waits for the database to perform the update before it returns the response to the requester. Thus, the response actually reflects the current status of the database. In distributed cloud systems, however, when we have multiple replicas, with or without CQRS, it is possible to improve performance, by using event brokers (queues) to update the data (between the service and the database, or between the database and its replicas, or both) in their own time, while the response to the client is being returned immediately.

  Cloud databases such as Microsoft Azure Cosmos DB, Amazon's AWS DynamoDB, Apache Cassandra, or Google Cloud Firestore support eventual consistency natively. This means data does not get updated or replicated immediately, while our app can benefit from high performance and low latency.

- **Data lakes and data warehouses**: It is definitely worth mentioning data lakes. Given all the power we have with data handling, processing, and storage, we may need to handle large volumes of data, which comes from various sources, and then process the data for different needs so it can be consumed efficiently.

  As depicted in the diagram below, a data lake uses ETL processes to ingest data from multiple source (various storage, databases, apps persisting data, or streams from IoT devices). The data then gets processed, sanitized, formatted, and indexed; then it can be consumed by insight and analytics tools, such as BI tools, dashboards, and apps, or into a large data warehouse, which is a large database in which the data is stored in a specific structure, for a specific purpose, or consumed and processed by machine learning, AI or other data science apps. Additionally, governance is applied to the data that is stored, in order to keep track of data lineage (where a specific datum actually came from) and policies such as anonymization and access authorization.

  With this setup, data lakes are common for holding data from many sources and are complex and large-scale. Cloud providers use their resources and offer cloud-based data lake solutions for our native app, with relative ease and good performance. Services such as AWS Lake Formation, Google's BigLake, which unifies data lakes & data warehouses, or Azure Data Lake are provided out of the box.

The following figure shows a typical architectural scheme of a data lake, and how its components interact:

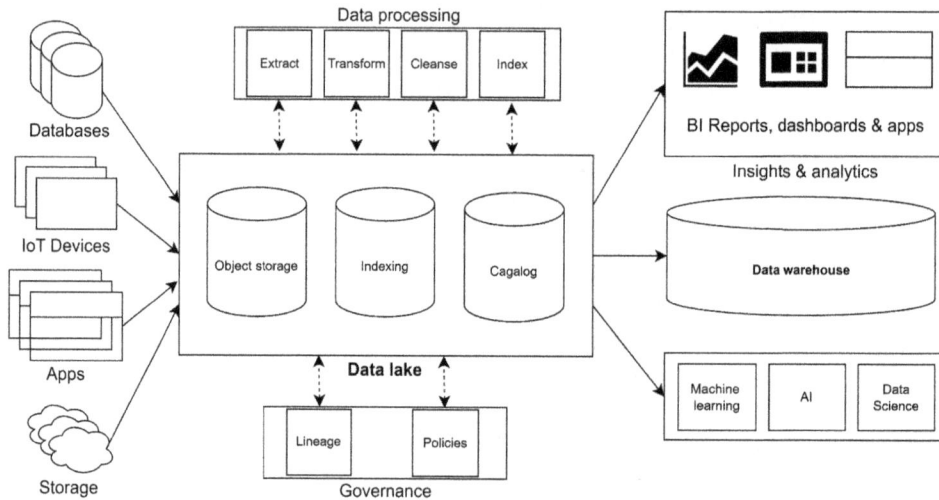

Figure 7.2: *Architectural diagram of a data lake*

Conclusion

In this chapter, we looked at cloud computing, its main features, and design considerations in relation to microservices and performance.

In the next chapter, we will explore the importance of monitoring in managing system performance. We will look at the various instrumentation points in the solution architecture, techniques to instrument the components, and integration points to gather key attributes, along with different tools and techniques to measure those attributes.

Key learnings

- We learned about design and architectural considerations when building a modern, scalable application.
- We discussed HPC, which is also offered as an extreme service.
- We looked at cloud tenancy and virtualization.
- We listed types of built-in cloud services and managed apps.
- We listed the 12-factor principles of building a modern app.
- We learned about scalability and elasticity.
- We discussed the challenges of microservices development, deployment, management, and scalability, which affect complexity and performance.
- We looked at the options cloud-native applications have for improved performance with computing power and networking optimization.
- We discussed ways cloud-native apps can keep high performance with proper data and storage management techniques and tools.

CHAPTER 8
Designing Performance Monitoring

Introduction

We have mentioned monitoring as an important aspect of performance measurement several times. In this chapter, we will elaborate more on the importance of performance monitoring in managing system performance. We will describe the various instrumentation points in the solution architecture, techniques to instrument the components, and integration points to gather key attributes, along with different tools and techniques to measure those attributes. In the evolution of artificial intelligence/machine learning algorithms, how it helps in performance monitoring to detect issues and help identify the cause. OpenTelemetry is an evolving observability framework to capture relevant information as part of traces. Here, we will talk about the AWS open-source Distro of the OpenTelemetry library for auto instrumentation as well as manual SDK-based instrumentation to collect metrics, events, logs, and traces.

Structure

This chapter contains the following topics:

- Concepts and tooling
- Common deployment architectures
- Infrastructure and software limitations

- Key components in the architecture
- Metrics, events, logs, and traces
- AWS Distro for OpenTelemetry
- List of key attributes to measure from each component
- Data collectors and aggregators
- Application performance management
- Anomaly detection and suspect ranking
- Predictive analytics

Objectives

In this chapter, we are going to look at methods of collecting and analyzing data about our system's health and performance. We will discuss a few fronts in which we can measure, we will also explain how the tools get deployed, how they work, and what we can infer from them.

Concepts and tooling

As we are trying to get a glimpse of how our application runs, what it does, and how well it does Since there are many moving parts involved, we will first look at what we can learn, what kind of data is to be collected, and how. Later, we will look at a typical deployment of those tooling options.

Logging

Most basically, we consider logging. Logging is considered even when we do not have special performance or performance monitoring needs. Logging normally gives us an insight into what our code does (which modules and which functions were invoked, and when), plus any additional information we choose to share with the world, with different levels of distinction (we could choose that some deep verbose messages are reported only when we set the logging level preference to DEBUG, while logging critical parts, for example when we catch or do not catch a runtime exception, should be logged at any log level setting).

Some tools help aggregate and collect logs, such as *Elasticsearch*, which, as its name implies, is an actual search engine framework and a database aggregator of information. It has become the de facto standard open-source logging database. We will look further into Elasticsearch, with its suite of tools (the ELK Stack and the Elastic APM), with a running example in *Chapter 13, Golden Signals, KPI, Metrics, and Tools*.

Log lines sometimes follow a standard structure (of a timestamp, optionally the entry log level, and a textual string), but logs are collected in an unstructured manner. Anyone can write or not write whatever they want in their logs. This will differ between modules, too. Logs are meant to be informative for error analysis and debugging, but generally are not meant for performance metrics.

Telemetry

Telemetry is the method of remotely measuring, capturing, and transmitting data via sensors and communication systems, serving as a crucial mechanism for monitoring and understanding various systems and environments.

Telemetry primarily emphasizes the *acquisition of raw data* rather than its interpretation. We are referring to raw numbers here. It encompasses the gathering of diverse metrics, such as performance statistics, error rates, and resource utilization, enabling a deeper understanding of system behavior and facilitating informed decision-making. We would normally collect telemetry from two main areas:

- **Application telemetry**: It is where we collect runtime information about our application and its environment (hardware and operating system). Here, we can get performance insights about how our application runs, where the bottlenecks (the functions that slow us down) are, track events such as API calls, and learn about environmental measures such as CPU, storage and RAM utilization.

- **Network telemetry**: It is where we collect data related to network conditions and performance, such as bandwidth usage, speed, and other network measures.

Instrumentation

Telemetry, which represents numbers, is often collected by **instrumentation tools**. Instrumentation may be done through a library that integrates with our code or with the binary executables, or it may be an external tool or plugin that integrates with our **integrated development environment** (IDE) or with its debugger. This helps produce and collect traces and metrics on the runtime and behavior.

Another close concept is **profiling**, which analyses our code's execution in detail. We will explore this concept in the next chapter.

Application performance monitoring

Application performance monitoring (APM) is a framework that collects logs and performance telemetry at runtime. That is a general term, but there are some specific APM frameworks, some more technology-oriented, like specific frameworks for .NET or Java. Since technology solutions shift towards complex, multi-service, cloud-native, technology-agnostic implementations, APM vendors, such as *Middleware* or *New Relic*, provide more and more extensive end-to-end monitoring tools to collect the runtime data of any app.

A close term is **infrastructure performance monitoring (IPM)**, which relates to runtime frameworks that focus on the performance of infrastructure (cloud or non-cloud) components rather than the running application.

Monitoring and observability

Observability is probably the most important term in this chapter. Now that we have clarified, we collect telemetry data (the numbers) using instrumentation tools connected to an application performance monitoring framework; the next question is: *what do we do with all that huge amount of data?*

Monitoring is mostly rendered into monitoring logs and informative dashboards, where we can see the data. We can see chart trends and tables, where we can learn how fast or slow things are or when we are running out of memory, storage, or CPU power. Furthermore, a monitoring framework can produce events that loop back into our cloud host and trigger actions (for example, scale-out and provision another server). Still, looking at the data may not be easy to follow up on, and we may want to ask questions like *why is this or that happening? Why is our response slow?* Those are valid and fair questions, but in order to get appropriate insights and to be able to answer them, we would need a deeper look at our system. It may run dozens or hundreds of microservices scattered all over the place, chatting to each other. Following the path of a specific request, originating from the frontend to its final destination, requires a clear process. Obtaining traces and in-depth information about the events that occurred demands robust tracking and analysis mechanisms.

Observability takes monitoring to the next level. Observability frameworks not only monitor but also provide information about context, helping us connect the dots and understand where this data came from, which services it went through, and in which logs we should look for additional clues.

Observability provides a detailed view of system events, while monitoring offers a comprehensive view of overall system health. Observability allows us to follow data trails from end users' requests to system response, allowing for exact root cause analysis and efficient remediation. On the other hand, monitoring tools continuously collect and aggregate data related to system performance using predefined metrics, making monitoring specific metrics and components practical.

In one sentence, observability helps us turn the data collected by monitoring into information and knowledge by which we can act.

Benchmarking

Another commonly used term in the context of performance inspection is **benchmarking**. To prevent confusion, let us clarify and understand it here. When we do performance engineering, in many cases, we want to see how we stand in relation to what we expect from the product or what our requirements specify. Sometimes, we do not have those, or at least we do not have those yet. The term benchmark comes from the physical world, where measures of height or altitude are placed or chiseled on permanent landmarks of stone or wood.

Benchmarking ranks performance and other metrics in comparison to the rest of the world. It tries to establish a global scale of products and places competitors on the scale according to how they rank. This is done through competitive tests with similar tools across the bench. Hence, it is possible to find comparative lists online comparing different benchmark results of CPUs, network adapters, storage devices, graphic cards, and other hardware components.

In our software development world, there are benchmark tools to evaluate applications too. For example, Google's Android dev tools include the libraries **Macrobench** and **Microbench** which help benchmark our app's operations in specific comparable conditions.

Benchmarking our complex cloud-native app can help us evaluate where we rate in comparison to industry standards. Cloud benchmarking tools help evaluate how well our components and services do, how well they scale, or simply how fast pages load in comparison to other benchmarked ones. Tools like *Kubestone* or *GTmetrix* are used for this purpose.

Benchmarking is an important concept, and we have mentioned it here as a side note. We will revisit it with a bit more detail in *Chapter 12, Performance Benchmarking*.

Common deployment architectures

With the confusions out of the way, and distinctions between logging, telemetry, instrumentation, monitoring, APM, observability and benchmarking, let us see how all this works in the real world.

In a classic scenario, we used to integrate our application with a matched technology APM and/or logging framework. For example, for a Java app, we may use the most popular library, log4j (or log4j2), which is not just a popular library but also an integral part of many Java-based applications, such as Apache, one of the most popularly used web servers. For following up on performance, we would use an APM that matches our technology well, such as *Glowroot* or *JavaMelody*. Each of the two aid frameworks would produce its data records, and if we ran into issues, we would have to go and inspect what was captured to get some insights and make decisions.

The following figure shows such a classic setup: an app with several modules, each of which interacts with a logging framework and is tracked with an APM framework, both produce logs, which are then analyzed by a performance expert:

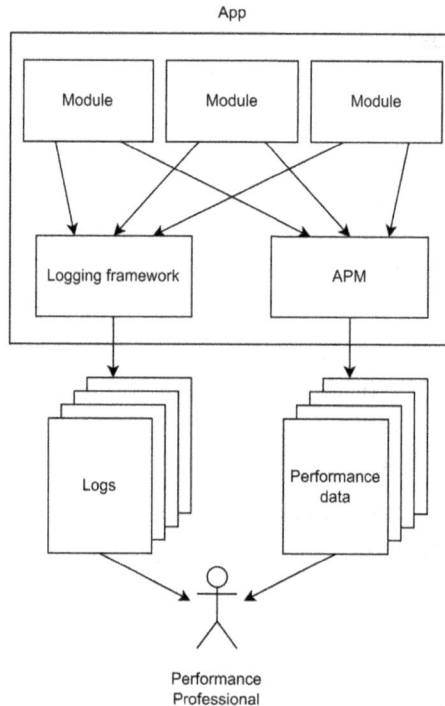

Figure 8.1: Classic logging and monitoring setup

With a more relevant and modern setup, we may run multiple services across multiple machines or virtual machines. We would have to put in place data collection applications, which are commonly called **agents**.

Agents are used for many purposes, usually to be able to communicate from an internal or secluded network machine to the outside world. Connecting from a central system to each dynamically provisioned machine is not easy, so the trick is to connect from the machine outwards to the central system. Build agents run on servers in order to connect to CI/CD services such as Microsoft Azure pipelines. Logging aggregators such as Elasticsearch run their agents to collect logs from multiple servers/machines.

Similarly, performance monitoring and telemetry frameworks have their agents installed on the servers in order to collect various data, such as logs and performance metrics. They can integrate with the running services, either by inspecting the runtime environment or with libraries integrating into the code for deeper instrumentation and tracing. They can also collect data from the operating system, data about hardware utilization, networking, and activity.

The data collected by agents finds its way to the aggregation systems, to provide central logs, performance dashboards, and other traces, and can also trigger alerts whenever required to inform about thresholds being exceeded, critical fails, issues, and performance problems.

The following figure shows such a contemporary setup of a distributed app, running in the cloud, split into separate services, running independently on different platforms and machines, alongside agents of a robust observability framework producing logs, metrics, traces, feeding visual dashboards, and sending out alerts:

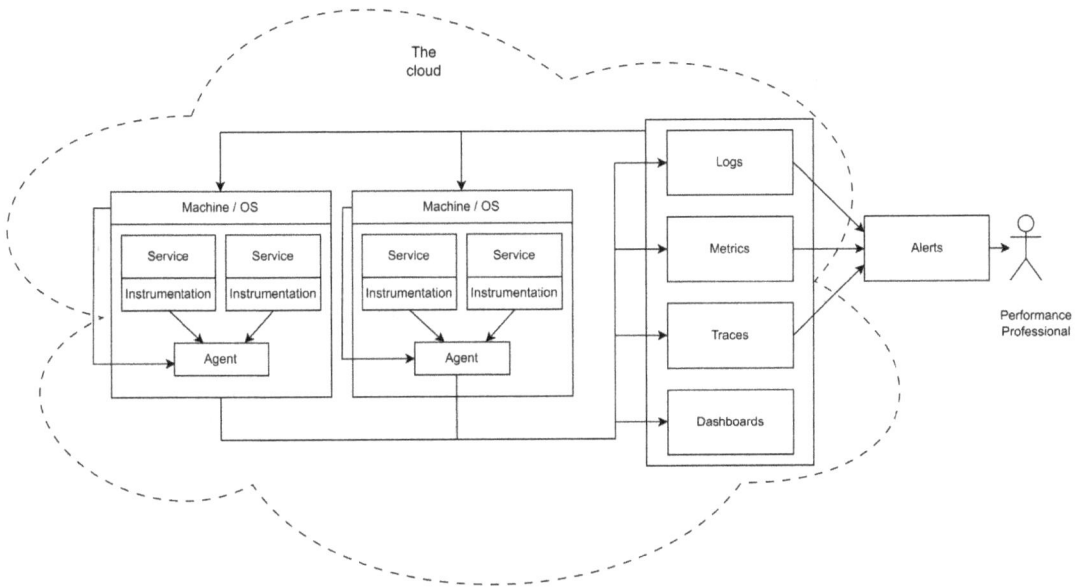

Figure 8.2: A modern observability framework with a distributed cloud app

Modern observability tools pack in a lot of power in order to serve as a central information collection point, to give as many insights as possible with deep observability, as well as added features like machine learning, predictive analytics, and advanced analytic tools to help us get end-to-end trace views on requests and incidents. An even more holistic approach includes the option to automate actions back to our infrastructure so that the collected data translates to automatic remedy (spinning up another server, increasing resources, restarting a system, etc.).

Prometheus is one example of an open-source, widely used monitoring and metric collection system, with detailed, configurable dashboards, logs, and alerting systems, and integrations to many programming frameworks, APIs, and external tools. *Grafana* is an aiding tool that adds smart dashboards and observability options. Products of vendors such as *Splunk* or *DataDog*, and products like *IBM Instana* and *Netdata* also provide such elaborate monitoring services, as well as intelligent end-to-end coverage, analysis, tracing, and action tools.

In a solid system, we would have a decoupled connection between the telemetry data instrumentation collectors and agents, and the monitoring/observability tool. That way, we can use a different observability framework and/or change the telemetry/data collection tool if necessary.

Infrastructure and software limitations

We have growing complexities of cloud-native, wide, scalable, sophisticated microservice applications, with performance and observability monitoring tools, trying to catch up and bring as much data as possible, and with the growing data, trying to make sense of it all for us humans.

With that, there are several limitations that can impact the effectiveness and accuracy of monitoring systems, which are as follows:

- **Limited visibility into third-party services**: Performance monitoring tools become more and more sophisticated and smart. Trying to keep the holistic approach of capturing absolutely everything, they still may have limited visibility into third-party services or external dependencies that our application relies on. This can make it challenging to identify and diagnose performance issues that originate from these external services.

- **Sampling rate and data granularity**: Some performance monitoring tools may use sampling or aggregate data at a coarse granularity, which can lead to inaccuracies or missed insights, especially during periods of high traffic or when monitoring short-lived transactions.

- **Overhead and instrumentation impact**: With the large amount of data that we keep mentioning, the instrumentation is great and helps us collect a lot of it. However, instrumenting applications or infrastructure may introduce overhead and impact the performance of the monitored systems themselves. Excessive instrumentation or inefficient monitoring implementations can exacerbate this issue.

- **Network latency and packet loss**: Monitoring systems may be subject to network latency and packet loss, particularly when collecting data from distributed or remote locations. This can affect the timeliness and accuracy of performance metrics, especially in geographically dispersed environments.

- **Data storage and retention costs**: We are dealing with a lot of data here, which can grow rapidly. Storing and retaining performance monitoring data can incur significant costs, especially for large-scale deployments or when storing high-resolution data over extended periods. Balancing data retention policies with storage costs is a common challenge for performance monitoring systems.

- **Security and privacy concerns**: Performance monitoring tools may capture sensitive or confidential information, such as user data or system configurations. Ensuring the security and privacy of monitored data, especially in regulated industries or environments, is essential but can introduce complexity and limitations.

- **Scaling and elasticity**: Performance monitoring systems must be able to scale and adapt to changes in workload and infrastructure. However, scaling monitoring systems *themselves* can be challenging, particularly when monitoring dynamic or elastic environments such as cloud-based or containerized deployments.

- **Integration with legacy systems**: New shiny end-to-end intelligent observability frameworks are great, and they do try to have easy integrations with many technologies, programming languages, environments and tools. However, integrating them with legacy or proprietary systems may be difficult due to compatibility issues, lack of standardized interfaces, or limited support for modern monitoring protocols and technologies.

Key components in the architecture

We have already roughly explained how performance data collection works. Here are some components that usually take part in such a system. These components may vary depending on the specific requirements of the monitoring system and the technologies involved, but some common components include the following:

- **Agents**: As explained previously, data collection agents are software client modules deployed on monitored systems, applications, or network devices. They are responsible for gathering performance data from various sources, such as system metrics, application logs, network traffic, and user interactions.

- **Monitoring probes and sensors**: This is part of a specific type of monitoring, commonly referred to as **real-time performance monitoring (RPM)**. Those are hardware or software components that passively or actively monitor network traffic, application behavior, or system performance. They capture data at different points in the network or infrastructure and transmit it to the monitoring system for analysis.

  For example, *Juniper SRX* firewalls and gateways are hardware network components that have the capabilities of probing (testing access) and sensing (testing speed) of connections going through them. Such data can also be added to the pool.

- **Data aggregation and processing**: The data aggregation and processing layer collects raw performance data from data collection agents, monitoring probes, or polling engines and aggregates, normalizes, and processes it into a standardized format. This layer may also perform data enrichment, correlation, and deduplication to enhance the quality and usability of the collected data.

- **Data storage**: Data storage and persistence components store the processed performance data in a centralized repository or database. This allows historical data to be retained for trend analysis, capacity planning, and troubleshooting purposes. Common storage solutions include relational databases, time-series databases, and distributed storage systems.

- **Alerting and notification services**: Alerting services monitor the processed performance data in real time and trigger alerts or notifications based on predefined thresholds or conditions. Alerts may be sent via email, SMS, instant messaging, or integrated with incident management systems for automated response.

- **Analysis and observability tools**: Those may include an option to explore the data in-depth, see correlations, and follow requests as they pass through our labyrinth of components and services. Insights may be backed up by any smart tools, user interface for smart navigation, machine learning for deep analysis, and connection with other logs, which may help us pinpoint guilty components and root causes of failures, performance hits, or any undesired behavior.

- **Visualization and reporting tools**: Visualization and reporting tools present performance data in a user-friendly and actionable format, such as dashboards, charts, graphs, and reports. These tools enable users to analyze trends, identify anomalies, and gain insights into system performance and behavior.

- **Configuration and administration**: We also need an interface with which we can configure monitoring settings, define monitoring policies, manage monitored devices, and access monitoring reports and dashboards. It allows administrators to customize and fine-tune the monitoring system to meet specific requirements.

Metrics, events, logs, and traces

We spoke about concepts such as telemetry and benchmarking, performance monitoring/observability systems, what their components are, and how they interact, deploy, and work together. Performance monitoring means collecting huge masses of data. At the core of all this massive data collection and basic analysis, in order to actually understand what is going on, are four elements which need, abbreviated shortly as **metrics, events, logs and traces** (**MELT**), and we will detail here what they are, how they relate to each other, and what we can learn from them.

Events

It makes sense to abbreviate the terms as MELT, as it is easy to remember, but at the core of this collection of terms is E, for Events, as they are the starting point of the data journey.

Basically, events represent *something* that happened in the system. For example:

- A request was sent
- A request was received
- A function was invoked
- Data was stored
- A file was saved
- A database query was fired
- A response was sent

We rely on those events to understand what the system was doing and, generally, what happened. Events are pointers to events that happened across our system.

Metrics

Continuing to mix up the convenient MELT abbreviation, from E, we move to M, as in Metrics. We have already mentioned metrics a number of times, since they are such an important part of any performance measurements: they *are* the measurements. If we want to define or validate performance requirements, KPIs, benchmarks, or standards, we would need to get some data collected, and that data is numbers. Metrics are the numbers representing what we want to achieve and are also the numbers representing what we have measured and learned. Metrics measure things like the following:

- % of CPU utilization
- Number of requests per second
- Response time
- Server uptime
- Transaction success rate
- Load time

A performance monitoring system would collect telemetry data using agents, probes, services, and code-integrated frameworks and build runtime metrics from them. Metrics are time-based, which means we would normally want to know how they perform over a period of time. They are aggregated contextual statistics. It is not uncommon to see on a performance dashboard the current CPU usage, how many requests are being handled per second at the moment, the server's uptime, or error rates. This is crucial information to collect and compare to our expectations from the system.

Logs

As mentioned earlier, logging is a fundamental type of data collection and debugging. It is sometimes referenced to what is known as the **wolf fence** debugging algorithm, proposed in 1982 by *Edward John Gauss*, a mathematics professor at the *University of Alaska*:

There's one wolf in Alaska, how do you find it? First, build a fence down the middle of the state, wait for the wolf to howl, and determine which side of the fence it is on. Repeat process on that side only, until you get to the point where you can see the wolf). In other words, put in a few print statements until you find the statement that is failing (then maybe work backwards from the tracks to find out where the wolf/bug comes from).

This is rather reminiscent of another popular predator analogy: *catching a lion in the desert* binary search algorithm, in which we cut the searched list in half every time, until we get the item.

In contrast to metrics, which in the end represent cold, hard numbers that come from accurate measurements, logging is unregulated and fluid. There are a few common types of logs, mostly text-based (although can also be structured as JSON, XML, or any other format, there are even logs stored as binary data), in which every developer prints out whatever they deem important for them to know in case something fails.

Modern logging frameworks, such as *Elasticsearch* or *Loki,* help us plug any service and any piece of code with ease and collect all logs on a central server, where we can read, search, visualize, and analyze them upon need. They support multiple formats, easy to configure and consume.

Traces

Logging is all good and nice. It helps us locate and analyze bugs based on whatever we output. This is an important feature of pretty much any app. Not for nothing is it considered a fundamental part of debugging, and one would argue that no developer can survive without it. It is easy on a small desktop app when we need to look up some error source, but with complex cloud-based systems, things become much trickier.

Our app may be scaled out to multiple servers, running multiple copies of each of the many services, distributed modules and components, sharded databases, and each such component runs a logger of its own, which may result in enormous amounts of logged data. Finding the root cause of an error or a performance issue may be extremely complicated: we would have to track which services a request or action has gone through, as it had bounced through them before it failed or hung. This is where distributed tracing comes in.

Distributed tracing tracks requests as they flow from frontend devices to backend services and databases. Tracing keeps a unique ID, which gets attached to each request, as well as identification of the parent caller of the request. Hence, we can build sophisticated log tools that show how requests propagate through our system and are forwarded from one service to another.

That way, we can understand and follow, as in the example chart in *Figure 8.3*. The request went from the user's web app (1), to one of the nodes running the cart service (2), then to the data persistence service (3), which invoked a database query (4), as well as a call to update the catalog (5). Upon completion, the call was returned from the database to the data persistence service (6), which in turn returned the response to the cart service (7) and got reflected in the web app (8), to the user (9).

Combined with metrics, which give us measurements of how things went, if this flow had a bug, we could trace exactly which nodes it had gone through, and how much each call took, we could look in to logs relevant specifically for this one call as it had gone through our nodes.

The sequence of calls, which can be traced in its original order of execution, between services and components, can be followed through in the following figure:

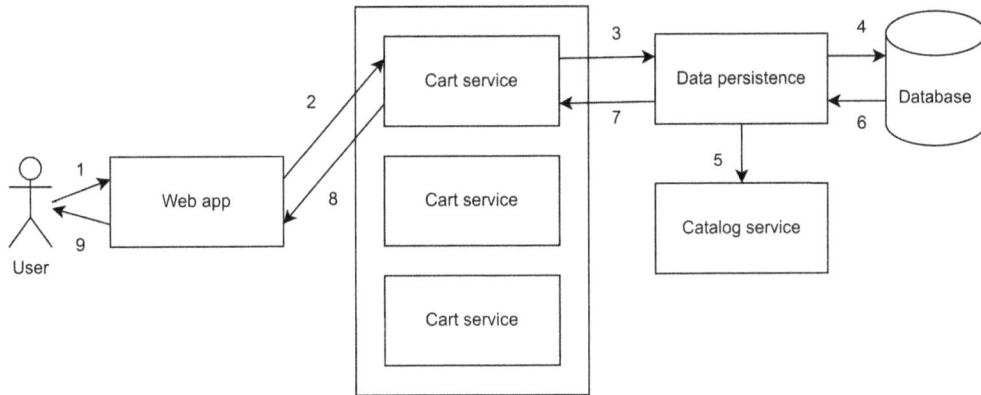

Figure 8.3: *Tracing a web request execution*

Sometimes we would also have something like *Figure 8.4* (simplified), known as a **flame chart**, or a **waterflow chart** (it seems water and flames do not cancel out in this case). On the Y axis, we see services that were invoked, top to bottom, while the X axis, left to right, shows time. In the example below, we see that the **add to cart action** took a staggering 34 seconds. We can see which services it has gone through, and we see that most of the time spent was on the persistence layer, probably waiting for the database to complete its query. From here, too, we can connect to exact logs file to get deeper insights into what was going on.

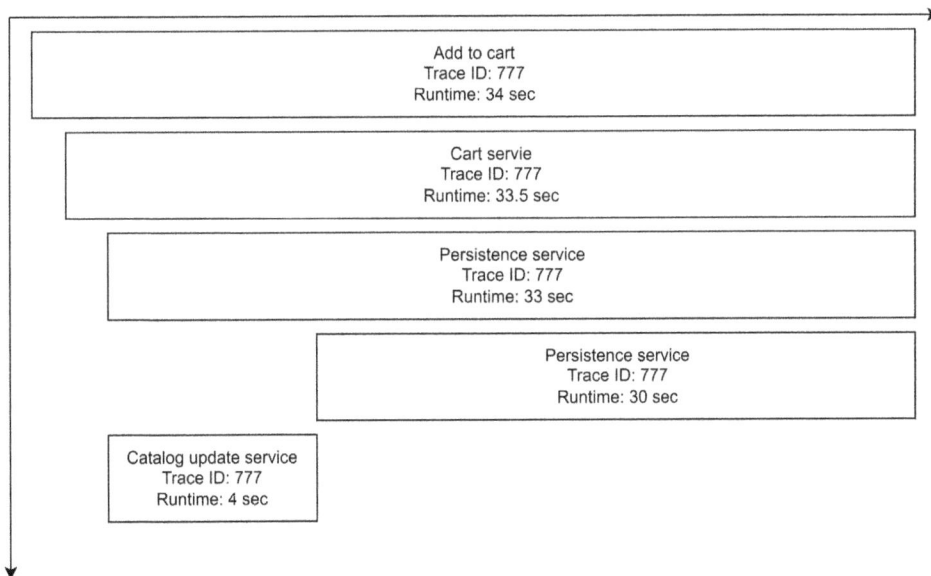

Figure 8.4: *A simplified waterflow chart, tracking time spend on each service*

Each of the items in the chart is referred to as a **span**. It would normally show information about the service, which parent service called it, and how much time it took to return, to get a detailed call chain of our execution. The chart above is over-simplified. An elaborate observability tool will give us a lot of information on each request, including its traceability chain, details about the request itself and its content, exception logs and stack traces, database queries, information debug logs, and any custom information we configured it to collect for us.

AWS Distro for OpenTelemetry

In this section, we introduce OpenTelemetry, an important tool that has become a standard of telemetry collection and data, and one of its most popular implementations on Amazon's AWS cloud.

OpenTelemetry

Such an informative chapter about monitoring and observability cannot be complete without mentioning one of the utmost (rightfully) favored tools in this area: **OpenTelemetry**.

OpenTelemetry, sometimes called **OTel**, is a project by the **Cloud Native Computing Foundation** (**CNCF**), which we mentioned in the previous chapter.

OpenTelemetry is an instrumentation tool that collects telemetry. It helps collect data, such as traces, metrics, and logs, in a uniform open standard format and sends it off to a monitoring/observability backend. As specified in the official documentation, it is an observability framework and toolkit designed to **create and manage telemetry data** such as **traces**, **metrics**, and **logs**. Crucially, OpenTelemetry is vendor- and tool-agnostic, meaning that it can be used with a broad variety of observability backends, including open-source tools like Jaeger and Prometheus (both are also projects of the CNCF), as well as commercial offerings.

OpenTelemetry is focused on... well, telemetry. It relies on a standard data format specification (called the **OpenTelemetry Protocol**, or **OTLP**) and includes a toolset, which helps us collect raw data, through instrumentation, with supporting code libraries (APIs and SDKs). OTLP is encoded either as JSON or in a binary format.

At the time this book is written, OTel's libraries are in 11 extremely common programming languages (C++, C#, Erlang, Go, Java, JavaScript, PHP, Python, Ruby, Rust, and Swift), and more language integrations are in plan. Those libraries also include integrations with major code libraries in those languages (for example, if we write our app in Node.js, and use the popular web server, Express, OTel supports seamlessly connecting with it, out of the box).

It also includes a configurable component called the **OpenTelemetry Collector**, which is a highly flexible data adapter, with which we can connect to pretty much any source of metrics and data, process the data on the fly, and send it on to our central monitoring/ observability backend server in the same open protocol format.

Speaking of monitoring & observability backend servers, all the major ones natively support the OpenTelemetry Protocol standard: Datadog, New Relic, Splunk, Honeycomb, Lightstep, X-Ray, CloudWatch, and others. The main thing to note is that OpenTelemetry, on one hand, seamlessly connects to our product and natively collects metrics, logs, and traces, and on the other hand, is completely **decoupled** from the observability backend.

On the OpenTelemetry website, opentelemetry.io, we can find a Registry section, which includes the huge list of all the code modules and libraries that are natively supported by OpenTelemetry, as well as additional tools, such as the *OpenTelemetry Collector Builder*, with which we can build custom executables of the OpenTelemetry Collector with extended data collection definitions.

Data collection of OpenTelemetry in a distributed cloud environment is done with OpenTelemetry agents, which are deployed onto our containers cluster. As part of the Kubernetes cluster, we only have to install an OpenTelemetry operator on our cluster, and it will take care of the rest. Plugging the OpenTelemetry infrastructure into our cluster will easily collect data of all the requests that are fired and other information and send it upstream to the observability backend.

Combining OTel's broad connectivity to many data sources (programming libraries) on one hand, and to a wide variety of monitoring/observability backends on the other hand, in addition to the fact that it's free and widely supported by the open-source community, make it an extremely useful, usable, versatile tool, and one of the most popular ones. The Swiss army knife of Telemetry data. In 2022, it became the 2nd most popular project of the CNCF and the 3rd most popular project of its parent foundation, the Linux Foundation; both were mentioned in the previous chapter.

A typical deployment diagram, in contrast to the general deployment one, may look something like *Figure 8.5*:

- We have services deployed with different technologies, Node, Python, .NET, Go, or any other.

- We integrate each with its OpenTelemetry library.

- On each cluster node, we deploy an OpenTelemetry agent.

- OpenTelemetry produces metrics, logs, and traces in OLTP format.

- The collected data is fed to an observability framework, which could be Datadog, Splunk, New Relic, AppDynamics, Prometheus, or any other.

- Given all the data collected and delivered, it is easily consumable, understandable, and useful for analysis of our system and potential issues, with proper distributed tracing, accurate metrics, and detailed logs, all interconnected.

In conclusion, the diagram depicts the versatility of OpenTelemetry, showing how it extends common apps, by standardizing its protocols and formats, allowing it a wide integration with various operating systems, programming languages, runtime environments and observability frameworks:

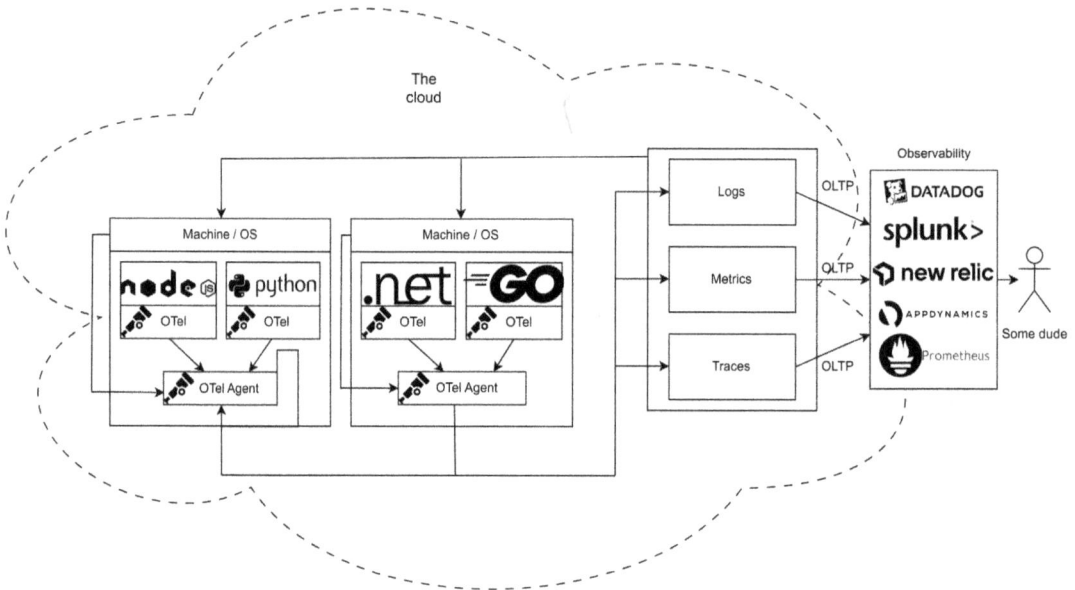

Figure 8.5: The versatility of OpenTelemetry

AWS Distro for OpenTelemetry

As mentioned above, OpenTelemetry is both agnostic and extremely popular due to its inherent advantages: wide support of programming languages, seamless native support of code libraries, and an open standard adopted by all big players in the observability universe.

It is only natural for major cloud providers to offer support for **OTel** as an integrated part of their services. Amazon's *AWS Distro for Open Telemetry* is one of them, on which we will elaborate a bit later. Similarly, on *Microsoft's Azure cloud*, we have native support for OpenTelemetry-based data collection (with **OTLP**) to power the experiences within *Azure Monitor Application Insights*, which is Azure's observability platform. Similarly, OpenTelemetry works with *Google Cloud Observability*. Such cloud-specific implementations also have added-value features, as each cloud provider can add native integration to its other cloud-native offered services.

AWS Distro for OpenTelemetry (ADOT), is an AWS native offering of Amazon's cloud platform, which uses OpenTelemetry in integration with other major AWS services. It is basically the same basic open source OTel framework, but customized and optimized to connect to AWS services (saying Amazon AWS services is a double redundancy, as A in AWS stands for Amazon and S stands for Services). It was made to easily route its data to the AWS observability tools, out of the box. In short, just like other built-in AWS offerings, ADOT is a prebuilt service that we can just choose to use and configure with well-documented features, clear code-to-infrastructure setup, easy to integrate, and easy to run.

Given the popularity and standardization of OTel, ADOT is a common solution that is accepted and recognized by many potential customers running their projects on AWS.

ADOT comes with its own prebuilt **AWS Distro for OpenTelemetry Collector**, which is configured to work with Amazon's services. It is built to integrate with native AWS observability/analysis backends, such as AWS X-Ray, Amazon CloudWatch, Amazon Managed Service for Prometheus, and other third-party partner monitoring solutions. It also comes with a bunch of supported data processors, exporters, and extensions, such as **sigv4authextension**, which supports AWS Signature version 4, for authenticating and signing requests within AWS.

List of key attributes to measure from each component

There are many cloud-native app components, to say the least, and infinite possibilities of what we can measure in order to get insights. However, for reference, we have collected a few key attribute examples that we may consider measuring on our telemetry data collection framework and route to the observability/analysis backend. They are more specific per resource type, how it is meant to be used, and what information we may need to make of the collected data.

General machine metrics

On most machines/virtual machines/nodes, we want to look at the general hardware usage rates and runtime issues. Such metrics include the following:

- **Error rate**: Percentage of HTTP requests that result in errors or failures.
- **CPU utilization**: Percentage of CPU capacity utilized by the web server.
- **Memory utilization**: Percentage of available memory used by the web server.

On different servers, services, and applications, different specific metrics can be collected. Such metrics may include the following:

- **Web servers**:
    - **Response time:** Time taken to respond to HTTP requests.
    - **Request rate:** Number of HTTP requests processed per unit of time.
- **Application servers**:
    - **Transaction throughput**: Rate of completed transactions processed by the application server.

- o **Average transaction response time**: Average time taken to process and respond to transactions.
- **Databases**:
  - o **Query execution time**: Time taken to execute database queries.
  - o **Database throughput**: Rate of transactions processed by the database.
  - o **Buffer cache hit ratio**: Percentage of data retrieved from the database buffer cache.
  - o **Lock waits**: Number of times processes wait for database locks.
  - o **Index usage**: Percentage of queries that utilize database indexes.
- **Load balancers**:
  - o **Request distribution**: Distribution of incoming requests among backend servers.
  - o **Response time**: Time taken to process and respond to requests by the load balancer.
  - o **Health checks**: Status of backend server health checks and response time.
- **Caching servers**:
  - o **Cache hit ratio**: Percentage of requests served from the cache.
  - o **Cache miss rate**: Percentage of requests that result in cache misses.
  - o **Cache size**: Total size of the cache and percentage of capacity used.
  - o **Eviction rate**: The rate at which items are evicted from the cache.
- **Message queues**:
  - o **Queue depth**: Number of messages currently in the queue.
  - o **Message throughput**: Rate of messages processed by the message queue.
  - o **Latency**: Time taken for messages to be processed and dequeued.
- **Content Delivery Networks (CDNs)**:
  - o **Cache hit ratio**: Percentage of requests served from the CDN cache.
  - o **Cache miss rate**: Percentage of requests that result in cache misses.
  - o **Bandwidth usage**: Amount of data transferred by the CDN.
  - o **Response time**: Time taken to respond to requests by the CDN.

Data collectors and aggregators

We have already discussed the importance of data aggregation when it comes to complex data flying around in events, requests, queries, and logs between many microservices, components, cloud services, and applications.

Data aggregation and processing layer

This is a critical component of any performance monitoring system responsible for collecting, processing, and organizing performance data from various sources within the IT infrastructure. Those will include agents, probes, and sensors. Primary functions include the following:

- Collecting raw performance data from various sources.

- Aggregating, normalizing, and transforming raw data into a standardized format suitable for analysis.

- Enriching data with additional contextual information, metadata, or annotations to enhance its relevance and usability.

- Correlating and integrating data from multiple sources to provide a comprehensive view of system performance.

- Filtering and deduplicating data to remove noise, redundant information, or irrelevant data points.

- The data aggregation and processing layer may employ distributed processing techniques, such as stream processing or batch processing, to handle large volumes of data efficiently.

Data aggregators

Data aggregators consolidate and combine performance data from multiple sources into a unified view. Some of their properties are as follows:

- **Scalability**: Data aggregators are designed to handle large volumes of data from diverse sources, supporting horizontal scalability and distributed architectures.

- **Reliability**: Data aggregators ensure data integrity, consistency, and availability, employing fault-tolerant mechanisms and replication strategies to mitigate the risk of data loss or corruption.

- **Real-time processing**: Data aggregators may support real-time or near real-time data processing to provide timely insights into system performance and facilitate proactive monitoring and troubleshooting.

- **Flexible data integration**: Data aggregators support integration with various data sources, protocols, and formats, enabling seamless aggregation and consolidation of heterogeneous data.

Data aggregators often implement advanced data aggregation algorithms, compression techniques, and data partitioning strategies to optimize performance, reduce latency, and minimize resource utilization.

Data transformation and normalization

Data transformation and normalization processes standardize and harmonize raw performance data from diverse sources into a common schema or format, making it easier to analyze, query, and visualize. Here is what we can expect:

- **Schema mapping**: Mapping raw data fields to a common schema or data model to ensure consistency and interoperability across different data sources.

- **Data cleansing**: Identifying and correcting errors, inconsistencies, or outliers in the raw data to improve data quality and reliability.

- **Data enrichment**: Enhancing raw data with additional metadata, contextual information, or derived attributes to provide deeper insights and facilitate analysis.

- **Data normalization**: Normalizing data values to a standardized scale or format to facilitate comparisons, calculations, and aggregation.

Data transformation and normalization processes may be automated using **Extract, Transform & Load** (**ETL**) tools, data integration platforms, or custom scripts tailored to specific data sources and requirements.

Application performance management

Both application performance monitoring and application performance management have the same acronym, APM, so this may be confusing for someone seeking information about one or the other. However, the two are very much related. As we have seen, application telemetry, monitoring, and eventually observability and traceability are all about collecting data from services, as well as other components, some cloud offerings, some hardware (or virtualized hardware) devices, and some from our own (virtual or real) machines and their operating systems.

When we talk about application performance management, it is focused mostly on meaningful data and behavior insights from the standpoint of our application itself. A primary goal is to measure end-user experience (top-down monitoring): time measures of full round-trip time of fundamental requests to the server and back, and timing of business transactions, with full analytics. Secondary measures may include more detailed measures of operations and response times of specific components.

In terms of tooling, methodologies, data, and how everything is orchestrated, collected, aggregated, observed, and analyzed, it corresponds to everything we have covered so far.

Anomaly detection and suspect ranking

We spoke at length about the aspects of application performance management, how we measure telemetries, collect data of metrics and logs, send them, aggregate, store, and analyze the data (or, better, let machines analyze it).

We have also spoken a lot about how we define performance requirements, how to formulate what we would want to expect from our app in terms of various performance metrics, and generally how to check whether we are near or far from what they are required to do.

However, running a performance observability / analytics / monitoring system can also give us additional insights about our app runtime, which may include unexpected behaviors, which we can refer to as measurement anomalies.

By definition, anomalies are events that happen outside the norm. In our context of performance monitoring and troubleshooting, they help us identify abnormal or unusual patterns in system behavior and prioritize them based on their severity or impact. In order to do that, we would have to know what **normal** is, so we can detect abnormal behaviors.

In an analytics graph, this may look something like the graph shown in *Figure 8.6*, where we see an unusual spike up (or down). Our system can detect such unexpected changes if it has an idea of what the normal data looks like, and / or if we set a threshold beyond it, we would consider an anomaly.

An anomaly in measurements in a monitoring graph may look something like the following figure:

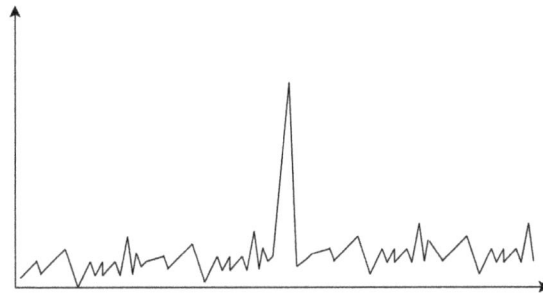

Figure 8.6: An anomaly in measurements

If we consider anomaly detection based on our ongoing data, we could use automatic identification of deviations or irregularities in performance metrics, such as response times, CPU utilization, or error rates, that deviate significantly from normal or expected behavior. Anomalies may indicate potential performance issues, failures, or security threats within the system. Techniques for anomaly detection include statistical analysis, machine learning algorithms, and pattern recognition. Once anomalies are detected, they are typically flagged for further investigation or action.

Even home-based systems such as Google Analytics employ performance anomalies detection algorithms, which can alert us on performance anomalies (such as unusually long page load times), so we can try to understand what caused it, and try to mitigate that.

Anomalies may indicate causes such as:

- Errors/bugs with our code or a 3rd party library
- Unexpectedly large resource sizes
- Traffic errors
- Bots
- Security threats and attacks
- Infrastructure problems

In fact, there are an endless number of events that can cause a performance anomaly, and if we have an analytics system that can detect performance anomalies, we can benefit from it by detecting and analyzing potential problems or external causes. It would be useful to have a rating of potential anomalies, so we can know which ones to pay more attention to, and which we can ignore. This is called **suspect ranking**: The process of prioritizing detected anomalies based on their perceived severity, impact, or relevance to the organization's objectives.

Suspect ranking algorithms assign a score or ranking to each anomaly, considering factors such as the magnitude of deviation, frequency of occurrence, potential business impact, and contextual information. High-ranking suspects are typically investigated and addressed first, while lower-ranking suspects may receive less immediate attention. Suspect ranking helps focus resources and efforts on resolving the most critical performance issues efficiently.

Together, anomaly detection and suspect ranking enable organizations to proactively identify and address performance anomalies, mitigate risks, and optimize system reliability and availability. These techniques are essential components of modern performance monitoring and management practices, helping organizations maintain optimal performance levels and deliver superior user experiences.

Predictive analytics

> *The future is certain. It is just not known.*
>
> — *Johnny Rich, The Human Script*

In an overly simplified manner, with anomaly detection, we look into the past data to detect at present when something goes out of range. With predictive analytics, we look into the future to try to extrapolate the behavior of our system. In the area of performance analytics, there are mainly three areas, on which we can study and try to predict. Those may be included in our monitoring statistics, in order to better prepare for changing trends and avoid peak surprises. Of course, this is a statistical extrapolation **guestimation**, and not a prophecy, but it is better to be partially prepared than overload and crash the system. The accuracy of those predictions depends on a multitude of factors and on the volume of input data we had collected. The more data we rely on, the better the accuracy of our guesses will be (depending also on our analysis/machine learning model).

User load

From hourly data of our system's usage load over at least a few months (the more, the better, of course), we can learn quite a lot about our users' habits, at what times, days, dates, events, etc., they use our system more.

This prediction cannot take into account things like the emergence of new technologies, changes in user behavior, and other disruptive factors. On the other hand, with adaptive learning (ingesting new real-time usage data) and especially in a distributed system, any additional data about our users that we can collect, normalize, and include, and with a well-trained neural network, we may get pretty high accuracy, as high as 75% and more, for the most part, of our expected user load.

Response time

On the other end (opposite the user's load and behavior) of telemetry monitoring and data collection is the data about our system's behavior. APM tools collect a lot of information about our hardware's utilization and metrics, such as response times, latency, database queries, etc. Those can be correlated to user load to help us see what we can expect, also in this context. Again, there is no guarantee, and the more data we collect and correlate, the higher our accuracy will be, and it can go pretty high, especially if we predict the load properly in advance. This can help us plan for better response times in general and in relation to our users' load, so we can give them a better, more performant, consistent experience (as opposed to if our servers crash or stall due to our miss-preparation, our users would get no experience at all).

Infrastructure capacity

In direct relation to our user load prediction and expected response time, we may also want to ensure our hardware can carry the load in the first place. Again, data correlation can help us see if the currently (or future) provisioned infrastructure would be capable of taking the predicted number of users, again, in order to keep our system healthy, efficient, and fast.

Effective data collection, along with the right models and algorithms in place, can help us deliver a better, consistent experience with relatively high accuracy, plan for the future, and avoid failures. The key factor is, of course, the quality and quantity of data that we collect, and as long as we take those as recommendations. Combining this with the real-time response of the monitored system (e.g., scale out or in when we cross a certain threshold) to the well-collected data, if we build this data on the right performance KPIs, it may save us a great deal of money and trouble.

Conclusion

In this chapter, we looked at collecting, aggregating, and making sense of performance information from our system level.

In the next chapter, we will get back into our code and our machine, and look at how we can profile our code to get information about its runtime and potential performance issues.

Key learnings

- We learned about performance monitoring terms and concepts: logging, telemetry, instrumentation, APM, monitoring, observability, and benchmarking.
- We looked at deployment architectures of logging and monitoring system's components.
- We listed possible infrastructure and software limitations in performance data collection.
- We listed tools and components that we can deploy to collect, aggregate, store, observe, and analyze our data.
- We inspected events, metrics, logs, and traces (ordered differently and abbreviated as MELT, which is easier to memorize).
- We learned about OpenTelemetry, and AWS Distro for OpenTelemetry.
- We looked at potential attributes we can measure and gather at different levels and components.
- We learned about data collectors and aggregators.
- We briefly mentioned the application performance management concept.
- We spoke about statistics, anomaly detection, and future prediction of analytics.

Join our book's Discord space

Join the book's Discord Workspace for Latest updates, Offers, Tech happenings around the world, New Release and Sessions with the Authors:

https://discord.bpbonline.com

CHAPTER 9

Tools and Techniques for Code Profiling

Introduction

In this chapter, we will explore tools and techniques to help us analyze and improve our code, both in terms of style and standards and in terms of performance. Profiling is a costly operation. This chapter elaborates on different techniques to run a minimal overhead profiler in production to collect relevant telemetry information. Here, we also elaborate on the steps to instrument a profiling tool, capturing snapshots and analyzing them to get inferences for application and operating system layers.

Structure

This chapter contains the following topics:

- Static vs. dynamic profiling
- Profiler collection methods
- Instrumentation
- Choosing the right profiling tool
- Common challenges
- Profile code and runtime with VisualVM
- Continuous profiling using pprof

- Linux kernel profiling using eBPF
- Automation for gathering profiler snapshots
- Code profiling best practices

Objectives

In this chapter, we will not only discuss profiling but also look into a few of the leading tools of different technologies, programming languages, platforms, depths, and practices. By doing so, we will learn about practices, pitfalls, and considerations.

Static vs. dynamic profiling

In this chapter, we are looking into profiling. We are referring to the two terms in the title as types of **code profiling**, although it is more common to address those as **code analysis**. Much like with other terms in this book, we will outline and explain precisely what we are talking about in detail, but some people use code profiling and code analysis interchangeably. It is also common that code **analysis** is more attributed to **static**, and code **profiling** is attributed to **dynamic**.

Both static and dynamic profiling/analysis are techniques used to ensure code quality, identify bugs, and improve overall software reliability. Static code analysis checks how our code is at rest (i.e., how it is written), while dynamic code profiling checks it in execution. Obviously, each technique measures different aspects of our code. By combining both, we can comprehensively evaluate and improve the quality, performance, and security of our software applications throughout the development lifecycle.

In the next two sections we will explain what each of those analysis strategies is, but as we are mostly interested in performance, we focus in this chapter more on how well our code performs at runtime, so the majority of details and tools discussed will be about dynamic profiling.

Static code analysis

Static code analysis involves examining source code *without executing it*, typically using automated tools to detect issues such as coding standards violations, potential security vulnerabilities, and logical errors. This analysis helps developers identify and address issues early in the development process, reducing the likelihood of bugs and vulnerabilities in the deployed software. They use commonly known popular (or custom-defined) patterns for syntax and structures. We can learn the following about how our code can be improved with static code analysis tools:

- **Coding standards and custom rules**: Probably the most common use of static code analysis tools, is to verify adherence to coding standards, defined by organizations or coding guidelines such as MISRA C/C++, CERT C, or PEP 8 for Python, and custom rules for keeping standards such as naming, letter-casing, lengths of functions, variables' names, proper comments, indentation and whitespaces (depending on the programming language and its relation to whitespaces and indentations).

- **Code quality**: Code analysis tools can provide metrics and measurements of code quality, such as complexity metrics, code coverage, cyclomatic complexity, and maintainability index.

- **Security and vulnerability detection**: Static code analysis tools can scan code for security vulnerabilities, including common vulnerabilities such as buffer overflows, SQL injection, **cross-site scripting** (**XSS**), and injection attacks. They also identify potential security weaknesses related to authentication, authorization, and data validation.

- **Memory leak detection**: It is definitely not the most common use, but a well-configured tool may be capable of detecting memory leaks and analyzing code to identify potential memory allocation and deallocation issues that could lead to memory leaks or inefficient memory usage.

- **Performance optimization**: Some static analysis tools can analyze code to detect potential performance bottlenecks, inefficient algorithms, or resource-intensive operations. They provide suggestions for optimizing code to improve performance and efficiency.

Popular static code analysis tools include **SonarQube**, **ESLint** (for JavaScript), **PyLint** (for Python), **Cppcheck** (for C/C++), and **Checkmarx** (for multiple languages).

Dynamic code profiling

Dynamic code analysis is about analyzing code while it is executing, either manually (for example, by marking execution points in our program with debug information) or with the help of specialized tools. Dynamic analysis helps developers uncover runtime errors that may not be apparent through static tools alone. By monitoring the program while it executes, a dynamic profiler can detect issues like null pointers or arithmetic exceptions. It can also track memory allocations, helping us identify objects that have not been properly deallocated, which then result in gradual memory leaks. Other examples include keeping track of CPU utilization and I/O operations, to analyze slow-downs, or measuring execution times of functions, or even of individual lines of code, giving us insights on problematic execution bottlenecks. By mapping which parts of the code are executed, we can also get insights on code coverage, helping us detect which code areas are hit more, and which very rarely or none at all. A profiler may reveal that a specific function is called much more frequently than expected, indicating a potential optimization opportunity. Execution time measurements might identify a database query that takes significantly longer than others, highlighting a performance bottleneck, to name a few examples.

Some of the metrics that are typically tracked by dynamic profilers include:

- **Execution time**: Profilers measure how much time the program spends in each function, helping identify performance bottlenecks. This is especially useful when we wish to analyze performance, to see how much time we spend in each function, and how many times a function gets called. This gives a useful insight into where our program spends most of its time.

- **Function call hierarchy**: Apart from execution time, profilers can build a call graph showing the sequence of function calls and their relationships, aiding in understanding program flow. Again, this is very useful for analyzing what's going on, where the execution goes, and what it does. With that, profiling helps analyze the time spent in each function, identifying bottlenecks.

- **Memory usage and CPU utilization**: Profilers can monitor memory allocation and deallocation patterns, detecting memory leaks or excessive memory consumption. With that, we can also analyze CPU usage to identify areas of high computational load or inefficient algorithms.

Dynamic profiling is useful for optimizing performance, diagnosing bugs, and improving the overall quality of software. By identifying hotspots and inefficiencies in the code, developers can make targeted optimizations to improve performance and resource utilization. Additionally, dynamic profiling can help identify areas of the codebase that may benefit from refactoring or restructuring to improve maintainability and readability.

Example with Python's cProfile and pyinstrument

In Python, we have standard libraries like **time** and **timeit** that help us measure execution times of our code, tools like *cProfile*, and *line_profiler*, which also collect data about our execution times but with more details about the number of times functions were invoke, and the time spent in each, and statistical profilers like **pyinstrument** which takes the intricate data collection, and can give smarter performance-oriented reports (for example, by eliminating intermediate functions which are insignificant to our performance analysis).

Other mentionable tools are *gprof*, which is a profiler for **GNU Compiler Collection** (**GCC**) that generates call graphs and execution profiles for C and C++ programs, and **Java Mission Control**, which, as can be inferred by its name, is a profiling and diagnostics tool for Java, providing real-time monitoring and analysis of JVM performance.

As a typical example, let us consider Python's popular **cProfile** module, which is the easiest to refer to, as it is a native library of Python and easy to use since we can place it anywhere in our code where we want to take some measures.

Below is an example of an inefficient Python program, with a few wasteful functions that have no functional value. They don't process inputs or outputs, but they do cost time, and run the CPU with costly empty loops, or introduce delays by sleeping:

```python
import cProfile
import time

def do_some_work():
    # Just waste some time
    time.sleep(3)

def costly_process():
    # just a long loop of nothing
    for i in range (10 ** 7):
        pass

def even_more_costly_process():
    # an even longer loop of nothing
    for i in range (10 ** 8):
        pass
    # ... and do some more nothing
    costly_process()

def do_some_stuff():
    costly_process()
    even_more_costly_process()
    time.sleep(4)

def main():
    do_some_work()
    costly_process()
    even_more_costly_process()
    do_some_stuff()

if __name__ == '__main__':
    print("Running...")
    cProfile.run('main()', sort='cumtime')
```

In the code given above:

- We import **cProfile** (as a profiling tool) and **time**, in order to invoke **sleep**, which just stops execution for a given number of seconds.

- We have a number of functions that draw time for no purpose, either by sleeping, looping a large number of empty iterations, and/or calling each other.

- We have a **main** function that calls all the other functions.

- At the program's entry point (the last three lines), we use **cProfile** to wrap and execute the **main** function and give results sorted by **cumtime**, which means sorting the results by cumulative execution time.

    Before that, we print the message "Running...", just to give an indication that we are executing, and that the long wait is not a total freeze.

When we run this program, we get the output of informative results displayed below (I called the file **demo.py**). Executing the command line:

python demo.py

We get the results from the Python interpreter:

```
Running...

14 function calls in 13.287 seconds

Ordered by: cumulative time

ncalls    tottime    percall    cumtime    percall    filename:lineno(function)
     1      0.000      0.000     13.287     13.287    {built-in method builtins.exec}
     1      0.000      0.000     13.287     13.287    <string>:1(<module>)
     1      0.000      0.000     13.287     13.287    demo.py:25(main)
     1      0.000      0.000      7.100      7.100    demo.py:20(do_some_stuff)
     2      7.006      3.503      7.006      3.503    {built-in method time.sleep}
     2      5.222      2.611      5.739      2.869    demo.py:13(even_more_costly_process)
     1      0.000      0.000      3.002      3.002    demo.py:4(do_some_work)
     4      1.059      0.265      1.059      0.265    demo.py:8(costly_process)
     1      0.000      0.000      0.000      0.000    {method 'disable' of '_lsprof.Profiler' objects}
```

We see an output table of results with the following columns:

- **ncalls**: The number of times a function was called.

- **tottime**: The total time (of all the calls) spent on the function's code itself (**not counting** calls to other functions).

- **percall**: Referring to the previous column (**tottime**), this is the average time we spent in the functions call itself, per call (that is **tottime/ncalls**).

- **cumtime**: The cumulative time (of all the calls) spent on a function (**including** calls to other functions).

- **percall**: Referring to the previous column (**cumtime**), this is the average time we spent in the function (including external calls), per call (that is **cumtime/ncalls**).

The total execution time of the program was 13.287 seconds. Here is what we can learn from this output table, in terms of rows, which are sorted by cumulative time of every profiled function:

- **The first two rows** are for Python's built-in execution functions that actually run the program. They do nothing except invoke the program, so naturally, their cumulative execution time is 13.287 seconds, but their total distilled time wasted is 0, and each was called just once.

- **The 3rd row**, we have the call to **main** (as indicated in parenthesis). We see it comes from **demo.py**, line 25. Again, **main** was called just once, and did nothing except dispatch other functions, hence its total time was still 0, and the cumulative time it had to wait while executing was 13.287 seconds.

- **In all the next rows (except the last**, which is reserved to the profiler itself), things become interesting.

We see calls to our methods (sorted by descending cumulative time), **do_some_stuff**, **sleep** (not our function but still wasted time), **even_more_costly_process**, **do_some_work** and **costly_process**.

We can see the most called method was **costly_process**, which was invoked 4 times, and took a total cumulative time of 1.059 seconds. The method **costly_process** runs a long loop with a large number of iterations but does not invoke other methods, therefore its total execution time is equal to its cumulative time (no other methods were invoked by it, or while it was running).

We also see that the most wasted time was on the **sleep** function, which took a total of 7.006 seconds (3.503 per call and was called twice).

Our own-built, most costly function was **even_more_costly_process**, which took pure execution time of 5.222 seconds (2.611 seconds per each of the 2 times it was called) and cumulative total time of 5.739 seconds (2.869 seconds per each of the 2 times it was called).

With this simple implementation and analysis, we can learn a lot about our code's behavior. We can sort the generated results by any column we choose, and detect bottlenecks, costly operations, learn which functions were called the most, and which ones wasted the most time. Quite a powerful tool.

Another example would be to use the profiling library, **pyinstrument**. Here, we removed the **cProfile** wrap from the last line of the program, and just called **main()** normally.

```
...
if __name__ == '__main__':
    print("Running...")
    main()
```

We ran the program with **pyinstrument**, like so:

```
pyinstrument --renderer=html demo.py
```

This generates an HTML report, which opens directly in the browser, and the result looks like this:

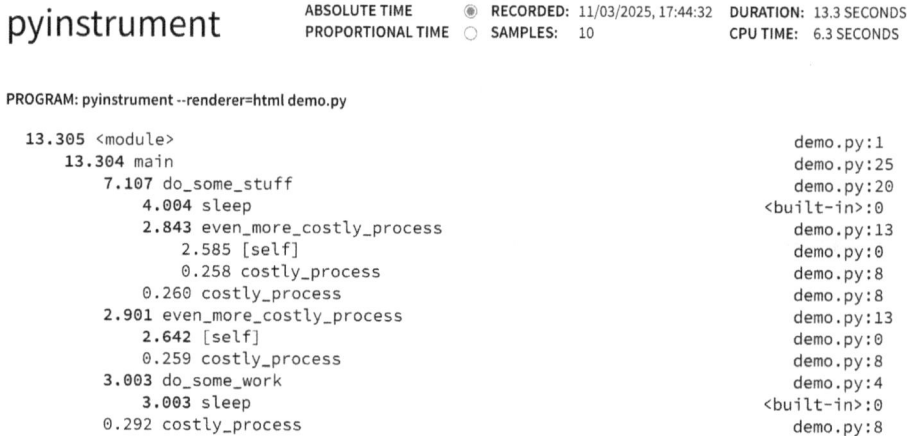

```
pyinstrument          ABSOLUTE TIME        ◉  RECORDED:  11/03/2025, 17:44:32   DURATION:  13.3 SECONDS
                      PROPORTIONAL TIME    ○  SAMPLES:   10                      CPU TIME:  6.3 SECONDS


PROGRAM: pyinstrument --renderer=html demo.py

   13.305 <module>                                                                    demo.py:1
      13.304 main                                                                     demo.py:25
         7.107 do_some_stuff                                                          demo.py:20
            4.004 sleep                                                               <built-in>:0
            2.843 even_more_costly_process                                           demo.py:13
               2.585 [self]                                                          demo.py:0
               0.258 costly_process                                                  demo.py:8
            0.260 costly_process                                                     demo.py:8
         2.901 even_more_costly_process                                              demo.py:13
            2.642 [self]                                                             demo.py:0
            0.259 costly_process                                                     demo.py:8
         3.003 do_some_work                                                          demo.py:4
            3.003 sleep                                                              <built-in>:0
         0.292 costly_process                                                        demo.py:8
```

Figure 9.1: Hierarchical HTML report produced by pyinstrument

We have a collapsible (interactive) tree of the entire execution process. We can see which function called which (and which file and line it resides in), and how much time was wasted on each call, cumulatively. Again, a powerful, easy tool to get insights for our program.

Profiler collection methods

In the previous section, we explained static and dynamic code analysis, and took a detailed look at two examples of dynamic code profiling tools. There are several tools, implementing different methods of profiling, each with its own strengths and weaknesses. Here, we will list a few methods and mention corresponding tools and how they work.

Sampling

Sampling profiling collects statistical data about the program's execution state and function calls, CPU, and memory utilization periodically at specified intervals (hence: **sampling**).

Sampling is the most commonly used technique by profilers. Sampled data at any point is referred to as a **snapshot**.

It provides a high-level overview of program behavior without instrumenting the code extensively. It is a good starting place to find areas to speed up our application. The collected data is analyzed to create a model of where the time was spent in the application. If we need accurate measurements of call times or are looking for performance issues in an application for the first time, then we may want to use sampling. It has less accuracy in the number of calls but is low cost to the profiler and has little effect on the execution of the application being profiled. Tools in the Performance Profiler that utilize the sampling method include the CPU usage tool.

Speaking more technically, the operating system interrupts the CPU at regular intervals (time slices) to execute process switches. At that point, a sampling profiler will record the currently executed instruction (the execution point) for the application it is profiling. This is as short an operation as can possibly be implemented. The contents of one CPU register are copied to memory. Using debug information linked to the application's executable, the profiler later correlates the recorded execution points with the routine and source code line they belong to. What the profiling finally yields is the frequency with which a given routine or source line was executing at a given period in the application's run, or over the entire run.

Sampling tools are powerful because they run closely to the hardware and the operating system's kernel, and do not require changing our application, but due to their nature of work (sampling periodically, rather than continuous collection of data), their accuracy is not as high as other profilers. Some tools include the following:

- **perf**: A built-in Linux command line tool, which works closely with the Linux kernel, and can measure various CPU performance counters, tracepoints, and a few other metric sources. It is capable of lightweight profiling in sampling fashion.

- **Google Performance Tools (GPrefTools)**: It is a set of tools for performance profiling and memory checking. One of the main advantages of the CPU profiler is a very nice graphical output, low overhead, and very simple use (the profiled application doesn't require any recompilation, and the profiling is enabled by simply preloading the profiler's library. Also, an optional library linking is possible when compiling).

- **Intel VTune Profiler**: It is a performance analysis tool that uses the Sampling Driver Kit to collect hardware event-based data on Linux systems. The Sampling Driver Kit is a component that enables detailed profiling by installing specialized kernel drivers (although VTune can also operate in a driverless mode in environments where driver installation is not possible. This allows advanced analysis of system performance under various conditions). With that, VTune Profiler samples the CPU activity directly through the system's kernel.

- **py-spy**: For Python specifics, we have **py-spy**, a sampling profiler that lets us visualize what our program is spending time on without restarting the program or modifying the code in any way. py-spy is extremely low overhead as it is written in Rust for speed and does not run in the same process as the profiled Python program. This means py-spy is safe to use against production Python code. py-spy works from the command line and takes either the process ID of the program or the command line of the Python program we want to run. It has three sub-commands: **record**, **top**, and **dump**. One advantage of py-spy is that it can profile a multi-threaded python process as well by passing the options.

Instrumentation

Instrumentation profiling was demonstrated in the previous section of dynamic code profiling. It collects detailed information about the work that is performed by an application during a profiling run. Data collection is done by tools that either inject code into a binary file that captures timing information or by using callback hooks to collect and emit exact timing and call count information while an application runs. The instrumentation method has a high overhead when compared to sampling-based approaches. Tools in the Performance Profiler that use instrumentation include: The **.NET Object Allocation Tool**, which is a profiler built into Microsoft Visual Studio (not Visual Studio Code). Since it is built into Microsoft's native .NET development environment, it has a good relation to the running application, allowing powerful metrics collection.

Similar to the .NET tools, which are native to the runtime and development environment, Java profiling tools work at the JVM level and monitor Java bytecode. They help in monitoring tasks like thread execution, objects creation, execution of methods, and garbage collection. They track all the important **Java Virtual Machine (JVM)** details such as CPU usage, memory consumption, and garbage collection. Those tools include **VisualVM**, which we will look into later, **Jprofiler**, **Java Mission Control**, and **NetBeans profiler**, which is bundled into the NetBeans development environment.

We have already looked at some Python instrumentation profilers: **pyinstrument** and **cProfile**. Others include **timeit**, which gives detailed runtime execution-times analysis.

Line profiling

Digging deeper than the function levels of standard instrumentation tools, the higher granularity line-level profiling instruments measure the execution time of individual lines of code. This allows developers to pinpoint exactly which lines of code are the most time-consuming. A line profiler report looks something like this (this one is produced by a Python line profiler):

```
Line #       Hits       Time  Per Hit  % Time Line Contents
==============================================================
  149                                           @profile
  150                                           def Proc2(IntParIO):
  151      50000       82003     1.6     13.5      IntLoc = IntParIO + 10
  152      50000       63162     1.3     10.4      while 1:
  153      50000       69065     1.4     11.4         if Char1Glob == 'A':
  154      50000       66354     1.3     10.9             IntLoc = IntLoc - 1
  155      50000       67263     1.3     11.1             IntParIO = IntLoc - IntGlob
  156      50000       65494     1.3     10.8             EnumLoc = Ident1
  157      50000       68001     1.4     11.2         if EnumLoc == Ident1:
  158      50000       63739     1.3     10.5             break
  159      50000       61575     1.2     10.1      return IntParIO
```

Figure 9.2: *A detailed profiling report per code lines, produced by Python's line_profiler*

Some examples of line-level profiling tools include:

- The most popular line profiler for Python has the original name… **line_profiler**! The example table above is of **line_profiler**. Each row in the report corresponds to an actual code line; we can see how many times the line was executed and how much time it took.

- Besides the popular built-in .NET tools, which can provide line-level reports, another popular, powerful profiler is called **ANTS**, which can produce detailed reports at many levels.

Continuous profiling

Continuous profiling basically uses the other profiling sampling strategies and combines them into a continuous progression of an overview of our code/system, giving visibility of progression and trends over time, issuing notifications and alerts.

One open-source example of a continuous profiler is **gProfiler** by **Granulate**, which also provides the platform to collect and display the collected profiling results, hosted in the cloud, or locally.

Another flavor of continuous profiling relates to the continuous nature of development, measuring how the applications' function calls improve or deteriorate from one released version to the next. Something like performance profiling regression test. This is also described below in the section describing *Go's pprof* tool.

Choosing the right profiling tool

Each profiling method has its own trade-offs in terms of overhead, accuracy, and level of detail. The choice of profiling method depends on the specific goals of performance analysis and the nature of the program being profiled. Combining multiple profiling methods may provide a comprehensive view of the program's performance characteristics and help identify optimization opportunities more effectively.

Choosing the right code profiling tool depends on several factors, including but not limited to:

- **The balance between accuracy, overhead and our needs:** As noticed a few times, choosing the right tool is a matter of balancing accuracy (sampling has hardly any effect on performance, but collects the data periodically, which is far less accurate) and overhead (profilers that work closely with the code, especially each and every line, give high granularity and accuracy, but may add a significant overhead to the runtime). Consider the accuracy of the profiling results and the overhead introduced by the profiling tool. Some tools may have higher overhead, which can affect the performance of your application. Choose a tool that provides accurate results with minimal impact on runtime performance.

  Consider the profiling method that best suits your needs. Determine whether you need time profiling, memory profiling, line-level profiling, function-level profiling, or another type of profiling. Some tools support multiple profiling methods, while others specialize in specific areas.

- **Supported programming language/framework, and compatibility with your IDE:** Ensure that the profiling tool supports the programming language of your application. Different tools are available for languages like Python, Java, C/C++, and others. Choose a tool that is compatible with your codebase.

  Also, ensure that the profiling tool is compatible with your development environment, including IDEs, text editors, and build systems. Choose a tool that seamlessly integrates with your existing tools and workflows for a smoother development experience.

- **Ease of use**: Choose a profiling tool that is easy to use and integrate into your development workflow. Look for tools with clear documentation, intuitive interfaces, and good community support. Avoid tools that require extensive setup or configuration.

- **Visualization and analysis features:** Look for profiling tools that offer visualization and analysis features to help you interpret the profiling data effectively. Tools with graphical interfaces, interactive visualizations, and advanced analysis capabilities can make it easier to identify performance issues and optimize your code.

- **Cost and licensing**: This one should go without saying, but evaluate the cost and licensing terms of the profiling tool, especially if you're considering commercial or proprietary tools. Some tools may require a paid license for full functionality, while others are open-source or offer free versions with limited features.

Common challenges

Code profiling and instrumentation are powerful techniques for gaining deep insights into our code's behavior and performance. They help identify bottlenecks, optimize resource usage, and uncover hidden issues, making them invaluable for improving software efficiency. However, these techniques come with challenges, some of which are listed below.

Overhead

The timer calls, which an instrumenting profiler inserts at the start and end of each profiled routine, take some time themselves. To account for this, at the start of each run, instrumenting profilers measure the overhead incurred from the instrumenting process - they calibrate themselves, and they later subtract this overhead from performance measurements. This usually works out very well.

However, when a routine is very short, another effect due to the instrumentation becomes important. Modern processors are quite dependent on the order of execution for branch predictions and other CPU optimizations. Inevitably, inserting a timing operation at the start and end of a very small routine disturbs the way it would execute in the CPU, absent the timing calls. If you have a small routine that is called millions of times, an instrumenting profiler will not yield an accurate time comparison between this routine and larger routines. If you ignore this, you may spend a great deal of effort optimizing routines that are not the real bottlenecks.

Profiling production applications introduces risks and challenges, as profiling tools may interfere with normal traffic and operations. Profiling in production environments requires careful planning, risk mitigation strategies, and minimization of disruption to users and services.

Sampling vs. instrumentation

Profiling techniques can be broadly categorized into sampling-based and instrumentation-based approaches. Sampling-based profilers periodically sample the program's execution state, while instrumentation-based profilers modify the program to collect performance data. Choosing the right profiling technique depends on factors such as accuracy, overhead, and compatibility with the application.

Complexity of analysis, debugging, and troubleshooting

Profiling data can be voluminous and complex, making it challenging to analyze and interpret effectively. Profilers generate a wealth of performance metrics, call graphs, and execution traces that require careful analysis and visualization to identify performance bottlenecks and trends.

Profiling often goes hand in hand with debugging and troubleshooting efforts, especially when investigating performance issues or unexpected behavior. Combining profiling data with debugging tools and techniques can be challenging, requiring expertise in both areas.

Resource constraints

Resource constraints refer to the limited system resources, such as CPU, memory, disk I/O, or network bandwidth, available during the profiling process.

Profiling tools often introduce additional overhead by collecting detailed performance data, which can consume significant resources. This can lead to a skewed representation of the code's true performance, especially in resource-constrained environments like embedded systems, low-power devices, or heavily loaded production servers. For instance, excessive memory usage or CPU cycles by the profiling tool itself may cause slower execution, leading to inaccuracies in the measurements and making it difficult to isolate the actual performance bottlenecks of the application. Managing this overhead is a critical challenge in effective profiling.

Profiling across distributed systems

Profiling applications that span multiple services, microservices, or distributed systems poses additional challenges. Coordinating profiling efforts, aggregating data from multiple sources, and correlating performance metrics across distributed components require specialized tools and techniques.

Security and privacy concerns

Profiling applications may involve capturing sensitive data, such as user inputs, credentials, or personally identifiable information. Ensuring the security and privacy of profiling data, complying with regulatory requirements, and protecting against data breaches are critical considerations when profiling applications.

Profile code and runtime with VisualVM

In the section about dynamic code profiling, we demonstrated two tools for processing and profiling Python code. In this section, we will look at a Java profiler, VisualVM.

VisualVM was first released in 2005. It was initially developed by *Tomas Hurka* as an open-source project hosted on `java.net`. It is a popular Java profiling tool that provides a visual interface for monitoring, analyzing, and troubleshooting Java applications running on the JVM, hence its name. Over the years, VisualVM has evolved with updates and new features, becoming a popular tool among Java developers for performance tuning and debugging.

Furthermore, it used to be bundled as part of the official JDK, up until version 8. As of the beginning of 2022 and JDK version 9, VisualVM is no longer part of the JDK, but it's a free, open-source project, available as a separate download from the VisualVM website and can be installed and used alongside JDK installations. Additionally, other Java distributions or development environments may include VisualVM or similar profiling tools as part of their offerings. For example, NetBeans includes VisualVM as an integrated part, and 3 other popular IDEs: Eclipse, IntelliJ IDEA, and Visual Studio Code, include plugins, natively developed by VisualVM, for easy direct integrations.

Java VisualVM supports local and remote profiling, as well as memory and CPU profiling. Connecting to remote applications requires providing credentials (hostname/IP and password as necessary) but does not provide support for ssh tunneling. We can also choose to enable real-time profiling with instant updates (typically every 2 seconds).

As can be inferred by its name, VisualVM is a rather visual tool, giving a graphical view of what is going on with processes running on the Java VM. Installation and integration are easy and quick, as long as we have a running Java and JDK installed and configured, and it gives a live view on utilized CPU, Java classes, running threads, memory heap allocation, and other metrics of the runtime environment and application executed, with or without the integrated IDE.

One interesting advantage of Java VisualVM is that we can extend it to develop new functionalities as plugins. We can then add these plugins to Java VisualVM's built-in update center.

As an example, let us look at the code block below, which uses an empty class called **Dummy**. The program runs a loop of 1 million iterations; in each iteration, it creates a **Dummy** object and adds it to an **ArrayList**. It also creates a string of characters, named **result**, and appends the iteration counter to it, separated by a space, using the + operator.

One anecdote worth noting is that appending to string using the + operator is considered bad practice, since by appending to a string with such concatenation, we create a new string every time, and that using the specialized **StringBuilder** class is the right way to go. However, this is no longer true, since the Java compiler, as of version 6, automatically transforms + concatenations to **StringBuilder** implementations, for optimization and to avoid such performance gaps.

In any case, this program does nothing and takes a while to load, run, and allocate memory. Below is the code:

```
import java.util.ArrayList;
import java.util.List;

public class PoorPerformanceExample {
    public static void main(String[] args) {
        long startTime = System.currentTimeMillis();
        List<Dummy> DummyCollection = new ArrayList();

        String result = "";
        for (int i = 0; i < 1000000; i++) {
```

```
        result += " " + i; // Inefficient string concatenation
        DummyCollection.add(new Dummy());
    }


    long endTime = System.currentTimeMillis();
    System.out.println("Result: " + result);
     System.out.println("Execution time: " + (endTime - startTime) + "
milliseconds");
    }
}
```

For this demonstration, the code was compiled and executed on an Ubuntu Linux machine, on Eclipse IDE, connected to VisualVM with the provided plugin. Following is a screenshot of the execution monitor in Visual VM. We can see four quadrants:

- On the upper left, the CPU usage.
- On the bottom left, a graph counting the allocated Java classes.
- On the upper right, we see the memory heap allocation; as we can see, it is going a bit crazy.
- On the bottom right, we see a graph of the number of active threads.

Take a look at the following figure:

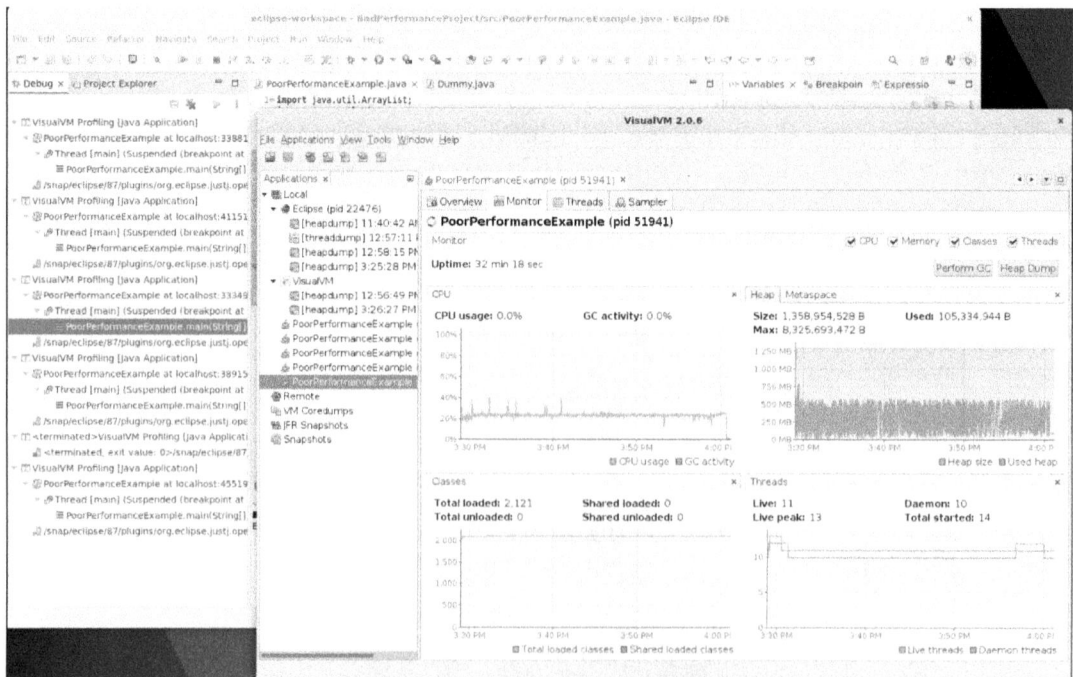

Figure 9.3: VisualVM runtime monitor with Eclipse

Another example of collected information on the same VisualVM, made while running our wasteful code, is a detailed sample of the heap data allocation during execution.

As we can see in the screenshot below, we have a memory heap histogram, which lists the memory allocations, sizes, and number of objects. The table is sorted by number of instances (**Live Objects**). At the top highlighted row, we can see that there are 1 million objects of type **Dummy**, taking 16 million bytes of memory. 2 rows below it, we see the highest memory allocation (**Live Bytes**) is occupied by byte arrays (**byte[]**), consisting of 16,205 objects, taking roughly 42 megabytes.

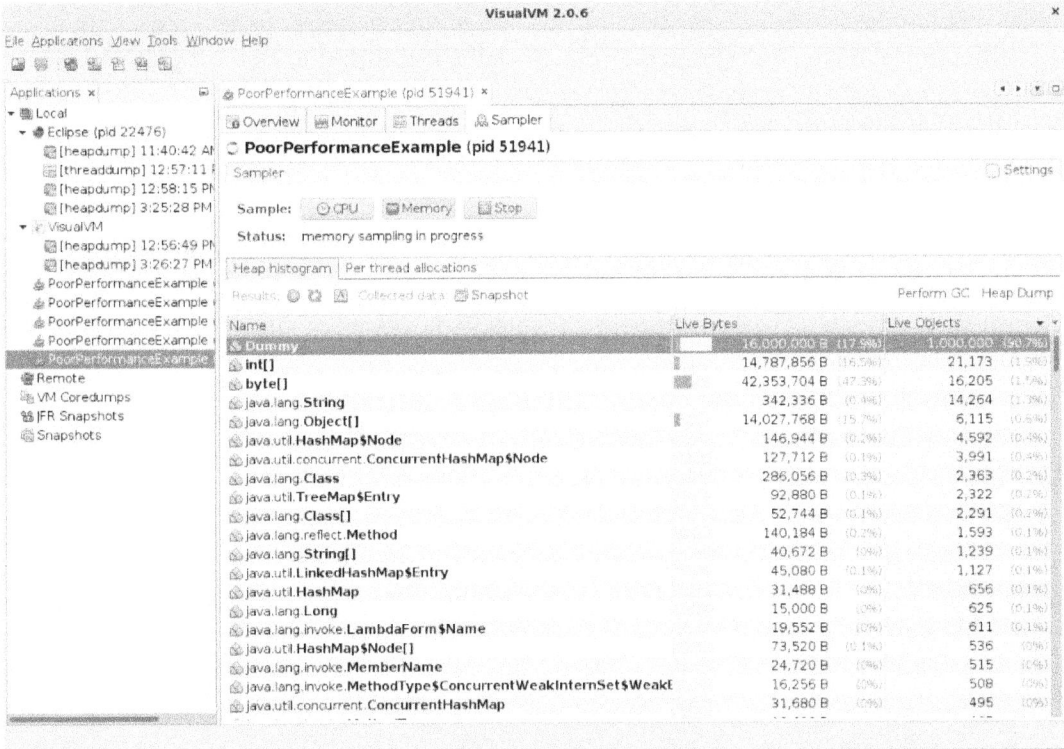

Figure 9.4: A sampled memory heap histogram in VisualVM

Continuous profiling using pprof

We have looked at a couple of profiling tools in Python, and at VisualVM, which is a Java tool. In this section, we will look at pprof, which is built as a general profiling assistant, but mostly connected to the Go programming language (Golang).

Golang

Go is relatively new (developed by Google in 2007) and has advantages as a modern, developed, strongly typed, compiled programming language. It is **somewhat** object-oriented in its own unorthodox way; it is built for efficiency, utilizing multiple core architectures of modern processors. Go gets compiled directly to machine binary code, and it's considered a fast language, easy to learn.

protobuf

protobuf (Protocol Buffers) is a language-neutral, platform-neutral, lightweight, extensible format for serializing structured data. Google developed protobuf as an internal project, then made it open source. It works by transforming the data into key-value pairs first, hence making the structure very dynamic also for scalable storage, without directly using in-memory structures and pointers, or elaborate formats such as XML or JSON, then the formatted data gets encoded to a lightweight binary format, which can be transmitted over the network efficiently and fast. Elaborate documentation at the official website **protobuf.dev** explains the structure and encoding in detail. The serialization specification is referred to as a "**proto file**", with a **.proto** extension.

Google provides specialized tools in many languages to serialize and deserialize proto data easily. Although at this time, there are not many tools, except Google's Go and pprof, that actually use it. One example is a commercial profiler for Java named **JProfiler**, which offers the option to export profiling data in protobuf format, and of course pprof, which we are looking at in this section.

pprof

pprof is an open-source tool developed by Google for visualization and analysis of profiling data. pprof reads a collection of profiling samples in **profile.proto** format and generates reports to visualize and help analyze the data. It can generate both text and graphical reports (through the use of the dot visualization package: **graphviz**, that needs to be installed separately, but in fact is the only external tool we need in order to run pprof and produce graphical reports. Everything else is built into the Go framework).

Basically, since protobuf is an open standard, and pprof is an open tool, any profiler that provides sampled data in proto format, can be read and visualized by pprof. Google's Go profiling libraries provide seamless integration between profiling tools, the proto format, and visualization/analysis of the data.

pprof works by running an integrated HTTP server in our Go code and connecting to it via a **command line interface** (**CLI**) or a web browser, where we can see the collected data snapshots. Data can be sampled and collected at any point in time.

Naturally, pprof is also natively integrated into Google's cloud services, specifically Google's Cloud Profiler, which gives many observability options based on profiling data and pprof generated artefacts. To quickly demonstrate how to work with pprof and Go:

```go
package main

import (
    "fmt"
    "math/rand"
    "net/http"
    _ "net/http/pprof"
    "os"
    "runtime/pprof"
    "time"
)

func main() {
    // Expose pprof HTTP endpoints
    go func() {
        fmt.Println("Starting pprof server on http://localhost:6060")
        http.ListenAndServe("localhost:6060", nil)
    }()

    // Simulate low-performance code
    for i := 0; i < 1000000; i++ {
        // Introduce artificial delay to simulate low performance
        time.Sleep(time.Duration(rand.Intn(10)) * time.Millisecond)
        // Perform some CPU-bound computation
        _ = expensiveComputation()
    }

    // Generate heap profile
    hf, err := os.Create("heap_profile.prof")
    if err != nil {
        fmt.Println("Error creating heap profile:", err)
        return
    }
    defer hf.Close()
    if err := pprof.WriteHeapProfile(hf); err != nil {
```

```
        fmt.Println("Error writing heap profile:", err)
        return
    }


    fmt.Println("Program execution complete")
}

func expensiveComputation() int {
    // Simulate CPU-bound computation
    result := 0
    for i := 0; i < 10000; i++ {
        result += i
    }
    return result
}
```

What we can see in this program, except for the **expensiveComputation** function at the bottom, if we look at the main function, the first part in it is a nested **go function**, which exposes an endpoint of profiling on port 6060.

To run this example, we execute go in a terminal window, and we get a notification that pprof is actually running as a server for profiled data on the aforementioned port, with the command line:

go run .

We get a message that our server is started:

Starting pprof server on http://localhost:6060

The endpoint of the profiled data would actually be on the following URL:

http://localhost:6060/debug/pprof/profile

This URL actually points to a gzipped protobuf file containing profiler info.

What we can do at this point, except opening it in a browser, is downloading it, either through a browser or from the terminal using **wget**:

wget http://localhost:6060/debug/pprof/profile

This will download the **profile** file, which we can open with pprof, for analysis, like so:

go tool pprof -http=:8888 profile

This will run pprof's frontend in a browser, on port 8888, which looks like this:

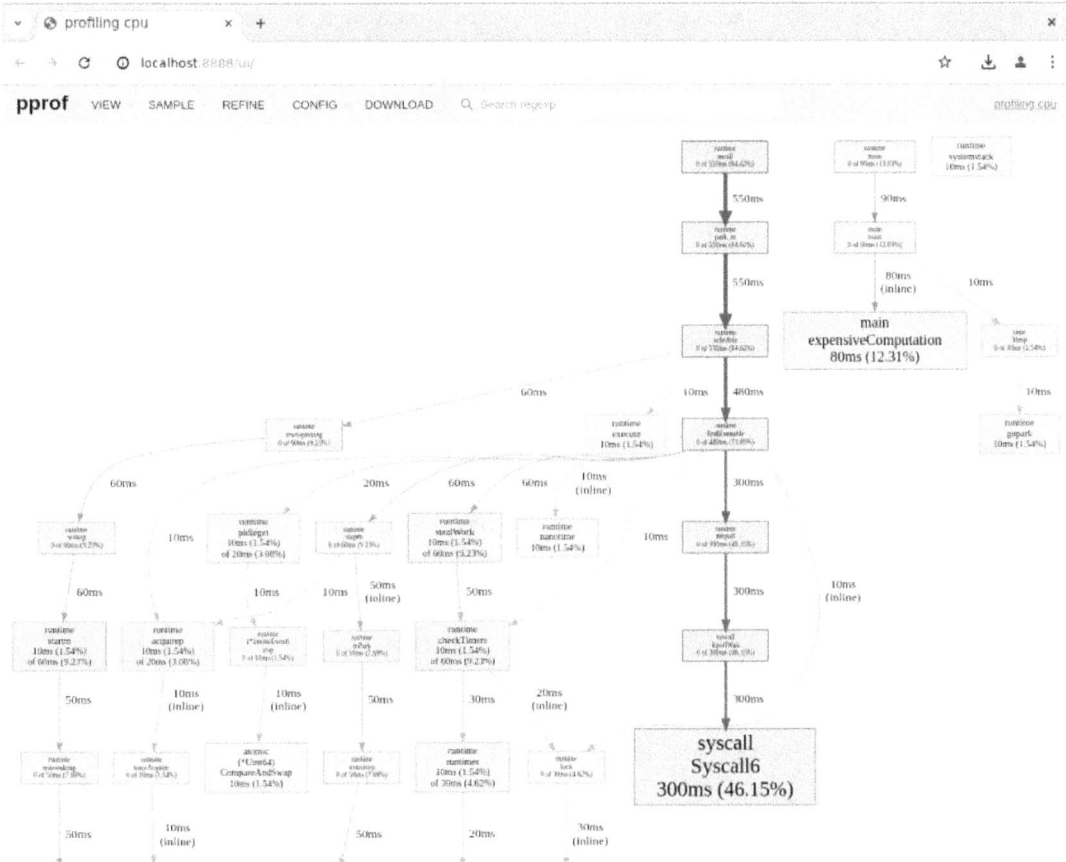

Figure 9.5: pprof call diagram with graphic execution measures

There is a lot of information present here; we see all the calls throughout all the functions of our programs, their timing, and CPU usage. Even the size of the rectangles has a meaning-the smaller they are, the less significant they are in our execution.

The UI is elaborate and gives a lot of information except this diagram. It is easy to set up and requires almost nothing to run it. A powerful native Go tool.

Continuous profiling

A bit like with continuous integration, which allows us to dynamically merge changes in our code and deliver them, the idea behind continuous profiling, is to collect data snapshots, and to visualize differences and trends, to connect what's changed to what is gone worse between code versions. Go's pprof tool has command line options to take 2 versions of Go binaries (into which the version can be embedded) and compare their profiled data. It gives the same artefacts (like graphs) of the profiled samples but showing difference in metrics such as latency and memory usage. To achieve continuous profiling, we can:

- Use the Go profiler, and manually run pprof's comparison features, to see how the measured metrics changed between versions.

- Automate pprof's analysis with taken snapshot samples.

- Use Google's Cloud Profiler, which gives a usable observability UI and integrating with pprof's continuous profiling features.

- Use tools such as **conprof** or **profefe**, or **pyroscope** that give a wide variety of usable features of continuous profiling with pprof right on our desktop.

With continuous profiling, we can use the same Go tools we saw above, but they are adjusted to comparative measures, with which we can see not just call times and CPU utilization, but also differences between versions.

Linux kernel profiling using eBPF

Extended Berkeley Packet Filter (**eBPF**) is a newer version of the technology called **Berkeley Packet Filter** (**BPF**). As its name implies, it was originally intended for filtering/ analyzing/monitoring network packets at the operating system's kernel level, but it is now much more capable and usable than that.

A modern computer's operating system uses virtual memory to provide separate address spaces called **user space** and **kernel space** for application execution. This separation serves to provide memory protection and hardware protection from malicious or errant software behavior. Kernel space is strictly reserved for running a privileged operating system kernel code, and most device drivers. In contrast, user space is the memory area where application software and some drivers execute, typically one address space per process. For security and smooth operation, the two memory spaces are kept strictly separated.

If we wish to write a regular user program (like many profilers) that monitors aspects such as network packets, memory usage, CPU utilization, file access at the kernel level, we'd have to use a specialized API of the operating system's kernel. This works, but adds some overhead, may not be efficient or accurate, and there may be security restrictions to overcome.

BPF was developed in 1992 (as the B in the acronym implies, at *Berkley University*) as a special property of the kernel itself, where applications can run directly. BPF was first intended for packet inspection and filtering (hence the PF), but later was extended (hence the E in eBPF) to support additional functionality. It became an extremely usable tool for the relatively easy creation of kernel-based, ultra-low-level, high-performance tools for security, tracing, filtering, and monitoring. eBPF is a relatively new technology that was developed in 2014, with the involvement of the open-source community, Meta, Google, Microsoft, Netflix, and other giants.

The main breakthrough idea of eBPF is that we can actually extend the kernel's functionality, running whatever we need in a privileged (sandboxed) kernel space, without rewriting or recompiling (and deploying) the entire kernel's code. Perhaps to a modern application developer, this seems trivial, but it certainly is not.

In the ultra-simplified following figure, we see how a profiling app may work through the kernel's API without eBPF (left), and as a kernel extension directly with eBPF (right):

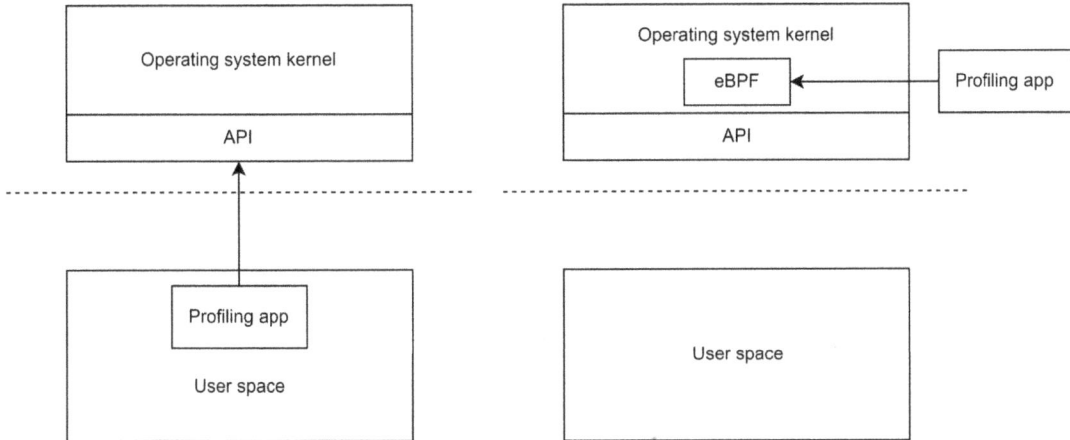

Figure 9.6: Profiling from the inside with eBPF vs. through the kernel's API

eBPF itself does not have a specific native programming language. It is a **virtual machine** (**VM**) within the Linux kernel that executes bytecode generated from programs written in various languages. As a result, eBPF programs can be written in different languages as long as they can compile down to the eBPF bytecode format.

C is the traditional language for writing eBPF programs. It offers direct access to the Linux kernel APIs and provides low-level control over system resources. Many eBPF tools, libraries, and examples are written in C. eBPF Assembly is another low-level language specifically designed for writing eBPF programs. It offers fine-grained control over eBPF instructions and is used for writing performance-critical or specialized eBPF programs.

Other languages, such as Python, have gained popularity due to their ease of use and higher-level abstractions. Libraries and bindings, such as those provided by **BPF Compiler Collection** (**BCC**) for Python, allow developers to write eBPF programs using Python syntax while leveraging the underlying eBPF infrastructure.

We cannot discuss eBPF without mentioning one of the largest, richest open-source resources built for it: BCC. BCC is a collection of tools and libraries for creating eBPF programs. It includes various tools for tracing, profiling, and monitoring system performance, such as bpftrace, bpfcc, and bcc-tools. BCC is widely used in the Linux community and provides powerful capabilities for observability. Another well-known toolset is **Cilium**, which is more for developing cloud-native eBPF-powered utilities for container-based applications. Some commercial profiling/monitoring products such as Sysdig, Datadog, New Relic and Tracee, use eBPF for their functionality.

As a quick demo of how eBPF works with Python, let us look at the following piece of simple code, that follows on CPU latency, bridged to run eBPF procedures with help of the BCC library. For this demonstration, the code was executed on Ubuntu Linux 22.04 (with kernel version 6.5.0-28. Mind you that eBPF is included in Linux kernels from version 4.x).

First, for this to happen, we would have to make sure that the **Python-BCC** utilities are installed on the system. Notice that this example is run on Ubuntu Linux, hence uses the **apt** package manager, and runs with elevated privileges, using **sudo**:

```
sudo apt install -y python-bcc
```

Then we add the BCC path to the **PYTHONPATH** environment variable. That is important for the Python code to be able to compile and run eBPF code. Again, this example is on Linux, using Bash syntax:

```
export PYTHONPATH=$(dirname `find /usr/lib -name bcc`):$PYTHONPAT
```

Then, in terms of Python libraries for the sample code, we would need to install **BCC** and **Pytest**, using **pip**:

```
pip install bcc pytest
```

> **Note: The string variable bpf_code, which includes the function measure_latency, actually contains code written in C. The Python program then uses the BPF object, to attach to the code the kernel. The main function runs a loop, that prints to the screen the CPU latency data.**

Our eBPF latency profiler, which is named **ebpf_profiling.py** is as follows:

```
import os
import sys
import ctypes as ct
from bcc import BPF

bpf_code = """
#include <uapi/linux/ptrace.h>

BPF_PERF_OUTPUT(events);

struct event_t {
    u64 start_ts;
    u64 end_ts;
    u64 latency;
};
```

```
int measure_latency(struct pt_regs *ctx) {
    u64 start_ts = bpf_ktime_get_ns();
    u64 pid = bpf_get_current_pid_tgid();

    u64 end_ts = bpf_ktime_get_ns();
    u64 latency = end_ts - start_ts;

    struct event_t event = {
        .start_ts = start_ts,
        .end_ts = end_ts,
        .latency = latency,
    };
    events.perf_submit(ctx, &event, sizeof(event));
    return 0;
}
"""

bpf = BPF(text=bpf_code)

# Attach eBPF program to syscalls of interest
bpf.attach_kprobe(event=bpf.get_syscall_fnname("getpid"), fn_name="measure_
latency")

# Define output handler
def print_event(cpu, data, size):
    class PerfEvent(ct.Structure):
        _fields_ = [("start_ts", ct.c_ulonglong),
                    ("end_ts", ct.c_ulonglong),
                    ("latency", ct.c_ulonglong)]

    event = ct.cast(data, ct.POINTER(PerfEvent)).contents
    print(f"Latency: {event.latency / 1e6} milliseconds")

# Output handler callback
bpf["events"].open_perf_buffer(print_event)
```

```
# Main loop
while True:
    try:
        bpf.perf_buffer_poll()
    except KeyboardInterrupt:
        sys.exit()
```

One last note for anyone who wishes to run this code, since this code requires kernel access, you would have to run this code as root, with **sudo**.

sudo python ebpf_profiling.py

Once running, the main loop will start throwing to the screen the current latency readings:

```
Latency: 5.5e-05 milliseconds
Latency: 0.000122 milliseconds
Latency: 3.4e-05 milliseconds
Latency: 0.00012 milliseconds
Latency: 0.000123 milliseconds
Latency: 3.5e-05 milliseconds
Latency: 0.000355 milliseconds
Latency: 5.3e-05 milliseconds
Latency: 0.00011 milliseconds
Latency: 3.7e-05 milliseconds
Latency: 0.000123 milliseconds
Latency: 0.000119 milliseconds
Latency: 0.000104 milliseconds
Latency: 3.2e-05 milliseconds
```

...

Just like that, we have just built an inner-kernel CPU latency profiler.

Running a low-performance app that badly affects the CPU, alongside this simple CPU profiler would show, in fluctuating latency measures, as seen above.

Automation for gathering profiler snapshots

As mentioned in this chapter and in the previous one, many profilers collect snapshots of data at regular intervals and connect to a robust observability framework for powerful analysis dashboards, logs, graphs, alerts, etc. Here, we have also demonstrated how we can put our hands on profiling tools in Python, Java, Go, and the OS kernel itself (with eBPF). Each of those demos, includes some runtime to collect profiling snapshots.

On a live system, we may want to automate gathering profiler snapshots, which involves creating a system or process that automatically collects performance data at regular intervals or in response to specific events. This approach enables continuous monitoring of application and system performance, allowing developers and administrators to identify performance issues, track trends, and make informed decisions for optimization and troubleshooting. The process would normally consist of:

- **Define metrics and events**: Identify the performance metrics, events, and behaviors that you want to monitor. These may include CPU usage, memory usage, disk I/O, network activity, latency, and application-specific metrics. Determine which profiler tools or mechanisms are best suited for collecting the desired data.

- **Select a profiler**: Choose a profiler tool or framework that supports automated data collection and analysis. This could be a built-in profiler provided by your programming language or runtime environment, a third-party monitoring tool, or a custom solution built using libraries or APIs.

- **Configure automated collection**: Set up automated processes to collect profiler snapshots at regular intervals or in response to specific triggers. This may involve scheduling tasks using cron jobs, setting up monitoring agents or daemons, or integrating with **continuous integration (CI)** pipelines.

- **Capture snapshots**: Execute the automated collection process to capture profiler snapshots according to the defined schedule or triggers. Ensure that the profiler tool collects relevant data with minimal overhead and interference to the running application or system.

- **Store and manage snapshots**: Store the collected profiler snapshots in a centralized location or data repository for analysis and archiving. Implement data retention policies to manage the storage of historical snapshots and ensure compliance with privacy and security requirements.

- **Analyze and visualize data**: Use analysis and visualization tools to process and interpret the collected profiler snapshots. Identify performance trends, anomalies, and areas for optimization based on the analyzed data. Generate reports, dashboards, or alerts to communicate findings to stakeholders.

- **Iterate and optimize**: Continuously monitor performance metrics and profiler snapshots over time to track changes and improvements. Use insights gained from automated profiling to optimize code, infrastructure, and resource utilization for better performance and scalability.

Code profiling best practices

To conclude this diverse chapter with many demonstrations, practices, and libraries, here are a few base best practices to follow when thinking about setting up profiling:

- **Profile early and often**: Start profiling early in the development process, ideally during the design and implementation phases. Profile regularly throughout the development lifecycle, including during testing, debugging, and optimization stages. Continuously monitor performance to detect regressions and track improvements.

- **Use the right tools**: Choose appropriate profiling tools and techniques based on your application stack, programming language, and performance objectives. Use built-in profilers provided by programming languages and frameworks, as well as third-party profiling tools and monitoring solutions tailored to your specific needs.

- **Choose your scope**: Decide on the granularity of your profiling, such as function, module, class, or line level. The scope should align with your goals and the complexity of your code. For broad performance optimization, higher-level profiling might be sufficient, while debugging specific issues may require more granular profiling.

- **Measure various metrics**: Ensure the profiler allows you to measure various performance metrics, such as memory and OS usage, execution time, and overall application performance. This flexibility will enable you to address a wide range of performance issues.

- **Identify hot/critical paths**: Use profilers to find the parts of your code that consume the most CPU or memory. Improving these **hot paths** can significantly enhance overall performance. Profilers are also useful for detecting memory leaks and understanding the performance of dependency calls and transactions.

- **Profile under realistic conditions**: Profile your application under realistic workloads, traffic patterns, and usage scenarios that closely resemble production environments. Use representative data sets, simulate typical user interactions, and account for variations in user behavior and system conditions.

- **Monitor and measure continuously**: Implement continuous monitoring and measurement of performance metrics in production environments. Use monitoring tools, logging frameworks, and profiling solutions to collect real-time performance data, detect anomalies, and respond to performance issues promptly.

Conclusion

In this chapter, we took a deep and diverse look into code analysis and system profiling, what kinds of tools are out there, how to actually use them properly, and what their best practices and pitfalls are.

In the next chapter, we will further look at performance testing, what we need to take care of, and some best practices in order to produce and conduct good automated relevant tests.

Key learnings

- We explained static code analysis and what we can get from it.
- We explained code profiling and what we can get from it too.
- We saw how we can profile Python with some common libraries.
- We learned about the different profiling methods and how they work.
- We learned about some considerations when choosing a profiling tool.
- We learned what VisualVM is and how we can profile Java code with it.
- We looked at some common challenges in profiling.
- We talked about pprof, how to profile Go code with it, and how it does continuous profiling.
- We learned what eBPF is and how to profile the operating system's kernel with it.
- We discussed profiling automation.
- We listed some best practices for profiling.

Join our book's Discord space

Join the book's Discord Workspace for Latest updates, Offers, Tech happenings around the world, New Release and Sessions with the Authors:

https://discord.bpbonline.com

CHAPTER 10

Performance Testing, Checklist to Best Practices

Introduction

In this chapter, and in the next few, we are going to talk in detail about automation and execution of tests in terms of preparation, development, execution, and things to note, arranging test data, various types of test measurements, and comparing them to requirements and preset key performance indicators, analyze them, and keep track. This touches on multiple areas, from development, data, quality assurance, automation, DevOps, and potentially a few more.

We will talk about best practices of performance testing, workload, automated test script development, and relevant tools (and we will look at JMeter as a popular functional workload testing tool).

Structure

This chapter contains the following topics:

- Performance validation checklist
- Script development
- Leverage functional test suite to create JMeter scripts
- Workload model to scenario mapping

- Environment preparation
- Production vs. performance test environments
- Performance testing tools
- Performance testing best practices

Objectives

We will learn about the process of developing a performance test plan, from the first steps of analysis through developing automated scripted performance tests and running them under different workload models on a well-matched test environment.

Performance validation checklist

We start our test modeling with a list of things we may want to pay attention to before, during, and after the tests.

System analysis

First, we would want to understand our system setup, environment, architecture, and risks.

The following are some points we can use for laying out, analyzing, and better understanding our system:

- Understand the system's architecture.
- Identify critical business flows.
- Identify in-scope and out-of-scope components.
- Understand the in-scope components.
- Understand the impact of changes on all the in-scope components.
- Assess the risks: review and sign off on the risk assessment document.

Test plan

At this stage, we collect, map, and define the requirements, research and decide on testing, profiling, and monitoring tools, and test data. Not just what we would like to ensure, but also how we define the completion of the project and successful tests.

The following are some action points for creating a test plan, in order to better profile and validate our system's performance:

- Set performance testing project timelines.
- Gather non-functional requirements.
- Decide on types of non-functional tests to be conducted.

- Non-functional requirements mapping.
- Decide on the test data approach.
- Decide on a performance testing tool.
- Decide on a server monitoring tool.
- Decide on a profiling tool.
- Prepare a detailed test approach and planning for each type of performance test.
- Prepare a detailed test data generation approach.
- Review and sign off on the test plan.

Test execution

Planning is all nice and good, but at some point, we would have to actually create the test scripts, run them, and collect all the results, stats, and logs.

The following list outlines some typical steps for running various tests:

1. Create test data.
2. Server restart (upon need or before every test).
3. Perform a smoke test.
4. Gather server stats.
5. Run the tests.
6. Collect test results.
7. Collect stats from the monitoring tool during the test period.
8. Collect server logs.
9. Collect dumps.
10. Analyze the test results.
11. Discuss the results with the project team and developers. Discuss bottlenecks, findings, recommendations, and resolutions.

Report

In the post-test-execution phase, we need to review the results, make a Boolean binary decision on the state of the project, and produce a report:

1. Collect the test artifacts.
2. In case of critical findings, make a decision on go/no-go.
3. Formulate recommendations.
4. Decide on further plan/performance tuning etc.
5. Complete a test report.
6. Review and sign off on the test report.

Script development

We are talking about performance testing, comparison, monitoring, profiling, and instrumenting, all of which involve measurable, exact metrics. We need consistency, accuracy, and high coverage to be able to detect issues efficiently and early.

We have already established the importance of test automation in our context. As mentioned a number of times, performance is sometimes a matter of feeling, but it goes down to the experience of the end-user, and the customer is always right. As our system grows, scales, and spans, we would not want to impact the API responses, the UI load time, or the database calls; everything can boil down to milliseconds or, in a much worse case, seconds. To catch things before they go south, we may want to be more proactive than reactive, and performance testing ahead of time is the way to go: to serve and protect. To detect issues early, make sure all relevant teams are aware of issues when they are caught, and improve our product in general. Automation of performance tests helps continuous performance and reliability testing, and a more effective, efficient testing and development process. It also allows repeating tests as many times as we need on any environment, comparing results to see whether our infrastructure and hardware can handle the load, and viewing trends of improvement or regression between versions.

Scripted automated tests are on the border between testing and programming. When choosing a framework to test, we need to know what we intend to test and find the scripting tool and framework that work best for us, according to the project we are trying to test and what language it is built with.

Apart from the various types of scripted tests, we have the instrumentation and profiling tools we discussed and demonstrated in the previous chapter, and wrapping up the tests, and other integration and delivery stages of our project, we would have to write CI/CD pipeline definitions and scripts that help tie everything together, run the tests we chose to automate, build, pack, shrink, copy and deploy.

Some automation tools provide both scripted options, as well as low-code/no-code definition of steps through a UI, which may or may not produce a written script eventually. Sticking to a written script may not suit every tester, but it comes with advantages normally related to code writing, such as easy version control, reusability of components, functions, and modules, flexibility to parametrize functions, and better performance.

To differentiate and as a quick summary, here are typical testing routines with a small note about how they are scripted/written, what they test, and how they run:

- **Performance tests: load tests, profiling, and instrumentation**: Those were mentioned in detail in the previous chapter and throughout the book. Be it with specific technology frameworks, such as Python's cProfile or pyinstrument, or Java's VisualVM, more standard tools (or standard wannabe) such as Go's pprof, or tools that profile at the kernel like eBPF, we include tests with our code, or on the runtime environment, and collect stats, either at the application's build-time, runtime, or while specific other tests are running, to isolate execution and gather performance measurements. Performance tests may be categorized according to how we intend to measure performance, whether we perform load tests, stress tests, spike tests, endurance tests, scalability tests, volume tests, etc.

- **Unit tests**: Unit tests focus on individual units or components of the software in isolation (e.g., functions, methods, classes) in order to validate that each unit behaves as expected.

  Unit tests are written in a framework that matches the programming language in which our code is, hence, most naturally developed by the programmer who wrote the code. With unit tests, we want to keep the code execution confined just to one single tested unit (e.g., a single function), but our code does not normally run in a vacuum. It interacts with other functions, classes, modules, and data. Thus, in order to keep the test execution confined to just one single specific unit, all the external interactions and data are simulated (mocked) by a dedicated mocking framework. We isolate the execution just to the tested unit, and not, for example, trigger real events or make real database calls. This also helps simulate all kinds of edge cases and situations.

  For proper unit tests, we need to thoroughly understand the programming language and testing framework. We write test cases to cover different scenarios and edge cases for each unit, including potential execution time measurements.

- **Integration tests**: Taking the unit tests to the next level, we want to test not just the single isolated unit, but how units interact with one another, or the end-to-end flow of scenarios. With integration tests we would aim to validate that integrated components work together correctly. For that, we would need to understand the software architecture and dependencies between components and write test cases to cover integration points and data flows. Integration tests can also take into account performance measurements and metrics.

  Since integration points may be many and diverse, integration test scripts and tools vary. From executing scripted executions of our code, through initiating execution through API calls with tools like Postman (and its automated counterpart Newman) or with JMeter, which we will look into in the next section, or to triggering flows and execution through the UI with frontend testing frameworks, such as Selenium. The tools and technologies used depend on the depth of the tests and how **far** or **close** they are to the code or to the user interface.

- **Functional tests**: Functional tests take it up another notch, to testing the functionality of the software from an end-user perspective. Here, we would want to validate that the software meets the specified functional requirements. For that, we would have to understand the application's behavior and user workflows.

  Functional tests also depend on the system's functions, how it runs, where it runs, and what it does. We write test cases to cover different use cases and user scenarios.

With that arsenal of testing tools, scripting considerations, and frameworks according to our needs, we can divide our execution batches, and decide when to run which: **regression tests** (testing to ensure that new features or updates to the software do not harm existing functionality, or introduce new critical bugs), **smoke tests** (testing the minimum viable basic functionality of the software to ensure that it is stable and deployable), or any other routine tests that execute **during development**, or when new **changes are pushed**, or just **before, during or after deployment**.

Leverage functional test suite to create JMeter scripts

As outlined in the previous section, scripts and automated tests come in many flavors, technologies, and tools. When the subject of automated testing is brought up, the common reference would be the UI functional tests with a tool like Selenium (it would also mostly be Selenium, if we are testing a web application). However, for obvious reasons, we are mostly focusing on functional performance tests. Hence, we will take a closer look into scripting such tests with the exemplary ultra-versatile tool, JMeter.

As can be inferred right from the first letter, JMeter is a **Java-based test tool**. When mentioning **functional tests**, in relation to tools like JMeter, we refer to testing functionality of APIs, endpoints of services of different types, web URLs, or databases, as functional entry points to our system. JMeter is made exactly for this.

With JMeter, we can create tests that issue requests to any endpoint, populating them with any data, parameters, headers, etc. We **trigger requests** simulating **user load** (also to be referred to as workload, which we will look into in the next section. With JMeter, we can specify, for example, how many concurrent users to simulate, how many concurrent requests to issue, and how to loop them multiple times); we can also specify custom rules and assertions of what we expect in response and enrich our tests with custom functions code.

JMeter can export its findings to **HTML dashboard reports** (or, by default, to CSV files, which can be consumed by any tool or dashboard). If some of this functionality sounds to you awfully close to tools like Postman + Newman, you would be right. The core functionality of creating requests and assessing responses is a core of Postman, too, but the combined, consistent reporting features of JMeter are preferable. JMeter has many tricks up its sleeve, which are not part of Postman.

JMeter supports additional features, running tests **not just against HTTP URL endpoints**, but also tests that include sampling all kinds of server applications such as **FTP servers**, **LDAP** directory servers, mail servers such as **SMTP**, triggering direct **queries against databases**, and many more, making it much more versatile, and superior to request samplers such as Postman. Some of those features can be seen in the following figure of JMeter's sophisticated, yet easy-to-use UI:

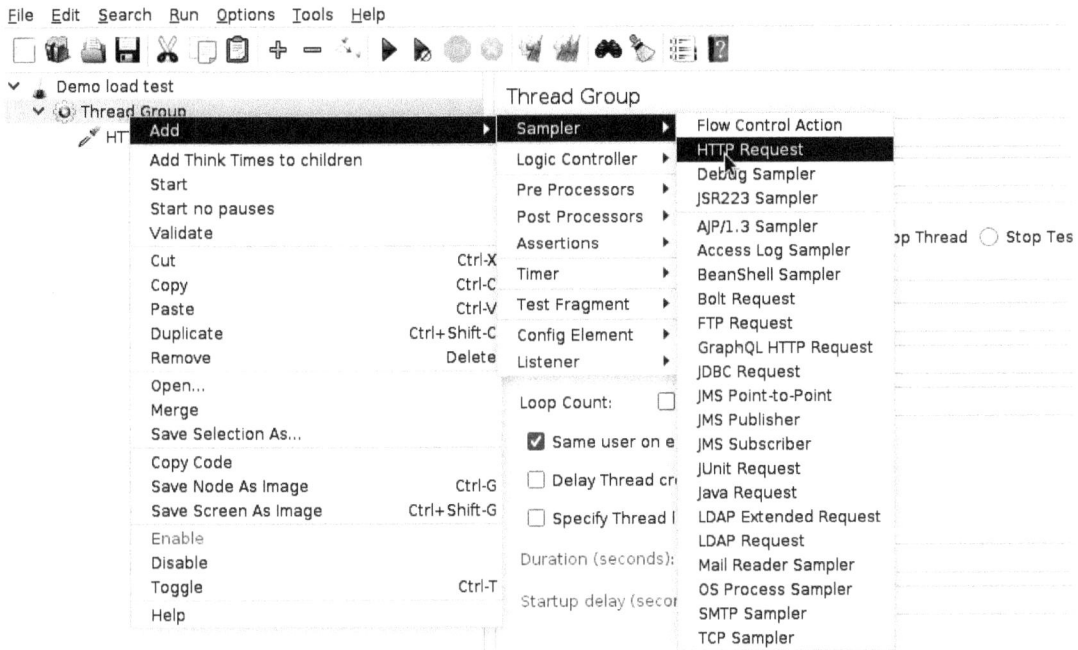

Figure 10.1: Adding an HTTP request to test in JMeter

Since JMeter was written in Java, it can run on any system (which has Java runtime on it), and measure any project, run against any server; it is basically **technologically agnostic**.

JMeter is a very large tool, with loads of features and customization options, to the level of being overwhelmingly packed. Test scripts can be produced in 3 ways, or a combination thereof:

1. Manually writing the script code
2. Creating the steps using the very handy JMeter UI
3. For tests of websites and services accessible via a browser, JMeter comes with its own proxy module, with which we intercept the browser's traffic, and record the activity that goes through, then have JMeter replay it as a test script, with additional simulated conditions of load or customized parameters.

In the following screenshot, we demonstrate setting up a simple test for running an HTTP request against a local running HTTP Apache server (running on **localhost**). Note that we can set up workload parameters for running the request in a loop (in this case, 10 iterations), simulating multiple users (in this case, 100), with time intervals (in this case, 2 seconds). Following that, we can see the simple report of this test operation. Of course, as we mentioned, this tool has a huge amount of versatile options, allowing us to test and measure the performance of many functions of many different servers and services under heavy load, with highly customizable options, and giving readable, useful reports and dashboards for analysis.

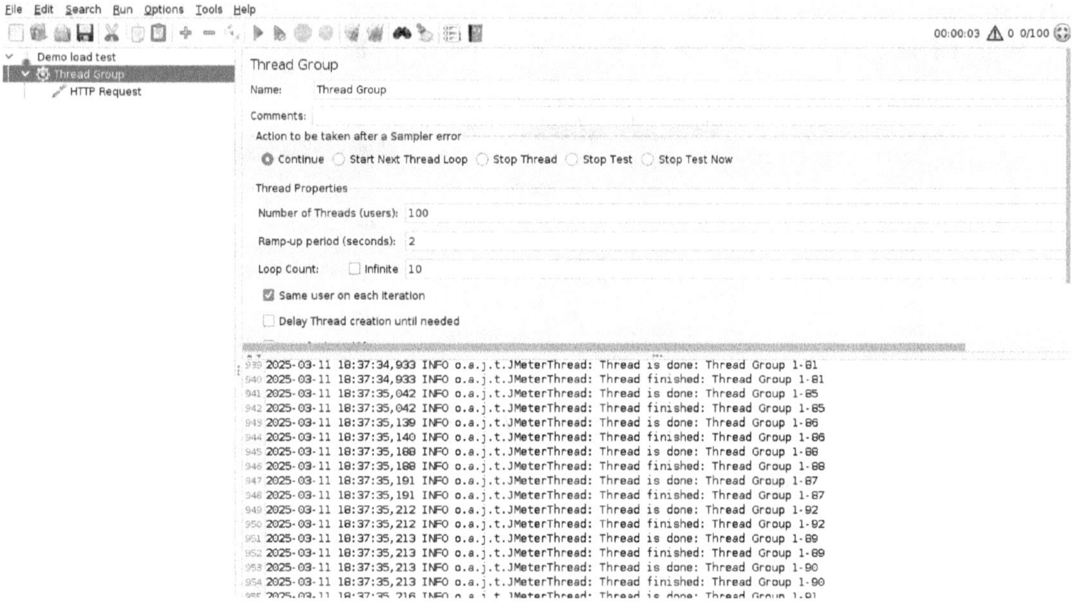

Figure 10.2: Defining and running a threaded test in JMeter

Workload model to scenario mapping

In order to script our tests, we need to come up with our test plan. In parallel to outlining clear definitions of our product's functional and non-functional requirements, on the other hand, when it comes to testing and measuring, we need to outline scenarios or proper test cases, which accumulate into a clear test plan.

We would naturally want our testable scenarios to simulate real-world conditions, that is, to consider the load distribution on the system in each case, which is commonly referred to as **workload**. We looked at the simulated workload with JMeter in the previous section. Adding workload as a manifestation of testable requirements to an identified, defined testable scenario is what we refer to as **workload modeling.** With workload modeling, we can define what we expect to be production conditions and produce load tests that simulate those conditions to check how the application behaves and reacts, but not just in theory and anticipated scenarios. If we encounter an actual production problem caused by a heavy load, we could replicate and simulate similar workload conditions and test them in isolation with an appropriate tool, such as JMeter.

We are referring here to the term **users** a lot, but it is worth mentioning that users are not a single homogenous, equal definition. Users are tied to the tested scenarios, so when we come to define a workload model, we should also differentiate the types of users that are relevant to us (regular users, administrators, guests, unauthenticated users, etc).

With that, we can define our model's metrics, which may be many. Some aspects, as we saw in the previous section, for example:

- The number of users
- The number of requests per seconds ("hit count")
- The time between different actions ("think time")
- The number of simultaneous users or transactions
- The time between iterations ("pacing")
- The number of iterations to run
- Page response time
- Data throughput

Once we have defined a workload model, we map it to specific test scenarios. Of course, not all workflow model metrics are relevant to all scenarios. It is our job to mix and match and map the relevant ones. Some steps in that area would be:

1. **Identify the key user scenarios** that need to be tested. These should represent the most critical and common user interactions with the system. For example:

   a. User login and browsing.

   b. Product search and viewing details.

   c. Adding items to the cart and checkout.

2. For each scenario, define user profiles that perform the actions. This includes understanding different user types and their specific behaviors. For example:

   a. Regular user logs in, searches for products, views product details, and checks out.

   b. Guest user: Browses products, views details, and signs up for an account.

3. Map out the specific transactions and think times for each scenario. Think time should be realistic, reflecting how long users typically take between actions. For example:

   a. User logs in (think time: 2-5 seconds).

   b. User searches for a product (think time: 3-7 seconds).

   c. User views product details (think time: 5-10 seconds).

   d. User adds product to cart and checks out (think time: 4-8 seconds).

4. Define the load patterns for each scenario. This includes modeling how we see the user load change over time and how we expect it to grow.

   a. The time it takes to reach the target number of users or transactions ("Ramp-up time"). For example: **Increase from 0 to 100 users over 10 minutes**.

   b. The duration for which the target load is maintained ("Steady state"). For example: **Maintain 100 users for 30 minutes**.

c. The time it takes to decrease the load back to zero ("Ramp down time"). For example: **Decrease from 100 to 0 users over 10 minutes**.

Thus, we would normally imagine a surge of load, followed by a steady load for some time, and relief and decrease of the load, which may look something like this:

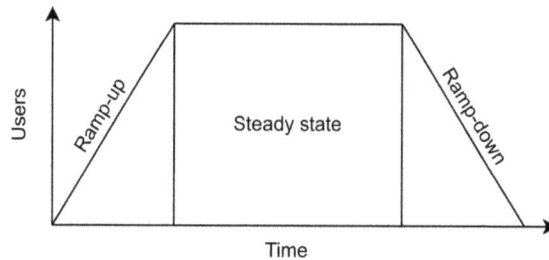

Figure 10.3: Typical expected usage load of users over time

Once we have the model defined, we understand which users we address, and how we expect them to behave, we can build our test, configure our testing tool (as demonstrated with JMeter), execute the tests against our designated environment, and analyze the results.

In conclusion, transforming a workload model into scenario mapping involves a detailed understanding and accurate simulation of user behavior and system interactions. By following these steps, we can ensure that our performance tests are realistic and provide valuable insights into how our system performs under different conditions.

Environment preparation

The importance of a proper test environment cannot be emphasized enough. A test environment is where we can experiment, test, crash, try new applications, modules, features, components, or even train new users. Specifically, for performance and load tests, it would be best to test our system in a realistic environment, which is as close as possible to the live production one. This is easier said than done, as we may encounter organizational, technological, or security challenges. Not every organization would invest in a full-blown live environment with all its bells and whistles, and in a test environment with the same scale and magnitude. We usually would not expect the same number of servers, bandwidth, and networking features, or database sizes on the test environment to match those of the production environment. This is also not easy to maintain, in order to keep close to the real production environment.

It is not impossible to run certain **tests** and checks in production, but this is definitely not recommended, even if the system is not in use outside its commonly loaded hours; the risk is just too big. In general, a production environment should not be meddled with at all. We could consider a few options for our test environment:

- **The least probable scenario**: A copy of the production environment. The best scenario, but hard to achieve and maintain, heavy, expensive, and time-consuming.

- **The intermediate solution**: A carved-out part of the production environment. Not to include everything, but with those relevant parts that we deem relevant for our tests kept as faithful to the original setup as possible. This will still give a somewhat reliable result when running load and performance tests.

- **The most common budget-setup**: A lower specs (mostly partial) copy of the production environment. Less servers, less components, and/or components of lower specs. This will most probably not give reliable results in terms of performance, as results may be far from the ones on a full production setup.

When preparing and building our test environment, we should be careful and take sufficient time to work on a reliable environment that is both isolated and resembles our production environment as much as possible.

Production vs. performance test environments

A few aspects to keep in mind, while on the topic of test environment are some common differentiators between the live production environment, and the one meant for testing, as those differences can significantly impact the accuracy and relevance of our test results.

Production environment

The production environment is where the actual end-users interact with the application. It is the live environment where the application is deployed for real-world use. Some important characteristics to keep in mind:

- **Real data**: Probably the most important thing to note. The production databases contain real user data and transactions. Those are at the core of our system, so we should be extra careful with them. Running manual queries against a production database is extremely sensitive.

- **Full scale and live traffic.** The live environment operates at full scale with the expected number of concurrent users and workloads. Real servers, services, allocations, provisions, actions. They are all alive and in use by real users, interacting and sending requests.

- **High availability.** Not always, but in the great majority of cases, the production environment is typically configured for high availability, redundancy, and reliability. It is not expected to go down, crash, or be unavailable.

- **Security.** As our project's portal to the world, it is implemented with full security measures to protect user data and privacy, as per our requirements.

As can be inferred from those characteristics, the pros of the production environment are in the context of performance measurements, observability, and data collection. It is the real deal. It is accurate, and shows real actual performance metrics, as it reflects real user interactions and behaviors.

The workload is realistic. Tests that are executed are of the actual system under actual normal usage conditions.

However, we should be extremely careful with it and mind the cons:

- **Risk of disruption**: Performance testing in production can disrupt live users and affect the business. In physics, we speak about the observer effect in the double-slit experiment, which entails the alteration of the behavior of particles (e.g., electrons) when they are being measured and observed. Here, in a very different way, but matching effect, when we take measurements in an effort to improve performance, we actually disrupt it and skew the results.

- **Limited testing scenarios**: This cannot be emphasized enough; be careful with the live environment. We cannot test everything freely. It is difficult to simulate extreme conditions without affecting real users, and one wrong click can have disastrous consequences.

Performance test environment

The performance test environment is a dedicated setup that mimics the production environment for the purpose of testing the application's performance under controlled conditions. In contrast to the production environment, it is:

- **Isolated setup**: Any test environment is isolated and separate from the production environment to avoid any impact on live users.

- **Controlled data**: In a test environment, we would not have real production data. Instead, we would normally use synthetic or anonymized data for testing. This is good, because we can tweak the data to match specific scenarios we would want to test (for example, synthetically create a huge database and see how it behaves), but also bad, because it does not always reflect reality.

- **Scalable setup and similar configuration**: The test environment would be configured to simulate different levels of load and stress conditions, again, try to mimic the real world. We would also ideally mirror the production environment in terms of hardware, software, network configurations, and data volume. As much as possible, that is.

The advantages taken by the test environment are a mirror image of the disadvantages of testing the production environment:

- **Safe for testing**: We can conduct extensive tests without affecting real users.

- **Flexible and repeatable**: We can simulate various load conditions, including peak loads and edge cases. Tests can be repeated under the same conditions to compare results.

Some cons to bear in mind, however, are mostly of cost and accuracy:

- Maintaining a separate environment can be expensive.
- Differences from the production environment can lead to less accurate performance predictions.

Test environment considerations

In order to ensure the quality and reliability of our tests, there are some aspects we may want to consider:

- Ensure the test environment closely mirrors the production environment. This includes hardware specifications, network configurations, software versions, and data volumes.
- Use realistic data that mimics production data in terms of volume, structure, and characteristics. Anonymize sensitive data to comply with privacy regulations.
- Accurately simulate user workload patterns, including peak usage times and concurrent user sessions. Use tools like JMeter, LoadRunner, or Gatling to generate the required load.
- Monitor system resources such as CPU, memory, disk I/O, and network bandwidth during testing. Use monitoring tools to capture detailed performance metrics.
- Test the system's ability to scale under increased load. This includes both vertical scaling (adding more resources to existing machines) and horizontal scaling (adding more machines).
- Simulate failure scenarios such as server crashes, network outages, and database failures to test the system's resilience and recovery mechanisms.
- Implement necessary security measures to protect the test environment, especially if it contains sensitive data or is accessible from outside the organization.

Performance testing tools

In this section, we will look at some of the considerations for choosing a specific test tool or framework to measure our performance. We will also look at a few real-world popular tool examples.

The right tool for the job

We have explored a few performance measurement and test tools from different angles and needs, both in this and in previous chapters. Choosing the right tool involves evaluating several factors to ensure the tool aligns with our project's specific requirements and constraints.

- **Project requirements**:
  - **Matching the tool to our application**: Most basically, choosing a matched tool to our technology. Whether it is web-based, mobile, desktop, or a combination, some tools are better suited for specific types of applications.
  - **Matching the tool to the used protocols**: We should ensure the tool supports the protocols our application uses (e.g., HTTP, HTTPS, FTP, SOAP, REST, or specific services such as LDAP, SMTP, FTP, SSH, etc.).
- **Methods for measuring scalability and performance**:
  - **Assessing our workload simulation**: We consider how many virtual users the tool should be able to simulate. Our choice should be able to handle the expected number of concurrent users.
  - **Assessing how our tool affects resources**: We assess a tool's impact on system resources during testing to avoid false positives due to tool-induced bottlenecks.
- **Ease of use per user type**: As we have seen, there are various options for producing workload and performance tests using a tool like JMeter. The right tool should fit whoever uses it. A manual QA engineer who is not specialized in coding may prefer UI interaction, while a test automation engineer or a developer may be more comfortable with the flexibility of programmatically doing everything.
  - **UI**: Not all tools support it, but a tool with an intuitive and user-friendly interface can significantly reduce the learning curve, and suit people who are not seasoned or feel comfortable with code.
  - **Scripting**: We evaluate the ease of creating and maintaining test scripts. Some may use a proprietary language or with declarative scripts.
  - **Record/replay**: That is another capability not all tools have, but this may be beneficial and cut development times. The ability to record activity with all its parameters, settings, and customizations, producing test cases we can easily adapt and replay, is a comfortable hybrid between intuitive UI generation and scripting.
- **Integration and extensibility**: Our tests do not run in a vacuum. We may want to consider what we can connect our tool with.
  - **CI/CD integration**: It is not the worst idea to use CI/CD pipelines and ensure the tool integrates seamlessly with our existing DevOps tools, so we can trigger tests before, during, or after deployment.

    Again, eventually, CI/CD tools run pipeline scripts (either declarative scripts or programmatic ones), and many natively use isolated containers, in which we can run pretty much any custom tool, including any performance test tool, and with that, our scripts, too. But a native easy integration through a native pre-built plugin of a CI/CD tool, such as Jenkins or Microsoft Azure DevOps, may help make the integration smoother and easier.

- o **Plugins and extensions**: Another useful consideration is whether the tool supports plugins or extensions that can enhance its functionality or adapt it to specific needs. JMeter may be a powerful Swiss-Army knife, but there may always be a feature missing.

- **Reporting and analysis**:
  - o **Real-time monitoring**: A useful capability is monitoring and reporting during tests.
  - o **Detailed reports**: Customizable detailed reports that can help identify performance bottlenecks and other issues.
  - o **Dashboarding and integration**: Some tools, like JMeter, feature integration with dashboards and external systems to get a detailed, versatile overview of their measurements and results.

- **Community and support**: One of the reasons to use a popular tool, is its community back. Things like documentation and tutorials, community support (mostly for open tools), and/or vendor support (for commercial tools) help to get up to speed with the tool of your choice, and learn about its best practices, features, and capabilities, including ones that are less trivial.

- **Cost and licensing**: For choosing any dev tool, we should consider budget constraints. Open-source tools like Apache JMeter and Gatling can be cost-effective, while commercial tools like LoadRunner and NeoLoad might offer more features but at a higher cost.

  Understanding the licensing model of the tool is also important. Some tools charge based on the number of virtual users, while others might have a subscription-based pricing model.

Mentionable performance testing tools

Following is a list of a few popular performance testing tools that are worth mentioning and knowing:

- **Apache JMeter**: As it is mentioned throughout this chapter, it is first on the list, also, for being one of the most popular open-source performance testing tools. As mentioned in detail in the previous section, it was initially designed for web applications, but it has evolved to test a wide range of applications and service types.

- **BlazeMeter**: BlazeMeter is a cloud-based load-testing platform that is fully compatible with Apache JMeter test scripts. It is capable of running tests from multiple cloud locations. It supports detailed real-time reporting and analysis, with high scalability to simulate thousands of users.

It is ideal for cloud-based load testing and for teams that are already using JMeter.

- **LoadRunner**: Another popular tool of choice is LoadRunner, developed by MicroFocus (currently OpenText). It is a comprehensive performance testing tool used by enterprises to test system behavior and performance. It comes with its own UI and is suitable for large-scale performance testing of applications across multiple protocols and complex environments.

  Among its features are protocol variety - supporting over 50 protocols, including web, mobile, database, and legacy systems, the scalable capability of simulating millions of users, detailed performance analysis, and reporting capabilities.

- **Gatling**: Gatling is an open-source load and performance testing framework based on Scala, Akka, and Netty. It is optimized for high performance and scalability, providing real-time metrics and reports. Based on the Scala programming language, Gatling's test scripts are written in Scala, which makes it a powerful programming tool that allows users to write complex test scenarios and logic. Since the release of version 3.7 in 2021, Gatling has supported Java in the bundled version and via plugins for Maven and Gradle.

  It supports easy integration with CI/CD pipelines and is considered a good choice for continuous integration and continuous delivery workflows, and for applications requiring high performance and scalability.

- **Neoload**: NeoLoad is a powerful performance testing tool designed for enterprises and supports large-scale load testing. It is built to simulate realistic user behavior and provides comprehensive performance metrics and analysis. It has seamless integrations with DevOps toolchains and is considered good for enterprise-level performance testing with a focus on realistic user behavior and DevOps integration.

Selecting the right performance testing tool requires a thorough understanding of our project's needs and constraints. By considering factors such as the type of application, scalability, ease of use, integration, reporting, support, and cost, we can choose a tool that will effectively help us identify and address performance issues. Whether we opt for open-source tools like Apache JMeter and Gatling, or commercial solutions like LoadRunner and NeoLoad, the key is to ensure the tool aligns with our specific performance testing objectives.

Performance testing best practices

Some ground rules that keep coming up when discussing performance testing best practices are: **test everything that is relevant** (although **local tests** of specific features and **controlled load** can help detect bottlenecks and issues in advance), **test early**, and **test often**.

The sooner we start testing, we will get a better picture of our performance status, which will help us establish a baseline of our status in order to see later improvements or regressions.

There is an infinite number of best practices for performance testing.

With everything mentioned in this chapter, we would conclude a few more base best practices, which basically boil down to: keep your tests real. Make them reflect reality as much as possible, so that we can learn from them how our system really behaves.

The following are a few points to note when planning performance tests:

- Set up an effective performance testing environment. That is, to mimic the production environment as much as possible.

- Strategically outline, design, and plan the tests. Performance metrics should align with business goals and predefined requirements, and tests should match those in order to validate the state of the system in relation to expectations. Workload models should also be considered accordingly.

- Test data should also be considered seriously. It should be kept consistent and realistic as much as possible, in order for the tests to reflect reality.

- Choose the right tool for the job (see *The right tool for the job* in the previous section). Take into account all the proper considerations, in order to maximize the benefit of the tests and their results.

- Follow on results over time. Make sure to keep track of performance regressions and issues ahead of time (that is, before the customer complains about them), and achieve continuous improvement.

Conclusion

In this chapter, we kick-started performance tests, from definition to execution, on a properly set test environment, outline its characteristics and our test tools, and look at JMeter as a versatile example.

In the next chapter, we will look further into automated tests, and discuss test data, how to define it, prepare it, and use it for our tests.

Key learnings

- We listed the main tasks to include in system analysis, building a test plan, test execution, and reporting.

- We discussed the aspects of automated test script development: various kinds of automated tests to be built for different needs.

- We learned about JMeter, what it is, what are its useful features, and how it works.
- We listed the properties of various performance test tools, the criteria to choose the right one for the right needs, and a few popular ones.
- We learned about workload modeling, and how they are combined with test scenarios.
- We learned about test environment preparation, the differences between the test and production environments, and what we need to know in order to set it up.

Join our book's Discord space

Join the book's Discord Workspace for Latest updates, Offers, Tech happenings around the world, New Release and Sessions with the Authors:

https://discord.bpbonline.com

CHAPTER 11
Test Data Management

Introduction

Performance testing simulates the real-world usage pattern in lower regions, and it is important to run the simulation with a unique set of users to avoid caching and backend contention and observe the actual production system behavior in the performance test region.

Test data management (**TDM**) is, in fact, a critical aspect of software development and testing that involves the creation, provisioning, and maintenance of data sets used for testing applications. The goal of TDM is to ensure that the test data accurately reflects real-world scenarios while maintaining data privacy and security. Effective TDM practices help organizations streamline their testing processes, improve test coverage, and enhance the quality of their software. By managing test data efficiently, teams can reduce the time and effort required for testing, minimize the risk of defects in production, and ensure compliance with data protection regulations.

This chapter details the approach to define the various characteristics aligned to the business use case with the right mixture, as well as the strategy to set up that data in the systems for usage.

Structure

This chapter contains the following topics:

- Test data requirement definition
- Test data characteristic classification
- Strategy to setup test data
- Test data clean-up and reuse
- Service virtualization
- Automation
- Data security

Objectives

In this chapter, we detail how test data is managed, created, handled, and secured. The concept of test data is sometimes taken for granted, or not minded enough, while, in fact, TDM is a field in its own right. We will introduce the concepts, definitions, strategies, security measures, and automation tools involved.

Test data requirement definition

As part of our setup for testing the behavior of our application and setting up the conditions to simulate real scenarios, we need to process data accordingly, too. Preparing data for automated tests involves generating and organizing data sets that accurately reflect real-world scenarios and usage patterns. This process includes creating realistic test data, anonymizing sensitive information, and ensuring data consistency and completeness. Tools and scripts are often used to automate data generation and seeding into databases, enabling the replication of various conditions the application might encounter. Proper data preparation is crucial for reliable and efficient automated testing, helping to identify potential issues and validate performance under expected workloads.

The data used in performance testing must closely mirror real-world usage to provide meaningful insights into how our application will perform in a production environment. In this section, we list some considerations and principles for defining performance test data requirements.

- **Understand the application and its data**: The structure of the data. First and foremost, we need to understand the application's data model, including database schema, data types, relationships, and constraints.
  - o **Usage of the data**: Analyze how users interact with the application to determine data creation, modification, and deletion patterns.

o **The volume of the data**: Estimate the amount of data typically stored and processed by the application in production.

- **Identify data requirements for different scenarios**: Different performance test scenarios may require different types of data. Key scenarios were already mentioned in previous chapters, including:

    o **Load testing**: Requires a volume of data that mimics the expected production load.

    o **Stress testing**: May require even larger volumes of data to push the system to its limits.

    o **Endurance testing**: Needs data that supports long-duration tests to check for issues like memory leaks.

    o **Spike testing**: Requires data that can handle sudden increases in load.

- **Define data characteristics**: Here, we need to address characteristics such as the amount of data (volume) required to simulate real-world conditions (This includes the number of records in databases, file sizes, and other relevant metrics), the inclusion of different types of data (variety) the application will handle, such as text, numbers, images, and multimedia files, data distribution, including a mix of common, rare, and edge-case data, data relationships and interdependencies, and referential integrity to simulate realistic interactions within the database.

- **Data sources**: Here we define the various sources where our test data can come from. That may be:

    o **Production data**: If allowed, we use (preferably anonymized) production data to get the most realistic test data. Ensure compliance with data privacy and security regulations.

    o **Synthetic data**: Synthetically generated data, that mimics production data patterns. We use data generation tools to create realistic and varied data sets. The benefit is that we can make an infinite amount of synthetic pseudo-data.

    o **Hybrid**: We may combine production and synthetic data to ensure a comprehensive and realistic data set.

- **Data preparation**: Depending on the source of our data, we need to prepare it for testing.

    If we use production data, we would most probably need to anonymize or mask sensitive information to protect privacy and comply with regulations.

    If we use synthetically generated data, we would need to utilize the tools to automate the creation of large volumes of test data. Tools like **JMeter**, **Data Factory**, and others may help generate realistic data sets.

    Depending on the generated data, we may need to write scripts to seed databases and other data stores with the required volume and variety of test data. That is, in order for our application to run tests on prepopulated data stores, containing our test data.

- **Data maintenance**: It is also important to maintain our data to keep it relevant. We should regularly refresh the test data, to ensure it remains relevant and reflects any changes in the application or its usage patterns and reflect changes in production.

  We should also implement procedures to clean up test data after tests are completed to maintain an optimal test environment.

Test data characteristics classification

In the previous section, we listed some of the aspects and considerations we need to account for when defining our test data and briefly mentioned the characteristics of the data classification. In this section, we will zoom in on some characteristics of our data. By considering factors such as volume, variety, complexity, distribution, lifecycle, quality, volume-to-variety ratio, sensitivity, and state, we can ensure that our data sets are realistic and cover a wide range of scenarios. This thorough approach helps identify potential performance issues and ensures that the application can handle real-world conditions efficiently and reliably.

Garbage in, garbage out: About data quality

Probably the most important characteristic of our data. At the core of our application's processing, persisting, runtime, and results sits its data. The quality of our tests relies, among other factors, on the quality of our test data. The commonly used expression **Garbage in, garbage out** relates to how our program responds to data. Feed your application biased or poor-quality data; it will produce a result of similar quality.

Especially with synthetically generated data, which can be anything we want it to be, and as big as we want it to be, it is important to produce it fast but also with sufficient quality results.

We would want to make sure our data is diverse, valid, and relevant for our tests (this does not mean that every test should pass, of course. It is important to test edge cases and invalid cases just as well). We should test with both valid data (Correct and logically accurate, which represents typical, expected input) and invalid data (Incorrect or logically inconsistent data used to test the system's validation and error-handling capabilities).

Additional data characteristics

In addition to paying attention to data quality, here are a few other properties to note and keep in mind:

- **Data volume**: Here, we consider the size of our dataset, which depends on the type of test we perform.

- o **High volume data**: To be used to simulate heavy loads and stress the system to identify performance limits.

  - o **Low volume small datasets**: Usually used for basic functionality tests and to ensure that even minimal data conditions are handled correctly.

- **Data variety and complexity**: Here, we consider the types and structures of data that we test through in order to address different test cases and scenarios, and partially in order to address varied cases and see how the system handles them.

  We use different data types, such as text, numbers, dates, multimedia files, etc., and varied data structures, including structured (e.g., databases), semi-structured (e.g., JSON, XML), and unstructured data (e.g., images, videos).

  The complexity of the data also varies. From simple data, which is straightforward and isolated, used for testing basic operations and functions, to large, complex data, interrelated and multi-faceted data that tests the system's handling of complex interactions and dependencies.

- **Data distribution**: Here, we address the property of distribution and normalization of our data. That is, how our data varies in size, load, and other characteristics. With **uniform distribution**, data is distributed evenly to test consistent performance across the system. But data distribution can be **skewed** and distributed unevenly to test how the system handles peaks and variations in load.

  This depends on our test strategy and the types of scenarios we wish to address.

- **Data lifecycle**: Evaluating whether our data changes, evolves, or grows. Our data may be static, unchanging, and remain constant throughout the tests, to provide baseline performance metrics. In some cases, we would want to use dynamic data, which is continuously changing, that may sometimes simulate real-time user interactions and updates.

- **Data sensitivity**: It is crucial to be aware of sensitive data, especially if we rely on real production data. Sensitive data that includes personal or confidential information requires anonymization and secure handling, while non-sensitive data does not pose privacy or security risks.

Strategy to setup test data

Talking about the characteristics of test data and how to create the right data for the right tests, in theory, is all nice and good. It is easy, if we know the project, its expected performance, weak points, potential bugs, edge cases, and other produced test cases, to come up with proper test data that follows our needs. But as the known proverb of the modern world says, in theory - there is no difference between theory and practice, but in practice, there is. Things are seldom so easy and simple.

Test data management

Our fast-paced DevOps world of automation, frequent changes, automated deployments, and ever-continuous delivery are not easy to keep up with. Testers must make fast decisions too, detect issues, and respond to them quickly. We are talking about highly complex systems, with complex distributed components and lots of moving parts, which get deployed and change frequently, for which our tests, as well as our test data, need to adjust in order to accommodate.

In contrast, sometimes we deal with legacy systems, where data is difficult to pull out, or sometimes inaccessible at all due to restrictions and policies.

TDM is the process by which we get the data in order to evaluate our application's needs, requirements, performance, and behavior. Regardless of the source of the data, be it pulled from the actual production sources (and processed appropriately), or synthetically generated. TDM may involve all relevant parties: developers, testers, data experts, security experts, DevOps, governance and compliance stakeholders, and others.

As part of our process, we would want to detect and fix bugs as early as possible. The sooner we detect issues, the less costly it will be. The later in the process we handle bugs, it is believed and sometimes mentioned that the trend of the effort cost of fixing them rises at an exponential rate, in relation to the development timeline progress. Bugs and issues, performance misbehaviors, and crashes detected when the product is already in production can cost a whole lot (that is the exact figure) of money, time, and effort to fix. With large service and product companies, millions of dollars.

This movement of adopting tests and remedies as early as possible, sometimes referred to as shift-left, was already mentioned here in *Chapter 2, Performance Driven Development*.

The **Gartner hype cycle** is a graphical presentation developed, used, and branded by the American research, advisory, and information technology firm Gartner to represent the maturity, adoption, and social application of specific technologies. The hype cycle claims to provide a graphical and conceptual presentation of the maturity of emerging technologies through five phases. Gartner is the world's biggest firm in this field, and one of the most influential ones. Due to its size, scale, and magnitude, many companies see Gartner and the business analytical information and reports it publishes as a reliable global compass of trends.

The graph below is Gartner's hype cycle for Agile and DevOps for the year 2022, showing the level of expectations from a trend or technology on the Y axis, and the progression of the five key phases of a technology's life cycle, as it becomes hyped, to the point of becoming a productive and usable (given the picturesque metaphoric names **technology trigger, peak of inflated expectations, trough of disillusionment, slope of enlightenment and plateau of productivity**) on the X axis. The idea is to show how emerging technologies and tools evolve on their path to becoming mainstream and relevant.

The first stage **technology trigger** is where it gets introduced, then as the expectations from the new technology rise, it heads up towards the **peak of inflated expectations**. After the boom of the expectations peak, the hype usually goes down, as more and more organizations adopt the hyped technology, while going down the **trough of disillusionment**, where they realize whether the hype was justified, and whether they should keep using it. The ones that survive the drop of disillusionment continue to the **slope of enlightenment**, where further development and experiments are conducted, until the technology becomes mainstream and widely adopted productively, onto the **plateau of productivity**.

In the 2022 graph given in *Figure 11.1*, we can see **DevOps TDM** is not only included, but at the very peak of expectations. Marking it as an emerging technologically important subject. This was also a marker for many companies to pay attention to TDM and consider adopting it.

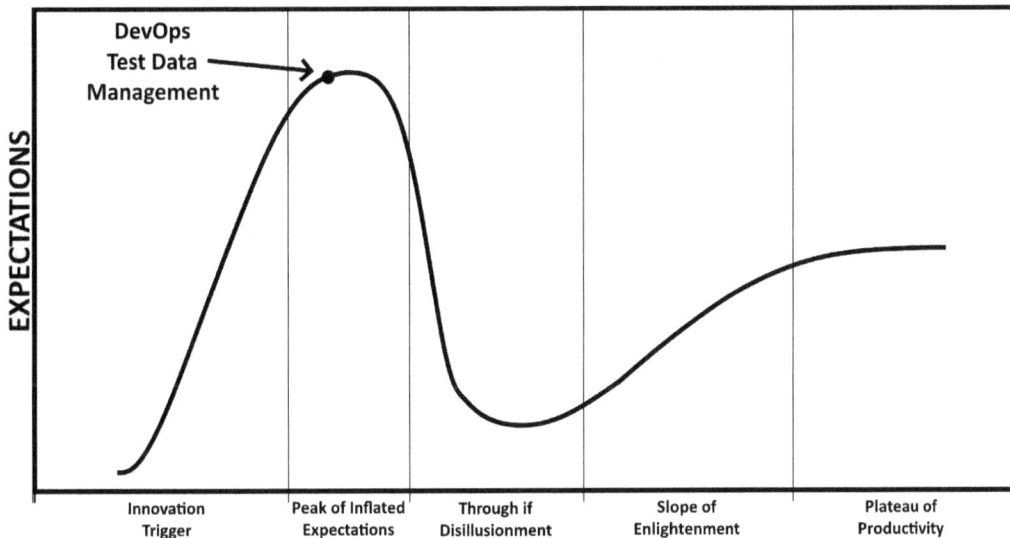

Figure 11.1: *Test data management in the peak of rising technologies in 2022*

In the following year, 2023, we see that TDM has passed the peak and is now entering the **trough of disillusionment**, which means it passed the big hype, and now the technology/ field needs to actually prove itself in order to stay relevant.

HypeCycle for Agile and DevOps 2023

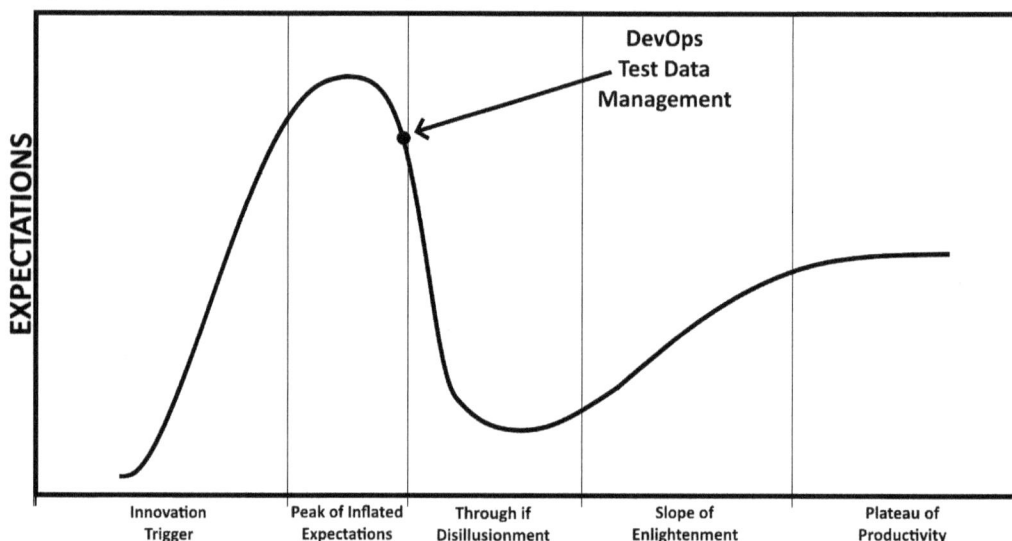

Figure 11.2: *Test data management on the path to disillusionment in 2023*

> **Note: Gartner's graphs and info are proprietary, so we only included an exact copy of the graph representation and the position of the DevOps TDM item on each. At the time this chapter is written, there are no conclusions for 2024 as of yet, but it is clear that TDM is still very relevant, being used and developed, as it remains a necessary tool for testing complex systems.**

Relying on production data

Our production environment runs our actual stable product and has all the needed data. Why don't we just take the data from there?

Without proper tools in place, the process of relying on production data is lengthy and complex. We have to extract data from production sources, make a copy of it, and map the relationships; then, we would most probably have to scrub, anonymize, clean, format, sanitize, or mask the data and transfer it to our **dev/test/staging** environments. Additionally, we expect test data to be specific, consistent, compliant, sufficient, etc. The data may come from different sources, relying on different technologies and environments.

Test data warehouse

A different strategy for TDM is to use a large central data store, which contains all the necessary data, for all the application's needs, both for production runtime and for testing. Putting all the data in one place has its complexities, but with that we gain consistency and use of holistic features of the warehouse, such as central management, data subsetting, masking, uniform integration, data versioning and archiving, and more.

Synthesized data

Working around the difficulties of dealing with production data, which is usually large, sensitive, secure, and contains private information, is to produce our own data. Production information is also biased, as it reflects cases of current users and their usage cases, and is not guaranteed to contain data with wide variety and diversity, while synthetically generated data can contain any desirable data for any test cases we may need or desire, real or not. The data creation is driven by sets of predefined rules that copy our production data, logic, definitions, relations, and conditions.

We do not jeopardize, expose, or risk production data; we can produce as much data as we want in order to test any type of system load, any use case, and any test case.

Synthetic data can be generated with automated tools, based on rule logic, or by machine learning, which uses algorithms to learn patterns and relationships of our original data, and generate new test data based on those learned patterns. This involves training a machine-learning model on our original dataset. Besides the complexities of training a model properly, this method has its own challenges, such as we would still need access to production data, but we can create tons of realistic, rich, and compliant data based on what we had trained our model on. Machine-learning data is all nice and good, but one more crucial point, is that it has to be trained on preexisting data. New features, for which there is no data yet, cannot be processed, and no data can be generated for them in this way. Same is true for uncovered test cases, such as negative tests, as such data probably does not exist in our data store.

Test data clean-up and reuse

As can be inferred already, test data and TDM are serious business, regardless of how the data was fetched, copied, modified, generated, or made up. Data is at the core of our system, and test data is a big part of the test setup and our test environment. There are quite some pitfalls along the way, and we definitely should plan and use them wisely. But at the end of the test cycle, a strategy for handling the data afterwards is important to have. In the 21st century, we are all in favor of recycling and reusing. Reusing and recycling our test data means using the same, or similar, test data for different test cases, scenarios, or cycles. This helps save time, resources, and costs of creating new test data.

Cleaning up and reusing test data effectively requires a combination of automated tools, strategic planning, and robust processes. By implementing automated cleanup scripts, tagging data, using archiving solutions, and setting up isolated environments, organizations can maintain clean and efficient test environments. For data reuse, techniques like data pooling, versioning, subsetting, and parameterization help maximize the value of existing data sets, saving time and resources while ensuring consistent and comprehensive testing.

Proper data management not only enhances testing efficiency but also contributes to maintaining high data quality and compliance with regulatory standards. Some techniques and methods to achieve this efficiently include:

- **Automated cleanup scripts**: For data cleanup, we can produce scripts to automate the process of identifying and deleting obsolete or expired test data, or we can use database management tools to automate cleanup tasks, such as SQL scripts for purging old data and restoring the data to its initial state.

- **Tagging and metadata, data versioning, and snapshots**: We can assign tags or metadata to test data to indicate its purpose, creation date, and expiration date, facilitating easier identification for cleanup. With that, we can implement lifecycle management policies to automatically remove or archive data based on its age or usage.

  Taking snapshots of our test data (and/or our test environment) at specific points in time, may allow quick restoration and reuse of data. Implementing version control for test data, to track changes and manage different versions of data for various testing scenarios, can also help us quickly reset our data to its initial/ previous/any desired state.

- **Scheduled cleanup jobs**: Automated scheduled jobs can be triggered to run cleanup scripts at regular intervals, ensuring that test environments remain clean. Another option is to integrate cleanup tasks into CI/CD pipelines to automatically clean up data after test executions.

- **Data archival**: Archiving important essential data, which is infrequently used, to archival storage, reducing the active dataset size while retaining access to historical data. With that, we can use cost-effective storage solutions for archived data, such as cloud-based storage with infrequent access.

- **Environment isolation**: Dedicated environments isolating test data or schemas simplify cleanup without affecting other datasets. We can segment data by project, team, or test type to ensure that only relevant data is cleaned up.

- **Data templates and parameterization**: Data templates of our common data structures or test scenarios that can be quickly populated with actual data for reuse can help accelerate data reuse. Similarly, we can use parameterization to create flexible and adaptable data sets that can be reused across multiple test cases with different inputs.

- **Data subsets and masking**: Subsetting the data, we can create smaller, representative parts of large datasets to use in different tests, reducing the need to recreate data. If the data contains sensitive information, we apply masking to protect sensitive information in reusable data sets, ensuring compliance with data privacy regulations.

Service virtualization

One strategy to lower the scale and efforts of large-system testing is service virtualization. In the following sections, we will briefly introduce this concept.

Principle

When we want to minimize our tests without reducing the results, we can consider virtual services over real, full-blown ones. We mentioned unit testing in the past, which mostly uses simulated mocked responses or mocked modules in order to test just one specific unit of code and see how it behaves in various scenarios. Service virtualization has a similar, larger-scale purpose.

Regardless of whether our application relies on microservice architecture or not, there will always be APIs and external services to communicate with. External services can be developed internally or externally; they may not even be operational or ready for testing yet, they may be offline, or maybe not in an optimal setup for us to test our module's behavior and performance. We would still want to test it somehow.

Service virtualization allows us to emulate the runtime of our dependent systems and services. It allows us to control the behavior, the test data, and the performance characteristics. Our tested component still runs as it should, not minding that it is actually communicating with a virtualized isolated service, while, in fact, we run a controlled slice of the entire system, not needing a whole robust test environment. The data is also managed here; we slice up our test data just to what our tested piece needs.

The simplified diagram below demonstrates how our tested service can run on our test environment, or a dedicated test machine, against virtual services, and a specifically reduced test dataset (left), rather than spinning up and deploying the entire array of services, databases, and replicating the entire production setup (right).

With that, we can eliminate the complexities of setting up an entire test environment for any need; we can create virtualized containerized services, even in the realm of our CI/CD pipeline, and test right in there. This helps us get to much more streamlined continuous testing, which is much more lightweight, adaptable, and independent of external factors. It also cuts the dependency on environment access, and security restrictions.

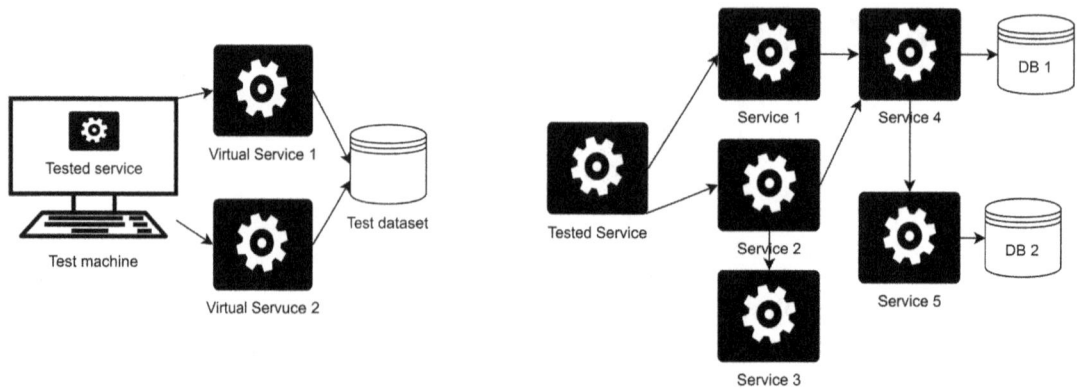

Figure 11.3: *Virtualized service testing vs. full test environment (reduced example)*

Benefits

Benefits of virtualized services include:

- Fully test software and detect defects earlier, using virtual data that covers every possible scenario.
- Avoid project delays by simulating unavailable or incomplete components.
- Create stable environments for API testing, free from system dependencies and constraints.
- Provide distributed and outsourced teams with parallel access to the secure environments they need.
- Drastically reduce pre-production infrastructure costs and avoid the risk of costly data breaches.
- Expose virtual data to distributed test and development teams in parallel and on demand.

Automation

TDM tools are large and complex, handling the abundance of tasks of creating the data (copying it from production or other data sources, or synthetically producing it), and processing it, manipulating it, securing it, with features like masking, data tokenization, and synthetic data generation. Of course, with all these required features, by automating data management and maintenance, automation tools ensure that our testing is conducted accurately and efficiently. This reduces the time and resources required for testing and increases overall efficiency by facilitating data sharing among team members.

In general, we would look for tools that are capable of fulfilling the base requirements:

- Provision data from one or more sources. Extract data from whichever data sources we need. Alternately, it produces its own data artificially.

- Subsetting of the data, to be able to slice just what's important for our tests.
- Masking/anonymizing the data for improved security.
- Transform the data, with arbitrary rules, to match the test cases and requirements.

With that, many tools offer additional, more advanced features.

Large-scale tooling

In contrast to other areas of automation, TDM tools are mostly robust and costly, and aimed for enterprise scale usage. Tools such as **IBM InfoSphere Optim TDM**, **CA Test Data Manager**, and **Solix Enterprise Data Management Suite**, are wide suites with elaborate features such as data management at the business level, data analysis capabilities, data management policies enforcement, synthetic data generation, data synchronization, date masking and complex data manipulation options, and other capabilities, as per the tool.

Much like we have seen with observability frameworks, enterprise-grade tests data management tools provide a wide, end-to-end experience, are usually backed up by big brands (see above, for example, IBM and CA), and come packed with strong features, easy to integrate, and supported as services by large cloud platforms too.

Open options

The second option is to use free/open-source tools built for data/test-data management. In contrast to the large-scale tools, the open-source options usually suffer from common deficiencies. Open-source tools tend to focus on one aspect of the TDM funnel. Some tools help teams create synthetic data, while others may focus on data anonymization. However, no single tool is an end-to-end TDM solution. Single-function offerings may seem tempting as a short-term fix, but they end up costing plenty in the long run.

They also tend to have less support and maintenance (depending on the community and contributors) and, at times, a steeper learning curve, both for usability and integration. On the flip side, they are free (depending on the usage license).

Databucket is an open-source, Java-based, Docker container-powered TDM tool made to work with PostgreSQL and MySQL/MariaDB databases. It delivers features to effectively create and maintain test data and metadata for extensive tests on multiple projects, environments, and various integrated tools at the same time. Databucket stores data in elastic structures, which gives a ready approach to maintaining constantly changing test data in the software development process.

A more targeted tool may be **Faker**, which is a Python-based, data generation library. It can bootstrap a database, create good-looking XML documents, fill in data for stress tests, and anonymize data taken from a production service.

Jailer is a Java-based tool, for database subsetting and data anonymization. It allows the creation of smaller, meaningful subsets of our data, as described earlier. It also offers data masking capabilities to protect sensitive information. It supports a wide range of database systems and is particularly useful for projects that require selective data extraction.

There are many other such tools and libraries, some more targeted and focused than others, it is up to automation experts to decide what suits their needs and budget best.

Self developed scripts

Another option, for smaller scale work, or for less costly projects, is **Bring Your Own Script** (**BYOS**), that is to build our own data handling scripts. This provides flexibility and is specifically built to accommodate our product's datastores and schemas but requires significant effort to develop properly.

It could be, of course, a hybrid solution between a robust tool, like **DATAPROF**, a code library like **Faker**, and a custom script written for the job.

As a simple example of test data automation, we will use the Python code below, with the popular **Faker** library, to generate and insert test data. Our test data resides in a local *MariaDB* database.

In order to connect the Python code to the MariaDB database, we will be using the standard **mysql** client connector Python library. The code inserts 1,000 dummy test records into the **employees** table, which has six columns:

- **emp_no** (employee number, a unique integer)
- **first_name** (first name, a string)
- **last_name** (last name, a string)
- **gender** (gender, an enumerated string, which contains either M or F)
- **birth_date** and **hire_date** (both are date fields, that can be populated with a typical yyyy-mm-dd string)

The code is super simple, lightweight, and easy to use and understand. It first initializes a Faker instance with a hard-coded seed, which is used for its randomization.

Then it establishes a connection to the local database named **employees**, running on the **localhost** server (127.0.0.1) on the standard port 3306, with user **root**, and password **password**.

The next part is a **for** loop of 1000 iterations, running from 0 to 999. Each iteration runs an SQL **INSERT** statement, to insert a single record into the table.

> Note: Before the cursor.execute operation is run, the fake object generates all the data: valid first names, last names, M or F genders, and dates.

After the 1000 iterations loop is finished, the SQL operations get committed to the database, and the connection is closed.

```python
import mysql.connector
from mysql.connector import Error
from faker import Faker

# Initialize the faker object
Faker.seed(33422)
fake = Faker()

# Connect to the local MariaDB database
conn = mysql.connector.connect(
    host="127.0.0.1",
    database="employees",
    user="root",
    password="password",
    auth_plugin="mysql_native_password",
    ssl_disabled=True
)
cursor = conn.cursor()

# Insert fake records!
for i in range(1000):
    firstname = fake.first_name()
    lastname = fake.last_name()
    gender = fake.random_element(["M", "F"])
    date_of_birth = fake.date_of_birth()
    hire_date = fake.date()

    print(f"Inserting[{i}]: {firstname} {lastname}")
    cursor.execute('insert into employees (\
            emp_no, \
            first_name, \
            last_name, \
            gender, \
            birth_date, \
            hire_date\
```

```
        ) \
    values (%s, \'%s\', \'%s\', \'%s\', \'%s\', \'%s\')' \
            %(i, \
                firstname, \
                lastname,
                gender, \
                date_of_birth, \
                hire_date
                )
        )

# Commit the operations, and close the connection
conn.commit()
conn.close()
```

Running the code is simple and straightforward, and prints out the 1000 names of the employees that were inserted (on each loop iteration, the print statement outputs the data).

```
$ python insert_data.py
Inserting[0]: Richard Cohen
Inserting[1]: Wendy Gray
Inserting[2]: Andrea Navarro
Inserting[3]: Roy English
Inserting[4]: Christopher Maxwell
Inserting[5]: Travis Hoover
Inserting[6]: Rhonda Hall
Inserting[7]: Sandra Hansen
Inserting[8]: Jacqueline Young
...
Inserting[994]: Derek Casey
Inserting[995]: Laura Franklin
Inserting[996]: Victoria Jordan
Inserting[997]: Catherine Hawkins
Inserting[998]: Christian Haney
Inserting[999]: Julie Zamora
```

A simple look at our database will show the records are safely stored in the table. We are using DBeaver as a client UI to connect to the database, and query with a simple **SELECT** statement.

Following is a screenshot of DBeaver, querying our synthetic test data:

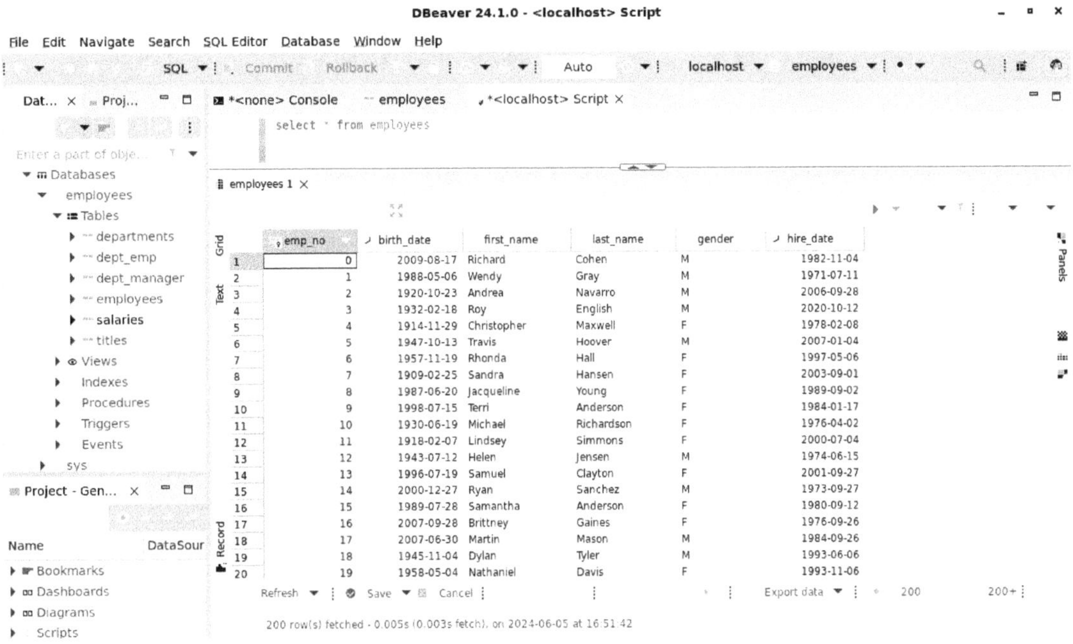

Figure 11.4: Generated test data in MySQL

Data security

Keeping data secure is always crucial because it involves ensuring that sensitive information used in software testing is protected from unauthorized access, breaches, and misuse. Especially if we pull production data (which mostly contains real, trusted, sensitive information) into testing (which is, by definition, a less secure environment for experiments), we have to ensure that some key points are followed to keep the test data safe. Most of the measures listed below should come as no surprise, as they are basic data security practices, though some, like masking and anonymization, should be considered, especially in TDM.

Implementing these practices would help us maintain the confidentiality, integrity, and availability of test data, thereby safeguarding sensitive information from security threats.

- **Masking and anonymization**: This is normally the first aspect mentioned when it comes to test data security. Information cannot leak if it is not there in the first place. We either change or remove it so that the test data had the same **structure** as the production data but with different content.

- Data masking involves obscuring original data with modified content (characters or numbers) to ensure sensitive information is not exposed. Masked data retains the functional characteristics needed for testing but does not reveal actual sensitive information.

- Anonymization of the data involves removing or modifying personal identifiers from data sets so that individuals cannot be readily identified. Unlike masking, anonymization aims to make it impossible to trace back to the original data.

- For example, in a credit card number, the first four numbers may be fictitious while the other digits are rendered untraceable. There are both commercial and open-source technologies that simplify TDM, with built-in features for data masking and anonymization that have been available over time with ease.

- **Compliance with regulations**: Closely related to masking and anonymization, is keeping the data compliant and adhering to regulations: Ensuring that our TDM practices comply with relevant data protection laws and regulations, such as **General Data Protection Regulation (GDPR)**, **Health Insurance Portability and Accountability Act (HIPAA)**, and others. This includes implementing measures to protect personal data and conducting regular compliance reviews.

- **Subsetting**: Minimize risk, do not take data portion you do not need. Creating smaller, representative samples of the full data set can help minimize the amount of sensitive information exposed during testing. This involves selecting a subset of data that retains the characteristics necessary for testing while reducing the overall data volume.

- **Data lifecycle management**: Do not keep the data forever. Again, as part of reducing risk by not keeping what is not necessary, managing the entire lifecycle of test data from creation, usage, and storage to destruction ensures that data is securely deleted or archived once it is no longer needed for testing purposes.

- **Encryption**: Another basic core security measure that is highly recommended is to keep the data encrypted. This works both for data-at-rest encryption (encrypted data is stored on disks or backups, so it cannot be read without a certificate/ key), as well as data-in-transit encryption (ensure that data being transferred over networks is encrypted to prevent interception by unauthorized parties. Use encrypted secure protocols such as SSH/SFTP or HTTPS).

- **Access control**: Limit who can access the data in the first place. Implementing role-based authorization helps control who can access which data, based on the user's role within the organization, or explicit permissions, allowing only authorized personnel to access sensitive test data. A good strategy would be the **least privilege principle**, which denotes that users are granted the minimum levels of access needed to perform their job functions and no more.

- **Audit and logging**: Implementing access control is an important measure, to keep people from accessing our data, but despite this measure, if we suspect that somehow the data has been accessed in a bad way, it would be good if we had kept detailed records (audit logs) of who accessed or modified the data, when, and what changes were made.

- The data is also alive and evolves over time. It is also a good practice to conduct audits on a regular basis, to ensure compliance with data security policies, and to identify any potential security gaps.

- **Secure test environments**: Another important practice is not just keeping the data itself secure, but also keeping prying hands off the data by keeping the environment secure altogether: ensuring that the environments where test data is stored and processed are secure. This includes implementing security measures such as firewalls, intrusion detection systems, and secure access protocols.

- **Training and awareness**: Finally, keeping the personnel who have their hands on the data educated is important. With all the security measures in place that can help prevent mishaps, improper access, and leaks, it is still important to conduct regular training and awareness programs for employees to educate them about data security best practices and the importance of protecting test data.

Conclusion

In this chapter, we looked at the concept of TDM, which is a wider topic than most people consider. We discussed the considerations we need to make to prepare our test data, how to get it or generate it, and how to keep it safe.

In the next chapter, we look closer at the actual tests, what kind of tests we can perform, and how to build and run them.

Key learnings

- We discussed the process of defining the requirements of our test data.
- We discussed the required characteristics of our data.
- We learned about data setup strategies.
- We learned about cleaning up and reusing data for various tests.
- We discussed the concept of service virtualization.
- We mentioned automation tools for TDM.
- We detailed security measures for keeping our test data safe.

Join our book's Discord space

Join the book's Discord Workspace for Latest updates, Offers, Tech happenings around the world, New Release and Sessions with the Authors:

https://discord.bpbonline.com

## CHAPTER 12

Performance Benchmarking

Introduction

Prepare your app for the holiday season. It is not just about making it shiny and festive; we want to know that with increased and extreme conditions, it would not lag, crash, slow down, lose data, or waste memory or storage.

Once the foundation is ready, after we have defined our objectives, data, environment, and proper test cases, we need to understand what we are going to build on top of it. This chapter talks about the various performance tests that are needed to validate the non-functional requirements of the system. It also explains the difference between baselining and various other measurements post-optimization to measure the improvement. It is a continuous journey, so we are discussing the frameworks to integrate continuous validation as part of the CI/CD pipeline.

Structure

This chapter contains the following topics:

- Types of performance testing
- Smoke testing
- Single-user isolation testing
- Load testing

- Volume testing
- Endurance testing
- Readiness checklist
- Scenario setup
- Performance baselining and benchmarking
- Continuous performance validation using Jenkins and JMeter

Objectives

This is a practical chapter. We will look at different types of performance tests and get to know the idea behind them and how they differ. We will also look at how to run load tests with **Locust**. We will review a detailed list of items to account for when running all kinds of tests, we will learn about benchmarks and baselines (and the differences between them), and we will learn about continuous CI/CD testing integration between Jenkins and JMeter, with a detailed instructional demo.

Types of performance testing

As we have looked in previous chapters at a number of different types of tests, methodologies, and tools, from system telemetry measures, runtime instrumentation, profiling libraries, cloud integration, to test data management, in this chapter, we shall outline different typical types of test execution patterns, why they exist, what are their principles and how to conduct them properly. Different types of tests come to accommodate different needs and help us release better products by assessing and ensuring their qualities.

In the following sections, we will look deeply at and understand different typical characteristics of performance tests; some try to challenge our system with the number of users sending requests, some with a large amount of data, and some over long periods of time. Some are meant to detect immediate critical issues, while others show evolution over time.

Smoke testing

Smoke testing, also known as **build verification testing** or **confidence testing**, is a preliminary testing process that evaluates whether the most crucial functions of a software application work correctly after a new build or update. It serves as a checkpoint to determine whether the software is stable enough for further, more rigorous testing.

Different types of initial validation tests

Some confuse smoke tests with sanity, regression, or re-testing, as they are all used for initial validation of the software. Just as a quick clarification, they are all related in a way:

- **Sanity tests**: They are a minimal set of tests, usually the first ones run **before any other tests**, to make sure the overall status of the system is good. Sanity tests are quick validations; more often than not, they are executed manually and may not even follow predefined, strict test plans.

- **Smoke tests**: They are at the focus of this section, after executing the sanity test, before running more rigorous tests, to check the stability of our system. Smoke tests cover critical functionality of our system to see if they are intact.

- **Regression tests**: They are performed once new features are introduced in our system. Regression tests are based on the system requirements and the system features that implement them, that is, to confirm that changes and new features did not impact the system in a negative way.

- **Re-tests**: They are repeated tests for functionality that had failed in the past in order to verify fixes and changes, and to see if the detected defects were handled successfully. The same test procedure that detected the defect is repeated, with the same test data, in order to see that the system behaves better.

Aspects of smoke tests

Smoke tests are an essential practice in the software development lifecycle, acting as a gatekeeper to ensure that only stable builds undergo more comprehensive testing. By quickly identifying major issues, it helps maintain the quality and reliability of the software product. To sum up some key aspects of smoke tests:

- **Purpose**: The primary goal of smoke tests is to catch major issues early in the development cycle, ensuring that the core functionalities of the application are working as expected before moving on to more detailed testing phases. This helps save time and resources by identifying critical problems early.

- **Scope**: Smoke testing focuses on the most critical and basic features of the application, such as launching the application, logging in, basic navigation, and simple operations that are essential for the application's operation. It does not get into detailed testing of all functionalities.

- **Frequency**: Smoke tests are typically run whenever a new build is created, especially after bug fixes, updates, or any changes in the codebase. This helps ensure that recent changes have not introduced new defects and that the build is ready for more detailed testing.

- **Automation**: Given its repetitive and essential nature, smoke testing is often automated. Automated smoke tests can quickly verify the integrity of a new build, providing immediate feedback to developers and reducing the time required for manual testing.

- **Process structure**: Once we have a new build of our application, we get it deployed onto our test environment, after which we can trigger smoke tests, to verify critical functions are intact. The executed tests produce reports (automatically as test logs or standard format such as Junit, or by manually writing reports of manually executed tests). The results get analyzed, and appropriate decisions are made. If the build passes smoke tests, we proceed to more comprehensive testing. If it fails, the build is rejected, and the issues are reported to the development team for fixes.

- **Benefits**: Smoke tests help **catch critical issues early**, preventing defective builds from progressing further in the testing cycle. By quickly identifying unstable builds, smoke tests help focus resources on builds that are more likely to succeed in detailed testing. Successful smoke tests provide confidence that the build's basic functionalities are intact, setting a solid foundation for further testing.

Examples

Some examples of smoke tests can include:

- Verifying that the application launches successfully.
- Ensuring that users can log in and log out.
- Checking that the main navigation links work.
- Testing basic operations like creating, reading, updating, and deleting records.

Single-user isolation testing

A great deal of what we are focusing on in this book, and in general, when performance is being considered, engineered, planned, tested, and analyzed, is mostly on server capabilities, things like how much traffic we can handle, how we handle caches and architectural components smartly, or how well the application works with the hardware, optimizing runtime through telemetry and profiling tools. However, there are other types of tests, which come down to the direct, single-user experience and how well our application performs on the end-user's device. Here, instead of the macro big picture of high traffic through a complex distributed system, we zoom in and focus on how things look from close range, eye-to-eye with our application.

Single-user isolation performance testing (sometimes referred to as **client-side performance testing**) is a type of performance testing focused on evaluating the performance of a software application when it is accessed by a single user. This testing aims to establish a performance baseline, which can be used for comparison against multi-user performance tests, such as load tests. As depicted in *Figure 12.1*, we are focusing on the user:

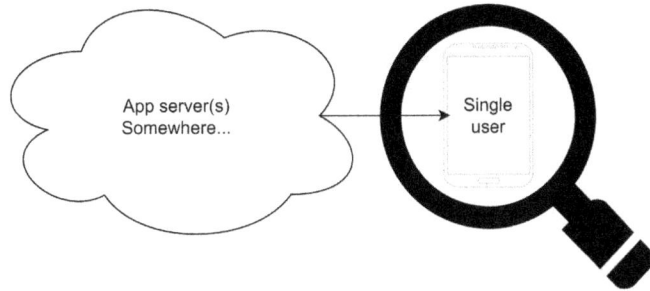

Figure 12.1: Focus on the single user

The main goal of single-user isolation tests is to measure the application's performance under **minimal load** conditions. This helps in identifying the inherent performance characteristics of the application without the influence of multiple concurrent users.

This kind of testing is typically limited to a single user performing a series of actions or transactions. It assesses response times, resource usage (CPU, memory, disk I/O), and other performance metrics when the application is not subjected to high load or stress.

There are several reasons for us to want to do that. With this testing approach, we can establish a baseline for our performance metrics, which can be used for comparison with results from load, stress, and other performance tests. It also helps in the early identification of performance issues that might be inherent to the application logic or code, independent of multi-user interactions. Also, isolating a single user's performance makes it easier to pinpoint issues, as there are no confounding factors from multiple users. By isolating a single user's interactions with the application, single-user isolation testing provides clear insights into the application's performance without the complications introduced by multiple concurrent users. This makes it a vital step in the performance testing process, ensuring that the application's core functionalities perform well in isolation before more complex scenarios are tested.

The process of such a test is quite similar to other performance tests:

1. The testing environment is configured to mimic the production environment as closely as possible, but with only one user interacting with the system. Tests are performed from the user's perspective; thus, they are run on real (or simulated) devices that the user is expected to use.

2. The single user performs a set of predefined actions, such as logging in, navigating through the application, performing CRUD operations, and logging out.

3. Performance testing tools like Apache JMeter, LoadRunner, and others can be configured for single-user isolation tests by setting the number of users to one.

4. During the test, various performance metrics are monitored and recorded, such as response times, system resource utilization, and any errors or exceptions.

5. The collected data is analyzed to identify any performance issues or bottlenecks that occur even under minimal load.

Such test cases may include:

- Establishing initial performance benchmarks for new applications or features.
- Checking that performance remains consistent after code changes or optimizations.
- Investigating performance issues reported by users to determine if they occur under isolated conditions.

Load testing

With load testing, we analyze how our application performs under **expected user loads**. The primary objective is to identify performance bottlenecks, ensure stability, and validate the application's ability to handle the anticipated volume of traffic. The main goal is to ensure that an application can handle the number of users or transactions it is expected to encounter in a production environment. This helps identify performance bottlenecks and ensures that the application remains responsive and functional under load.

Load testing examines the performance characteristics of an application by simulating a specified number of users or transactions. It focuses on key performance metrics such as response time, throughput, resource utilization (CPU, memory, disk I/O), and error rates.

This normally works by running multiple requests/actions by a number of virtual users, over time. For example, if we anticipate 2000 users hitting our application at any given time, we create a test plan that fires 2000 requests, representing the users, continuously over a moderate amount of time, for example, 1 hour. The number of concurrent requests usually starts from 1, gradually rises to the anticipated number, and stays there for the duration of the test, then gradually gets reduced back to 0. This pattern is represented in the following graph:

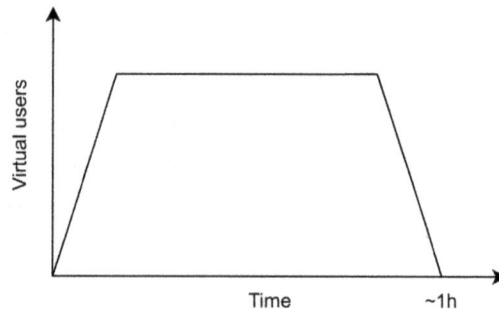

Figure 12.2: A typical load test pattern with the duration of 1 hour

Among the benefits of load tests are:

- **Performance validation and capacity planning**: Load tests ensure that our application meets performance requirements under expected load conditions. Thus, they also help determine the infrastructure needed to support the expected user load, aiding in capacity planning and resource allocation.

- **Bottleneck identification**: Load tests help identify and address performance bottlenecks, such as slow database queries, inefficient code, or inadequate server resources.

- **Improved user experience**: Load tests ensure that the application remains responsive and provides a good user experience under load.

Several tools are available for load testing, each with its strengths and features. Popular load-testing tools include **Apache JMeter**, **LoadRunner**, **Gatling**, **BlazeMeter**, and **NeoLoad**. However, as a quick, simple example of a load testing tool, and for consistency with Python, which we are accustomed to in this book, we shall demonstrate the (rightfully) very popular tool, **Locust**, which was briefly mentioned in *Chapter 2, Performance Driven Development*. Locust is extremely easy to use and quite powerful, and for the sake of clarity and cleanliness, we will demonstrate how to set up a minimal, useful, usable, powerful load test very quickly. With Locust, we can get an informative dashboard with tables, information, charts, export tools, and multiple reports for our load tests, literally within minutes, by following the steps outlined:

Our setup will end up looking as depicted in *Figure 12.3*:

- Our dummy server, running on Python's built-in web server on port 8080, represents our tested service, the one we will invoke load-simulating test requests to.

- Our coded tests (basically just sending a request to the root path of the service) written in Python, and executed under Locust.

- The Locust web UI, running on port 8089, giving us the option to trigger our tests with load parameters, as well as displaying the statistics and results in convenient dashboards. Now, look at the following figure:

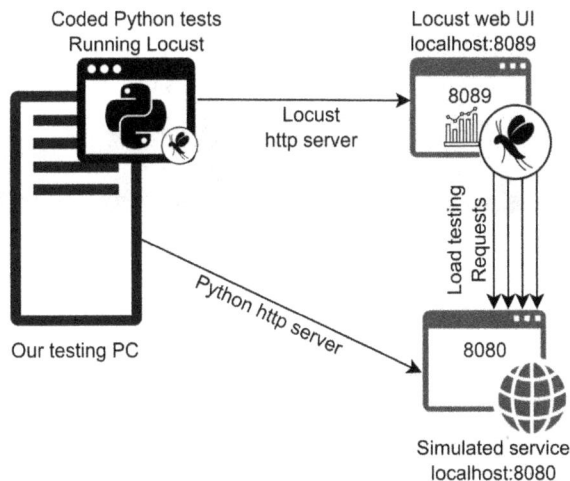

Figure 12.3: Our Locust demo setup

Here is how we set this up:

1. **Locust installation**: On our Python environment (or virtual environment), running **pip install locust** will install the tool. We can verify that by running **locust -V** to display the current active installed version of Locust:

```
$ locust -V
locust 2.29.0 from /home/alon/demo/.venv/lib/python3.10/site-packages/
locust (Python 3.10.12, OpenSSL 3.0.2)
```

2. **Server simulation:** To get started, to simulate our server, the easiest way to spin up a dummy web server with Python, is using the built-in http server, by running:

```
python -m http.server -b 0.0.0.0 8080
```

3. This will instantly start a web server on port 8080, serving the local directory. To serve some response content, we create an HTML file, **index.html**, and place it in the same folder where we ran the Python server from. This is the content of the file:

```
<html>
    <head>
        <title>Load test demo</title>
    </head>
    <body>
        Hello, performance engineer!
    </body>
</html>
```

This represents our tested service. Locust can now run performance tests by firing requests at it.

As seen in the following figure, once the server is running, opening a browser and navigating to **http://localhost:8080**, renders our HTML file:

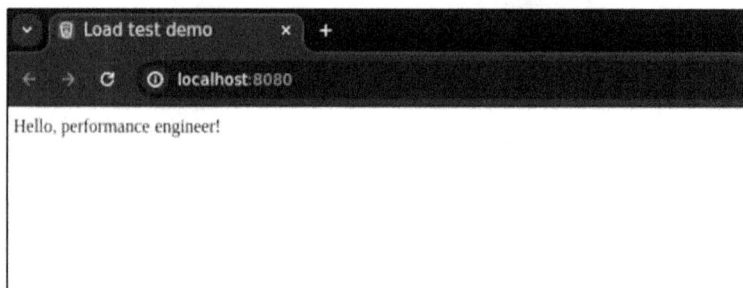

Figure 12.4: Python web server is up and running

4. **Creating the test**: Now that we have Locust set up and a test server, we can create our test. To do that, we create a Python source file named **locust.py**. For simplicity, we are including minimal code in **locust.py**. This is its content:

```
from locust import HttpUser, task

class LoadTestDemo (HttpUser):
    @task
    def root_request(self):
        self.client.get("/")
```

We import tools from the Locust library: **HttpUser**, which simulates virtual users, and **task**, that marks test procedures. We also create a class named **LoadTestDemo**, with one test named **root_request**, which sends requests to the root path of our web server, marked with a slash **/**.

5. To run Locust now, all we have to do is run the command **locust** in the terminal, and we get a notification that Locust has started:

$ locust

demo_server/INFO/locust.main: Starting   web   interface   at http://0.0.0.0:8089

demo_server/INFO/locust.main: Starting Locust 2.29.0

Locust started its own web interface at **http://localhost:8089**. If we navigate to this address, we are presented with the following simple user interface, which allows us to configure the test parameters:

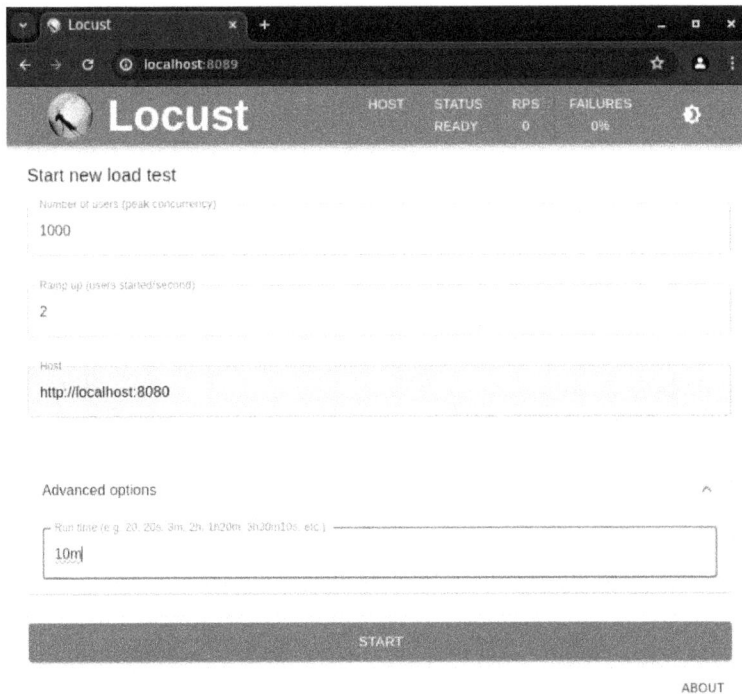

Figure 12.5: Setting Locust test parameters on the main page

As can be seen in the example above, we are running a test against our server, at **http://localhost:8080**, with a load of **1000** users, incremented by **2** users every second, and running an overall test with this load for **10 minutes**. Now, we can click **START** to start the test, and we get the following statistics page, with a table of the results, shown in *Figure 12.6*.

Note: The table has one row of results of tests performed by invoking a GET request to the root path /. This request is generated by the small test we included in our python file. If we had additional tests performed, more corresponding rows would be included in the table.

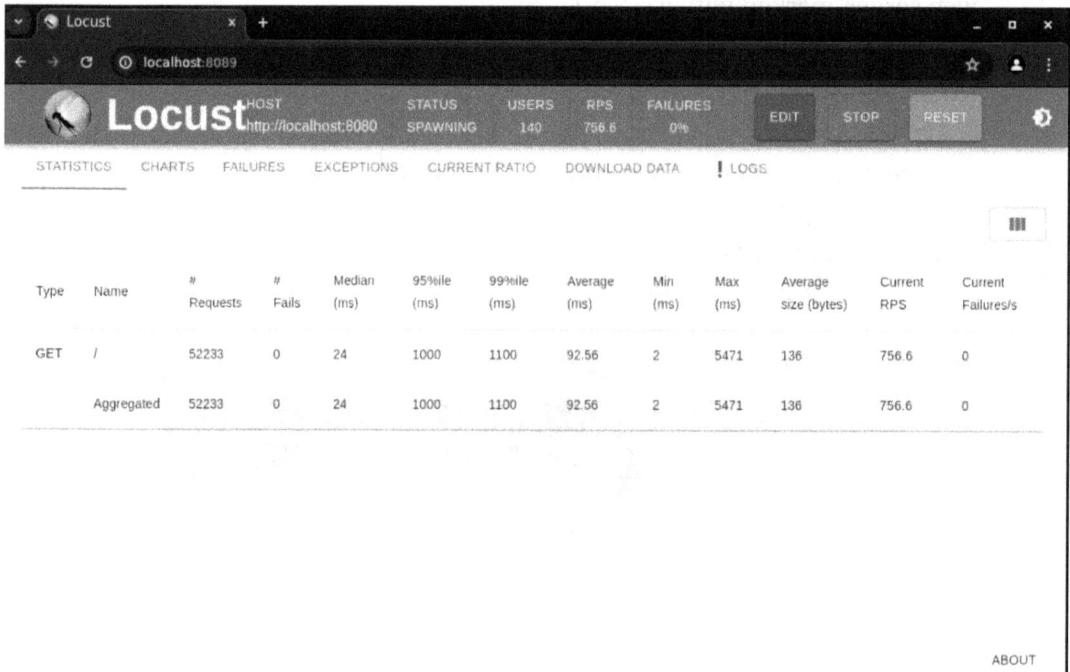

Type	Name	# Requests	# Fails	Median (ms)	95%ile (ms)	99%ile (ms)	Average (ms)	Min (ms)	Max (ms)	Average size (bytes)	Current RPS	Current Failures/s
GET	/	52233	0	24	1000	1100	92.56	2	5471	136	756.6	0
	Aggregated	52233	0	24	1000	1100	92.56	2	5471	136	756.6	0

Figure 12.6: Locust statistics page

Now that we have Locust running, we are getting a lot of useful information about our tests, how they are executed, the rate of requests and response times, like in the table above, or in the **CHARTS** tab:

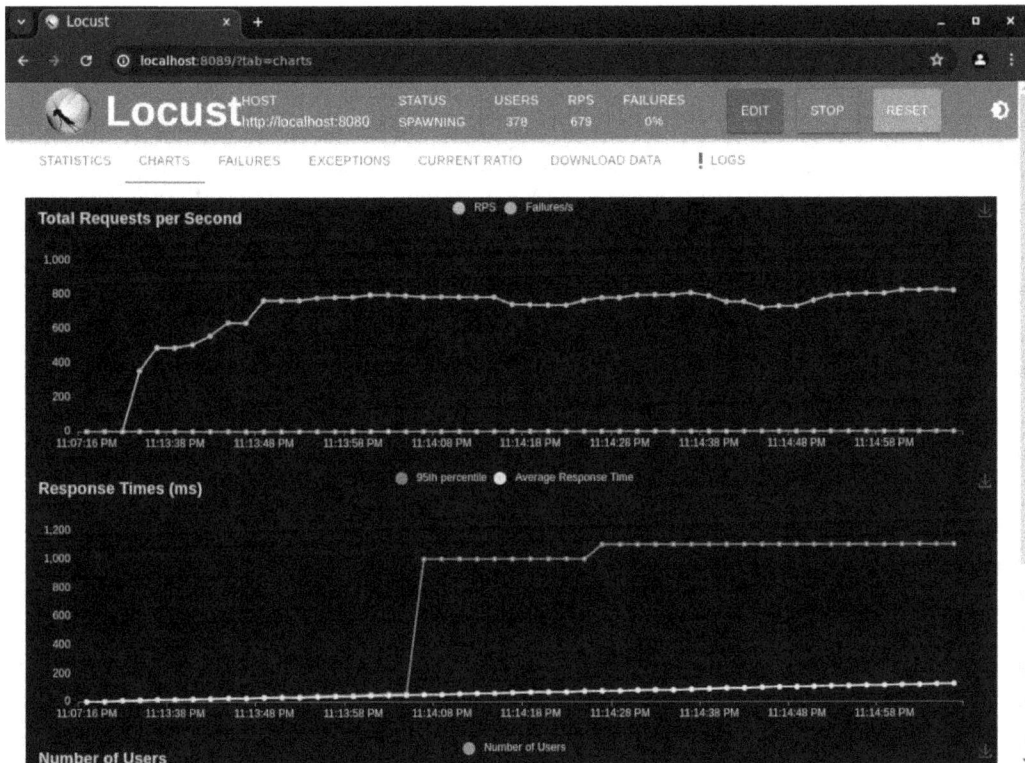

Figure 12.7: Locust test results charts

To summarize, load tests are essential for ensuring our application can handle expected user traffic efficiently and reliably. By identifying and addressing performance issues early, load testing helps deliver a robust and scalable application that provides a positive user experience under load.

Stress testing

Unlike load tests, which come to simulate the standard use of our application, with stress tests, we go to the extremes. The purpose of stress testing is to find the stepping-up breaking point by executing the most accessed transactions (typically) with an increasing number of users, until the system fails. A stress test will find and indicate for us the maximum number of users that the system can handle, with the infrastructure on which it is installed, and how long it takes to recover regular functioning after the system has been down for a period.

To conduct stress tests, we gradually increase the number of virtual users over time, let the system try to handle the increased number for a while, until we find the breaking point where the system cannot handle the load anymore. Something like the scheme depicted in the following figure:

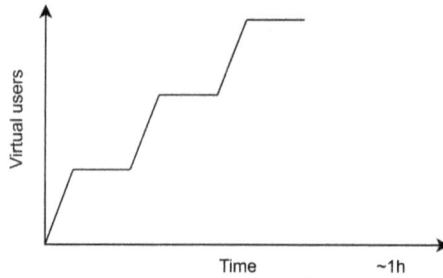

Figure 12.8: *A typical stress test pattern with gradually increasing load*

It is important to perform stress testing on a website whenever there is a spike or a sudden surge in traffic. If you fail to accommodate this sudden traffic, it may result in loss of revenue and repute. stress testing is also required for the following reasons:

- To check whether the system works under abnormal conditions.
- Display appropriate error messages when the system is under stress.
- System failure under extreme conditions could result in enormous revenue loss.
- Prepare the website for extreme conditions by executing the stress tests.

There are many tools for running stress tests, such as the elaborate JMeter we looked at in detail in *Chapter 10, Performance Testing, Checklist to Best Practices*. Another option is Locust, which we examined previously in this chapter, as its web interface allows us to gradually increase the load on every test by ramping up the number of users per second. With that, we can gradually bring the system to its knees and see at what point it cannot handle the load anymore, in a well-controlled, systematic manner. Once our system starts crashing, we stop the test.

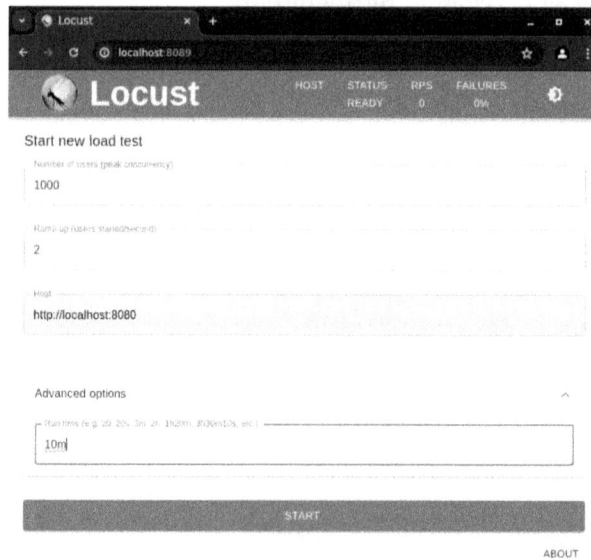

Figure 12.9 *Stress testing with Locust*

Volume testing

No, we are not talking here about testing the microphone and speakers of the sound system. We are also not necessarily talking about the scalability of the load of users on our system. In contrast to load tests and stress tests, with volume testing, we are trying to challenge our system with high volumes of data in order to see how well it can handle them. While we are at it, we would want to collect regular performance data, such as stability, response time, throughput, telemetry, etc. Volume testing is sometimes referred to as **flood testing** or **batch testing**.

Volumes are usually tested in a few potential places. Either at the database level, by preparing very large quantities of data, using test data management automation tools, as we have covered in *Chapter 11, Test Data Management,* or by flooding the system with transactions in large batches, seeing how well it handles them, or by running many transactions or data procedures at the same time, for example, a high number of data processed on the database, like many tax calculation routines running against the database all at once.

Volume testing focuses on the data-handling capabilities of the system rather than the number of concurrent users. It typically involves testing database performance, data storage mechanisms, data retrieval processes, and overall system performance with large datasets.

Normally, this would help us:

- To verify that our application can handle large volumes of data without performance degradation or crashes.

- To ensure that our system can process, manage, and retrieve data efficiently under high data volume conditions.

- To identify potential bottlenecks related to database size, data processing, and storage capacity.

Typical examples where volume tests would be desirable may be, for example, with an e-commerce application, where volume testing involves loading the database with millions of product listings, user accounts, and transaction records to ensure that the application can handle the data volume without performance issues, or with a banking system, where volume testing could include processing large numbers of transactions and customer records to verify the system's ability to maintain performance and data integrity.

Volume testing design and execution processes depend a lot on our system's structure, architecture, technologies, etc. The idea remains the same: define and run whatever relevant performance tests but do it with large volumes of data.

1. **Define objectives**: First, we determine the specific goals of our volume testing, such as testing the performance of the database under high data volume or assessing the system's response times with large datasets.

2. **Prepare test environment**: As with any test, we set up a test environment that closely resembles the production environment, ensuring that it can handle the expected volume of data.

3. **Generate data**: Here is the pickle. We create or simulate large datasets that will be used for testing. This data should be representative of real-world scenarios. Test data management, synthetic data generators, or pseudo-production data (if it is big enough, secure, and properly anonymized) are recommended to be used here.

4. **Execute the tests**: Now, we load the large datasets into the system and execute various operations, such as data entry, updates, queries, and deletions.

5. **Monitor performance**: Obviously, we track key performance metrics, including response times, transaction times, CPU and memory usage, disk I/O, and database performance.

6. **Analyze the results**: Finally, we analyze the collected data to identify any performance issues or bottlenecks and determine the system's ability to handle the volume of data.

All in all, it is a very straightforward process, but the emphasis is on the data stored or crunched during the test.

Endurance testing

With load and stress testing, we increase the number of users; with volume testing, we increase the amount of data; and with endurance testing, we increase the amount of time.

Again, we are talking about a variant of load testing. Similar to load testing, we play our tests with a certain number of virtual users over a certain period of time. However, when we want to check the endurance of our system, we would want to see how it can keep up with those users for an extended amount of time (hours). We would want to see how our system behaves when it has to actually handle a large number of operations over a long time. This is what we call **endurance testing**, or sometimes referred to as **soak testing**, an action scheme as represented by the following chart:

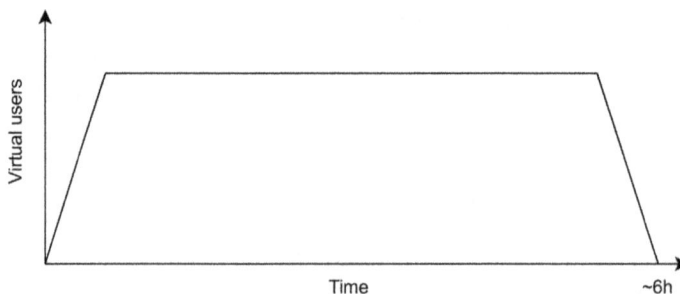

Figure 12.10: A typical endurance test pattern with a duration of 6 hours

The aim of such lengthy tests is to check **stability**: to ensure our system remains stable over long periods of continuous operation, to detect issues such as **memory leaks**, database **connection leaks**, and other **resource leaks** that could degrade performance over time (those are sometimes difficult to find, but over time, they add up!), to observe any gradual **performance degradation**, such as increased response times or reduced throughput, and to evaluate how our system handles **sustained load** and continuous operation.

In terms of scope, we are aiming for tests that run for **extended periods**, sometimes even days or weeks, to simulate real-world usage. The system is subjected to a **steady, consistent load** to mimic typical user behavior over a long time, and we focus on critical paths and high-usage areas of the application to ensure sustained performance.

The benefits, as already pointed out above, apart from the fact that this is yet another form of challenging the performance of the system, to see if it can work efficiently nonstop over time, thus helping us optimize it in terms of resources and bottlenecks, we can also better detect issues like memory leaks, which are sometimes detected only on a larger scale of operations.

In terms of tools, processes, and test plans, this is again very individual and depends on our system's architecture, technology stack, and objectives. The difference is how we execute the tests and let them run for as long as we see fit.

Readiness checklist

With all our performance benchmarks, tests, and analysis, we want our app to be ready for real-world traffic under various conditions. This may be with a high number of users, bombarding it over time, peak traffic, sudden traffic increase anomalies, and large amounts of data. Of course, we do not need to follow all the sections of the checklist; this all depends on the nature of our system, our expectations from it, our KPIs and goals, and how we expect it to be used. Typical items we may want to consider for our checklist are:

- **Goals**:
    - **KPIs defined**: In order to determine if our system is ready, it is best to first define what we expect from it. We identify and document key performance indicators such as response time, throughput, and resource utilization.
    - **Performance goals**: Once we have defined our KPIs, we translate them into performance goals and acceptable thresholds. We can then see how the system measures up to those expectations, on different scenarios and different types of tests (as detailed in the previous sections, with load tests, stress tests, volume tests, endurance tests etc.). We are basically trying all kinds of techniques to break those expectations, to see where we fail.

- **Environment:**
  - To be sure we are ready for the real world, we would need a production-like performance test environment. It should closely mirror the production environment in terms of hardware, software, network configuration, and security settings, as much as possible.
  - **Stability:** We should also run our tests on a test environment that is stable enough, where all relevant components are functioning correctly.
- **Load testing scenarios:**
  - **Load scenarios:** We should define load scenarios that simulate real-world usage patterns, including normal load and also under extreme load conditions.
  - **Distribution:** We should simulate load from multiple geographic locations if applicable.
  - **Peak load:** We need to test the system under peak traffic conditions to ensure it can handle the maximum expected user load.
  - **Sudden traffic spikes:** We simulate sudden increases in traffic to test the system's ability to handle traffic spikes and anomalies.
- **Stress testing scenarios:**
  - **Limits:** We should identify and test the upper limits of the system by gradually increasing the load until the system fails.
  - **Resource degradation:** We monitor the system's behavior under extreme stress to identify potential performance degradation points.
- **Endurance testing scenarios:**
  - **Long-term stability:** We run our tests over extended periods to ensure the system remains stable under continuous load.
  - **Resource leaks:** Over time, we try to identify and address issues such as memory leaks, database connection leaks, and other resource leaks.
- **Volume testing scenarios:**
  - **Large data handling:** We test the system's ability to handle large volumes of data, including data entry, storage, and retrieval operations.
  - **Database Performance:** We ensure the database performance is not adversely affected by large datasets.
- **Scalability, resilience, and failover testing scenarios:**
  - We can scale either horizontally (by adding more servers) or vertically (by increasing the resources on our servers), or both. Thus, we can see how it behaves in scaling scenarios and how those affect its performance.

- o On the other hand, we can simulate various failure scenarios, where we experience a hit on our running resources (e.g., server crashes, network failures) to ensure the system can recover gracefully and that performance is not hit.
- o **Failover**: We test the effectiveness of failover mechanisms and disaster recovery processes. Again, those can have an effect on performance.
- **Resource utilization monitoring testing**:
  - o We monitor metrics such as CPU, memory, and disk I/O usage to ensure resources are used efficiently.
  - o **Network**: We also monitor the network traffic to ensure there are no bottlenecks.
- **Application performance monitoring**:
  - o **Real-time monitoring**: APM tools will help us monitor application performance in real-time, during and after tests are executed.
  - o **Alerts and notifications**: With our monitoring framework, we also set up alerts for performance anomalies and threshold breaches.
- **Security testing scenarios**:
  - o **Load and stress under security constraints**: We would want to ensure that security measures do not significantly impact our system's performance under load, as they may introduce overheads.
- **User experience (UX) testing scenarios**:
  - o **Response time**: Most significantly, we would want to ensure response times are within acceptable limits for end-users.
  - o **Consistent performance**: We would also want to ensure consistent performance across different user devices and network conditions.
- **Analysis, reporting, optimization, and tuning**:
  - o **Detailed reporting**: Tracing our findings and producing useful detailed reports is crucial, as it is the goal of the testing procedures to begin with. We document all our tests' results, including performance metrics, identified bottlenecks, and any issues encountered.
  - o **Performance review**: We review the test results with stakeholders and make necessary adjustments to the system.
  - o **Tuning**: In conclusion, from our reports, we would want to optimize our application's code, database queries, and infrastructure configuration based on test results.
  - o **Retest**: After our optimizations have been applied, we would want to ensure improvements are effective and no new issues are introduced.

Scenario setup

To establish useful cases/scenarios/strategies for our performance tests, there are some aspects and considerations we would want to look into. The following are those principles:

- When designing performance test scenarios, we should reflect the **real-world projections** that our users, customers, or systems experience when interacting with our software.

  This includes the configuration and setup of our **test environment**. It should reflect our production environment as much as possible so that our test scenarios rely on the fact that they are expected to be executed on similar configurations and conditions. We should know and consider that when we are planning and designing our test scenarios.

  This also derives the **tools** and **frameworks** we are going to use, and test cases are also affected by our **toolset capabilities**. This includes test tools, monitoring tools, or any other required tools.

- To design and implement test scenarios, we should first identify the **key scenarios** that cover the most important and frequent functionalities of our system. Then, we define the parameters and variables that affect the behavior and outcome of each scenario, such as user data, input values, or environmental conditions.

- Additionally, we create **realistic test data** that match the parameters and variables of each scenario and implement the **logic** and **flow** using the **features** and **functions** of our performance testing tool.

- First, we need to define the **performance testing objectives**. Those depend on our system and its **goals**. Those will help us define our testing goals. We are assisted here by predefined KPIs, **metrics**, or **findings of previous tests**, which we may want to improve.

  For example, if our system is a web application, we would want to make sure our application can handle an anticipated load of users and respond in a good timely manner.

  The process of running tests also feeds itself with **additional scenarios**, as we may uncover performance issues, which are appended to be re-tested once fixed.

- The **scope** of our tests is also reflected in our test cases. We define which **components**, servers, services, databases, etc., we will be testing, and what **metrics** we are going to measure for each component. Here, we also consider other parameters, such as which **user/profile/role** is being used for the simulated test. Other **security configurations** may be considered here, too.

- **Test scenarios** are derived from the above, and from the purpose of our system. We should consider the features we would want to test.

  If we are building a commerce system, we would look at functional features, such as browsing products, adding to cart, running through checkout, etc.

Another viewpoint is to isolate individual backend services we would want to check and challenge with performance tests.

Our scenarios also include test-appropriate parameters, such as what load we are going to simulate, for how long, and in what conditions.

- **Test methodologies** are derived from our defined goals, scope, and scenarios. We should consider the tools and types of tests we would want to perform, such as load tests, endurance tests, and volume tests, some of which are listed in this chapter.

Performance baselining and benchmarking

It is argued more than once throughout the book, when discussing performance tests, that we need to have clear metric goals for our tests. We need to define how we expect our software to behave. But suppose we start from zero, what can we expect? How do we decide on metrics to measure and improve? The term **industry standards** is sometimes mentioned in this context, but this is vague.

When we have a reference for our metrics, this is sometimes referred to as **comparison testing**. We run our tests and compare the results to **something** we can relate to, and that **something** may either be what we call industry standards (benchmarks. More on that in a bit), results of our previous execution (Baselines. More on that in a slightly further bit), or arbitrary requirements imposed on us by the client, business or other stakeholder involved (and no, **as fast as possible** is indeed a valid requirement, but it is not a comparative metric).

The terms **baseline** and **benchmark** are often used in comparison testing and are often confused and used interchangeably, though there are subtleties by which they differ.

Benchmarks: Someone already did it!

Benchmarks were mentioned briefly in *Chapter 8, Designing Performance Monitoring*. In the world of software engineering and products, there are rarely completely new revolutionary ideas and developments that have not been built before. That is why many developers can find answers to many of their challenges in StackOverflow, and AI can learn to code and repeat structures, patterns, and solutions that have been built many times before. Benchmarks are results of tests that have already been performed in the past and are now marked on the bench, figuratively speaking.

Suppose I wish to run a marathon. A marathon is a standardized race, where everybody knows the rules and length. All marathons are 42 km long. It has been published that a novice marathon male runner at the age of 50 runs a marathon, in average, in 4 minutes and 40 seconds. If I start practicing, that would be the benchmark for me, so while I train, I can measure and know how well I am doing in comparison to it.

Benchmarks are those **industry standards** everyone talks about. Benchmarks are popular with software and hardware performance. They rely on the results of past tests, for good or for bad.

If you assemble a new computer and you want to know how well the microprocessor you plan to buy performs, you can refer to past benchmark tests and see how well this processor did in comparison to other processors, which were tested in similar conditions. You can then know where on the global scale the specific processor is. You can also know there is a problem, or an overload, when your processor starts lagging and not living up to its benchmarked results. Many hardware profiling tools can run on our operating system, and measure not just how well it is doing, but also how well it is doing in comparison to publicly known benchmarks.

All this is also relevant for software performance testing. If we are building an e-commerce system, especially based on a popular framework, server, or service, and wish to measure its performance, we can compare collected metrics to public industry standard benchmarks. Finding relevant software performance benchmarks to compare against our own performance tests can be crucial for evaluating how well the application performs in real-world conditions. Benchmarks can come from various sources:

- **Industry standards and publications**: For example, **Standard Performance Evaluation Corporation** (**SPEC**, at **www.spec.org**) provides standardized benchmarks for a variety of industries, including SPEC CPU for processor performance, SPECjbb for Java server performance. Another example source is **Transaction Processing Performance Council** (**TPC** at *www.tpc.org*), which benchmarks are widely used for database and transaction processing systems.

- **Industry reports and case studies** are another source of public benchmark data. Popular reports and studies are published by institutes such as **Gartner** and **Forrester**. They often include performance benchmarks and comparisons for various types of software and platforms.

- There are also **open-source benchmarks**. **Apache Bench** is a simple and commonly used tool to benchmark web servers. It provides basic performance metrics for HTTP servers. Another example is **Phoronix Test Suite**, an open-source benchmark suite for various types of software and hardware.

- Many popular **performance testing tools** provide built-in benchmarks or have community-contributed benchmarks. **Apache JMeter** provides templates and example scripts for various performance testing scenarios, **Gatling** offers example scenarios and performance metrics that can be used as a reference, and **BlazeMeter** extends **JMeter** and provides additional benchmarks and test scenarios.

- Other sources for benchmarks may be **online communities and forums**, or the **software vendors themselves**. Oracle and Microsoft publish benchmarks of their databases and other software, and cloud providers such as **Amazon** and **Google** do too. There are some other **standardization-dedicated organizations,** such as **IEEE** or **ISO**, which also publish all kinds of benchmarks.

- Speaking about inventing the wheel, **competitors** that build software similar to ours, may also be a source of comparable benchmarks. We can check how well they are doing, in order to make sure we are doing at least as good, preferably better.

Those benchmarks can help us define our performance KPIs.

Baselines: Someone already did it! That was you!

Baselines are snapshots of test results, frozen in time forever. That is, while we run our performance tests and analyze the results, we may be able to know how well we compare to the expected benchmark results.

Regardless, once we ran our tests and got results, those results were our **baseline**. In future tests, we can refer to those previous results and see how much better or worse we did.

Going back to the marathon analogy, suppose we know the standard benchmark for a male my age is 4 minutes and 40 seconds, when I start training, I manage to run the marathon in 8 hours (that is, of course, a false example, as I will most probably not be able to complete a marathon even in 8 days). Now, we have a baseline to refer to. On further practices, we can see how well we are doing in comparison to the benchmarks and in comparison to our previously established baseline. Upon improvement, we establish new baselines to refer to.

This marathon measurement is, in fact, a performance test for me, and the same goes for our software performance tests. Whether or not we rely on benchmarks, we can always reference our previously established baselines. With new versions of our software, we can see if we are doing better or worse.

Continuous performance validation using Jenkins and JMeter

Integrating our performance tests with our system delivery mechanisms can help us ease the testing process and its repetitions, and give us immediate, continuous feedback if things worsen. In the following sections, we will discuss an example of such a setup.

Continuous deliveries

We have already looked at a number of performance test tools in this book and saw demos of how to simply set them up and run basic tests. For a mid-level developer these quick demos/tutorials should be sufficient to understand how to get started and continue from there.

We have also mentioned the evolution of the complexity of modern applications and how they are configured, delivered, deployed, and tested. The rise of DevOps has been an important step in establishing the link between the development of complex, distributed, modular software and the practices of deployment, integration, and delivery. Automation tools on all fronts help us achieve this goal, from continuous integration and continuous delivery servers to infrastructure-as-code scripting tools and others.

Jenkins FTW

One of the values of continuous delivery is that we can integrate many automatic steps to ensure everything is okay and acceptable with our software, on its way to deployment. Among the most popular tools lies Jenkins, which we mentioned in *Chapter 2, Performance Driven Development*, with 44% of the global market share for CI/CD in 2023, Jenkins is a very popular tool. As we mentioned in *Chapter 2, Performance Driven Development*, it is free (under MIT license), open source, easy to install and use, but also very powerful, and comes with a large ecosystem of software plugins, and prebuilt integrations.

Once we have a Jenkins server in control of our delivery pipelines, we can integrate testing into the process. This is extremely important, as we may put stoppers and thresholds to prevent faulty software to go any further. Having an automated, integrated delivery pipeline helps us **fire and forget**. Just push your code changes (after sufficiently testing them yourself, of course), Jenkins can get automatically triggered to start running the pipeline, and while doing so, running additional tests (those may be integrated with other modules, which the developer may have not tested individually, or may not have had to robustness of the other modules). Among the automated integrated tests of the CI/CD pipeline, we can run performance tests to make initial validation that our performance measures are still acceptable. This gives us an effortless, continuous validation of our system's performance, even before it reaches the hosting environment.

Continuous performance

As mentioned, Jenkins has a mammoth collection of plugins and extensions, which can be easily pulled in and integrated. Many of which are officially included with any Jenkins instance. One of which is the **Performance plugin for Jenkins**. The Performance plugin allows us to run performance tests as a build step of our Jenkins job or build reports from pre-existing test result files with ease. It has built-in integration with a few popular performance test tools, such as **JMeter, Junit,** and **Taurus**. We have met JMeter in *Chapter 10, Performance Testing, Checklist to Best Practices*, and saw a basic use of it. The official Jenkins documentation contains information about how JMeter is pre-integrated with Jenkins and how to use it right from the Performance plugin.

Generally, as we have established, Jenkins can run pretty much anything, including JMeter tests. The Performance plugin provides the connection between the Jenkins execution pipeline and the JMeter test results. Of course, like with other sections of this book, we are not just talking, but will also show exactly how it is done. One little point to note is that on the Jenkins documentation site, the instructions refer to running Jenkins and JMeter on a Windows environment, while our demo below shows how to do that with Linux and running Jenkins under Docker (Docker's Jenkins container runs under an Ubuntu image too). Note that Docker can also be run under Windows, on top of the **Windows Subsystem for Linux** (**WSL**) component.

Pre-setup of JMeter and a web server

We are going to keep things here really simple, to show how things work from the start.

Web server/tested service:

Of course, we can run tests against any server or service, but we are going to use the simplest possible server (which we encountered earlier, on the Locust demo in the *Load testing* section), the Python built-in **http server** module.

To start it, as in the previous example, on a Python-installed computer, all we need to execute is:

```
python -m http.server
```

Now, we have a server running on the default port, 8000 (unlike in the previous example, we are not specifying a port).

We have also placed an ultra-small **index.html** file in the same folder from which we ran that command (this is pretty much the same demo file mentioned in the previous example, too), and the meaning of *ultra-small* is that it contains just this:

```
<html>
    <body>
        Hello, tester!
    </body>
</html>
```

That is all there is to it. We have our server. Opening the browser and navigating to **http://localhost:8000** also confirms it:

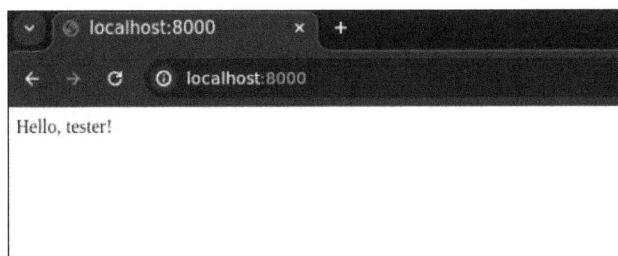

Figure 12.11: Python web server is up and running again

JMeter setup:

All it takes to run JMeter is to head over to the JMeter website (*jmeter.apache.org*) and download the latest release in the form of a zip file, to extract the zip, navigate to the **bin** subfolder, and run the JMeter script according to our operating system (**jmeter.sh** as a bash script on Linux or Mac, or **jmeter.cmd** as a batch script on Windows).

Keeping things really simple with JMeter, we will create a really simple test plan, hitting our micro-server. Pretty similar to what we saw in *Chapter 10, Performance Testing, Checklist to Best Practices*, the test plan sets a thread group of 100 virtual users, ramped up every 2 seconds, in a loop of 10 iterations, as depicted in the JMeter GUI:

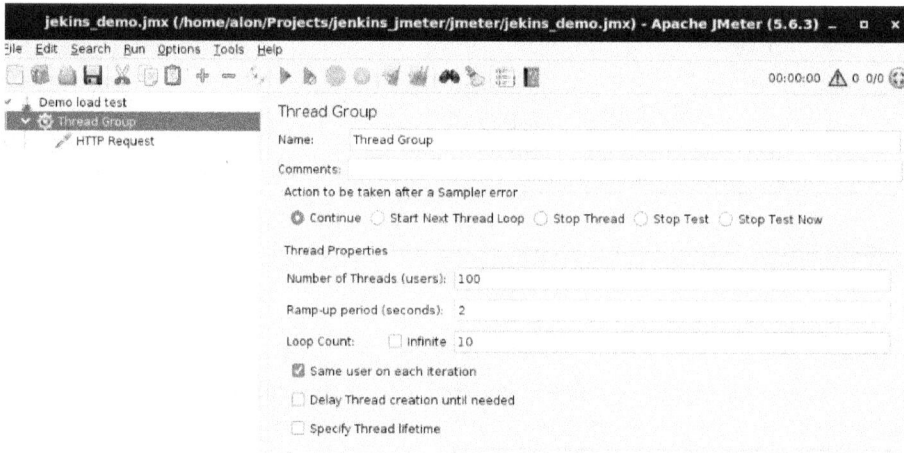

Figure 12.12: A simple initial test plan in JMeter's main UI

In terms of requests, it just hits localhost on port 8000, where our tiny server runs. To configure this, we click on HTTP Request in the JMeter tree and fill in the details of our server, as seen in the following figure:

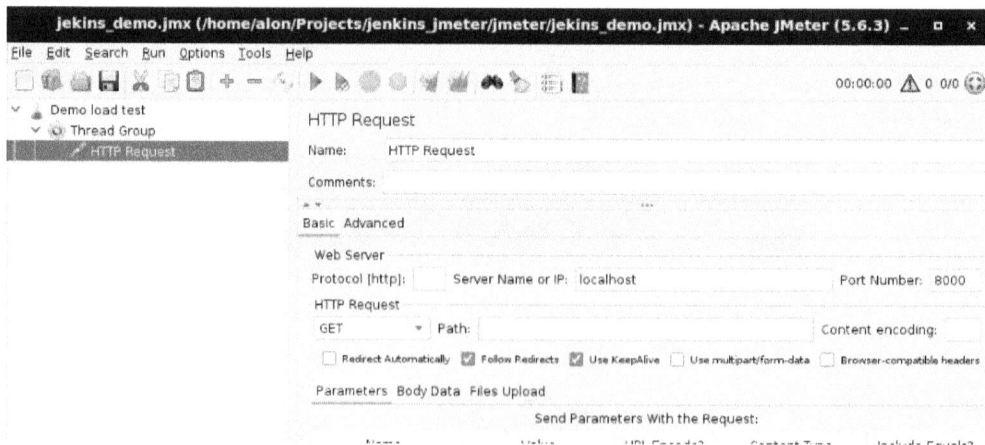

Figure 12.13: Setting up the server to hit with HTTP requests

This setup is sufficient for this demo. **The test plan must be saved first**, and we save it under the name `jenkins_demo.jmx` on the root folder of our JMeter (this is done by selecting the option on the JMeter GUI menu: **File | Save Test Plan As…**).

To prepare JMeter to interface properly with Jenkins, we need one additional small step, which is to add one line in one configuration text file. In the JMeter **bin** folder, there is one configuration file named **user.properties**, which contains arbitrary parameters we can refer to with JMeter's runtime. We are setting a parameter for the report output format, which will be set to XML So, at the bottom of the properties file, we append:

```
jmeter.save.saveservice.output_format=xml
```

And save. This will ensure that when we run JMeter inside Jenkins, the test results will be generated in XML format, which Jenkins can later integrate easily.

Jenkins

If setting up a Jenkins server seems intimidating to you, fear not. Just like with the previous items, we are keeping things to a minimum here, just to show how simply things can work. We are going to create one execution automated pipeline, have it run our JMeter test, and process the load test results.

The easiest way to run a Jenkins server is probably inside a Docker container. Although Jenkins is Java-based and can be easily downloaded and run on any Java-enabled machine with nearly zero effort, it also has an official Docker container at the public Docker repository, Dockerhub, which makes it even easier to get a full Jenkins environment with one terminal command line. The only thing we need is Docker. And here is how we run it:

```
docker run -p 8080:8080 -p 50000:50000 --net="host" --restart=on-failure -v
${PWD}/jmeter:/jmeter --name jenkins_jmeter jenkins/jenkins:lts-jdk17
```

Let us break this command line down to its components:

- **docker run**: This is the base docker command to run a container.
- **-p 8080:8080 -p 50000:50000**: These parameters open ports between our host server and the container. Port **8080** (for Jenkin's web UI) and **50000** (for accessing Jenkins agents running locally, or somewhere else).
- **--net="host"**: This parameter allows general network access between the host and the docker container. We need this since we want to be able to access our running server on localhost on port 8000, for the performance test from within the Docker container which runs Jenkins inside it.
- **--restart=on-failure**: This parameter tells Docker to restart the server in case of a crash.
- **-v ${PWD}/jmeter:/jmeter**: This parameter shares the JMeter folder between the host machine and the container. Jenkins needs to access the JMeter folder in order to trigger JMeter test plans and read the generated reports. In this case, the **jmeter**

folder under the current path (**PWD** in Linux), mapping it to **/jmeter** under the root folder inside the container.

- **--name jenkins_jmeter**: This parameter gives our container a name, so it is easy to manage. In this example it is arbitrarily called Jenkins_jmeter.

- **jenkins/jenkins:lts-jdk17**: This parameter tells Docker which image to run: we are requesting the Jenkins (**long term support** (**LTS**), stable version) image from DockerHub, based on Java JDK 17.

Running this command immediately gets the Jenkins server running locally on its default port 8080, so it is accessible on the URL **http://localhost:8080**. Note that the Jenkins server runs on port 8080 **inside** the container. We can access it from our operating system, since the **--net="host"** parameter was specified, and the host can access the server running **in the** container.

It takes a few trivial setup screens in the browser, and we have a full-blown Jenkins server, effortlessly, literally within less than 5 minutes. Those screens are briefly shown below. Jenkins provides a quick and easy setup wizard that can be clicked through to get the system up and running:

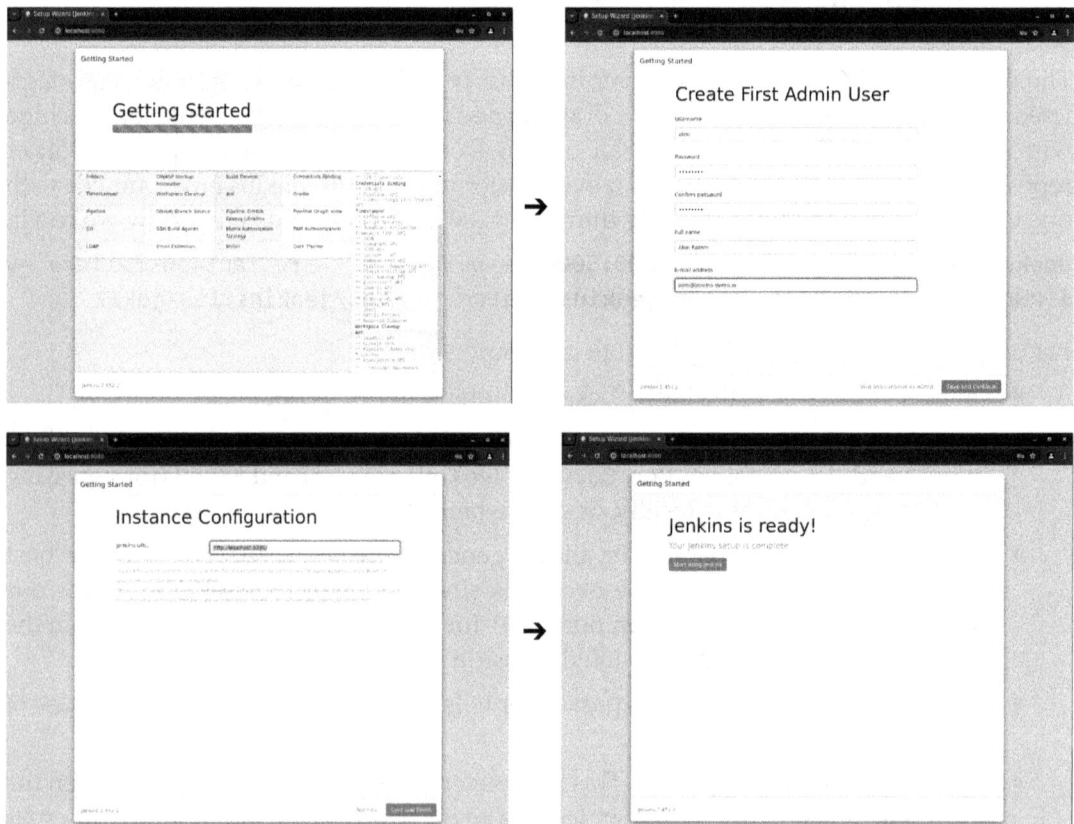

Figure 12.14: Jenkins setup wizard

Once installed, on the main Jenkins dashboard, we only have to navigate to **Manage Jenkins**, then clicking on **Plugins**, then under **Available plugins** we can quickly find the **Performance** plugin and install it in one click:

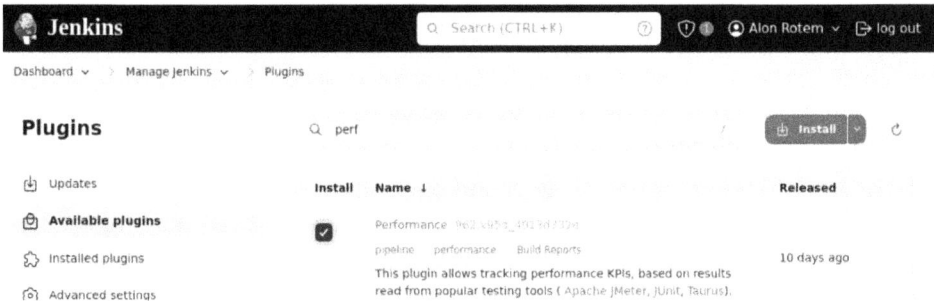

Figure 12.15: *Installing the Performance plugin in Jenkins*

Just like that, we have a running Jenkins server with the Performance plugin installed.

Creating and running a performance pipeline

Everything is now set up. We have a dummy server to test running on localhost, and we have a Docker container, which hosts Jenkins, as well as a mapped folder with the JMeter executables. All we have to do is create the pipeline. Follow these steps:

1. On the Jenkins dashboard, we click on + **New item**, on the next screen we name the item `JMeter_demo`, and choose the **Freestyle project** option, then click **OK**:

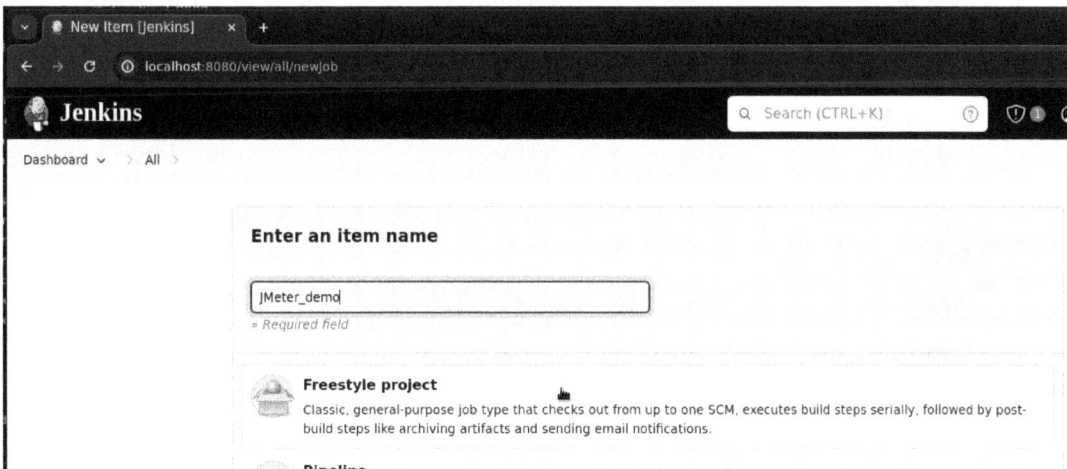

Figure 12.16: *Creating a test project*

2. Now, under the new pipeline, we need to add 2 items: a build step (to run the JMeter test) and a post-build step (to process the test results).

3. Under **Build steps**, choose **Add build step** | **Execute shell** (on the Jenkins documentation site, a script is added as a Windows batch command, while this demo uses Linux shell). And this is the script to put there:

```
OUT=jmeter.save.saveservice.output_format
JMX=/jmeter/jekins_demo.jmx
JTL=/jmeter/reports/jenkins.io.report.jtl
/jmeter/bin/jmeter -j $OUT=xml -n -t $JMX -l $JTL
```

What do we have here? 3 parameters, and one command to run. Note, again, that this is in Linux shell format.

- **OUT**: This parameter defines the output format. Note that this refers to the parameter we have put in JMeter's **user.properties** file, and its value there is set to **xml**.

- **JMX**: This parameter is the path of our saved test plan file from JMeter. Note that, as mentioned, it was placed under the root of the JMeter folder, but the path in Jenkins refers to the mapped **/jenkins** folder inside the container as a shared volume. This way Jenkins can execute the test plan.

- **JTL**: This parameter points to where the report is going to be saved, once the execution ends. Again, this is in under the **/jmeter** folder (inside the container) which is mapped to my JMeter folder on the host machine. The report filename and path are arbitrary.

- Lastly, the **/jmeter/bin/jmeter** command runs JMeter from its relative `bin` folder, with all the parameters we've just defined (and **-n** in order to avoid trying to open the JMeter UI).

4. Under **Post-build Actions**, click **Add post-build action** | **Publish performance test result report**. This is where the Performance plugin comes into play, processing the test results. All we need to put here is the path to the same JTL file we defined earlier, that is the output report, in the Source data files (autodetects format) field. So we just put the same path:

/jmeter/reports/jenkins.io.report.jtl

That is it. This is what our pipeline is supposed to look like at this point:

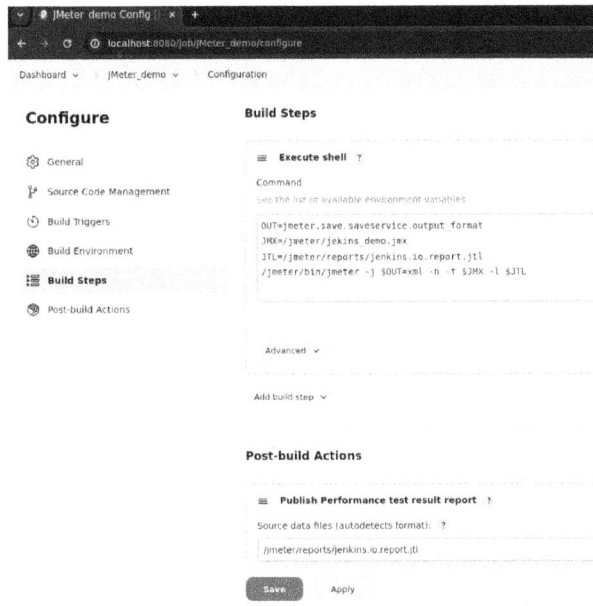

Figure 12.17: Simple initial JMeter pipeline

5. We can just save it.

6. Once saved, we can just click **Build Now**, to initiate an execution, as shown in the following figure:

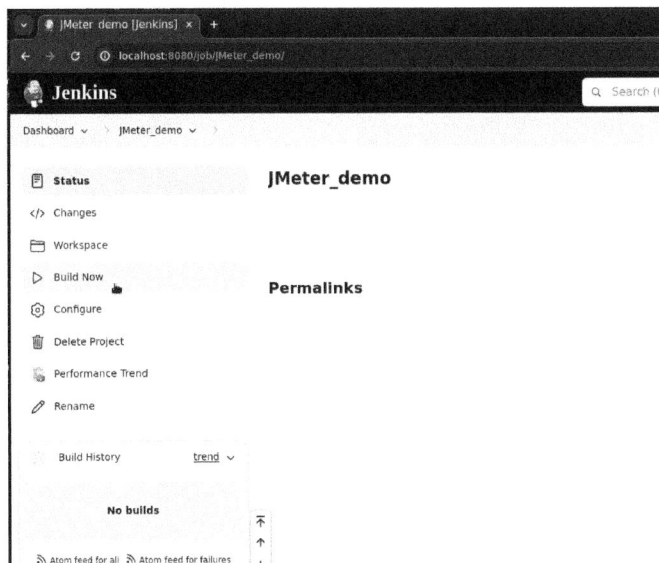

Figure 12.18: Running a pipeline build

7. After running the pipeline a couple of times, we already get runtime detailed reports and graphs on the pipeline's status page, as well as on the dedicated

Performance Trend page, as seen in the screenshots below. First is the execution results page:

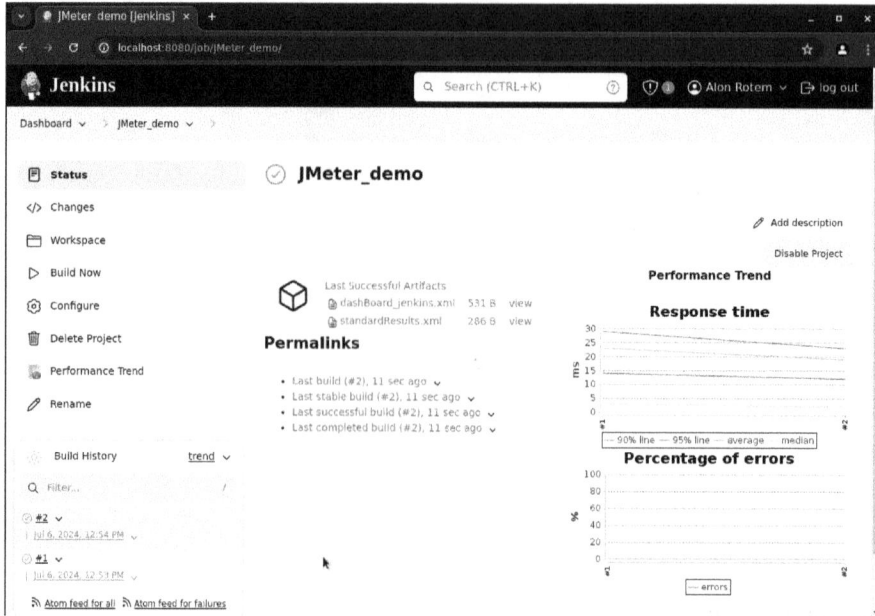

Figure 12.19: Running a pipeline build

8. Clicking **Performance Trend**, we are redirected to the informative performance analysis page, with detailed data and charts about our tests, as seen in the following:

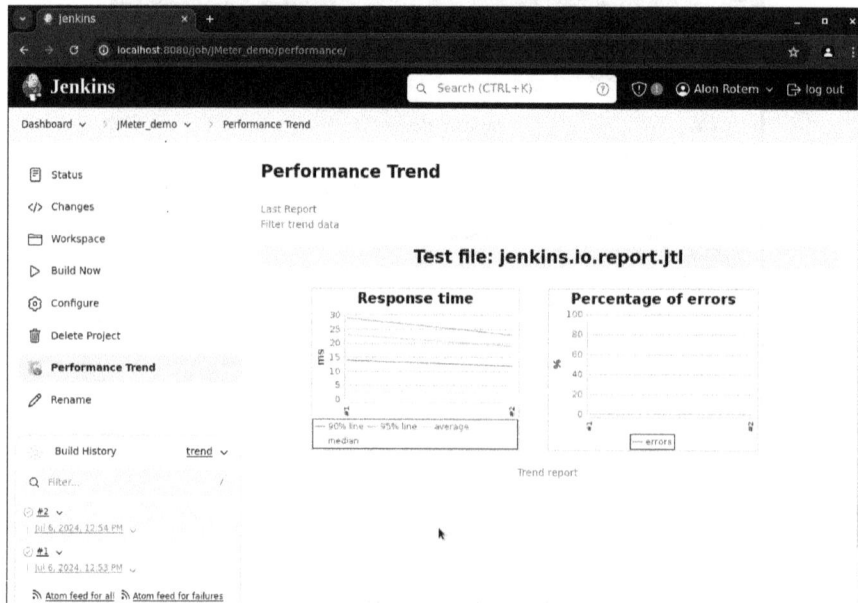

Figure 12.20: Test results in the Performance Trend section

Conclusion

In this chapter, we examined different approaches and methodologies for performance tests, and the key differences between them. We also looked at continuous performance validation with Jenkins.

In the next chapter, we will look at the numbers. Expected performance test results and indicators, metrics and measurements.

Key learnings

- We looked at test methodologies, key features, and aspects of different types of performance tests: smoke tests, isolated user tests, load tests, stress tests, volume tests, endurance tests.

- With that, we demonstrated how to use Locust as a tool to trigger various loads and test their performance behaviors.

- We reviewed a long list of key items to ensure running effective performance tests of all sorts.

- We learned about designing and planning test case scenarios, and what's important when doing that.

- We learned about baselines and benchmarks, and the differences between them.

- We took a dive to know how to perform continuous performance validation with Jenkins and JMeter, with a detailed simple example of how to set it up and run it, within minutes.

Join our book's Discord space

Join the book's Discord Workspace for Latest updates, Offers, Tech happenings around the world, New Release and Sessions with the Authors:

https://discord.bpbonline.com

CHAPTER 13

Golden Signals, KPI, Metrics, and Tools

Introduction

In previous chapters, we mentioned the importance of defining goals as our performance requirements, and in order to know how well our app is improving or declining in relation to our goals, those goals better be marked as hard cold numbers, commonly referred to as metrics, which we can follow.

In this chapter, we look again, in-depth, at different metrics and **key performance indicators** (**KPIs**) to measure various performance properties. This also includes the metrics for engineers to look at during the development and key metrics post-production, along with analytics for executive view. The performance monitoring attributes start from underlying infrastructure metrics for self or cloud-hosted or hybrid environments, application runtime metrics, and application behavior metrics, along with interfacing and third-party metrics.

Elastic APM is an open-source performance management platform. This chapter overviews and explains what Elastic components are and reviews different ways the Elastic suite can be set up and run to capture metrics, traces, and logs.

Structure

This chapter contains the following topics:

- Key performance indicators
- Different metrics for different participants
- Infrastructure components and usage management
- Application runtime vs. behavior metrics
- White box and black box monitoring
- Good to know statistics for third-party hosted content
- Performance monitoring with the open Elastic APM

Objectives

In this chapter, we will look further into metrics and measurements.

We will look at KPIs, what they are, in which fields they are used, and why they are important.

We will discuss different types of metrics which concern different participants in our projects. We will learn how and why it's important to meter our infrastructure usage and about different types of application metrics. We will explain white box and black box monitoring, the differences between them, and why they are important to be used together. We will briefly present and discuss some metrics that are important to consider when running our components on third-party hosting.

We will learn about the Elastic framework, with its wide ecosystem of products, and how to set up a full-blown data ingestion, storage, analysis, and observability with minimum effort and for free.

Key performance indicators

The importance of measurements has been mentioned across the previous chapters, as performance is elusive and better relies on cold, hard numbers, metrics, and measures. When those are mentioned, it is not uncommon to address the term **Key performance indicators** (which will be shortened to **KPIs** hereon).

Although KPIs are a well-known and understood term, they are most commonly attributed to business or project goals; as the word **Key** in the name implies, they are related to the main strategic success factors of the organization, team, or project. Most importantly, the practice with KPIs is to constantly compare them to the measured metrics in order to infer how well we are doing, to see a trend for better or for worse, and to position ourselves in relation to what we had established as goals.

The word **Indicators** tells that we are relying on numeric data, which we can measure and compare, and we are obviously talking about **Performance**, that is what those measures relate to, be it personal performance, team performance, or, sometimes, software performance, if we establish those metrics as strategic goals to achieve and keep.

KPIs provide valuable insights into the performance, efficiency, and overall quality of the development process. They enable organizations to prioritize tasks, monitor progress, and effectively communicate with their teams. With KPIs, resource allocation can be better optimized, workflow management improved, and transparency increased. Whether you are an engineering leader or a software developer, understanding and implementing the right KPIs is essential for success. Engineering leaders rely on KPI metrics to track engineering performance, project delivery, and software quality. Development teams benefit from clearer goals, improved focus, and better coordination. In summary, KPIs are our most important quantifiable measures of progress towards our intended outcome. Measurable values indicate how effectively an organization, project, or individual is achieving key business objectives. In the context of performance testing, KPIs should be critical metrics used to evaluate the performance, stability, and efficiency of a software application under various conditions. These indicators help determine whether the application meets performance requirements and expectations.

Quoting the famous words of *Peter Drucker*, an Austrian American author, one of the pioneering educators of management, being one of the leading founders of modern management theories and management education: **What gets measured, gets managed**. If we put in place ways with which we can measure our performance in a particular domain, then we are likely to manage our performance in that domain and, therefore, more likely to get the results that we want.

KPIs are commonly formulated as statements of what we want to achieve or as statements that are close to what we want to achieve (but are more difficult, more costly, or more difficult to measure, but still help us understand the current situation). The latter ones are rarer and are referred to as **proxy indicators**.

To create good KPIs, we need to ask the right questions:

1. What are our desired outcomes, and why do we want each of them?
2. How do we measure the progress?
3. How and by whom will the progress be reviewed to know whether or not we have achieved our targets?

Characteristics of good KPIs are:

- They provide **objective evidence** of progress towards achieving our desired outcome. That is, when we measure our performance metric and compare it to the KPI, we get a reliable number, which is not subject to opinion, bias, or prejudice.
- Good KPIs **measure the right things**, to inform better decision making.

- They link directly to the **organization's strategic imperatives**. We craft KPIs that should mirror our organization's priorities.

- KPIs should allow us to reliably **track how our performance changes** over time, so we can understand the trends in our performance, whether it is increasing, declining, or staying at a level.

- They have to **track things that matter** to us, such as timeliness or efficiency, effectiveness and quality, governance and compliance, behavior and performance, resource utilization, etc.

- **Follow the SMARTEST principle**: They should be Significant, Measurable, Achievable, Relevant, Trackable, Ethical, Supported, and Time-bound.

Not every measurable performance indicator is to be considered a KPI. As per the name, we are mostly seeking **key** indicators, i.e., the most significant ones. So much so that some companies consider methodology as proposed by *Gary Keller's* book *The one thing*, where he urges to focus on the one most important strength or goal rather than juggle too many targets at once. Quoting the proposed method for focus- *What one thing can I do such that it makes everything else easier or unnecessary?* This is an extreme version of goal setting and following, and definitely not for every company, manager, or scenario, but then again, we would have to consider which measure is a KPI by which we make our decisions and which is just a helpful metric we can measure.

Just one more anecdote worth noting is the differentiation between KPI and **Objective Key Results (OKR)**, as the two are sometimes confused, and the difference between them is not always clear to everyone. Again, the objective part of the OKR stands for a goal we are trying to fulfill and achieve, and key results are intermediate-defined achievements on our way to achieving that main objective. While KPIs are affected mostly by things we can do, influence, and improve, OKRs are goals that are not necessarily in our control, but are assisted by key results we can control and achieve. In a business context, for example, an OKR's objective can be something like signing up 10 new clients, while intermediate key results may be things like making 100 more sales calls (which may count as an achievable KPI).

Different metrics for different participants

KPIs and their respective metrics differ depending on the perspective of the person defining them. Each has different goals, metrics, methods of measurement, and a different definition of success. As we go higher up the scale, we get a higher view of our system and see it through the prism of different metric indicators. The following sections discuss a few examples of different success measures for different roles.

Engineers

Engineers' KPIs often focus on productivity, quality, and efficiency. Examples include:

- **Code quality:** The number of bugs per 1000 lines of code.
- **Code review completion rate**: Percentage of code reviews completed within a given time frame.
- **Deployment frequency**: How often code is successfully deployed to production.
- **Lead time for changes**: Time taken from committing a change to deploying it in production.
- **Cycle time**: Time from the start of work on an issue until its completion.
- **Customer-reported issues**: Number of issues reported by customers.
- **System uptime**: Percentage of time the system is operational and available.
- **Technical debt**: Amount of refactoring required to improve codebase health.

Architects

Architects' KPIs focus on system design, scalability, and alignment with business goals. Examples include:

- **Architecture compliance**: Adherence to architectural guidelines and standards.
- **System performance**: Response time, latency, and throughput of systems.
- **Scalability**: Ability of the system to handle increased load.
- **Reusability**: Number of components or modules reused across projects.
- **Cost efficiency**: Total cost of ownership of solutions designed.
- **Innovation rate**: Number of new technologies or methodologies adopted.
- **Technical debt ratio**: Ratio of technical debt to development effort.

Business analysts

Business analysts' KPIs are centered around requirements gathering, stakeholder satisfaction, and project outcomes. Examples include:

- **Requirements quality**: Number of requirement changes or clarifications needed post-delivery.
- **Stakeholder satisfaction**: Feedback scores from stakeholders.
- **Requirements coverage**: Percentage of requirements that are fully implemented.
- **Time to market**: Time taken from requirements gathering to product launch.
- **Project delivery rate**: Percentage of projects delivered on time and within budget.
- **Business value realization**: Measurable business impact of implemented solutions.

- **Change request frequency**: Number of change requests received post-requirements sign-off.

Executives

Executives' KPIs focus on overall business performance, strategy execution, and financial health. Examples include:

- **Revenue growth**: Year-over-year percentage increase in revenue.
- **Profit margin**: Net income as a percentage of revenue.
- **Market share**: Company's share of total market sales.
- **Customer satisfaction**: **Net Promoter Score (NPS)** or customer satisfaction index.
- **Operational efficiency**: Cost of operations as a percentage of revenue.
- **Employee engagement**: Employee satisfaction and retention rates.
- **Innovation rate**: Percentage of revenue from new products or services
- **Strategic goal achievement**: Progress towards long-term strategic goals.

These KPIs help ensure that each role within the organization is aligned with the overall objectives and can contribute to the company's success in measurable ways.

Infrastructure components and usage management

We have looked at infrastructure from various angles throughout this book. Here, we will discuss in a quick summary how we approach, map, distinguish, and manage infrastructure components and their usage.

This is true for any software-developing IT company, but in the modern world, actually, most of it counts for any company; as our digital workplace evolves, so does the IT infrastructure that sustains it. At its essence, the IT infrastructure represents a comprehensive collection of various technological components, which are not just a random assembly but a carefully orchestrated system assigned to support and drive the operational capabilities of our organization's IT environment and, of course, our developed projects. It encompasses a wide array of physical hardware, such as servers, routers, and switches, as well as essential vital software components, such as operating systems, applications, and management tools. These pieces work together to form a cohesive framework that underpins and propels our digital processes and needs. From communications to storage and software delivery, it is the backbone that enables our company's operations and success.

Both hardware and software components can be physically running on our premises on actual computers, but can equally be virtual and running in the cloud. There is little distinction already, as the world is well connected, we might as well rely on cloud resources, which we can control and manage, scale and duplicate, create, provision, or shut down, and pay for dynamically per actual usage. This brings a great deal of control and comfort. Within those boundaries also lies the setup of our delivery environment, where our software can be written, built, tested, packaged, deployed, and released. Good hardware and software asset management can enable us to drive growth and innovation in today's competitive world. This directly relates to our performance as a business, where we can keep track of our OKRs and KPIs, as well as the behavior and advantages of our software and other goals.

Managing our infrastructure components is orchestrating a big operation, with a lot of attention to detail. This task is not just oversight, and requires a proactive approach to ensure that every element operates at peak efficiency and reliability. Maintenance is a cornerstone of this process and requires routine checks and updates to prevent issues before they arise. Keeping all those components up to date means adopting new features and security policies and ensuring hardware and software compatibility.

All this in place adds a layer of complexity for keeping track of our software intact and its performance at peak, which is why virtualized and containerized environments may be helpful to maintain consistency of what we know that works well and keeping our projects running at optimal efficiency in an established, tested, consistent environment, although the virtual and containerized runtime services also rely on hardware resources in the end, and we'd need to monitor and observe that those also run properly.

Elaborate monitoring tools such as **Nagios XI**, which is community-supported and, as such, open-source (but not licensed free, although it includes a free tier), is a standard popular tool for monitoring hardware resources, web services, network performance, and many more. **SolarWinds Server & Application Monitor** is another option, being a commercial product that helps keep a close watch on our servers and services. This would help us at many levels: control costs, efficiency, performance measurement, downtime prevention, and overall usage outlook on our resources and their utilization.

Application runtime vs. behavior metrics

Following and measuring various metrics is important at many levels. Both for testing how our app does in terms of performance, how we achieve our KPIs, how our infrastructure resources are being utilized, and in general, to detect and prevent faults and downtime. With that, we can differentiate types of metrics; some are attributed to how our application behaves, and some are about how the user behaves with it. Here, we will list some examples for each of the two measurables and discuss the differences between them.

Application runtime

Application runtime metrics measure the performance and operational aspects of our application while it is running. These metrics help in understanding how well an application performs in real-time and can include:

- **CPU usage:** The amount of CPU resources consumed.
- **Memory usage:** The amount of memory being utilized.
- **Disk I/O:** Input/output operations on the disk.
- **Response time:** Time taken to respond to a request.
- **Error rates:** Frequency of errors occurring in the application.
- **Throughput**: Number of transactions processed over a given time period.
- **Uptime:** Duration the application is available and running.

Behavior metrics

Behavior metrics focus on how users interact with an application and how the application behaves under different conditions. These metrics provide insights into user experience and application efficiency. Examples include:

- **User engagement:** Number of active users, session length, and interaction frequency.
- **Usage patterns:** Common user actions and navigation paths.
- **Feature utilization:** How often specific features are used.
- **Conversion rates:** Percentage of users completing desired actions (e.g., purchases, sign-ups).
- **Abandonment rates:** Percentage of users who leave the application without completing tasks.
- **Load time:** Time taken for the application to load for users.
- **User feedback:** Ratings and reviews from users regarding their experience.

Key differences

Runtime metrics focus on technical performance and are used for optimizing application performance and identifying technical issues, while behavior metrics focus on user experience and interaction and are used for improving user experience and understanding user needs. Runtime metrics come from application monitoring tools and system logs, while behavior metrics are collected from user analytics and tracking tools. When we are looking deep into the inner workings of our application's runtime, it may be referred to as **white box** monitoring, while looking at behavioral patterns without considering internals, may be referred to as **black box** monitoring (see below).

By combining both types of metrics, organizations can ensure their applications run efficiently while providing a positive user experience.

White box and black box monitoring

So we have discussed metrics and KPIs, things we need to measure and monitor at different levels of hardware and software in order to maintain and track various goals of performance, from software to business needs. in previous chapters, we also discussed monitoring requirements, techniques, and tools. Later in this chapter, we will present another one, Elastic APM. For different needs, we may be required to monitor servers, applications, or hardware infrastructure components. For that, we distinguish the two types of monitoring discussed in this section, the black and white boxes. This relates to how we perceive the services we want to monitor.

Black box monitoring

The term black box is known in the world for mainly two meanings, and we are actually talking in this section about a third.

The first, most common association, is the black box of a plane, which is officially called a flight recorder (and is, in fact, painted orange, and not black), which monitors and logs flight information in real-time, in order to get those recordings and logs, in case something goes wrong (the reason it is called **black box**, is not clear. Some believe early flight recorders were painted black, while others think it refers to charring that can occur in post-accident fires, although the device is painted in strong bright orange to make it easily findable in such cases). Although the flight recorder is definitely a kind of hardware monitor, it has no relation to our case of black box.

A second meaning to the term **black box**, somewhat closer to our monitoring definition, is in engineering, where a black box refers to a technical component, of which we do not know the inner workings. A black, or opaque box, that does **something**, but we don't know (or should not care) how it does it. In software development, this is pretty common, as we often deal with closed-source components and libraries (or overly complex ones we should not, or have no desire to, look into, analyze, or reverse-engineer).

In a monitoring sense, the **black box** has a close meaning to the engineered opaque black box, in the sense that we observe the monitored component as a single unit that **does something**, but we are interested in outer, exterior measures (hardware metrics), and not the inner workings (software metrics). The black box refers to the monitoring of servers, with a focus on system areas such as disk space, CPU utilization, memory loads, etc.

With that, black box monitoring, also as the name may imply, is more about the box (i.e., hardware). That is, for example, monitoring network devices, such as switches, load balancers, routers, for their system metrics, or actual server computers, storage devices, processors etc. Figuratively, we can say that with black box monitoring, we look at the box itself, metaphorically from the outside. That way, we observe the outputs and consequences of our system without looking into the inner workings of it.

White box monitoring

If **black box** is opaque, we can figuratively relate to **white box** as see-through. With white box, we are looking into the box, to see what is actually running on it. That is software. With a white box, we are looking straight with our x-ray vision and observing the inner workings of our applications, services, and runtime. From HTTP requests, to response codes, to SQL queries, users and loads, errors and logs, exceptions, crashes, and everything around application metrics.

This gives us granular insights into the internal workings of our system. We can say that in contrast to black box monitoring, where the main question is **what?** with white box monitoring, we ask more **how?**.

Insights of white box monitoring include refined data about the performance and health of individual components of our system. This level of detail helps us diagnose and troubleshoot issues more effectively. This is often done by instrumenting the code with monitoring hooks or using tools that can extract data from within the application. We looked at some of those tools closely in *Chapter 9, Tools and Techniques for Code Profiling*. White box is commonly useful for debugging and optimizing our applications, as it allows us to better understand what is happening inside our system at any given time, helping us with early detection of issues, tracing and analyzing root cause thereof, performance tuning, and enhanced overall reliability.

Traditionally, monitoring (be it black or white) used to be the work of system administrators. As DevOps culture has risen and become more and more dominant, software developers take more responsibility for monitoring their applications in a white box, while system monitoring in black boxes is left for the DevOps engineers. Implementation of white box tools (depending on the tool and its deployment) can still be in the hands of DevOps at times.

In fact, both boxes are equally important as they give an insight into our runtime. A **black box** alert (i.e., a server crash) may trigger us to look further into the "white box" logs and see what caused it (an abundance of heavy SQL queries). It makes us more sensitive to our system's behavior (as opposed to the days when the black box was the primary tooling on production environments), helping us achieve more stable systems, exceed our goals, and improve performance and other aspects of our complex systems.

Good to know statistics for third-party hosted content

When hosting our application on a third-party platform (cloud or physical), fully (or partially, what we refer to as **hybrid deployment mode**), it is essential to monitor all metrics and statistics to ensure performance, reliability, and efficient resource usage. As the environment is out of our hands, it is good to know what is going on so that we can either adjust our application to its hosting environment or improve the hosting conditions.

Many of those metrics/statistics overlap other measurables we should pay attention to in any way, but we may want to pay attention to aspects of security, vulnerability, compliance, and performance assurance to ensure our end user experience does not get harmed. Depending on our setup, cost is another factor we might want to pay attention to.

In a remote or hybrid setup where at least some of the components run in the cloud, several key performance metrics are crucial. Some of these include:

- **Underlying infrastructure metrics**:
  - ○ **Network latency:** This is critical for ensuring smooth communication between on-premise and cloud components.
  - ○ **Resource utilization:** Monitoring CPU, memory, and storage use across both environments for optimal performance and cost management.
  - ○ **Uptime/downtime:** Ensuring high availability and quick issue resolution in both environments.
- **Application runtime metrics**:
  - ○ **Response time:** This is important for assessing performance consistency between on-premises and cloud-hosted applications.
  - ○ **Error rates:** Identifying and resolving application-specific issues quickly.
- **Interfacing and third-party metrics**:
  - ○ **API response time:** Ensuring efficient communication and data exchange between hybrid components.
  - ○ **SLA adherence:** Verifying that third-party services meet their performance guarantees.
- **Security Metrics**:
  - ○ **Access controls:** Ensuring secure access across different environments.
  - ○ **Threat detection:** Monitoring for security incidents in both on-premises and cloud setups.

Those metrics, and others, help us maintain seamless performance, security, and reliability across a hybrid or remote infrastructure.

Performance monitoring with the open Elastic APM

Adding to the arsenal of performance monitoring tools we have already looked at in previous chapters, we will now discuss Elastic's APM tools. Elastic has been a popular, established player in the world of IT tools for quite some years. Elastic builds self-managed and software-as-a-service offerings for search, logging, security, observability, and analytics use cases. Elastic's tools are considered high quality, and they are all open-source and free to use, which is among the reasons they have become so popular and adopted by software companies all over the world. Elastic also runs its own Elastic Cloud, which supports deployments of its products natively, which is a paid platform.

ELK stack

Elastic ships an entire suite, not to say ecosystem, of products which are designed to work well together. Among those are Elasticsearch, Logstash, and Kibana, as they are commonly set up together, they are known by the abbreviation ELK. Here are the ELK products, and what they are used for:

- **Elasticsearch**: Elasticsearch is the main central product among the Elastic toolset. It's a distributed, RESTful search and analytics engine. As the heart of the Elastic stack, it centralizes and stores data for fast search, fine-tuned relevancy, and powerful analytics that scale. Elastic is a powerful server, first released in 2014, originally written in Java, and has no user interface of its own. It's based on another pre-existing open-source Java-based search engine, Apache Lucene.

- **Beats**: The B of Beats is not included in the ELK acronym, but it's definitely an integral part of the classic ELK setup. Beats are a set of data shippers, that is, data collectors. They send data from hundreds or thousands of machines and systems to Logstash (see below) or directly to Elasticsearch. Beats can collect data from files, network, native operating system logs (such as Windows event logs), and other sources.

- **Logstash**: Logstash is a data processing pipeline that ingests data, transforms it, and then sends it to a data server. Logstash consolidates data from different sources, predominantly (but not always) from Beats, streamlines and unifies the data collection, and delivers it natively to Elasticsearch.

- **Kibana**: Kibana brings a complex user interface into the setup. Kibana is an elaborate web-based dashboard, that provides visualization capabilities on top of the content which is indexed on Elasticsearch. Users can create various charts and maps on top of large volumes of data. Kibana also provides presentation tools, such as Canvas, that allow users to create slide decks that pull live data directly from Elasticsearch.

The ELK stack flow starts from Beats, which collects various data and feeds it into Logstash, which delivers all the ingested data to the Elasticsearch database, which then gets visualized in Kibana. This is a powerful setup, which can be extended into a large observability platform with the help of additional tools.

Additional notable tools

Elastic's wide range of products, in addition to the traditional ELK stack, and to Elastic Cloud as a runtime platform, include various tools. Some of these are:

- **Web Crawler**: As the name implies, Web Crawler is a website scanner and indexing tool that goes through the entire website data (or configured parts of it), indexing and optimizing it, and stores it for search, offline browsing, or any other purpose.

- **Elastic agents and fleet**: Elastic agents are lightweight small data collection programs, to be running on any server, to collect and send metrics to Elastic's stack. Fleet, one of the features of Kibana, allows management of multiple agents running on different servers, for collecting that data.

- **OpenTelemetry integration**: We have looked at **OpenTelemetry (OTel)** in *Chapter 8, Designing Performance Monitoring*. OTel is an instrumentation tool that helps collect data, such as traces, metrics, and logs, in a uniform open standard format and sends it off to a monitoring/observability backend, supported by many observability platforms as a standard. The Elastic ecosystem supports OTel natively.

- **Elastic Search AI Platform**: Elastic has also incorporated generative AI and machine learning features into its platform as of 2023, injecting new capabilities into its search, observability, and security, allowing users of the Elastic Cloud to build AI-powered apps. Combined with Elastic's data processing and handling capabilities, and its complex observability, the additional context-aware generative AI and machine learning help reduce labor-intensive troubleshooting, streamline triage activities, help with anomaly detection, and other useful features.

Elastic APM

With all the power of Elastic's tools, which form a system that specializes in data collection, ingestion, processing, searching, and visualizing, it is only natural to bake them all into a powerful observability tool.

The Elastic APM Server is freely available with the ELK stack. It was written in the Go language and receives data from different Elastic agents that we can configure with our applications and services. It receives data in JSON format and through HTTP API requests, groups the data into documents that Elasticsearch can index, and sends them to Elasticsearch.

Elastic stack creates the APM Server by utilizing the Beats' framework features. The APM Server is a separate component that is usually installed on a dedicated machine, sits between the APM agents and Elasticsearch and converts the data that it receives from the agents before sending it on to Elasticsearch. Controlling, viewing and producing reports and dashboards of the Elastic APM observability server can be easily done on the Kibana web UI.

In *Figure 13.1*, we can see a typical simplified setup of Elastic APM. Data is being collected by Elastic agents from any server we require. The agent streams the data to the Elastic APM Server, which ingests it, uniforms it and sends it on to Elasticsearch, which stores it, and gets visualized on the Kibana web UI in the form of informative observability dashboards.

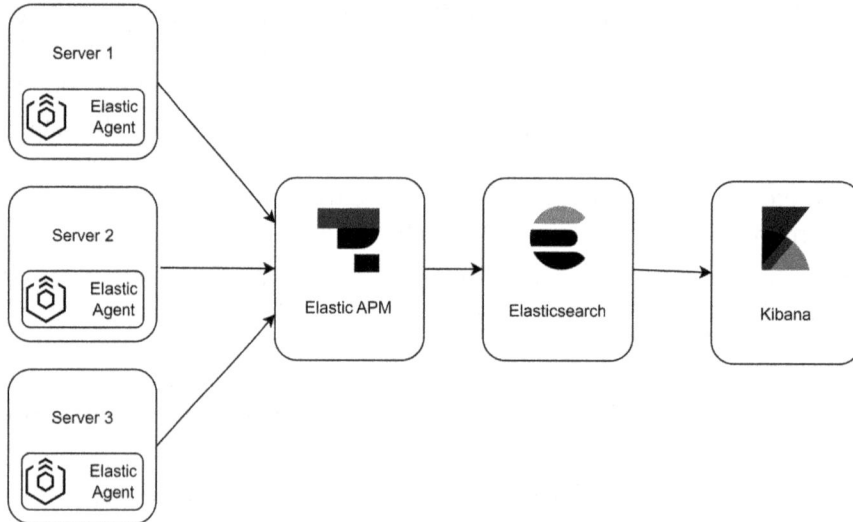

Figure 13.1: Typical simple Elastic APM setup

Making it all work

With the richness of the useful Elastic ecosystem tools, one might think that setting up an entire robust complex Elastic system, such as a full-blown APM, is a complicated process. And they'd be right.

Using the Elastic Cloud can help as an integrated platform in which it is simpler to provision Elastic tools, with or without AI components (or, for example, the wide Search AI Lake, for handling large amounts of data with Elastic tools).

The cheapest option is to self-manage and set up Elastic components manually, which are free to download and install and can be set up on any computer, be it physical, virtual, or cloud-based. The deployment scheme depends on our system setup, which computers we have, and how they are connected.

Elastic provides detailed documentation for each of their components, explaining how to install and configure it on various operating systems.

In conclusion, it is not rocket science to learn how to setup each component, connect it, configure it, and end up with a cluster of servers, running a powerful data platform, with various data ingestions, a highly searchable large database, and a usable fully featured web UI, with reports, logs, dashboards, interactive graphs, and charts, and it is all completely open and free to self-manage, self-install and run.

There is a yet even easier way to get started with deploying and running a fully featured Elastic system, and that is using Docker containers. With Docker, we do not even have to work hard on installation and initial configuration. Elastic supports Docker, and official images of Elasticsearch, Kibana, Logstash, Elastic APM Server, Beats data importers, Elastic agents, and others are hosted in the free, official Docker image repository, DockerHub.

This means that by simply running any of those official containers, we already have a proper, fully installed, running Elastic component. Then, we only need to make sure they can connect and work together. It does not get much easier than that.

But it does. Indeed, we can boot a few Docker containers and make them run together, interconnected, as if we have an entire group of servers running a full Elastic architecture, but. to have it even faster and with a single command line, we can use Docker Compose. Instead of starting each container separately, with Docker Compose, we can trigger the entire collection of containers, with interconnected network, storage volumes, and dependencies. Docker Compose can be run from a single yaml file and triggered in a single command from our terminal.

Here is an example Docker Compose file, named **docker-compose.yml**:

```
version: '3'
services:
  elasticsearch:
    container_name: elasticsearch
    image: docker.elastic.co/elasticsearch/elasticsearch:8.7.1
        environment:  ['CLI_JAVA_OPTS=-Xms2g  -Xmx2g','bootstrap.memory_
lock=true','discovery.type=single-node','xpack.security.enabled=false',
'xpack.security.enrollment.enabled=false']
    ports:
      - 9200:9200
    networks:
      - elastic
    ulimits:
      memlock:
        soft: -1
        hard: -1
      nofile:
        soft: 65536
        hard: 65536
    deploy:
```

```
    resources:
        limits:
            cpus: '2.0'
        reservations:
            cpus: '1.0'


  kibana:
    image: docker.elastic.co/kibana/kibana:8.7.1
    container_name: kibana
    environment:
        XPACK_ENCRYPTEDSAVEDOBJECTS_ENCRYPTIONKEY: d1a66dfd-c4d3-4a0a-8290-
2abcb83ab3aa
    ports:
      - 5601:5601
    networks:
      - elastic
    deploy:
      resources:
        limits:
            cpus: '2.0'
        reservations:
            cpus: '1.0'


networks:
  elastic:
```

The file above is a super basic example of a Docker Compose file. If we have Docker and Docker Compose installed, and the above file, all we have to do is to navigate to the folder where the file is stored, and run: **docker compose up -d**. This will bring up Elasticsearch, running on port 9200, and Kibana, running o port 5601. In the following screenshot, we can see the initial JSON response from the Elasticsearch server by opening a browser and navigating to localhost on port 9200:

```
Pretty-print ☐

{
  "name" : "0e1f32d85292",
  "cluster_name" : "docker-cluster",
  "cluster_uuid" : "nxh2sZ5gRX-rzTpRCWFZGA",
  "version" : {
    "number" : "8.7.1",
    "build_flavor" : "default",
    "build_type" : "docker",
    "build_hash" : "f229ed3f893a515d590d0f39b05f68913e2d9b53",
    "build_date" : "2023-04-27T04:33:42.127815583Z",
    "build_snapshot" : false,
    "lucene_version" : "9.5.0",
    "minimum_wire_compatibility_version" : "7.17.0",
    "minimum_index_compatibility_version" : "7.0.0"
  },
  "tagline" : "You Know, for Search"
}
```

Figure 13.2: *Elasticsearch running in a Docker container on port 9200*

By navigating to localhost on port 5601, we access the very usable Kibana UI, as can be seen in *Figure 13.3:*

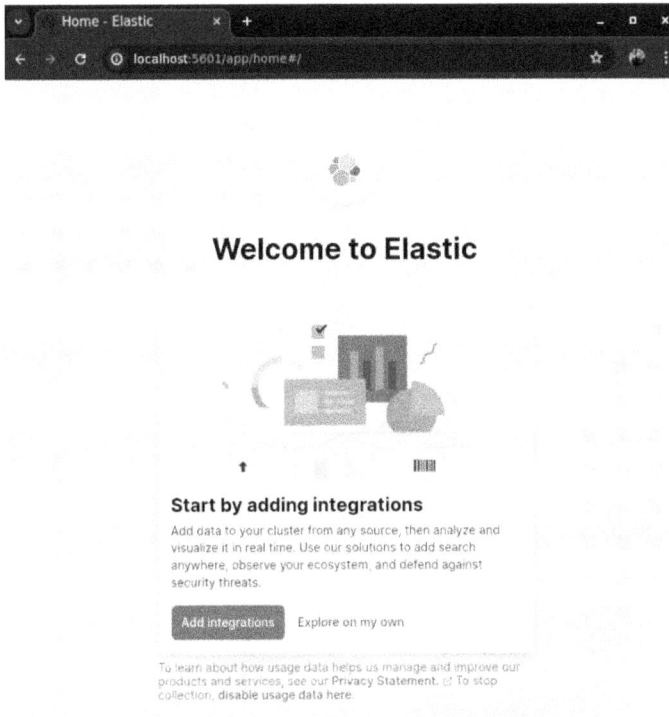

Figure 13.3: *Kibana running in a Docker container on port 6501*

Thus, with a single plain text file, and one command, we started a basic Elastic system. Furthermore, Elastic supports Docker Compose officially too. A more detailed Docker Compose sample is not just part of the Elastic documentation, but a matching, official, maintained setup, can also be found in GitHub.

The repository belongs to **elkninja** and is named **elastic-stack-docker-part-two**. It is officially addressed by Elastic's documentation, and it contains a Docker Compose yaml file, with detailed configurations for building and running each component.

It even creates self-signed SSL certificates, so we can experiment running Kibana's web servers in secure mode with HTTPS. This is not a good security to be run on publicly accessible production environments; as for that, we will need an encryption certificate signed by a recognized certificate authority, but for testing purposes, the self-signed certificate is definitely enough. SSL certificates are required in order to have our servers run on HTTPS and not HTTP, and this, as a security measure, is required for running fleet, agents, and the Elastic APM.

The proposed, supported Docker Compose sample repository runs a number of containers, which include:

- Elasticsearch
- Kibana
- Beats
- Logstash
- Fleet server
- A sample web app for generating data or errors for APM testing.

Cloning the official GitHub repository, with 13 small files, and running this entire setup takes less than 5 minutes, and we've got a big, free, full Elastic setup we can start playing with, customizing, fixing and adjusting to suit our needs.

Of course, this setup is *not* production ready. Docker Compose runs all the containers in one place, on a single computer. In a real production setup, we would want to run each of the Elastic services separately and configure it to our needs, but as a starting point it cannot get much easier than this Docker Compose option, and with that, we can start configuring and testing the Elastic services to ensure they match our architecture and requirements. Let us see the following figure:

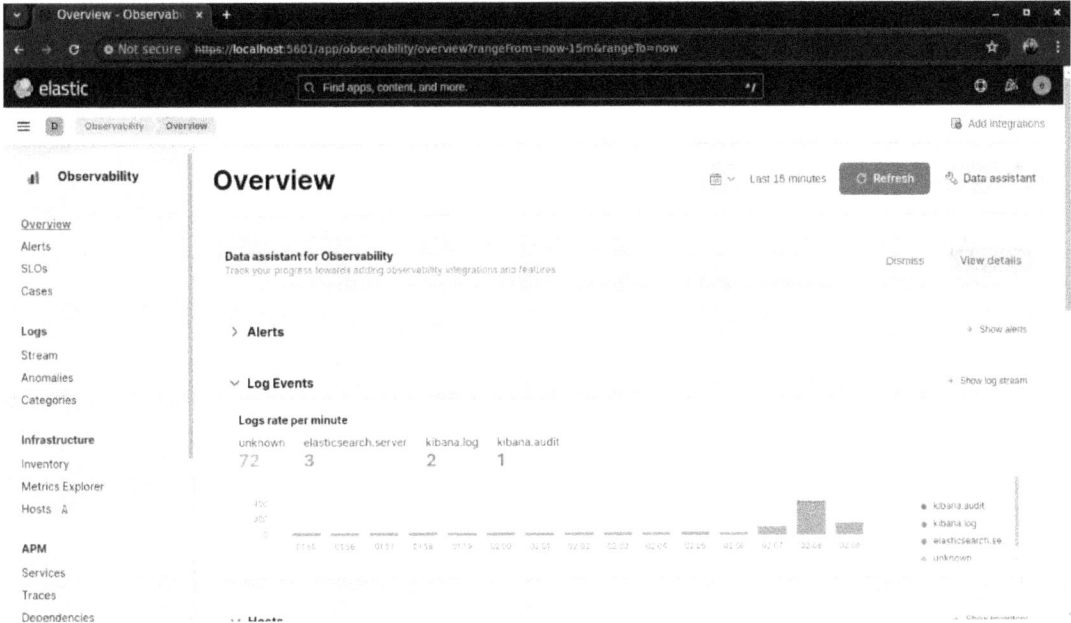

Figure 13.4: *Full observability dashboard running with APM from Docker Compose*

As can be seen in *Figure 13.4* above, a screenshot taken from the observability feature of Kibana, a fleet of one agent is running and sending its data to the Elastic APM, giving us a powerful dashboard. This is done by following the official Elastic tutorial with just a few steps, running it from a Docker Compose set of containers, with just one execution command line. From here, we can go deeper, as much as we need to, with the detailed Elastic documentation.

Conclusion

In this chapter, we looked into metrics and measurements from different angles. We looked at different types of metrics and how they are defined, used, collected, measured, and followed.

In the next chapter, we will look at correlation aspects based on the signals collected during the performance measurement, in order to arrive at the root cause for potential bottlenecks.

Key learnings

- We learned what KPIs are and what the theory behind them is.
- We looked at how different participants in a software project, such as engineers, architects, and executives, have different needs for different KPIs/metrics to collect and analyze.

- We discussed infrastructure components and why managing and tracking their usage is important.

- We discussed application runtime metrics vs. behavior metrics, the differences behind them, and why they are both important.

- We discussed white box monitoring vs black box monitoring, the differences behind them, and why they are both important.

- We reviewed some metrics that are important to trace if we are running some or all of our components on a remotely hosted deployment.

- We learned about the rich Elastic ecosystem, which components it consists of different options to get started with it, and how to bring up an entire data analytics system, with an observability framework, completely for free, and with minimum effort.

Join our book's Discord space

Join the book's Discord Workspace for Latest updates, Offers, Tech happenings around the world, New Release and Sessions with the Authors:

https://discord.bpbonline.com

CHAPTER 14
Performance Behavioral Correlation

Introduction

In the previous chapters, we discussed, in progression, benchmarking and monitoring tools, metrics, and KPIs. With this state where we have data collected, in this chapter, we will discuss topics of data analysis in order to get better conclusions from our data and get to actionable strategies.

Gathering timely information is vital to understanding the state and behavior of the system. This chapter details the correlation aspects based on the signals collected during the performance measurement to arrive at the root cause for potential bottlenecks. Here, we discuss the different parameters to look out for every symptom noticed and arrive at actionable outcomes for development to fix critical defects, as well as performance engineers to act upon for subsequent measurements.

Structure

This chapter includes the following topics:

- Common scenarios and root causes
- False positives and false negatives
- Correlation and suspect ranking
- Behavioral pattern analysis

- Concluding actionable outcomes
- Trending analysis
- Defect tracking and closure

Objectives

In this chapter, we will learn about analysis processes and how to get to know our potential problems better.

We will look at root cause analysis, how we investigate it, and how to analyze it. We will learn about various cases of false perceptions and test results in relation to reality when we detect false issues or do not detect issues at all. We will learn about data correlation and how to test our suspicion in relation to issues. We will learn about behavioral patterns, how we study them, and what we can make of them. We will look at actionable analysis and how it can help us get to concrete actions. We will learn in-depth about trend analysis and different methods to conduct it, and we will view a practical example of how this works. We will talk about keeping track of our issues and their cycle from detection to closure.

Common scenarios and root causes

Analysis of root issues and findings is an important step towards improvement and enhancement. In this section, we look at some basic methods of analysis, causes, and effects.

Root cause and root cause analysis

Root cause analysis (**RCA**) is a systematic process used to identify the underlying reasons for issues in many fields, including software bugs and performance issues. In the context of software development, RCA helps teams delve beyond surface-level symptoms to uncover fundamental problems that cause failures or inefficiencies. Sometimes, knowing there is a problem is not enough, and a simple symptom fix is not sufficient, as there may be a greater cause underneath the surface.

This process involves collecting data, analyzing patterns, and pinpointing the origin of issues to implement effective solutions. Analyzing and learning about root causes is commonly aided by various tools, some of which have been mentioned in detail throughout this book, such as collection of logs and traces, **application performance monitoring** (**APM**) and observability frameworks using standards such as OpenTelemetry, such were discussed in *Chapter 8, Designing Performance Monitoring*, or in-depth code analysis tools, profilers, instrumentation frameworks and line debuggers, which were discussed in *Chapter 9, Tools and Techniques for Code Profiling*. By addressing these root causes, developers can enhance software reliability, optimize performance, and prevent recurring issues, leading to more robust and efficient systems.

Here is a quick example:

Our web application experiences slow response times. We may think that our computing resources cannot handle the workload. Hence, the immediate solution might be to scale out and add more server instances to handle the increased load. This temporarily improves performance, but it may be that the underlying issue has not been investigated at all and remains unaddressed. Also, instead of considering improving, which would possibly make our app more efficient and effective, both with performance and with costs, by scaling it out, we increase our runtime expenses even more.

Instead, upon deeper investigation, the root cause analysis reveals that the slowness is due to inefficient database queries. Specifically, a critical query lacks proper indexing, causing significant delays. Additionally, it was discovered that there are memory leaks in the application code, leading to increased garbage collection times and some allocated memory not being deallocated at all.

By knowing this, instead of merely adding more servers, we can optimize the database queries by adding the necessary indexes and refactoring the code to eliminate memory leaks. This not only resolves the performance issue but also reduces the infrastructure costs by minimizing the need for additional server resources.

By focusing on the root cause rather than just the symptom, a more sustainable and cost-effective solution is implemented, preventing the issue from recurring and enhancing overall system performance.

Digging into common root cases with the fishbone diagram

The fishbone diagram was developed in the 1960s by *Kaoru Ishikawa*, who was a Japanese organizational theorist and a professor at the *University of Tokyo*. It became a popular method for outlining and investigating root causes in different scenarios. After him, it is also known as an **Ishikawa diagram**, a **herringbone diagram**, or simply a **cause-and-effect diagram**.

The fishbone diagram (sometimes portrayed as a fish, but in some cases just as a collection of interconnected lines) is an organized list of possible investigation directions and potential root causes we may want to consider under each of them. Mapping our problem this way may help us brainstorm causes and line them up in an organized manner, and then we can investigate them systematically.

Structure of the fishbone diagram:

- The head of the fish represents the defect, issue, or problem we are trying to solve.
- The head is connected to the central backbone, which connects to possible causes.

- To the fish backbone, ribs are connected, up and down. Each rib bone represents a category in our relevant field we could look into and investigate.

- From each rib representing a category, we split sub-areas and potential root causes we may want to check.

This structure gives a hierarchical bird-eye fishbone view of our investigation process to help us build our research toward getting down to the root of the problem and proposing resolutions.

Since root cause analysis is a technique used by various industries, not just software development, to investigate different problem types, some standard setup categories are developed to accommodate each industry. For example, if we are in an industrial field and we are presented with a manufacturing problem, we are likely to kick off our investigation with what is known as the **5 M's**. Those are: **M**anpower (the professionals and people involved), **M**achine (referring to equipment and technology), **M**aterial (raw materials, additional consumables, or any other), **M**ethod (the manufacturing process), and **M**easurement (our environment or any other relevant metric). The cause for a manufacturing problem most likely lies in the depths of one of those 5 M's.

The following is a possible root-cause fishbone diagram for tackling a performance/software engineering problem. The main categories listed are:

- Requirement issue (either in the requirements definition, interpretation, or the way it was communicated).

- An issue with our code (either does not comply with the requirements, implemented wrong, not tested properly, or lacking some skills).

- A testing issue (either tested using a wrong methodology, a test environment setup issue, or a mismatch of the test and the feature requirement).

- An environment issue (missing proper documentation, deployment problem, or any other unforeseen mismatched issue of our runtime).

The following figure shows those categories on a fishbone diagram for a possible follow-up and analysis of the software problem:

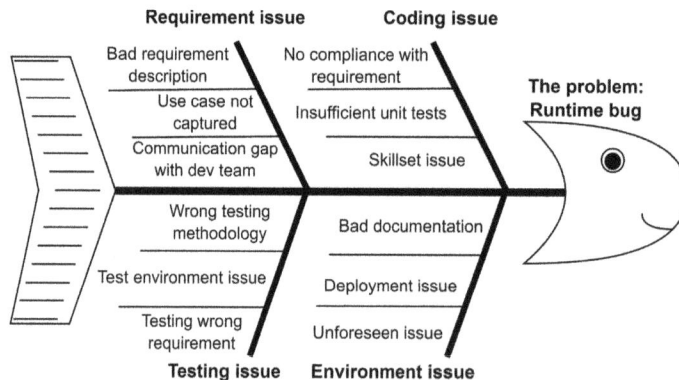

Figure 14.1: Fishbone diagram of software problem analysis

Following the flow of the fishbone diagram helps us define the cause-and-effect relation of our problem. With that diagram laid out, we can start systematically diving into the different categories to try to trace which of them is the root cause of our issue.

For each of the categories, we can use any of the profiling, testing, data collection, frameworks, observability platforms, logging, monitoring, and code analysis tools in our arsenal in order to finally detect where our bug originates from.

Analysis steps

Whether or not we outline our focus categories and analysis criteria, we might want to consider using some tools and methods in order to dig into the root cause of our problems, many of which are covered in this book and may include the following:

- **Monitoring and logging**: By implementing detailed monitoring and logging, we can capture performance metrics and error details. For that, we can use elaborate logging and monitoring tools such as ELK stack, which was discussed in depth and demonstrated in *Chapter 13, Golden signals, KPI, Metrics and Tools*, cloud-based tools, such as Amazon CloudWatch, AWS CloudTrail, AWS Config, Azure Monitor, Log Analytics, Policy, GCP Stackdriver Monitoring, Stackdriver Logging, and/or tools that implement OpenTelemetry, as **AWS Distro for OpenTelemetry** (**ADOT**), which was discussed in *Chapter 8, Designing Performance Monitoring*.

- **Profiling**: By using profiling tools, we identify bottlenecks in code and resource usage. Such tools were discussed in *Chapter 9, Tools and Techniques for Code Profiling*, including static and dynamic code analysis tools, like Python's cProfile, Java's VisualVM, or Go's pprof.

- **Load testing**: We perform load testing to simulate peak usage and identify scalability issues. We saw the different types of load tests in *Chapter 12, Performance Benchmarking*, where we also looked at tools such as Locust and JMeter.

- **Code review**: Conducting code reviews can help us find inefficient code patterns, potential memory leaks, as well as an abundance of other bugs and issues.

- **Database optimization**: Reviewing and optimizing database queries, adding indexes, and redesigning schemas, if necessary, can help increase our database runtime performance.

- **Network analysis**: Analyzing network traffic and configuration would help us identify latency and bandwidth issues.

- **Resource management**: Ensuring proper handling and release of resources like memory, file handles, and database connections is useful for avoiding leaks, crashes, and slowness.

- **Third-party services**: Causes for problems may arise from external services, not just our own, but together with our developed product, they make one whole system, where everything affects everything else. Monitoring and ensuring third-party services are reliable and performant is crucial, as those may cause problems in our product, too.

Common scenarios and root causes

Here are a few typical cases of performance-related issues we may run into, what we may think immediately, and some potential root causes that may cause them:

- Slow response times are caused by high CPU utilization. Handling such a symptom by scaling up to a stronger machine or scaling out to multiple servers may help mitigate the symptom.

  However, a root cause analysis may conclude inefficient code, excessive looping, or resource-intensive operations. This can also be caused by memory leaks, causing frequent garbage collection.

- Gradual increase in memory usage over time, leading to crashes or slow performance, we can assume this is caused by a memory leak.

  A root cause analysis may give deeper insights, such as objects being referenced longer than necessary, improper handling of resources like database connections or file handles, or circular references in JavaScript.

- Application performance degradation during peak usage times may be due to slow SQL queries.

  A deeper root cause insight may tell us we have unoptimized SQL queries, missing indexes, or excessive database locks. Inefficient schema design or a lack of query caching can also contribute.

- High response times due to network delays may suggest high network latency.

  Investigating the root cause may tell us we have poor network configuration, high latency links, or bandwidth bottlenecks. It could also be due to excessive API calls or inefficient data transfer methods.

- Slow read/write operations affecting application performance may be caused by disk I/O bottlenecks.

  Root causes may be high disk utilization due to large file operations, inadequate disk speeds, or insufficient disk resources. Fragmented disks or lack of SSDs in high I/O scenarios can be contributing factors.

- Frequent application errors leading to degraded **user experience** (**UX**) with high error rates may be a nuisance.

  Analyzing the root cause may reveal things like code bugs, improper exception handling, or third-party service failures. Misconfigurations or version incompatibilities can also cause increased error rates.

- We may encounter scalability issues in the form of performance degradation when scaling the application.

A root cause in such cases may be inefficient load balancing, lack of horizontal scaling capability, or stateful application components that don't scale well. Inefficient use of caching mechanisms can also be a problem.

- Our application may experience frequent crashes under high load or specific operations.

  Root causes may include unhandled exceptions, resource exhaustion (memory, threads), or race conditions. Bugs in third-party libraries or components can also cause crashes.

- On the front side of our application, we may encounter slow page load times, affecting UX.

  Root cause analysis may point to large, unoptimized images, excessive JavaScript execution, and too many HTTP requests. Poor CSS and JavaScript management, such as not minifying or bundling assets, can also contribute.

False positives and false negatives

Since testing and measuring are at the core of performance engineering, performance planning, and performance improvements, we have been discussing tests and test results analysis in length throughout this book. We have mentioned theories, techniques, methodologies, platforms, tools, analysis flows, and more. But in such a detailed book that touches so many test-related topics, we cannot leave out the important, yet sometimes elusive, topic of false-positive and false-negative results.

False-positive and false-negative refer to cases where we wrongly (hence the **false**) categorize the results. We either consider good results as bad or bad results as good. Since test results are crucial for our usage of the software, continued development and time spent on analysis, debugging, and improvements may be wasted if we treat the results wrongly. This can happen when we deal with borderline tests or get borderline results. To minimize false classifications, statistical significance and confidence intervals should be taken into account.

The confusion matrix

Before we discuss the meaning of false negatives in our context, we first need to understand the logic behind it. The concept of false-negative/false-positive results is not always well-known, and when it is taken into account, it has the tendency to be confusing. Surprisingly unrelated to this common confusion, the name of the logical tool that helps us map scenarios of test outcomes is called a **confusion matrix**, with which we can classify whether our test conclusions match our preliminary expectations. In our case, there are four options, as a matrix of 2x2 Boolean variables.

The confusion matrix (also known as **error matrix**) is used in machine learning to classify errors and to better visualize the performance of a complex algorithm. In our simple case of classifying the quality of test results, we differentiate the four options as follows:

		Test results	
		Positive	**Negative**
Predicted values	Positive	**True Positive (TP)** There is no issue (**positive**), and the results are good (**true**)	**False Positive (FP)** There is no issue (**positive**), But the test results detect a problem (which is a **false** detection)
	Negative	**False Negative (FN)** There is an issue (**negative**), But the tests results pass (which is a **false** detection)	**True Negative (TN)** There is an issue (**negative**), And the results reflect it, as they should be (**true**)

Table 14.1: Simple confusion matrix logic

Do not let the confusion table confuse you. This is *not* a typical logical truth table in which the intersections combine 2 Boolean values. Here, the terms **true** and **false** refer to whether the results match our expectations.

True, it is a good start. With true scenarios, the results are **true** to the actual situation:

- **True positive** is when the **positive** outcomes reflect **reality**, and they are what we had been expecting (i.e., we ran a test that was expected to pass, and it did pass without issues).

- **True negative** is when **bad results** reflect reality, and they are what we had been expecting (i.e., a bug. Our test was trying to unfold an issue – and indeed, it found it).

The problems start when our perception and observation are **false**. Our results (good or bad) are erroneous: we consider the situation wrongly. We marked the cells of those problematic scenarios in the confusion matrix above in grey:

- **False positive** is when the reality is actually good, and our test is expected to pass (**positive**), but it actually fails, indicating that there is an issue. But this indication is wrong (**false**).

- **False negative** is when, in reality, there is a problem (**negative**), but our tests actually pass, and the bug goes through undetected, but this indication is wrong (**false**).

In conclusion, we need to be aware of situations where our perception of reality is **false**. Either we detect a bug that is not there (**false positive**), or we do not detect a bug that *is* there (**false negative**). In both cases, the fault is ours.

False positive

With false positives, we fathom *a bug that is not there*. Here is a typical example:

- An automated testing tool flags a test case as failed due to an assumed bug in our software.

- The actual root cause of the false test result may be that the test case is actually written incorrectly or the environment is misconfigured.

- This makes the developers spend time investigating and fixing a non-existent issue, leading to wasted effort and potential delays.

False negative

With false negative, we let a *bug pass through undetected*. Here is a typical example:

- An automated testing tool passes a test case, indicating no issues, when there is actually a bug present.

- This can be due to a wrong test definition, a bug in the test implementation, or just a missed test case we did not cover. In any case, our tests may all pass despite an undetected bug.

- The bug goes unnoticed into production, potentially causing failures or performance issues for end users.

Correlation and suspect ranking

We mentioned the topic of suspect ranking briefly in *Chapter 8, Designing Performance Monitoring*, in the context of data anomaly detection. Here, we will look at it in the context of the correlation of factors in our tests.

Correlation vs. causation

In this chapter, we touch upon a few terms from the world of causality, statistics, and probability. We spoke earlier about root cause analysis, which brings forward the concept of cause and effect. **Cause-and-effect** describes a relationship between two events, where one event (the cause) leads to the other event (the effect). In software development, understanding these relationships helps with diagnosing and fixing bugs, optimizing performance, and improving system reliability.

Correlation is a statistical measure that describes the extent to which two variables are related. In the context of software testing and performance analysis, it helps identify relationships between different metrics or events.

Both with correlation and causation, we observe two sets of events, conditions, variables, or measures, and map how they relate to each other, but we should tread carefully here. Things may **appear** to be related, although they are **not**.

The creator of the iconic webcomic **xkcd**, *Randall Munroe*, is often attributed to the funny quote, *Every single person who confuses correlation and causation ends up dying*. This is funny because:

- There is indeed a **correlation** between the people who confuse the two terms and death. It is true that every single one of them ends up dead.

- However, since **everybody dies**, despite the correlation, the cause of their death is **not the confusion** of the terms (probably in most cases, that is).

  There is **correlation**, but **not causation**, although the sentence is formulated as if the confusion is the cause of those people's deaths (which, in turn, confuses correlation and causation).

When investigating our metrics, test results, and logs, we should be aware and careful not to confuse causation with correlation.

As an example, let us look at a typical visualization graph of two datasets. The thin line represents ice cream sales per month throughout the year, and the thick line represents the number of boat accidents over the same months. This is shown in the following chart:

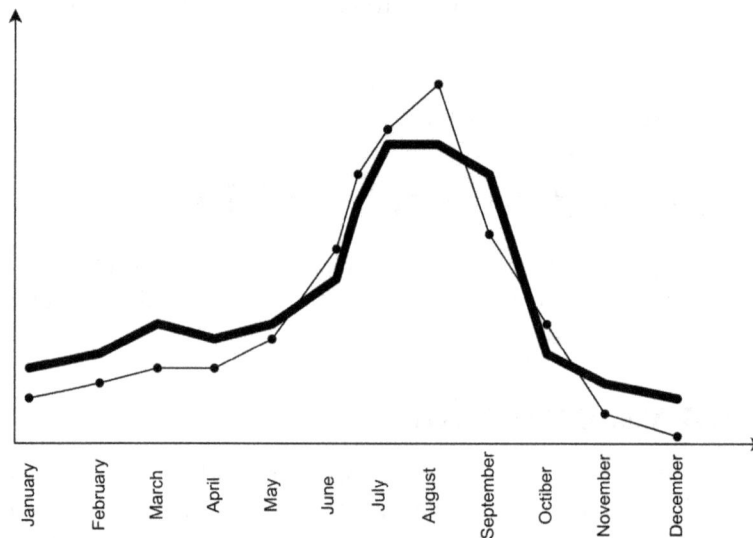

Figure 14.2: Ice cream sales vs. boat accidents

If we leave out the unmatched scale and units of the two datasets (ice cream sales are measured in thousands of liters, and boat accidents are measured as individual incidents), if we put them both in scale on a graph over one set of axes, we can definitely detect a matched pattern. However, we should be careful not to confuse correlation with causation. What we see is a correlation. During the colder months (in the northern hemisphere), ice cream sales are low. They climb steadily to a peak in the hottest months of July and August, then go as the weather cools down again, to nearly zero in December. The number of boat accidents shows a close trend. We see a definite climb towards the warmer months and a reduction during colder ones.

Looking at the two datasets overlayed, one may conclude that **ice cream causes boat accidents.** This may not be completely untrue (as a really good ice cream may distract the captain from keeping an eye on their surroundings), but of course, considering the reality, we know this is not the case. Ice cream is not the cause of boat accidents (and boat accidents do not increase the sales of ice cream). We are looking at **correlation, not causation**.

We can find many such examples of funny, misleading graphs online, showing clear correlations between completely real factors, which have absolutely no relation (for example, the number of babies born in the *United States* with a specific name between 1985 and 2015 and the number of robberies per 100,000 residents in a specific state over the same years). The bottom line: Be careful confusing correlation with causation; it may be lethal.

Suspect ranking

When looking at our bugs and issues, performance metrics, we can also sometimes detect anomalies, trends, and matched patterns. As we may be looking for the causes of our issues, we should pay attention to the **correlation** between factors.

For example, correlation analysis may reveal that increased memory usage correlates with certain feature deployments, indicating potential memory leaks. As explained earlier, we should be careful not to confuse causation with correlation, but looking at the data we may suspect there is a cause-and-effect relation between the recorded factors. However, correlation may lead us to suspect what *may be the cause*, but we need further investigation in order to prove or disprove the connection of causality.

Suspect ranking is a technique used to prioritize potential causes of software defects or performance issues. By analyzing factors such as recent code changes, historical bug data, and code complexity, the system ranks components or modules based on their likelihood of being the root cause.

The investigation flow may go as follows:

1. A new bug is reported.
2. Looking at the data, suspect ranking helps prioritize recently modified files or components, potentially with a history of similar bugs.
3. Guiding the developers to investigate these areas first. We can start by correlating the data we have to what we know, so we can prioritize our suspicions, list potential causes, and then perform a deeper analysis.

Here are a few examples of how this process progresses:

Example 1 Web application performance degradation

The symptom: Users report that a web application is slow during peak hours.

Correlation analysis:

1. We gather metrics on server CPU, memory usage, database query times, and network latency.

2. **Identify patterns**: We notice that high memory usage on the application server correlates with slow response times.

3. **Further investigation**: We analyze logs and trace transactions to identify memory leaks in the session management module.

Suspect ranking:

1. **Recent changes:** As this is a new issue, we prioritize investigating recent code changes related to session management.

2. **Historical data:** We check modules with a history of memory leaks.

3. **Complexity and usage**: We rank highly complex and frequently used modules higher for initial investigation.

Solution:

- We refactor session management code to fix the memory leak.
- We monitor post-deployment to ensure the issue is resolved.

Example 2 High error rates in API

The symptom: API error rates spike intermittently.

Correlation analysis:

1. We collect logs, error rates, API request counts, and network latency data.
2. We correlate error spikes with increased request counts and specific endpoints.
3. Detailed log analysis reveals that errors occur during database writes.

Suspect ranking:

1. **Recent deployments:** We investigate changes in the database schema and write logic.

2. **Frequency**: We focus on endpoints with high traffic.

3. **Past issues:** We check components that have previously caused similar errors.

Solution:

- We optimize database write operations.
- We implement more robust error handling for high-load scenarios.

Example 3 Database performance issues

The symptom: Database queries are significantly slower than expected.

Correlation analysis:

1. We monitor query execution times, index usage, and database server performance metrics.
2. We identify that slow queries correlate with high CPU usage on the database server.
3. As a deeper investigation, execution plans reveal missing indexes on frequently queried tables.

Suspect ranking:

1. **Heavy queries:** We prioritize optimization of the heaviest queries.
2. **Schema changes:** Looking into recent changes to the database schema.
3. **Table sizes:** We focus on large tables with high read/write activity.

Solution:

- We add necessary indexes to optimize query performance.
- We regularly review and optimize query plans.

Behavioral pattern analysis

Behavioral pattern analysis (BPA) is a method used to identify, interpret, and predict patterns in human behavior based on data-driven insights by examining recurring actions, decision-making processes, and interactions to detect trends, anomalies, or potential risks. BPA is widely applied in cybersecurity, psychology, marketing, and law enforcement to enhance understanding and improve decision-making. In this section, we discuss some of the aspects involved.

Analytics types

Looking into issues with our application, we may use different analysis techniques and tools. Another angle is analyzing behavioral patterns. This involves studying and interpreting the behaviors exhibited by users, systems, or components within a software environment to identify patterns and anomalies.

This type of analysis is crucial in various fields such as cybersecurity, UX design, performance monitoring, and marketing. More than ever, we want to understand our users, how they interact with our application, and which parts of it, for how long, what their journey looks like while using it. These kinds of analytical insights may be highly valuable for us as the owners of the app and are indeed at the heart of every modern application.

Some areas we may want to focus our attention on:

- **User behavior analysis (through analytics)**: With user behavior analysis, our goal is to understand how users interact with an application to improve UX, increase engagement, and optimize functionality.

  For example, analyzing click paths, session durations, and navigation flows to identify bottlenecks or areas causing user frustration.

- **System behavior analysis (through telemetry)**: With system behavior analysis, our goal is to monitor and analyze system performance and stability.

  For example, tracking CPU, memory usage, and response times to detect unusual patterns that might indicate underlying issues such as memory leaks or resource contention.

- **Security behavior analysis (through specific monitoring rules and alerts)**: With security behavior analysis, our goal is to detect and respond to security threats by identifying unusual patterns or anomalies.

  For example, monitoring login attempts, access patterns, and data transfers to detect potential security breaches or unauthorized access.

User behavior analysis

As briefly explained above, understanding how our users interact with the app may be crucial for our digital strategy, marketing needs, and performance improvements. It can help us make decisions on how to improve the UX and our business along the way. By understanding our users' motivations, journeys, preferences, and behavior, we can see our products and services see which paths we need to pay closer attention to, measure, improve, and maintain.

The world is not just Google Analytics. There is a wide range of user behavior analytics tools that help us track and measure, so we know what parts we need to improve.

The steps for successful behavior analytics are pretty straightforward, and we have reviewed and outlined similar processes throughout the book:

- **Define goals:** We start by clearly defining what we aim to achieve through the analysis. This could range from improving user satisfaction to increasing conversion rates, finding bottlenecks, or detecting problematic performance areas.

- **Select metrics relevant to our case:** We choose a set of metrics that align with our goals. These metrics serve as our guide and support for gaining detailed insights. Examples include funnel analysis, path analysis, trend analysis, feature analysis, event analysis, heatmap visualization, session recordings, load times, number of hits per action/page, etc.

- **Choose the tool for the job:** We utilize web or product analytics platforms to gather the necessary data. These tools can provide insights into user interactions, feature usage, and overall engagement with the application.

Tools implement different strategies besides simply *following which pages or areas* the user has gone through, such as **heatmaps** (which capture interactions such as taps or swipes, providing a visual representation of how users engage with the application's interface), **session replays** (which record activities, offering a detailed replay of user interactions with the application), **conversion funnels** (which track user progress towards completing a desired action, helping identify where users may be dropping off and why) or **surveys** (as simple as directly asking users questions to gain a better understanding of their perceptions and preferences regarding the application).

- **Analyze and visualize data:** Once data is collected, it should be visualized in an analytics dashboard for easy interpretation. Analyze the data for relevant insights and act upon them. This iterative process helps in assessing the impact of implemented changes.

- **Implement improvements based on insights:** We use the insights gained from the analysis to make targeted improvements to our product strategy. This could involve optimizing specific features, enhancing the user journey, or addressing identified pain points.

Proper user behavior analysis enables us to base our product development decisions on actual user data rather than assumptions, leading to more effective solutions. By understanding how users interact with our application, we can make informed adjustments to improve usability, performance, and overall user satisfaction. It can also help us predict future trends, allowing us to stay ahead of the curve and adapt our products accordingly.

User and entity behavior analytics

This is definitely the place to mention one more important term. User behavior analytics is a commonly used term, sometimes shortened as **UBA**. The term **user and entity behavior analytics (UEBA)** was coined by Gartner in 2015. UEBA tracks the activity of devices, applications, servers, and data. UEBA systems produce more data and provide more complex reporting options than UBA.

UEBA combines elaborate data collection of a wide range of users' behaviors, baselining the collected information, and detecting anomalies in it. The workflow starts with the collection of detailed telemetry, which commonly adds up to large volumes of intricate data. The data is then run through a funnel of machine learning, analyzing and detecting atypical deviations. For example, if the daily number of fetched records is, on average, five thousand per user, and for a specific user, we measure fifty thousand, that would indicate a deviation from the norm we need to look at. A user that normally logs in from the *East Coast* of the *USA* but suddenly logs in from South Africa, or a user that logs in two-three times a day, suddenly logs in 100 times in one day. Those are deviations that, with the right machine-learning algorithm in place, would be traced. Even deviations from normal sequences of actions may raise a flag. And that does not have to highlight one user among all others, but as part of several identified groups with different characteristics. With a large user base of thousands or tens of thousands of users, it would be impossible to apply such rules to detect problematic or abnormal behaviors without proper algorithms and techniques.

Apart from seeking anomalies and spotting problematic specimen, this can also help us baseline what the standards of our application are, how users normally behave with it, and where we need to reinforce and improve.

The added E in UEBA (rather than UBA, which focuses solely on **user** behavior) stands for **entities**. That is, we can follow the behavior of not just users but also non-human entities. Network devices, servers, virtual machines, and other resources may be taken into account here to give us a helpful picture of how our system is doing, how it behaves, which areas require attention or improvement, which areas require attention on a wider scale, and not just directly affected by users.

Concluding actionable outcomes

Indeed, we talk a lot about data collection in this book. It is at the core of understanding performance, what affects it, and where to look for traces of where the problems may lie. The craft of taking action is in itself an important aspect of improvement. Some would argue that it is the most important.

Actionable analytics

It has been said that in order to know our system and its weaknesses, we can collect data. Piles of loads and loads of data. We formulate our metrics, our KPIs, use tools that can monitor and record every possible piece of relevant or irrelevant information, and the data grows tremendously. Next, we should ask ourselves what we should do with all this data.

Actionable analytics takes our data forward into insights and information that can help drive business decisions. The goal of actionable analytics is to transform data into actionable recommendations that businesses can use to optimize their operations, improve customer experiences, and drive growth. While traditional analytics and reporting methods focus on data collection and analysis, actionable analytics is specifically designed to provide insights that can be acted upon to drive outcomes. It focuses on real-time insights that can affect decisions in the present, rather than relying on retrospective analysis of historical data. Actionable analytics require a deep understanding of the business goals, the customer needs, and the industry in order to guide relevant actions. The data alone is not enough.

Example flow, from definitions to actions

Let us look at an example: A SaaS company wants to improve the performance of its web application by reducing page load times and improving user experience.

Here is how the process may take place, from start to finish:

- **Define objectives**: In this example, we state that we wish to reduce the average page load time by 30% and decrease the error rate by 20%. This goal aligns with the company's broader strategy to enhance user experience and customer satisfaction.

- **Collect and integrate data**: For that, our data sources are:

  o Web server logs for detailed user interaction data.

  o Application performance monitoring tools like New Relic or Datadog.

  o Front-end performance data using tools like Google Lighthouse.

  o Error tracking systems like Sentry or Rollbar.

  We ensure data accuracy by validating against source systems and cleaning any inconsistencies. We then use an ETL process to consolidate data into a centralized data warehouse.

- **Analyze the data**: We analyze the data using various tools and techniques:

  o We examine past performance data to understand the average page load times and error rates. For that, we can use SQL queries to look at historical performance data.

  o As a diagnostic analysis, we investigate the factors contributing to slow page load times and high error rates. BI tools like Power BI create dashboards showing correlations between different performance metrics and application components.

  o Using machine learning models, we can predict future performance issues based on current trends. This is done with Python libraries, such as scikit-learn, to build predictive models identifying potential performance bottlenecks.

  o We generate recommendations for optimizing our application's performance. Optimization algorithms may help suggest improvements in coding practices, server configurations, and resource allocations.

- **Visualize insights**: For better insights that are easy to follow and conclude, we can use tools such as:

  o Dashboards in Power BI display current and historical performance metrics, including page load times and error rates.

  o Visual aids, such as line graphs that show performance trends over time and heatmaps, identify areas with frequent errors.

  o Custom-tailored reports deliver concrete data to developers, QA teams, and product managers.

- **Generate actionable recommendations**: With the collected data, we can come up with actual, concrete recommendations to follow, such as:

- o Optimize database queries to reduce load times.

- o Implement server-side caching to improve response times.

- o Minimize JavaScript payloads and defer non-critical resources.

- o Address frequent error patterns identified in the logs.

In our specific recommendations, we'd have to keep prioritization and focus on high-impact areas such as critical user pathways and frequently used features.

- **Make decisions**: Meetings are held with development teams, QA, and product managers to discuss insights and recommendations, evaluate the options for action, and consider the feasibility, potential impact, and resource requirements of different actions.

We get to finalize the optimization strategies to be implemented, based on the data-driven recommendations.

- **Implement actions**: Now we can translate our decisions into concrete action plans, assign responsibilities, and implement the actions as specified:

- o We create detailed plans for database optimization, server-side caching, and JavaScript payload reduction.

- o We schedule tasks and allocate time for developers to address identified performance issues.

- o We assign the development team to implement code and database optimizations.

- o We assign the DevOps team to configure server-side caching.

- **Monitor and Evaluate**: After implementing our decisions, we track our progress, using KPIs such as average page load times, error rates, and user satisfaction scores to monitor performance. Real-time dashboards in Power BI and monitoring tools like New Relic can give us relevant insights.

We can compare pre- and post-implementation performance metrics to evaluate the effectiveness of the actions and assess the progress. If desired improvements are not achieved, we can refine the interventions and make necessary adjustments.

- **Create a feedback loop**: Gathering input from developers, QA teams, and users on the process and outcomes, we collect relevant feedback with which we can learn and adapt; we identify areas for improvement in data collection, analysis, and decision-making.

As a measure of continuous improvement, we keep implementing changes to the analytics process to enhance accuracy and efficiency for future performance optimization initiatives.

Trending analysis

Trend analysis is a useful component of actionable analytics that involves examining data over time to identify consistent patterns or trends. By systematically analyzing historical data, we can uncover insights into how various factors have evolved and **predict future movements**.

This process can be applied across various domains, including sales, customer behavior, market dynamics, operational efficiency, or, in our case, trends of performance metrics.

Similar to other fields, trend analysis in performance engineering involves examining historical data of various performance metrics to identify patterns, trends, and anomalies. This analysis helps in understanding how performance metrics have evolved over time, how they operate under different conditions, and how to predict future behavior. This is crucial for maintaining and improving the performance of our products. It enables us to **identify** performance degradation, **understand the impact** of changes or updates, **predict** future performance issues, and make **data-driven decisions** to **optimize** our system's performance.

Like with other areas, we would follow key performance metrics, such as response time, throughput, error rates, resource utilization, or load and stress levels.

Despite the fact that this book is neither specialized in statistics nor in machine learning, we will mention here briefly some techniques and tools from both areas, since we are talking about trend analysis, and these are crucial elements used by most platforms and tools. Included in the following sections.

Statistical methods

Statistics plays a crucial role in trend analysis and predictions by providing methods and tools to understand historical data patterns and forecast future outcomes.

For trend analysis and historical data, some of the methods used are:

- **Descriptive statistics**: Basic statistical methods are here to give clarity on what has been happening with our data. Statistical functions such as mean, median, and mode help us measure and summarize central tendencies in the data. Calculating standard deviation and variance indicates the dispersion or variability in the dataset. Range and interquartile range provide insights into the spread and the degree of outliers in the data.

- **Time series analysis**: Taking a broader look at our data can give a better perspective. Techniques such as moving averages or exponential smoothing to smooth out short-term fluctuations, identify and highlight long-term trends. Testing and transforming data to ensure that statistical properties are constant over time, which is crucial for certain time series models.

- **Visualization**: Sometimes visual aids are important and make us identify trends just by observation. Line graphs plot data over time, to visually inspect trends. scatter plots help identify potential relationships between variables. Histograms and box plots help us understand data distribution and detect outliers. For example, the following diagram shows how we can infer scattered data points to an approximation line, showing us the trend:

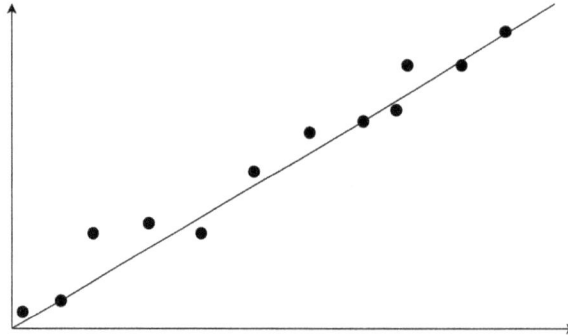

Figure 14.3: From scattered data points to a trending line

In terms of **future** analysis, extrapolation, and predictions, statistical functions also come to our aid.

- **Regression analysis**: With regression analysis we have a number of tools at hand. Linear regression may help predict how a dependent variable, based on the relationship with one or more independent variables, evolves. Extending linear regression to include multiple predictors can give us even more insight. Polynomial regression helps us model relationships that are not linear by fitting polynomial equations.

- **Time series forecasting**: **Auto-Regressive Integrated Moving Average (ARIMA)** combines auto-regression, differencing (to make data stationary), and moving averages to model time series data. Exponential smoothing models, such as Holt-Winters method, which accounts are useful for analyzing trends and seasonality. **Seasonal Decomposition of Time Series (STL)** decomposes data into seasonal, trend, and residual components for better forecasting.

Machine learning models

Machine learning models for trend and forecast analysis utilize sophisticated algorithms to capture complex patterns and relationships within data, making them particularly powerful for predicting future trends. Below is an overview of some key machine learning models and techniques used in trend forecasting. It is important to emphasize again that we are not focusing on machine learning theory and will not be exploring those models; we will just mention which they are, their names, and, with a few words, what they are and how they differ. It is important to note that machine learning is a highly powerful tool for extrapolating data, understanding patterns, and looking ahead. This can be a pointer for interested readers who would like to expand the depth of their knowledge about various relevant machine learning models.

- **Linear regression models**: Simple linear regression can help us model the relationship between two variables by fitting a linear equation to observed data. Multiple linear regression extends simple linear regression by using multiple predictors to model the relationship with the target variable.

- **Decision tree-based models**: Decision trees use a tree-like model of decisions to predict outcomes. They split the data into branches based on feature values, leading to a decision node. Random forests are an ensemble method that builds multiple decision trees and merges their results for more accurate and robust predictions. Finally, **gradient boosting machines** (**GBM**) build trees sequentially, where each new tree corrects the errors of the previous ones, leading to highly accurate models.

- **Neural networks**: Feedforward neural networks are basic neural network structures with multiple layers that can capture non-linear relationships in data. **Recurrent neural networks** (**RNN**) are designed for sequential data, making them suitable for time series forecasting. They maintain a memory of previous inputs in their hidden states. **Long short-term memory networks** (**LSTMs**) are a type of RNN that can capture long-term dependencies by using special units that control the flow of information. **Gated Recurrent Units** (**GRUs**) are similar to LSTMs but with a slightly simpler architecture, also effective for time series data.

- **Ensemble learning**: Bagging combines predictions from multiple models (like decision trees) to reduce variance and improve robustness. Boosting sequentially trains models, each one correcting errors from the previous model to improve accuracy. Stacking combines multiple different models and uses another model to learn how to best combine their predictions.

- **Probabilistic models**: Bayesian networks are probabilistic graphical models that represent variables and their conditional dependencies using directed acyclic graphs. **Hidden Markov Models** (**HMM**) are statistical models that represent systems with hidden states and are especially useful for modeling time series data with underlying processes.

- **Hybrid models**: ARIMA with machine learning, combines traditional time series models like ARIMA with machine learning models to capture both linear and non-linear patterns. DeepAR is a model developed by Amazon that uses RNNs for probabilistic forecasting of time series data.

Example flow

As an example, let us consider that our software company wants to improve the performance of its application. We have historical data on application performance metrics such as response time, error rates, CPU usage, and memory usage over the past year. The goal is to use trend analysis to identify performance degradation patterns, forecast future performance issues, and optimize the application's performance. To make this example, we will consider some fictional demo data of deteriorating performance and look at what a simplified version of the actual code for calculating our forecast may look like.

1. **Collect and prepare the data**: We collect time-series data for key performance metrics such as response time, error rates, CPU usage, memory usage, and disk I/O. Additional variables may include data on application updates, user load, and server configurations.

   The following table is what our collected data may look like:

Timestamp	Response Time ms	% Error Rate	% CPU Usage	MB Memory	User Load
2023-01-01 00:00	200	0.5	50	1024	1000
2023-01-01 01:00	210	0.6	52	1050	1200
...					
2023-12-31 23:00	300	1.0	70	2048	2000

Table 14.1: A summary table of various typical collected metrics

2. **Exploratory data analysis (EDA)** and **time series decomposition**: As descriptive statistics we calculate mean, median, variance, and standard deviation of performance metrics. We then visualize the data, using line charts to plot performance metrics over time to visually inspect trends and seasonal patterns. We can also plot response time, error rate, CPU usage, and memory usage over time to observe overall trends and periodic spikes. STL can help us decompose the time series data into trend, seasonal, and residual components to understand underlying patterns.

   The following is a simple Python code example of how this may look. To demonstrate the deterioration, in this example, in response time, we create some daily demo dummy data, in which all parameters are deteriorating over the period of the year 2023. We then analyze this data with the **statsmodels** library, creating a time series decomposition, plotting a graph, and exporting it to an image file, using the **matplotlib.pyplot** library.

```python
import pandas as pd
import matplotlib.pyplot as plt
import statsmodels.api as sm
from datetime import datetime

# ---------------- PREPARE DEMO DATA ----------------
# Function to create a date range
def create_date_range(start_date, end_date, freq='H'):
```

```
        return pd.date_range(start=start_date, end=end_date, freq=freq)

# Generate a date range for one year of hourly data
start_date = datetime(2023, 1, 1)
end_date = datetime(2023, 12, 31, 23)
dates = create_date_range(start_date, end_date)

# Number of data points
n = len(dates)

# Hardcoded performance data with a constant deterioration in response
time
data = {
    'Timestamp': dates,
    'Response Time (ms)': [200 + (i * 0.1) for i in range(n)],
    'Error Rate (%)': [0.5 + (0.01 * (i % 10)) for i in range(n)],
    'CPU Usage (%)': [50 + (i % 20) for i in range(n)],
    'Memory Usage (MB)': [1024 + (i % 1024) for i in range(n)],
    'User Load': [1000 + (i % 1000) for i in range(n)]
}

# Create DataFrame
performance_data = pd.DataFrame(data)
performance_data.set_index('Timestamp', inplace=True)

# ---------------- TIME SERIES DECOMPOSITION -----------------
# Perform time series decomposition on 'Response Time (ms)'
response_time_series = performance_data['Response Time (ms)']
decomposition   =   sm.tsa.seasonal_decompose(response_time_series,
model='multiplicative', period=24)

# Plot the decomposition results
fig, (ax1, ax2, ax3, ax4) = plt.subplots(4, 1, figsize=(15, 10),
sharex=True)

decomposition.observed.plot(ax=ax1)
ax1.set_ylabel('Observed')
```

```
decomposition.trend.plot(ax=ax2)
ax2.set_ylabel('Trend')

decomposition.seasonal.plot(ax=ax3)
ax3.set_ylabel('Seasonal')

decomposition.resid.plot(ax=ax4)
ax4.set_ylabel('Residual')

# ---------------- PLOT AND GRAPH ----------------
plt.suptitle('Time Series Decomposition of Response Time (ms)')
plt.savefig('time_series_decomposition.png')
plt.show()
```

After running this code, we get the following figure in a file named **time_series_decomposition.png**, shown:

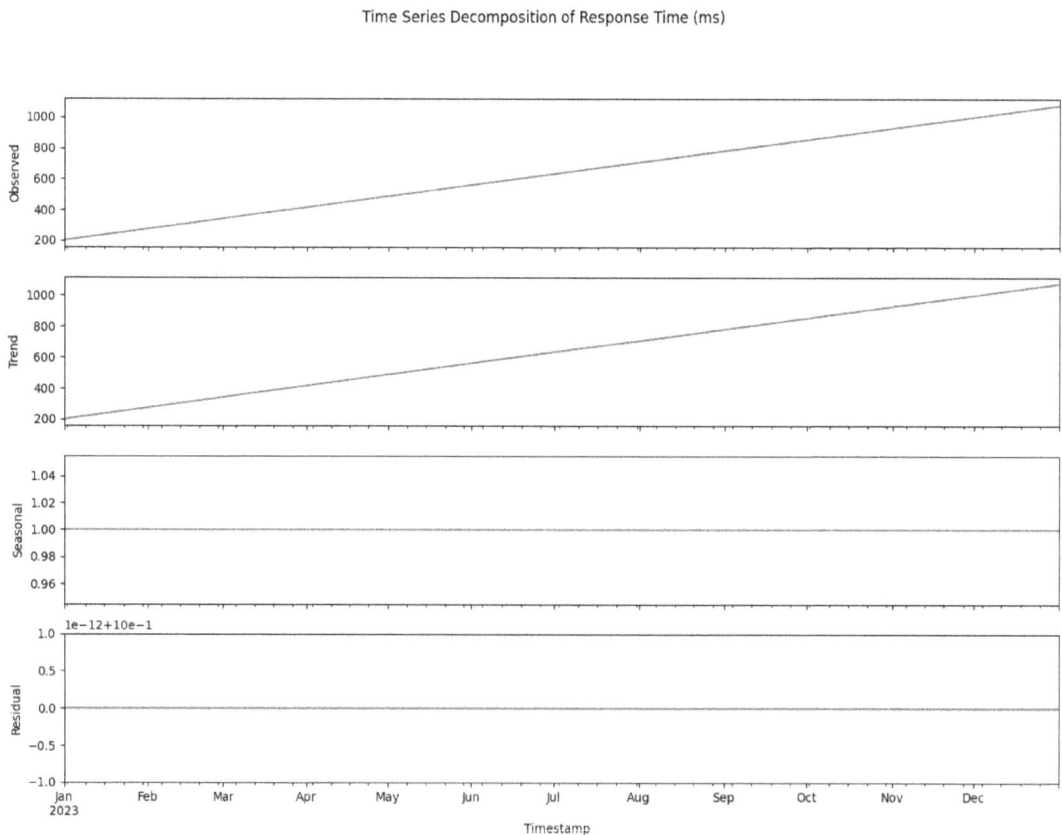

Figure 14.4: Time series decomposition line chart of deteriorating data

3. **Trend analysis**: As per this example, we can calculate moving averages to smooth out short-term fluctuations and highlight long-term trends. To do that, we add the following code to the bottom of our Python file:

```python
# ----------------- CLEAR THE PLOT -----------------
plt.cla()


# ----------------- MOVING AVERAGES TREND ANALYSIS -----------------
performance_data['Response Time - 24H MA'] = performance_data['Response
Time (ms)'].rolling(window=24).mean()

performance_data['Response Time - 7D MA'] = performance_data['Response
Time (ms)'].rolling(window=24*7).mean()


# Plot original data and moving averages
plt.figure(figsize=(15, 8))

plt.plot(performance_data.index,    performance_data['Response    Time
(ms)'], label='Original Response Time', color='blue')
plt.plot(performance_data.index, performance_data['Response Time -
24H MA'], label='24-Hour Moving Average', color='orange')
plt.plot(performance_data.index, performance_data['Response Time - 7D
MA'], label='7-Day Moving Average', color='green')

plt.xlabel('Timestamp')
plt.ylabel('Response Time (ms)')
plt.title('Response Time with Moving Averages')
plt.legend()
plt.grid(True)
plt.tight_layout()
plt.savefig('response_time_moving_averages.png')
plt.show()
```

Now, after running our code, we get an additional image, in a file named **response_time_moving_averages.png**, showing our trend in a line graph, comparing the original times, a 24-hour and a 7-day moving average, as we can see in the following figure:

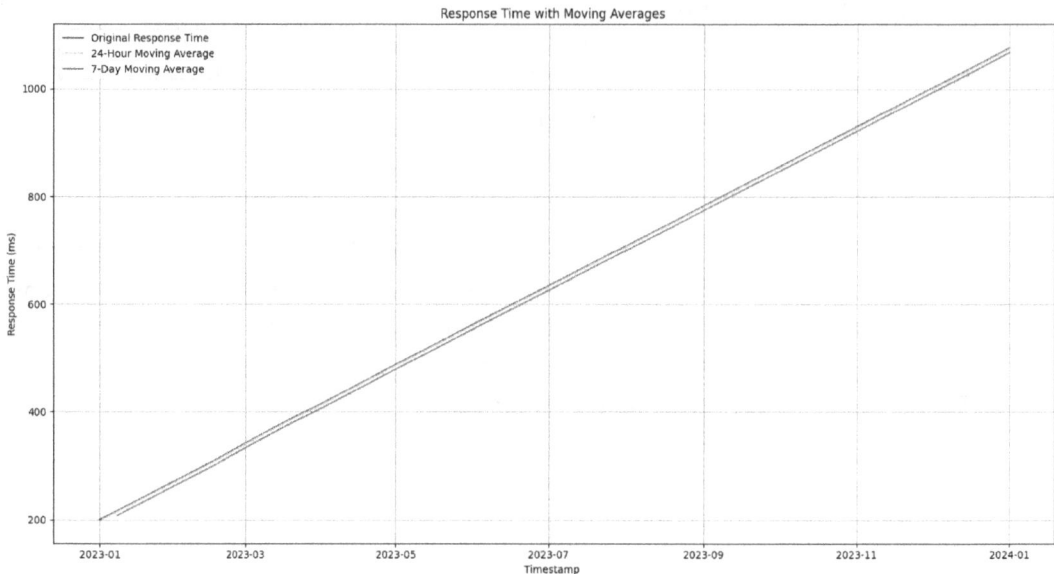

Figure 14.5: Trend analysis with moving averages of our deteriorating response time

4. **Forecasting**: In order to generate a forecast, we choose an appropriate model, such as ARIMA, Prophet, or LSTM, based on data characteristics. To do that, we add the following code to the bottom of our Python file:

```python
# ----------------- CLEAR THE PLOT -----------------
plt.cla()


# ----------------- ARIMA MODEL FORECAST -----------------
# Fit ARIMA model and make a forecast
response_time_series = performance_data['Response Time (ms)']
arima_model  =  auto_arima(response_time_series,  seasonal=False,
trace=True, error_action='ignore', suppress_warnings=True)
n_periods = 24 * 7  # Forecast for the next 7 days
forecast, conf_int = arima_model.predict(n_periods=n_periods, return_
conf_int=True)

# Create a DataFrame for the forecasted values
forecast_index  =  pd.date_range(start=performance_data.index[-1],
periods=n_periods + 1, freq='H')[1:]
forecast_df  =  pd.DataFrame(forecast,  index=forecast_index,
columns=['Forecast'])
```

```
# Plot original data, moving averages, and forecast
plt.figure(figsize=(15, 8))

plt.plot(forecast_df.index,    forecast_df['Forecast'],    label='ARIMA
Forecast', color='red')

# Plot forecast confidence intervals
plt.fill_between(forecast_index,  conf_int[:,  0],  conf_int[:,  1],
color='pink', alpha=0.3)

plt.xlabel('Timestamp')
plt.ylabel('Response Time (ms)')
plt.title('Response ARIMA Forecast')
plt.legend()
plt.grid(True)
plt.tight_layout()
plt.savefig('response_time_forecast.png')
plt.show()
```

Now, after running our code, we get an additional image, in a file named **response_ time_forecast.png**, showing our trend how the algorithm foresees our trend for the next 7 days, as can be seen in the following figure:

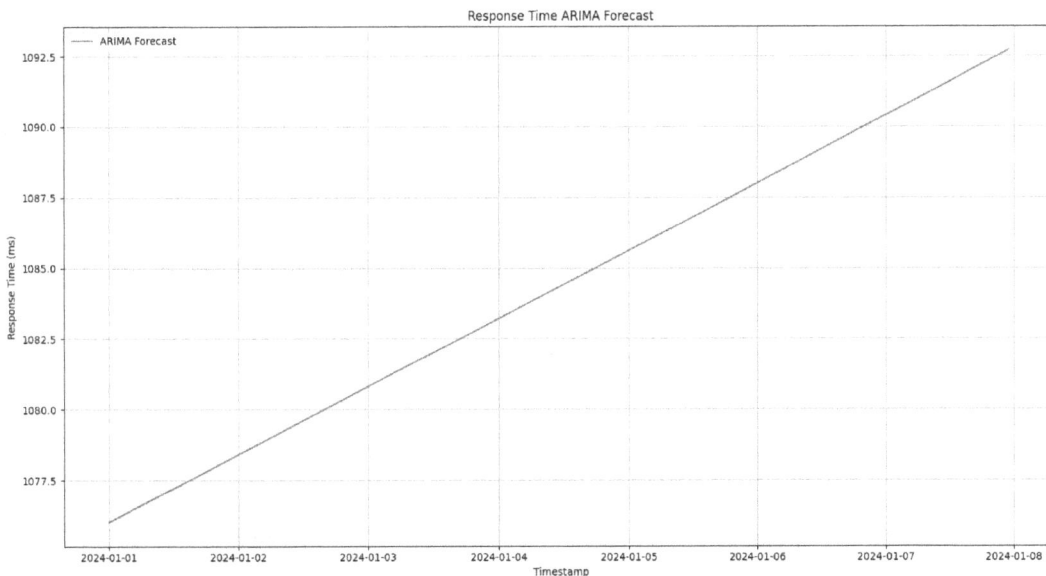

Figure 14.6: *ARIMA forecast of our deteriorating response time for the next 7 days*

5. **Implementing optimization strategies**: With all the collected data, analysis, and forecasting, we can strategize our forthcoming actions. We definitely see that our response time is deteriorating consistently. Of course, in the overly simplified example above, things are very clear and immediately visible. Needless to say, with real-life data, things are not so simple. In any case, once we get a glance into the future, we can take actions, such as adjusting server resources based on the forecasted user load to prevent CPU and memory bottlenecks, identify and optimize code segments that contribute to high response times and error rates, implement load balancing strategies to distribute user requests evenly across servers, etc.

Defect tracking and closure

As an integral part of our software development lifecycle, with our continuous, systematic progress and seeking improvement, following up on defects is an integral, not to say crucial, part of the process and of quality assurance. It ensures software defects (bugs) are identified, documented, tracked, and resolved in a good manner.

Tracking

The purpose of defect tracking is to monitor and manage defects from discovery to resolution, and to ensure that defects are addressed in a timely and efficient manner.

The lifecycle of a defect usually passes through some of the following steps:

- **Detection**: Defects are typically detected during various phases of software testing (unit testing, integration testing, system testing, etc.) or reported by end-users.

- **Reporting**: Detected defects are reported using a defect-tracking tool (like JIRA, Bugzilla, or Redmine). The report should include: a title, a detailed description of information about the defect, including steps to reproduce it, severity/priority – which are indicators of the defect's impact on the system and the urgency of its resolution, and additional information such as information about the environment where the defect was found (e.g., operating system, browser, etc.). Added attachments such as screenshots, logs, or any other relevant files may also be appended.

- **Triage**: The reported defects are reviewed by the team, which usually includes developers, testers, and project managers. They get categorized based on their severity and priority and assigned to appropriate developers or teams for resolution.

- **Tracking**: The status of each defect (e.g., New, In Progress, Resolved, Closed) is updated as work progresses. Continuous communication between testers, developers, and other stakeholders ensures that the status and progress of defect resolution are transparent and up to date.

Resolution and closure

The purpose of the resolution and closure phase is to resolve defects effectively and ensure they do not recur, and to confirm that the resolved defect has been thoroughly tested and closed.

We can relate to the following four phases:

1. **Resolution**: The developers analyze the defect to understand its root cause. The defect is fixed in the code. This might involve changes to the software's logic, database, user interface, or other components.

   The fix is initially tested by the developer to ensure it resolves the defect without introducing new issues.

2. **Verification**: The defect is tested by the QA team to ensure that the fix is effective and that the defect no longer exists. Additional testing is conducted to ensure that the fix hasn't affected other parts of the software (regression testing). This can be automated or manual.

3. **Closure**: Once the defect is verified, it is marked as closed in the defect tracking system. The closure report includes a confirmation that the defect has been fixed and retested, any relevant comments or notes on the fix, and sometimes, a final review or approval might be required from a QA manager or product owner before closing the defect.

4. **Metrics and reporting**: Data on defects is collected and analyzed to identify trends, common issues, and areas for improvement. Common metrics include defect density, defect resolution time, and defect detection efficiency. Regular reports are generated to provide insights into the defect management process and overall software quality.

The definition of done

In this context, we will just mention here yet another related crucial concept in software development, particularly within agile methodologies: The **definition of done** (**DoD**).

It represents a clear and shared understanding among the team of what must be achieved for a product increment, user story, or task to be considered complete. The DoD typically includes criteria such as all code being written, reviewed, and integrated; passing all relevant tests (unit, integration, and user acceptance); ensuring that all defects are identified, resolved, and closed; updating all necessary documentation; and verifying that the product meets both functional and non-functional requirements.

Sometimes, the DoD should be formulated and customized in order to match our project's definitions, specifications, and characteristics. We define what we can accept as a done task in this context. By adhering to a well-defined DoD, teams ensure consistency in deliverables, maintain high-quality standards, and avoid the accumulation of technical debt, thereby fostering greater transparency, accountability, and customer satisfaction.

In many cases, our process of defect tracking and closure is tightly related to our DoD, as part of our criteria for completion, in which we strive to have our system defect-free as much as possible. A new feature should be declared done, after a sufficient number of cycles, including proper testing, issue reporting and resolution, documentation and review, and verification.

Conclusion

In this chapter, we discussed handling defects, analyzing data, detecting problems, getting to the root cause, and managing our defects efficiently. This can help us release more stable, controlled, complete, higher-quality products.

In the next chapter, we will look at what happens after we release our product. How we manage the production environment, and how we keep managing our quality, observations, and communications after a successful deployment.

Key learnings

- We learned what root causes are and about root cause analysis.
- We learned how to analyze root causes with a fishbone diagram.
- We listed some common scenarios and their potential root causes.
- We learned about false positives, false negatives, detections, and everything in between. Differentiating them with a confusion matrix.
- We learned about correlation vs causation, data correlation, and how to approach it.
- We learned about suspect ranking and rating our suspicions when new issues are detected.
- We learned about behavioral pattern analytics and user behavior analysis.
- We learned about actionable analytics and how they help us conclude actionable outcomes.
- We learned about trend analysis with statistical methods and machine learning, and we looked at an example of such a trend analysis and forecast that actually takes place with the help of Python code.
- We learned about the defect tracking and closure lifecycle, how we normally keep track and triage issues, and how they correspond with the DoD.

CHAPTER 15

Post-Production Management

Introduction

In continuation to the previous chapters, where we focused on learning as much as possible about our product's metrics, aligning our KPIs, analyzing our collected data, and optimizing it for deployment into production, in this chapter, we discuss the key activities to be performed post-production release to manage non-functional requirements delivered to end users. This also includes the feedback loop from production incidents and problem management back to developers and solution architects. Here, we discuss the various teams involved; we look at ownership and the different roles in making software better and more performant.

Structure

The chapter covers the following topics:

- Alerting and dashboarding
- Learn from incidents
- Continuous improvement journey
- Identifying key stakeholders
- Defining and agreeing the level of ownership
- Performance engineering culture across teams

- Predictive analytics and projections
- Reporting to key stakeholders

Objectives

In this chapter, we will learn about building effective dashboards and alerts to help us follow the behavior of our software in the production environment. We will learn about operational conclusions from incidents we may encounter, how to learn fast by experimenting more, and how to use the cycle of trial and error, incidents, and improvements to create a continuous cycle of ever-finer improvement and perfection. We will learn about the different roles, and particularly about stakeholders in our project, why it is important to know who they are, and how to keep them informed. We will learn about responsibility, the RACI matrix, and different areas of ownership and what they mean. We will discuss how different teams and roles relate to performance engineering culture across the software development process. We will discuss again predictive analytics and data projections, this time through a post-deployment perspective, and we will talk about looping back informative reports to the right stakeholders, to keep everybody informed.

Alerting and dashboarding

The previous chapters were dedicated to preparing our software for deployment and running in the wild. We focused on quality and different types of performance-related tests, test tools, and test data, and runtime environments; we discussed measurements, metrics, and KPIs; we looked at monitoring and observability, and we talked about the analysis of our findings. With all that in place, we should be able to optimize and tweak our software and make it production-ready. It is only logical, then, that our next step would be deploying it in a live production runtime environment, and once it is alive and running there, there are some post-deployment sentinels we can put in place to ensure our application still runs properly.

A proper post-deployment dashboard can aggregate important metrics and useful real-time data, collected into presentable, easy-to-consume informatics and graphic elements. Some are tailored for developers, some for DevOps teams, and some for managers and stakeholders to keep an eye. This enables quick identification of any issues that may arise, ensuring that the software is still performing as expected and that users are having a positive experience.

If something does happen, and not all eyes are on the dashboard exactly when it does, alerting complements dashboarding by automatically notifying teams when certain thresholds or conditions are met, such as a spike in error rates or a drop in system performance. These alerts are critical because they allow teams to respond to potential problems before they escalate into larger issues that could impact users or business operations. By implementing effective post-deployment dashboarding and alerting, organizations can maintain high levels of uptime, quickly address incidents, and continuously improve their applications based on real-world usage data. This proactive approach not only ensures better reliability and performance but also enhances customer satisfaction by reducing the likelihood and impact of service disruptions.

Dashboarding best practices and key features

A good post-deployment dashboard is important for monitoring the health and performance of our applications in production. To be effective, it should be designed with several key principles and features in mind. Some of these are:

- **Real-time data**: Probably the most important aspect. Real-time monitoring is essential for promptly detecting and responding to issues as they arise. We strive to display live metrics such as response times, error rates, CPU/memory usage, and traffic load to give immediate insights into our system's current state.

- **User-friendly interface**: A dashboard is only as useful as its readability and ease of use are. We should use clear, intuitive visualizations (charts, graphs, gauges) and organize the dashboard in a way that prioritizes the most critical information. The design should allow us quick scanning and easy interpretation by various stakeholders.

- **Customizable views and reports**: Different team members (developers, operations, management) have different needs and priorities. By allowing users to customize the dashboard to display the metrics most relevant to them and provide options for generating and exporting reports, we increase our visibility and exposure and get more critical angles of analysis, understanding, and possible issues.

- **Key performance indicators (KPIs)**: We looked at KPIs in *Chapter 13, Golden signals, KPI, Metrics and Tools*. They provide us with a high-level overview of the system's health and are crucial for assessing whether the application is meeting its goals. Here, we may include metrics like uptime, average response time, request rate, error rate, and user engagement statistics. These should be clearly visible and easy to interpret.

- **Historical data and trends:** Historical data helps in identifying trends, understanding long-term performance, and diagnosing intermittent issues. For a good, useful, dashboard, we would include visualizations of data over time, such as graphs showing the last 24 hours, 7 days, or 30 days of performance. This can help us spot patterns and predict potential issues before they occur.

- **Error and exception tracking**: Quickly identifying and resolving errors is critical to maintaining a smooth user experience. Besides critical alerts (which we will discuss below), including logs or summaries of recent errors and exceptions, categorized by severity, is highly important, to give us critical information we need to address. Many observability tools include features for automatically capturing and displaying such information.

- **User experience metrics**: Understanding how our users interact with our application can help identify performance bottlenecks or usability issues. Again, this can be important and useful if we detect, for example, a significant drop in performance, with or without a load spike. We track metrics such as page load times, user session lengths, and conversion rates. Such metrics can and should be correlated with backend performance to give a complete picture.

- **Service and infrastructure health**: We discussed the importance of monitoring in *Chapter 7, Performance in the Clouds,* and *Chapter 8, Designing Performance Monitoring.* Monitoring our underlying infrastructure is crucial to ensuring the application remains stable and performant. Displaying the status of servers, databases, and third-party services, with indicators for issues like high latency, downtime, or connection failures, giving a real-time view of what is running, what is down, crashed, or scaled.

- **Security monitoring:** Security threats can compromise the integrity and availability of our application. Including security-related metrics such as failed login attempts, unusual access patterns, and vulnerabilities detected may be useful in quick identification and response to potential threats.

Alerting best practices and key features

Once we have our monitors and observability in place, it is also crucial to have effective alerts for promptly detecting and addressing issues in our production environment. Here are several key principles and features to keep in mind when designing our alerting system:

- **Relevant and actionable alerts**: Alerts should only trigger when action is required, preventing alert fatigue and ensuring that each notification is meaningful. Our consideration is to configure alerts for critical conditions such as system failures, performance degradation, or security breaches. Avoiding alerts on every minor issue is important; instead, we should focus on events that demand immediate attention.

- **Threshold-based triggers**: Continuing the previous bullet, setting appropriate thresholds would help avoid unnecessary alerts while ensuring that serious issues are detected. We can define thresholds for metrics like CPU usage, and memory consumption, which should be based on historical data and adjusted over time to reflect the normal operating conditions of our system.

- **Prioritization and severity levels**: Not all alerts are created equal. They differ in urgency and impact. Some require immediate action, while others can wait. We should categorize alerts by severity (e.g., critical, warning, informational) to ensure that higher severity alerts receive more attention. For example, a system outage would be a critical alert, while a minor increase in response time might be a warning. This should also be customizable, of course, as sometimes we would want to give some areas more attention. For example, we may expect a spike in sales before the holidays, but we can alert and pay closer attention to the number of requests or response times to address issues before they happen.

- **Clear and informative messages**: This cannot be emphasized enough. Engineers in all areas of software development, deployment, and others tend to include alerts and debug information, which is clear to them but may mean nothing to everyone else. This extends not just to monitors and alerts but to comments and internal and external documentation. Our alerts should provide enough context to understand the issue quickly without requiring extensive investigation. They should include key details in the alert message, such as what triggered the alert, the affected systems or services, and possible causes. Providing links to dashboards or logs where the issue can be investigated further is also helpful.

- **Timely notifications**: For relevance, not only the clarity of the information counts but also the timing. Alerts must be delivered quickly to ensure rapid response and mitigation, and to be relevant. Reliable notification channels (e.g., email, SMS, immediate internal organization Slack, or Teams messages) that can reach the relevant team members quickly, may be crucial. We should ensure that alerts are sent in real-time and that there is redundancy in notification methods to avoid missed alerts.

- **Escalation policies**: If an alert has not been acknowledged or resolved in a timely manner, it should escalate to ensure it gets the attention it needs. We should define escalation paths that automatically notify higher-level personnel if an alert is not addressed within a certain time frame. For example, if a critical alert is not acknowledged within 10 minutes, it might escalate to a senior engineer or manager.

- **Silencing and maintenance windows**: Another feature to plan and consider. Just as much as alerts are important, as mentioned in previous bullets, we would not want to overload with too many unnecessary ones; it is also important to be able to stop the alerting system, at times. During planned maintenance or deployments, alerts should be temporarily suppressed to avoid unnecessary noise. We should implement silencing features or schedule maintenance windows during which alerts are either paused or treated differently. This ensures that teams are not overwhelmed with alerts that are expected during these periods.

- **Automated remediation**: Do not let a human do a computer's job. In some cases, automated actions can resolve issues more quickly than human intervention. Where possible, we can configure alerts to trigger automated remediation actions, such as restarting a service, scaling resources, or rolling back a deployment. This can reduce downtime and the burden on the team.

- **Integration with incident management**: As another means of automation, alerts should be part of a broader incident management process to ensure structured and efficient handling of issues. Integrating alerts with incident management tools (e.g., PagerDuty, OpsGenie) can create incidents automatically, track their status, and facilitate post-incident reviews. This helps in managing alerts as part of a larger workflow.

Learn from incidents

As we strive to improve the quality of our software, deployment, environment, and resources, it is important to learn, review, and analyze cases where things went wrong so we can learn what happened and fix it for the future.

Fail fast, learn fast

As part of the continuous growth philosophy, by which we improve by learning from failures, the phrase **fail fast, learn fast** (or sometimes **fail fast, learn faster**) is associated with the principles of agile development, lean startup methodologies, and the broader tech and innovation culture. The idea is to start experimenting as quickly as possible, to see where we have problems, and to fix them in practical experimental iterations.

Here is an example:

Suppose we have to build a messaging system in one week.

One approach we can take is to spend our time researching about proper technologies, read technical documentation, and find which are the best patterns and libraries to use, in the process of perfecting our code, while relying only on minimal local tests. At the end of the development cycle, we have a finely crafted solution we can deploy, which is supposedly pretty good, obviously with some untested scenarios since we have not had the chance to run it in real conditions. With the approach of trying to build things right the first time (something like **measure twice, cut once**) our solution may follow good practices, but is probably better in theory than it is in real conditions.

Another approach we can take is to follow the **fail fast, learn fast** strategy. With this approach, we start raw. As fast as possible, as soon as we have something we can deploy and run, we do it. Our solution is far from perfect at first, but we can immediately get an idea about its real pain points and issues. We can then take it from there in small iterations of deploying it, detecting issues, addressing them quickly, deploying, and testing again, as many times as needed. At the end of this cycle, we still get an imperfect solution, but with this solution, some of the practical issues have already been apparent and addressed. In comparison to the result of the first approach, our solution here may appear to be more **quick and dirty**, but it is more likely to work better in production conditions, and the iterative learning process of our fails may have given us invaluable experience of how the product really behaves and what its practical defects are. Later on, we can refactor to perfect our code, patterns, etc. Thus, we failed fast but also learned a lot about how our project runs through experience and experiments.

The phrase **fail fast, learn fast** became widely recognized as a mantra in startups, product development, and even large corporations that adopted agile and lean practices. It emphasizes the importance of quickly identifying what does not work, learning from those failures, and applying that knowledge to improve or pivot the product or strategy.

That is, in comparison, for example, to big and heavy corporations, which can invest time in education and research, elaborate designs, and pre-work, in contrast to an agile, quickly adapting smaller organization, where results are needed fast. Then we can refine everything.

Learning from Incidents movement

This goes beyond just the intuitive practice of analyzing incidents and making conclusions. The **Learning from Incidents (LFI)** movement is a growing trend within software development, IT operations, and broader tech communities that emphasizes the importance of learning from system failures, outages, and other incidents. Rather than viewing incidents solely as problems to be fixed, this movement encourages organizations to see them as valuable learning opportunities. The LFI movement is closely aligned with the principles of **Site Reliability Engineering** (**SRE**), DevOps, and modern software development practices that prioritize resilience, continuous improvement, and a blameless culture.

Jeli is an end-to-end incident management platform built to ease the cost of coordination and communications during incidents and reduce the time to analyze and gain insights after an incident, ultimately surfacing burnout risks and patterns across organizations and technologies. It is a commercial enterprise-level product, with a free tier for small teams, including built-in integrations with a wide variety of systems, helpful built-in collaboration and communication tools, and AI-assisted analysis capabilities. Nora Jones, a former resilience engineer with Slack and Netflix, and the CEO and founder of Jeli, is also among the founders of the LFI movement and the initiator of a yearly international LFI conference.

LFI does not only mean learning lessons from failures, should they happen, because the assumption is that in a large complex system, there are always incidents. In fact, there is no time during which there are no incidents while the system is running. Eliminating critical ones, learning from them, thus making the system strong enough to run reliably, increasing its **resilience** (where the responsibility of **Site Reliability Engineers** – SREs, is to improve resilience, that is to make the software withstand failures). On the other side, **chaos engineers** try to cause an increase in incidents in order to test how resilient the software is. The bottom line is that we coexist and **live with the incidents** and **iteratively learn from them** to build a stronger product.

The LFI approach is more about **learning** and **applying our new knowledge** for the future, rather than just **fixing** and **closing** the issue. It is guided by several core principles:

- **Blameless post-mortems**: Focus on understanding the incident without assigning blame to individuals. This fosters an environment where team members can openly discuss failures and share insights.
- **Root cause analysis**: Investigate the deeper, systemic causes of incidents, rather than just addressing the symptoms. This helps in identifying and mitigating underlying issues.

- **Continuous improvement**: Use the insights gained from incidents to make ongoing improvements to systems, processes, and practices. This ensures that the organization becomes more resilient over time.

- **Systems thinking**: View incidents as the result of complex interactions within systems, not isolated mistakes. This encourages a holistic understanding of how different factors contribute to failures.

- **Knowledge sharing**: Document and share the lessons learned across the organization to prevent similar incidents and build collective knowledge.

- **Resilience building**: Focus on enhancing the system's ability to withstand, recover from, and adapt to disruptions, rather than just preventing failures.

LFI vs. the traditional approach

Here is an example of how the LFI approach may differ from the traditional approach to handling incidents. Suppose a cloud-based service we are using experiences an unexpected outage, causing downtime for our users. The issue is traced back to a misconfiguration in the load balancer, which led to a cascading failure across the system.

With the **traditional** approach of handling, we first apply an immediate fix: the engineering team quickly identifies the misconfiguration, reconfigures the load balancer, and restores the service. After conducting a brief investigation, where the person who made the configuration change is identified and reprimanded, our focus is on ensuring that the individual does not make the same mistake again. A brief incident report is created, documenting the issue and the fix, but it is not shared widely. The incident is closed, and the team moves on. No significant changes are made to the system or processes. The emphasis is on avoiding human error rather than addressing potential systemic issues.

With the LFI approach, after the immediate fix, the team conducts a blameless post-mortem to understand not just what happened, but why it happened. The discussion includes everyone involved in the incident, and the focus is on systemic causes rather than individual mistakes. We would want to understand *why* the incident happened. We know that it is because of a misconfigured load balancer, but we would want to really know why this happened in the first place. We would research deeper to find the root cause of the misconfiguration and discover that the load balancer's complex settings and insufficient documentation contributed to the mistake. We also find that the lack of automated testing for configuration changes allowed the error to go unnoticed. We conclude some actionable improvements: implement automated tests for configuration changes to catch errors before they affect production, update the documentation to make the configuration process clearer and easier to follow, improve monitoring to detect similar issues earlier, and alert the team before they escalate. We would also conduct knowledge sharing, by documenting and sharing the improvements in detail across the organization. This ensures that other teams can learn from our incident and apply similar improvements to their systems. One of the most important aspects of this approach is continuous learning: the incident is added to a repository of past incidents that our team regularly reviews to identify patterns and further improve our processes. We also conduct follow-ups to ensure that the changes are effectively implemented and working as intended.

Continuous improvement journey

We have been talking a lot about practices of the **software development lifecycle (SDLC)** and their iterative nature. Methodologies like agile, and modern processes of DevOps run in cycles from requirements to deployment, and looping back with conclusions, issues, incidents, bugs, and improvement suggestions. Complex software systems always run on incidents and, just like any creation, are never perfect. However, as with other crafts, repetitive revisits help polish and improve it. Continuous development and testing, continuous integration, and continuous delivery bring ever-finer continuous improvement.

One way to illustrate the power of small improvements is by calculating the accumulated improvement over time. If we consider measurable metrics by which we get better by 1% every day for a year, we accumulate an improvement of 1.01^{356}, which is a total of 37.78%. On the other hand, getting worse by 1% every day for a year sums up to 0.99^{365}, or a total of 0.025%. The difference is often depicted in a graph like the one below, where the horizontal dashed line represents the baseline of no change, and we can see how continuous improvement leads to growth, and continuous worsening leads to a steady, shallow decline.

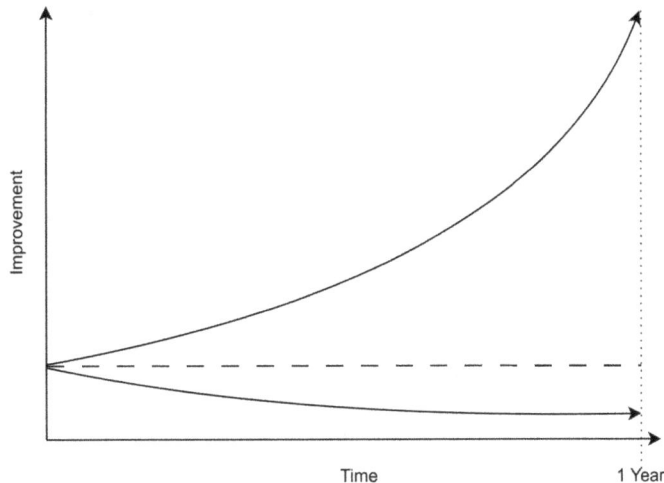

Figure 15.1: Continuous improvement vs continuous decline

Like LFI, the concept of **continuous improvement** may sound intuitive and trivial, but it has grown into a useful methodic movement with principles and guidelines, and not just in the software world. The continuous improvement journey is about making small, consistent changes that lead to big results over time. It is a mindset that involves everyone in the organization and touches every aspect of software development, from planning and coding to deployment and feedback. By embracing this journey, organizations can build more resilient, adaptive, and high-performing software development teams.

The Deming Cycle

Continuous improvement requires constant planning and checking. The Deming Cycle, sometimes referred to as **PDCA** in the abbreviation of its four steps: **Plan, Do, Check, Act**, was developed in the 1940s by *William Edwards Deming*, an American economist and engineer (and a musician and composer), and one of the founding fathers of quality control. It is a methodology for small cumulative improvements, adapted by many businesses, and a core part of Kaizen (see below).

As listed above, the Deming Cycle consists of four key steps:

1. **Plan:** This involves establishing the process through which our goals can be achieved. Much like with many methods described in this book, we need to start with a goal and a plan.

2. **Do:** This step is fairly self-explanatory, and it is where we execute our plans.

3. **Check:** Here, we assess our process and results, identifying areas where we may have fallen short or areas that could be improved.

4. **Act** (or sometimes: **Adjust**): This is the stage where we implement those modifications, come up with them, and improve our process for the coming cycles.

Following the four steps is done in a continuous loop, by which we keep polishing our product as well as our processes. The Deming Cycle is illustrated as follows:

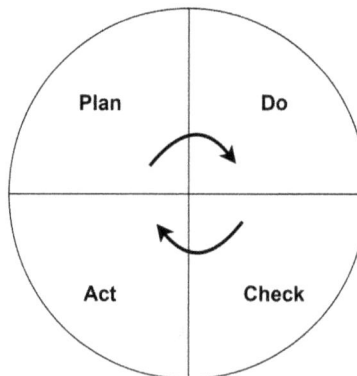

Figure 15.2: The Deming Cycle

Kaizen

Speaking of methodologies of continuous improvements, we must mention **Kaizen**, a Japanese term that translates to **change for the better** (or, in other words, **continuous**

improvement). It originated in Japan after World War II and became a core principle in lean manufacturing, particularly within the Toyota Production System. Kaizen emphasizes small, incremental improvements made regularly to improve efficiency, quality, and overall performance. While it began in manufacturing, Kaizen has since been widely adopted in various industries, including software development and business processes.

The key principle of Kaizen is continuous improvement. Kaizen is about making small, ongoing changes that collectively lead to significant improvements over time. The philosophy is that everyone in the organization, from top management to frontline workers, should be involved in identifying areas for improvement and implementing changes.

Main principles include:

- **Employee involvement**: Kaizen encourages participation from all employees. It fosters a culture where workers are empowered to suggest and implement improvements in their daily tasks. This democratization of innovation helps organizations tap into the collective knowledge and creativity of their workforce.

- **Standardization**: After improvements are made, new processes are standardized to ensure that the gains are maintained. This creates a stable foundation upon which further improvements can be built.

- **Incremental change**: Kaizen focuses on small, incremental changes rather than large, radical shifts. The idea is that small improvements are easier to manage, less disruptive, and more sustainable in the long term.

- **Process-oriented thinking**: The Kaizen philosophy emphasizes the importance of improving processes rather than just focusing on outcomes. By refining the way work is done, better results naturally follow.

- **Quality and efficiency**: Kaizen seeks to enhance both quality and efficiency simultaneously. It involves systematically eliminating waste (known as *Muda* in lean management) and ensuring that every step in a process adds value.

In the software industry, Kaizen is often applied within agile and DevOps environments, where continuous improvement is a core value. Examples include regular retrospectives at the end of each sprint to identify areas for small iterative improvement, incremental refactoring performed by developers to small parts of the code for improved quality (rather than waiting for a big refactoring project), and enhancements in automation of testing, deployment, and monitoring processes, which can lead to significant efficiency gains over time.

Identifying key stakeholders

Keeping things under control while we conduct changes and improvements is important, as sometimes continuous changes add up to have a large impact on our project's scope or definitions. Our project is seldom really just ours but almost always involves other parties, people, units, or organizations. Those who are defined as key stakeholders must be kept informed on important developments. It can be tricky to identify who the stakeholders are, but it is essential to figure out exactly who needs to be informed about delays, updates, or changes to the project's scope.

A stakeholder is anyone with an interest in our project's outcome. This includes members of the project team, managers, executives, project sponsors, customers, and end-users. We can tell a person, or an organization, is a stakeholder, if they are affected by the result of our project at some point in its lifecycle. Communicating effectively with all stakeholders is crucial, but different types of stakeholders require different types and levels of communication.

Key stakeholders are the ones with the most influence and authority to dictate whether our project is a success or a failure. We need to meet their goals because they have the power to make or break our project.

In the process of mapping who the key stakeholders are, we should consider customers, managers, team members, sponsors or financiers, executives, government agencies, contractors, owners, and even society itself in some cases.

Their relation to our project differs. For example, our end users are the ones who are directly affected by our software, being our most direct buy-in consumers. There are also indirect users and beneficiaries who rely on the outcomes of using our software without interacting with it directly.

Another example is our project team, which consists of the developers, project managers, partners, and team leads. Their job is to define the scope of the outcome and to make the software idea and requirements a reality. They have the most impact on the product, as it would not exist without them.

Between the producers (the project team), the consumers (who are most influenced by the product), and product owners and project managers (who help chart and scope our product's features), there are additional indirectly involved parties. Those may include regulatory bodies, institutes, suppliers, competitors, even governments, advocacy groups, non-profit organizations, or at some point, the general public. The span of the list of involved parties depends on our project, its purpose, scope, size, and expected impact. We can say that the tighter the circle and the closer the people in it to the project are, the more important they are to us and to our production, but the mission of identifying who the key stakeholders are is more about impact and influence over it, and by it.

The reasons we would want to recognize our key stakeholders are all about focused, efficient communications, in contrast to engaging and overwhelming a large list of correspondents. This may reduce risk, as we would know which stakeholders present a higher potential risk and engage them early in the project. To identify the key stakeholders, we would have to pay close attention to those who:

- Have direct contact with our product, such as customers, developers, project managers, and end users.

- Are the senior representatives of involved parties, such as managers, department leads, and directors.

- Contribute specific knowledge on which our project is shaped (subject matter experts).

- Are vital to our success. Those would be in the line of business partners, end users, and executives.

Those are people whose input is vital for our product's existence and success. Not all of them need to be involved at all times, but it is important to know who is who so we can strategize who to communicate with, what to do, and when.

On a software project, the list is usually narrow. The dev team, project managers, product owners, and possibly customer representatives would be the closest, most informed group, which takes part in all the important meetings.

Representatives of sales, marketing, customer service representatives, and technical support are also in the loops of greater communications but do not take part in all the internal meetings. Again, the larger the project and its impact, the bigger the list is, for example, if the product has a wide impact on the public or government operations. This can affect our strategy and stakeholders' lists dramatically.

Defining and agreeing the level of ownership

Another important task for ensuring clarity, accountability, and successful project delivery, especially in complex software projects, is to have an explicit definition of the roles of ownership, responsibility, and accountability, carried out by individuals or teams over different aspects of the project, including decision-making, execution, and outcomes.

RACI key roles

Not to confuse the definitions of the various terms used here, each of which represents a different level of ownership and different engagements. In today's projects, it is popular to differentiate the following roles:

- **Responsible**: The responsible person or people are the ones who *do the work* to complete a task or project. They are responsible for getting the job done. For example, in our software project, the developer who writes the code is the one **Responsible** for that task.

- **Accountable**: The accountable person is the one who is ultimately answerable for the task or project. They *ensure that the work gets done* and meets the required quality. There should only be one accountable person per task. For example, in our software project, the project manager might be **accountable** for ensuring the product is completed and delivered on time and works correctly.

- **Consulted**: The consulted person or people are the ones who *provide input, advice, or feedback*. They are consulted before decisions are made or when specific expertise is needed. For example, a designer might be **consulted** on how the website should look, giving their input before the developer starts coding.

- **Informed**: The informed person or people are the ones who need to be *kept up-to-date* on progress or decisions, but *do not have to be involved in the work* itself. For example, the marketing team might be **informed** about the project's progress, so they know when it will be ready to promote, but they are not directly involved in the development.

The **RACI matrix**, an acronym for **Responsible, Accountable, Consulted,** and **Informed**, is a tool for clarifying roles and responsibilities in a project. It lists the actual people who are involved in the project according to their level of engagement, as shown in the following table:

Responsible	Names of the responsible people, who do the work.
Accountable	Name of the accountable person who ensures the work is done.
Consulted	Names of people who give advice and input.
Informed	Names of the people who need to be kept in the loop about progress.

Table 15.1: RACI matrix structure

The RACI matrix helps ensure that everyone knows their role in a project, which makes it easier to get things done smoothly and efficiently.

Ownership

We can define what the different flavors of responsibility and engagement are as per the RACI matrix, but the question of ownership is many times more elusive. We can always, and many times will, ask who **owns** a piece of code. It would mostly mean the person who is in charge of that code. Either the person who wrote it or, at the moment, maintains it. Ownership may extend further, more loosely, to the entire dev team and further encompass every one of the RACI people, each with their own portion of the responsibility and ownership of the project and/or the code. Sometimes, the formal definition of ownership, either on a project, part of it, or even a specific piece of code, is summarized by the acronym AREA:

- **Accountability**: Same as with RACI, accountability means the person whose job is to ensure the work gets done.

- **Responsibility**: Again, same as with RACI, the responsible people are the ones who actually make it happen and do the actual work on the project.

- **Expertise**: People in the expertise pool are those who best understand the project or code. Either because they are the ones who have built it, and can inform how work should be done, or know it thoroughly in depth.

- **Authorization**: Authorized people are those who can commit or approve changes to code, data, or other assets associated with the project.

The AREA people may span from one person to an entire company, as long as the definitions overlap and cover all four requirements. Although they overlap, the ownership attributes are different from one another. Arguably, accountability is the most important on the list, as it puts the focus on one single person, who has to account for things being done, although he may not be the responsible or expert person who knows the code, or may not even have the authorization to access it directly. Therefore, many times, the dev team that delivers their part of the product can jointly be considered owners.

Once ownership levels are defined, they should be communicated clearly to all stakeholders. This can be done through project kickoff meetings, documentation (like a project charter or roles and responsibilities document), and ongoing communication throughout the project. We should ensure that everyone understands their role, the extent of their authority, and who they need to collaborate with.

Defining and agreeing on the level of ownership in a software project is a foundational step that ensures clarity, accountability, and successful collaboration. By taking a structured approach to assigning ownership and regularly reviewing it, project teams can enhance their efficiency, reduce risks, and achieve their goals more effectively. Defining ownership is important as it gives us:

- **Clarity and focus**: Clearly defined ownership prevents confusion and ensures that everyone knows their responsibilities, reducing overlap and gaps in the project.
- **Accountability**: When ownership is clearly defined, it is easier to hold individuals and teams accountable for their work, leading to higher quality and timely delivery.
- **Efficient decision-making**: Defined ownership helps streamline decision-making processes, as it is clear who has the authority to make decisions in each area.
- **Team alignment**: By agreeing on ownership levels, teams can work more effectively together, with a shared understanding of roles, responsibilities, and expectations.
- **Risk management**: Clear ownership helps identify potential risks early, as each owner is focused on their specific area of the project.

Performance engineering culture across teams

In this chapter, we are focusing on the final stages of a project cycle, deployment and control. We are defining and understanding ownership across teams and responsibilities. Throughout the book, we have looked at performance aspects and considerations throughout the entire lifecycle of the software development process. It is not intuitive and not always customary to consider performance throughout the project, but embracing a performance engineering culture across various teams in an organization involves fostering a mindset and practices that prioritize the performance, scalability, and reliability of software from the very beginning of development through to deployment and maintenance. Education is key, as most of the people in the different loops are not always aware of performance requirements to begin with. The following is a summary of how we can help different teams and roles consider embedding performance engineering into our project:

- **Product owners and business analysts**: They represent the customer's needs, outline the product's features, and are the ones who define and prioritize those features, aligning them with business objectives. As they do that, they should consider incorporating performance into the product's requirements. Ensure that those performance-related requirements, such as response times or scalability needs, are explicitly included in user stories and acceptance criteria.

  They need to work with technical teams to understand the trade-offs between adding new features and maintaining or improving performance, and collaborate with stakeholders to set clear, measurable performance goals that align with business needs.

- **Project managers**: Their role is to oversee project timelines, resources, and overall delivery, managing the timelines, stories, tasks, work rates, and rituals. To include performance considerations, they should integrate performance milestones, by including performance testing and optimization as key milestones in the project plan. Resources should be properly allocated for performance in time and budget for performance-related activities, such as load testing and performance tuning.

  It is also important that they encourage regular communication between development, QA, and operations teams to discuss performance issues and progress.

- **Developers**: They are the ones who write and maintain code, implement the features, and fix issues. As the rest of the teams, they should be provided with proper education about performance and best practices, with training on writing efficient code, design patterns and anti-patterns, optimizing database queries, and understanding performance bottlenecks, and tools such as profilers and code analysis libraries.

  This would help promote practices such as conducting performance code reviews and writing performance-conscious algorithms, helping to employ a performance-driven development culture. Of course, developers should be provided with the proper tools and resources for real-time performance monitoring, profiling, and testing within their development environment.

- **Quality assurance and testing teams**: Their job is to ensure the software meets quality standards, including performance. Here, we would encourage a shift-left testing approach to help QA teams incorporate performance testing early in the testing lifecycle, starting with unit and integration tests. Automated testing in general, and automated performance testing in particular, is also important, and integrating tests within the CI/CD pipeline can help us catch regressions early.

We should ensure performance tests use realistic load scenarios that mimic production environments, including varied user behaviors and data loads.

- **DevOps and operations teams**: They are the ones who manage deployment, infrastructure, and system reliability. They can help by implementing continuous monitoring tools to track performance metrics (e.g., latency, throughput, CPU usage) in real-time in production. Working closely with development teams to identify and resolve performance issues in the deployment pipeline and production environment can help tune up the performance, as well as automate scalability testing, by using infrastructure-as-code and automated scaling tests to ensure the system can handle varying loads and traffic spikes. Of course, incorporate all other tests into the deployment pipelines.
- **Database administrators (DBAs)**: They manage and optimize database performance. They can help us by optimizing queries and indexes, and regularly reviewing database structures, relationships, and interactions provided by developers, in order to improve performance. Also, by implementing tools to continuously monitor database performance, including query execution times, lock contention, and resource usage, we can uncover bottlenecks and unoptimized database implementations. For that, collaboration with the dev team will help design and implement better schemas.

Embracing the culture

To get started with performance-driven development projects, including all the relevant parties, we would have to take a few basic steps:

- **Educate** and understand performance engineering as a holistic discipline of ensuring that a system meets its performance requirements.
- **Equip teams with tools** for monitoring, profiling, and analyzing performance at different stages of development. Allow teams to run their own performance tests and analyze results without needing to rely on specialized teams, which promotes ownership.
- **Leadership should actively support and promote a performance engineering culture** by providing the necessary resources, tools, and training. Leaders should be aware and set an example by acknowledging and considering performance in their decision-making and communications.
- Encourage teams to **share their experiences and lessons learned** related to performance through internal presentations, documentation, or informal meetups.
- **Promote a performance-first mindset**, educate and train teams to ensure they understand the importance of performance and how their work impacts it. Provide training on performance best practices and tools.
- **Incorporate performance as early as possible** into the SDLC, not just as an afterthought during testing.

- Foster a culture where teams are always looking for ways to optimize and **continuously improve performance**, not just meet the minimum requirements.

- Build **cross-team collaboration**, by setting unified goals, and perceive performance as a **collective responsibility**. Regular meetings or stand-ups where teams discuss concerns, share insights, and collaborate on solving issues, performance-related and others.

- **Define clear metrics** like response time, throughput, resource utilization, and uptime. Setting baselines and targets that are aligned with business goals. These should be realistic and achievable but also drive improvement.

- **Monitor and measure continuously** to track performance metrics in real-time, providing visibility across all teams.

- **Shift left** and implement **performance testing practices** early in the SDLC, such as during unit testing or integration testing phases, rather than waiting until the end.

- Use **automated tools** to perform regular **performance tests** as part of the continuous integration and delivery pipeline. This helps identify performance regressions early.

- Regularly **simulate high loads and stress conditions** to ensure the system can handle real-world usage scenarios. Set **performance budgets** (e.g., maximum allowable load time or resource usage) and ensure that new features do not exceed these limits.

- During **code reviews**, include performance considerations, such as ensuring efficient algorithms, avoiding unnecessary computations, and optimizing database queries.

- Conduct **post-deployment** reviews to **analyze performance data**, identify areas for improvement, and incorporate learnings into future projects.

Predictive analytics and projections

We discussed data projection in *Chapter 4, Workload Modeling and Projection,* and pattern analysis and trends in *Chapter 14, Performance Behavioral Correlation.* We talked about the importance of understanding our metrics, telemetry, and measurements, and comparing them to benchmarks and to our KPIs and goals, to know how we stand in comparison to them. With the right tools, algorithms, statistics, machine learning, and other techniques, we can project trends and behaviors of the future, based on our experience of the past.

With the insights that predictive analytics of our data gives us, we can also decide on the right actions to take or **prescribe** ahead, before we encounter the consequences. Just to quickly sum up the three types of analytics we are talking about:

- **Descriptive analytics** answers the question, *What has happened?* by analyzing historical data. It involves summarizing and interpreting data to understand past performance and identify trends or patterns (understand the past).

For example, after deploying a new version of our application, we analyze logs to determine that the average response time increased by 20% compared to the previous version.

- **Predictive analytics** answers the question, *What is likely to happen?* by using statistical models and machine learning to forecast future outcomes based on historical data (Forecast the future).

  For example, using historical performance data, we predict that if the user load doubles during an upcoming marketing campaign, the application will experience a 40% increase in response time, potentially leading to slowdowns.

- **Prescriptive analytics** answers the question, *What should we do?* by recommending actions to achieve desired outcomes. It goes beyond prediction to suggest the best course of action based on data analysis (Recommend actions to influence future outcomes).

  For example, based on predictions of future performance issues, our analytics system suggests increasing server capacity or optimizing specific database queries to prevent the expected slowdown during the marketing campaign.

As this chapter is dedicated to the post-production world, predictive analytics and data projections are vital for post-deployment because they enable us to manage software performance proactively. By anticipating issues, optimizing resource use, improving user experience, and making data-driven decisions, predictive analytics helps us ensure that our software remains reliable, efficient, and cost-effective in a production environment.

To mention again a few of the main important benefits of post-production predictive analytics and projections:

- **Proactive issue prevention and early detection of problems**: Predictive analytics can identify trends or patterns that indicate potential performance issues before they impact users. For example, if the system predicts that memory usage will spike under certain conditions, you can address this proactively by optimizing the code or scaling resources.

- **Optimized resource management and capacity planning**: Data projections allow us to forecast future resource needs, such as CPU, memory, and storage. This ensures that the system is neither under-provisioned (leading to performance issues) nor over-provisioned (leading to unnecessary costs). Thus, by accurately predicting when and how resources will be needed, we can allocate them more efficiently, reducing operational costs while ensuring optimal performance.

- **Informed decision-making and data-driven decisions**: Post-deployment, our decisions about software updates, scaling, and optimization are better informed when based on predictive analytics. This reduces the risk of making changes that could negatively impact the performance of our software. Predictive insights can guide long-term planning, such as when to invest in new infrastructure, how to prepare for expected increases in user demand, or which features to optimize for better performance.

- **Continuous improvement and feedback loop**: We mentioned continuous improvement earlier. Predictive analytics creates a continuous feedback loop, where data from production informs future development and deployment strategies. This leads to a cycle of ongoing improvement in software performance. Over time, our system can *learn* from the data and become more accurate in its predictions, enabling increasingly refined performance management strategies.

- **Enhanced monitoring and alerting and smart alerts**: We also discussed dashboarding and alerting earlier in this chapter, and predictive analytics can trigger alerts not just based on current issues but on projected trends. For example, if the system predicts that disk space will run out in a week, it can alert the operations team well in advance, preventing a potential outage.

Reporting progress to key stakeholders

As the last part of our post-production loop, we complete the circle of monitoring, tracking, observing, analyzing, projecting, predicting, and reporting, closing a feedback channel back to the key stakeholders of the project is about keeping everyone informed, aligned, and engaged. Effective communication ensures that stakeholders are informed, aligned with the project's goals, and able to make informed decisions. Here is a breakdown of how to approach this task:

- **Understand the stakeholders' needs**: A stakeholder is a property, not a role. Different stakeholders have different needs and different levels of communication. We should determine who the key stakeholders are, for example, project sponsors, clients, product owners, team members, and executives. Each stakeholder may have different interests and concerns.

- Reports should be customized to address the specific needs and concerns of each stakeholder group. For example, executives might focus on high-level metrics like timelines and budgets, while technical stakeholders might be more interested in detailed progress and technical challenges.

- **Use clear and concise communication**: Transparency is key. We should clearly communicate the current status of the project, including any successes, challenges, or risks, and avoid jargon when communicating with non-technical stakeholders. Managers speak a different language than project managers and engineers.

- Using KPIs can help us show progress. These might include project milestones, budget usage, resource allocation, quality metrics, and timelines. Incorporating charts, graphs, and dashboards to visualize data, makes it easier for reportees to grasp complex information quickly.

- **Regular reporting cadence**: Consistency is important. Establishing a regular reporting cadence, such as weekly, bi-weekly, or monthly updates, depending on the project's pace and stakeholder expectations, would help reduce worries and concerns. We should also use consistent reporting formats and structures to make it easier for stakeholders to follow the project's progress over time.

- **Focus on outcomes and impact**: We need to differentiate between mere progress (e.g., tasks completed) and outcomes (e.g., features delivered that add value to the user) and emphasize how the work done contributes to achieving the project's goals. Relating project outcomes to broader business objectives shows how our project helps to achieve strategic goals, improve user experience, or generate revenue.

- **Address risks and issues**: Proactive risk management is highly important. We should report on any risks or issues that have been identified, along with the actions being taken to mitigate them. Of course, being honest about challenges, but also focus on the steps being taken to overcome them. If certain issues require input or decisions from stakeholders, make this clear and provide the necessary context to facilitate decision-making.

- **Seek feedback and engagement**: The report loopback is not one-directional. We should encourage stakeholders to ask questions, provide feedback, and engage in discussions during or after reporting sessions. This will help ensure that their concerns are addressed and that they remain invested in the project's success. Of course, we use the feedback received to improve the format, frequency, or content of future reports.

- **Celebrate successes**: The report loopback is not one-directional, and it is not just for ranting or reporting current or future issues. We should also regularly celebrate and communicate the completion of major milestones or successful outcomes. This not only keeps stakeholders informed but also boosts everybody's morale.

Conclusion

In this chapter, we discussed the key aspects of post-deployment production activities, what we need to take care of, who the key players are, and how to communicate with them effectively.

Points to remember

- We learned best practices for building dashboards and sending alerts for our deployed software.
- We learned about LFI and issues, and how this approach differs from **traditional** incident management.

- We learned about continuous improvement and why it is important in the long run. We looked at the Deming Cycle and the Kaizen methodology.
- We talked about key stakeholders, who they are, how to identify them, and why it is important for our process.
- We learned about different levels of ownership, about the different roles in the RACI matrix, about the meaning of ownership, and how to define different areas of it. We also learned why clear definitions of ownership and responsibility are important.
- We looked at how performance engineering culture relates to different teams, and how to embrace and apply it.
- We looked at projections and descriptive, predictive, and prescriptive analytics, and why they matter in a production environment.
- We talked about the feedback loop of reports of measures, issues, progress, and decisions back to the different stakeholders.

Join our book's Discord space

Join the book's Discord Workspace for Latest updates, Offers, Tech happenings around the world, New Release and Sessions with the Authors:

https://discord.bpbonline.com

Index